THE WORLD TRANSFORMED

MODERN CIVILIZATION SINCE 1648

FIRST EDITION

by **Charles Carter** & **Terry Morris**

Shorter University

cognella®
academic publishing

Bassim Hamadeh, CEO and Publisher

Kassie Graves, Director of Acquisitions

Jamie Giganti, Senior Managing Editor

Jess Estrella, Senior Graphic Designer

Jennifer McCarthy, Acquisitions Editor

Gem Rabanera, Project Editor

Elizabeth Rowe, Licensing Coordinator

Christian Berk, Associate Production Editor

Kat Ragudos, Interior Designer

Cover image copyright © 2014 Depositphotos/Chris Hepburn

Printed in the United States of America.

ISBN: 978-1-5165-1462-5 (pb) / 978-1-5165-1463-2 (br)

cognella®
academic publishing

www.cognella.com   800-200-3908

CONTENTS

ACKNOWLEDGMENTS

Dr. Terry Morris would like to thank his wonderful wife, Janet, who gave countless hours editing the chapters he contributed. She not only brought her knowledge of grammar and style to the task, but also her sensitivity to what might not make as much sense to the student as it does to the author. The chapters he contributed to the text were immeasurably improved by her contribution and he is deeply grateful to her. Of course, any remaining errors are the responsibility of Dr. Morris. She also put up with a distracted and frequently absent husband for the months during which the work was being done.

Dr. Charles Carter would like to thank all of the team at Cognella, including Project Editor Gem Rabanera. He also would like to thank his mother, Glenda Carter, for her encouragement during his writing.

INTRODUCTION

DEFINING THE MODERN

The period covered by this course, from the mid-seventeenth century to the present, is known as the "modern period" or the "modern world." But when the modern period starts, what *modern* means, and when it ends, if indeed it has ended, are matters about which historians disagree. In the following chapters we will present our positions on these questions; in particular, when and where the modern world first arose, why and how it subsequently spread across the globe, what the consequences of these developments were, and, finally, whether or not this period is over. But before we can begin, we need to define what we mean by modern—that is the purpose of this introduction.

In truth, historians use the word *modern* in two different but related ways. The first refers to a period that began after the mid-seventeenth century, as indicated above. But modern is also used to mean an approach to life or a world view; so, one speaks of the "modern world view" as opposed to the "medieval." There is a connection between the two usages. We speak of the modern beginning in the seventeenth century because the ideas and cultural institutions that characterize it do not appear before that time. Yet, most places in the world remained traditional long after the modern period began in the West. They functioned in the modern period (usage 1), but were decidedly not modern (usage 2). Keeping this

distinction and connection in mind prevents confusion when we shift from one usage to the other.

Defining the modern, in the second usage, will also provide an opportunity for us to explain what we mean by the ways of life that preceded it and continued, in many parts of the world, after the mid-seventeenth century, the "traditional." Modern ideas about life tend to undermine traditional ones and replace them with a pattern that is similar everywhere it appears. If you have traveled outside Europe to any degree, you will have recognized that the "modern" parts of cities you visited all pretty much resemble American ones and are decidedly different from traditional images of these countries. Traditional buildings have been replaced by high-rise offices and apartments; power grids are everywhere, along with high-speed rail (Figure 0.1). About all that remains from the past—in these modernized areas, at least—are the historic buildings that tourists come to see in the first place, especially places of worship. Even private residences are "modernized" (i.e., westernized) in these areas. If you want to see the traditional society and people, you must go to the rural, mountainous, or otherwise underdeveloped areas.

One other observation: While modern ways tend to be homogenous, traditional ones will all be different, reflecting the differing ways of life people evolved all over the world before modernization came to influence them. We are not contrasting

modern from a unitary traditional way of life, but from many different traditional ways of life.

It is also important to recognize that the homogenizing effects of modernization will never be total. Traditional ways will never be entirely swallowed up by these forces. We will want to make sure we pay attention to these subtle variations as we go along.

Now we should be able to define the modern. We will do so using eight characteristics that help distinguish this way of life from those differing, traditional ones.

SCIENTIFIC WORLD VIEW

Historians rightly celebrate the scientific accomplishments of ancient Greece, China, or the medieval Arab world. Yet, the science that came to fruition in the seventeenth century, which we call "modern science," was largely unprecedented—even unique—in human history. Furthermore, it is largely because of the rise of this new science

and its accompanying rationalism that the modern world appeared first in the West, and not somewhere else.

As we examine in detail how this occurred in subsequent chapters, we will be content, for now, to suggest broadly what we mean. First, science, for modern society, became the *only* reliable way to determine the true from the false. If something were not "scientific," it must be mere opinion, not to be trusted as it was likely based on superstition. But science, by contrast, had a means of determining whether a claim was valid—the "scientific method," an approach to interrogating nature objectively through observation and experimentation. Through this means, and this means only, one could determine whether something was fact or fiction, "myth" or truth. Such people were not impressed with the argument that they should believe something because it was a religious teaching from the past, believed by their ancestors, or what the ancients had taught.

Historians refer to it as the "scientific world view." While not everyone relied completely upon science to explain all aspects of their existence in the seventeenth century, as we move into the nineteenth and then the twentieth centuries, more and more modernists did. Positivism, a mid-nineteenth century philosophical movement, for example, maintained that if something could not be explained empirically—that is, inductively—it could not be known, and more to the point, was not worth worrying about. God was one of those unknowable propositions since God was by definition not material.

This scientific world view also included the assumption the world is rational and understandable in human terms because it operates according to natural laws best expressed in mathematical terms. We are not dealing with a mysterious universe, no magic *a la* Harry Potter here, but a rational one we could understand through science and mathematics. When something happens, there is a reason for it, whether we know the reason or not. Humans have the job of uncovering these reasons and putting them to work in solving human problems.

This new scientific view was like the traditional Judeo-Christian one in that both argued this world existed for human consumption. Humans were not an indissoluble part of nature, but existed apart from nature, functioning as its conquerors and exploiters. This is significantly different from most other traditional points of view in the world, whether those of the Native American, or traditional tribal African, or Confucian-molded Asian societies. In all of these, man is part of the natural order, and finds his meaning and place within it.

Traditional societies had some idea of science. Modern western science grew out of the medieval scientific world that preceded it; it did not arise in a vacuum. But traditional societies found it difficult to think of nature as disconnected from themselves, and they generally subordinated their view of what moderns would call "the natural order of things" to their theological perceptions. Once an alien concept, like Aristotle and Ptolemy's cosmology from ancient Greece, worked its way into the medieval understanding of the universe, it acquired the imprimatur of the church and was, therefore, sacrosanct and beyond questioning. Chinese and Arab scientists made astounding discoveries, but these did not lead to any alteration in the traditional nature of their societies; on the contrary, they tended to reinforce them.

Finally, we are suggesting the scientific world view is the most important of our eight characteristics of the modern because the other seven, in due course, seek to define themselves in terms of it. You will notice each attempts to be "scientific" after its own fashion.

SECULAR OUTLOOK

Being modern means looking at the world in rational and scientific terms, and viewing the world as a rational place that operates according to rationally discernable principles. Therefore, we should not expect it to be affected by the intervention of the divine, at least not as an ordinary occurrence. We call this a secular outlook. It does not mean one is necessarily an atheist, only that one looks at most earthly events as natural phenomena. Earthquakes, falling in love, being guilty, and even being benevolent are all things subject to scientific and rational explanation. Religious considerations are reserved for such questions as: Why was I born? What will happen to me when I die? Why is there a universe in the first place? These are weighty questions and worthy of serious consideration, but they are not subject to rational and scientific investigation.

Traditional societies assume that whatever happens is somehow a product of the activity of their gods or God. On December 26, 2004, a tsunami struck the coast of Indonesia, killing nearly three hundred thousand people. The modernist way to explain this has to do with plate tectonics and an earthquake that produced this powerfully destructive force. More traditional explanations were also offered at the time. Some Christian clergy suggested it was a punishment from God for being Muslims and/or for persecuting Christians. Muslim clerics by contrast agreed it was a judgment from God, but for a different offense—the offense of not being good Muslims. The point was that what was a natural phenomenon to the modernist was understood as a theological one by these contemporary traditionalist religious leaders

Mercia Eliade, a twentieth-century scholar in comparative religions, argued that what he termed "archaic" societies made a deliberate effort to destroy any sense of the linearity of time, the sense that time went only forward. Instead, theirs was an attempt to have time be repetitive, or cyclical. Native American Cherokees, for example, in their "green corn" ceremonies abolish time and begin the universe all over again each year. Ancient Hindus or Celts viewed life in the universe as cyclical.

Not surprisingly, people in traditional societies, such as the ones Eliade described, valued what they had always done and looked with suspicion upon anything or anyone new. They accommodated change only by redefining it as part of their tradition, so that it was not new and disturbing to their sense of order. Their authorities were old, the older the better. Indeed, in most traditional societies there once was a time when things were perfect, a "Garden of Eden" or golden age, but since then things have degenerated.

By contrast, modern society emphasizes progress. Modernists believe things are getting better and better, and the future will be better still. History is less important to them because only that which is most up to date is of any value. The greatest authorities are the most recent ones. In short, modern society is secular, forward looking, and seeks its answers in the natural world, while traditional ones are mythological, backward looking, and find their answers by appealing to their traditions.

DEPENDENCY ON TECHNOLOGY

Closely linked to science in its modern form is technology. As the modern centuries have passed, the linkage has become more obvious, and today the two are clearly impossible without each other. Think of the role technology plays, for instance, in modern physics with its massive particle accelerators. Theories could never be tested without the work of the technologists who can design such equipment. At first, though, there was very little linkage between the two. The great pottery maker Josiah Wedgewood did not need science to develop his pottery, yet he helped found the British Royal Society for the very purpose of advancing science. He also brought a rational attitude to his work, not unlike that of Newton.

All humans, and even other animal species, depend upon their technologies for survival. Civilization itself was a by-product of the rise of agricultural technology. People around the globe have found ways to improve their lives by inventing things. How is this a trait that distinguished the modern from the traditional? It is more a matter of degree than of kind, although with the rise of the Internet it is fast becoming both. But the point is we are in much more trouble without our technologies than traditional peoples were without theirs. How long could you feed yourself without grocery stores and vehicles to get you to them? Without computers, much of our current business would be impossible to conduct. Most could not attend school without an automobile or computer. How often do you write someone a letter you actually put in the mail, rather than simply e-mailing or texting them? I'll bet you see the point.

INDUSTRIALIZATION AND URBANIZATION

Until the early nineteenth century, almost everyone on the planet lived a rural life. They were farmers, and even after the rise of cities, which gave rise to civilizations, most people lived in the country. But as a result of industrialization, humans moved into cities. This urbanization process first occurred in England, early in the nineteenth century, and although there are some places where it has not yet occurred, most nations of the world are today predominately urban. It is highly likely that during your lifetime the overwhelming majority of the earth's population will live in cities.

Industrialization meant a shift from hand manufacturing to machine production in factories. When people worked in factories (compared with working on farms) their work lives became highly regimented. The factory whistle dictated the rhythms of life more than the sun and the seasons. They needed places to live near where they worked, resulting in an increase in the number and size of cities, unprecedented in human history. Finally, industrialization changed the ways they thought. Before the industrial era, aristocratic values dominated European life and values, but after industrialization and the subsequent rise of the middle class, different sets of values came to compete for allegiances. Before, work was to be avoided; the nobility had others to do that for them. After industrialization, if you did not work, according to the new middle class, there was something wrong with you. The new factory working class also came to develop its own sense of values that sometimes clashed with those of their employers. Industrialization then will have major economic consequences, but political ones as well. In short, industrialization radically altered the ways people worked, lived, and thought.

Industrialization and urbanization radically changed family life. Having lots of children became a disadvantage. What children needed to know was no longer necessarily something their parents could teach them. As such, it became necessary for them to obtain most of their education from strangers rather than family members

Recently, with the rise of the computer and Internet, much has been written about the end of the industrial age and the beginning of the age of information. This is not changing where most people live, but it is altering how they work and think. We will look at these changes at the end of the course.

ECONOMIC INTERDEPENDENCE

To be interdependent is to depend upon one another. Today, no country can be unconcerned about what is happening to another's economies. *Schadenfreude* is certainly not an option, as serious economic problems in one part of the world often have an influence, at times deleterious, upon others.

Just before the American Civil War, Great Britain did away with slavery in its colonies. When the Civil War began, Great Britain was tempted to side with the South against the North because Britain depended upon the South to provide raw cotton for its factories. Without the cotton, the factories would have to close, causing a depression in the English economy. The North, with its blockade of the South, created a genuine economic problem for the British government. While Britain considered supporting the South, in the end it turned to its emerging empire, India and Egypt in particular, to supply its factories with cotton. But clearly, England's economy and that of the Southern Confederacy were interdependent.

This kind of relationship has only become more significant with the passage of time. Recent history provides a number of similar examples. The Great Depression in America had awful consequences for the economies of Latin America, which depended upon Americans to buy its raw materials. When Japan fell into a slump in the 1990s, our gasoline prices fell significantly but so did our sales to that part of the world.

Nor does the type of economy, capitalist or socialist, make any difference. We shall see nations have tried to become economically self-sufficient, especially in the twentieth century, but these efforts inevitably failed. For good or ill, as a result of modernization, all humans are connected and everyone's well-being depends to some degree on the well-being of everyone else.

DYNASTIC AND BUREAUCRATIC NATION-STATES

Throughout the world today, people belong to nation-states. Put simply, this is a political association made up of citizens of the political entity to which they all belong. People define themselves as being members of a nation and see their territory as sacred, inviolable, and nontransferrable.

In return, their nation demands their ultimate allegiance: before family, before religion (when beliefs conflict with the requirements of the state; e.g., polygamy and Mormonism), and, at times, even before individual self-interest.

Nor does the form of state matter, from democratic to authoritarian; it only matters that the ruling group cultivate a sense of belonging among the peoples who make it up. Once the nation-state concept took hold of human consciousness, it was easy for political leaders to use it to stir up animosities against other peoples and nations, leading to wars. Just how important this power is

will become evident when we have examined the two world wars of the twentieth century.

The nation-state did not arise all of a sudden but took until the early nineteenth century to become fully developed. In Chapter I, we will explore the first phase of its development with the emergence of the sovereign states of the seventeenth and eighteenth centuries. Most of these states were monarchies, and called "dynastic states," in reference to their ruling families (e.g., the Bourbons in France, the Hapsburgs in Austria-Hungary, or the Romanovs in Russia). As these names suggest, these states were defined as the personal possessions of the ruling family and as bodies of citizens, French, Austrian, or Russian.

Charles V, the sixteenth century Hapsburg ruler, provides the perfect example of such a ruler. His empire included Spain, and therefore the colonies of the new world, which he inherited from his mother; the Netherlands, the land of his birth from his father; and the Holy Roman Empire, in particular Austria, and parts of Italy from his grandfather. The point is, he inherited all these territories; they had nothing in common with one another except a shared ruler, Charles V.

The completion of the evolution of the nation-state system occurred late in the eighteenth century with the American and French revolutions. Thereafter, nation-states appear regularly, replacing traditional ones, to the present.

Closely connected with the emergence of the nation-state state was the growth of state bureaucracies. Bureaucracies are the hired officials who make a government work. In America, you might encounter them in the postal service, the military, the IRS, Social Security, and the myriad other federal agencies, and also state officials, or the local police.

Bureaucracies have a bad reputation. The adjectives "faceless' or "impersonal" are often linked with them. They can be, but without a bureaucracy no government would be able to exercise the power necessary to operate the nation, defend it against enemies, or advance its citizens' national interests, at least as the rulers see those interests.

Traditional societies were different in character. First, government was generally more personal. There was certainly no notion of "the people," of citizens. The state was ruled usually by a monarch who was aided by a group of officials, usually from the members of the aristocracy. The people's interests, whether free or unfree (serfs or slaves), were not supposed to be the primary concern of the ruling class. Indeed, it was quite the other way around; the people existed to serve the needs of the ruling class.

Furthermore, it was generally accepted that God had ordained society to be this way; to oppose the status quo in any way was an act of impiety, as well as political rebellion. More often than not, the ruler got his authority from God (the gods), and ruled in accordance with his perception of His or their wishes. Likewise, the clergy, in traditional states, were very much a part of the ruling elites and helped reinforce its control over the lower orders of society. As a group, they were wealthy and so had a vested interest in doing so. What this will mean in the early modern period is that those who favored modernization often looked upon established religious authorities, and at times their beliefs, as obstacles to reform to be overcome.

In the early European Middle Age, state treasuries were the personal property of the rulers rather than of the states they ruled. Such bureaucracies as existed were the personal servants of the ruler. By the late Middle Ages, these bodies began to resemble their modern successors. The nation-state did not fully exist in its contemporary form until after the French and American revolutions

early in the nineteenth century. We will see how this complicated transformation occurred in subsequent chapters.

MASS CULTURE

The seventh attribute of the modern world, which we are calling "mass culture," is the most recent to appear. Today, we increasingly live in a world in which no group is willing to take a back seat to any other group. We are of the opinion that everyone should be able to achieve whatever he or she wants and is capable of achieving. Yet it may seem obvious, before the American and French revolutions, that everywhere around the globe people assumed certain people in their societies, by rights, enjoyed more privileges, wealth, and power than did others. Those who were the victims of this arrangement believed in the justice of the system quite as much as those who benefitted from it. It was simply the way God had ordained things; we must recognize and submit to our betters, period, end of story. What makes the late eighteenth and early nineteenth centuries significant is that this period marked the first time in human history people began to raise questions about that proposition, and while their vision was rather limited (e.g., they did not oppose slavery and in some cases owned slaves themselves), their ideas were pregnant with the future.

Like all the traits we have mentioned, this one is a work in progress. Race is still a barrier to advancement, as is religion, or sexuality, or place of national origin. Being born to a wealthy family still confers advantages. The point is, while these barriers have not been fully erased, it is difficult if not impossible for any politician, in a state influenced by modernist ideas, to maintain they should not be. That is certainly a transforming force in human life wrought by modernization.

TIME

Moderns are often said to be slaves to time. We live by the clock. When we do not have to get up at a certain time to be at work or in class, we don't set our clocks, but woe be unto us if we don't and fail to meet an appointment or take a test. To be sure, an industrially based society must have the order and discipline the clock imposes upon us. Yet, at times, one hears longings for a simpler life.

Traditional life, in fact, was rather simpler where time was concerned. First, the seasons were far more important to life in this earlier era than in ours. People largely lived and worked in accordance with the hours of daylight, more in the spring and summer, and less in the fall and winter; generally they were awakened with the light and retired to bed after dark. Climate, too, was a greater factor in determining their actions. If it were freezing outside, or unbearably hot, it was difficult to work out of doors or even in. There are accounts of medieval banquets in which the wine froze in their metal goblets. So life was more responsive to the seasonal rhythms. Since the advent of electricity, we have come to ignore both light and temperature; we keep on working, night and day, 24–7. Modern life, then, is vastly more regimented by time than our pre-modern ancestors could have imagined.

COMPLICATIONS

We have tried to define the modern way of life and contrast it from the traditional that came before, and that to some degree persists today. We cannot conclude this introduction, however, without citing a couple complicating factors. First, the traits we have enumerated, and briefly defined, do not appear in Western Europe all at once (or even in a completed form) when they first appear. Recall the nation-state would take shape over an extended period, from its beginnings in the seventeenth century until its completion in the nineteenth. The same point can be made for most of the other characteristics.

Modernization did not spread throughout the world all at once either. It began in Western Europe and the colonial areas under English, Spanish, and French control. Thereafter, it spread to Eastern Europe, and, later still, to Africa and Asia. Its influences can be seen throughout the world today. You can find examples of the eight traits throughout the world.

You can also find survivals of more traditional ways of life. The spread of modernism (in the second sense of that word) has been challenged throughout the entire period covered by this course. The degree to which modernization transformed traditional structures—especially, but not exclusively, in areas outside its base of origins in Western Europe—varies; indeed, waxes and wanes, sometime seeming to be very powerful, while at others very much on the defensive. One quick illustration will have to suffice for now. In the late nineteenth century, when European nation-states were taking over the entire globe in what was called "the Era of New Imperialism," Japan saved itself from this fate by adopting Western ways of doing things, adapting them to its own uses. It even joined Western states in building an empire at the expense of Korea and Taiwan. Western ideas and institutions became all the rage. Traditional Japanese ideas had very little sway. But following World War I, when the Europeans treated the Japanese in ways they regarded as racists and shabby, traditionalist Japanese ideas began to regain influence, and by the 1930s, in part because of the Great Depression, Japan threw off the Western ideas it had embraced and became the champions of a movement to drive the Western foreigners out of Asia. Ultimately, this led to Pearl Harbor and our involvement in World War II.

We will see other examples of this waxing and waning as we progress through the period covered by the course. From the beginning, modernist ideas have challenged the traditional bases of civilizations around the world, and continue to do so. But do not think the story we are telling is simply the story of the rise and triumph of modernism. It is rather more complicated. It is the story of the struggle between modern and traditional ideas and institutions being waged since the seventeenth century, and continues to this day.

After World War II, several anti-modernist movements, postmodernism and feminism, arose in Western Europe, the heartland of modernization itself. The European empires also came to an end, and as states gained their independence from their former masters, a number of anti-Western movements also arose. Each of these, in its own way, challenged the intellectual and social assumptions of modernism.

The story we are telling you will not be finished when the course ends, but you will have acquired knowledge to better enable you to make sense of that world. It is the world you live in today, and will live in for most—if not all—of your life. That is information well worth your knowing.

FOR FURTHER READING

Eliade, Mircea. *The Sacred and the Profane. New York: Harcourt Inc., 1959.*

The Rise of the Sovereign State

As we suggested in the *Introduction*, the modern world is made up of nation-states. Of all the traits we identified in that chapter, this one is the most widely embraced. There is no place on the planet today in which pre-modern forms of state exist without reflecting, to some degree, the influence of the nation-state idea, and, in most cases, the premodern forms have been completely supplanted by it.

The nation-state originated in Europe in the mid-seventeenth century, but only became fully developed after the French and American revolutions. In this chapter, we will be examining the first phase in its development, the rise of the "sovereign state." We will look at the political institutions out of which it arose in the Late Middle Ages, including the Renaissance and the Reformation. Then we will address the political ideas that distinguish the modern from what went before, and finally, we will examine the various political systems that resulted therefrom.

EUROPEAN POLITICS BEFORE THE RISE OF THE SOVEREIGN STATE

The European Middle Ages, which spanned the sixth to the mid-seventeenth centuries[1] CE, developed a political arrangement called "feudalism." Land tenure of the ruling classes, including the clergy, was based upon their military service (vassalage) in return for land and peasants to work it, along with the right to govern them (independent jurisdiction).

---

1   These dates mean the Renaissance and Reformation are treated as part of the medieval. In part they are precursors of the modern as well, but here, the similarities with the medieval are more important than their differences from it.

1

Political power in this period is best defined as "suzerain." When a king gave lands to a duke in return for his services, the king forfeited all rights to that land, unless the duke did not live up to the terms of his agreement or died without heirs. His rights were "suzerain," not "sovereign."

Towns did not fit into the feudal system since the people who lived in them did not fight, were not serfs who worked the land, or clergy who prayed. The solution was to allow towns to purchase charters of liberties, which allowed them to operate independently. Towns became virtually self-governing. Of course, they paid a fine price for these freedoms to a local nobleman, or to a king who used the money to hire mercenary soldiers.

Churchmen were also part of this system. They held large amounts of land they exploited just like aristocrats and they played an important role in the rise of towns.

Beginning late in the eleventh century, Europe began to expand beyond its borders in what is known as the Crusades. These invasions of the Middle East in the name of religion seem rather absurd in modern times, but they were eloquent testimony to the resurgent Europe that had taken place.

By the twelfth century a rather sophisticated civilization had emerged. Kings became powerful and brought aristocrats under their control, and institutions of government and law took shape. England came to have a common law system upon which our legal system is based. Legislative institutions also grew up, such as Parliament in England, which by the thirteenth century even included townsmen among its members. Similar institutions arose throughout Europe. Many survive to this day.

Late in the Middle Ages, as towns became important economically and socially, a middle class came to be a political force to be reckoned with. Its influence was most pronounced in German, Dutch, and British towns. It is difficult to imagine the Protestant Reformation succeeding if these cities had not existed.

The Breakdown of the Medieval

In the modern state the notion of sovereignty supplants suzerainty. The difference between the two and how this new concept arose is our next inquiry.

First, we will examine how the new concept arose. The simplest way to put it is to suggest everything that was going well in the High Middle Ages (eleventh to early fourteenth centuries) began to come unhinged by the mid-fourteenth century. Perhaps the most devastating event was the recurring bubonic plague, which by some estimates reduced the population of Europe by at least a third, and perhaps more. With the populations contracted, so did the economy that ceased to expand as it had in previous centuries.

In the High Middle Ages, rulers in the emerging states of Europe had demonstrated great leadership skills. By the fourteenth century, they either died young, or were less capable than their predecessors had been. The result was a resurgence of the power of the aristocracy whose selfish interests did not make for well-governed societies. As a result, life became more insecure, and commerce became riskier and less rewarding.

While not menaced by the Mongols during this period, Western Europe was threatened by the Ottoman Turks, who destroyed the Byzantine Empire in 1453 and later took over parts of what is today Hungary and Rumania. On several occasions, they seemed about to conquer Vienna and many feared Christian civilization in Europe was in danger of being destroyed.

Intellectually, it was a time of ferment as well. In the late-medieval period, whatever happened came from the hand of God. Good things indicated God's pleasure; bad the opposite. As their situation in this period was anything but good, there had to be some religious reason involved. This led to new and at times heretical ideas. A number of mystical religious communities arose that did not require the institutional church to provide spiritual solace, and outright heresies, such as the Cathari, Waldensians, and Hussites also arose in this period. The Protestant Reformation of the sixteenth century then comes as no surprise.

By the late fifteenth century, every measure to explain why Europe had been strong, expansive, and prosperous now suggested just the opposite. Not surprisingly, people began to seek solutions to their problems. The Renaissance and Reformation make sense in this context. Renaissance thinkers wanted to go back to ancient Greece and Rome for inspiration. Many of these ideas will have a significant influence upon education, art, and philosophy in the West, but they did not provide the institutional basis for a new Western state-system. The Reformation is equally important because it destroyed the religious unity fundamental to medieval civilization, but neither the political ideas of Protestants nor of Roman Catholics would come to Europe's rescue by the early seventeenth century. For that we must look to the nation-state and the concept of sovereignty.

The Sovereign State

What is the concept of sovereignty? Simply put, it means ultimate authority is invested in an individual or group whose power is not conditional upon someone's failing to live up to an obligation, as it had been in the Middle Ages. The modern sovereign state is capable of taxing its citizens, raising armies, even taking one's property (with compensation). In the early modern period, sovereignty often included the power to force citizens either to embrace a common religion, or to move to a new location. Failure to make one or the other of these choices often led to execution.

Sovereignty can be invested in a single person (a "sovereign"); in a small group, as in the Netherlands; or in a larger group, as in England, where sovereignty was divided among the king and his parliament, lords, and commons.

There were some states that did not embrace this concept, in particular Poland and the Holy Roman Empire. Both no longer existed by the end of the Napoleonic Wars. We will examine how they operated, and how the absence of a sovereign state idea helps explain their destruction as states.

The concept was first articulated in France in response to the disorders of the sixteenth and seventeenth centuries stemming from the Reformation. A group of French thinkers, the *politiques*, seeking a way out of this turmoil, came to the conclusion ultimate authority had to be invested in some source, if anyone were to be safe. As monarchists, they embraced a royal absolutism and were early supporters of what came to be known as "divine right monarchy."

The English thinker Thomas Hobbes, in *Leviathan*, promoted a similar but secular idea. He postulated that, at some time in the past, humans lived without government in what he called a "state of nature." Life under these circumstances, he famously observed, was "solitary, poor, nasty, brutish and short." In response, people made a contract with a sovereign power to protect them and, in return, gave that individual or group all their rights. That power, being sovereign over them, could order them to do what he or they deemed necessary for the well-being of the state. Only when the people returned to the state of nature (through conquest or a breakdown of the system that gave them sovereignty) were they relieved of their obligation to total obedience.

Sovereignty can also be invested in a group and limited in its scope. The best spokesman for this notion was John Locke. In his *Two Treatises on Government*, he proposed a theory of government somewhat like England's limited monarchy with its king and Parliament, which came to prevail in England after the Glorious Revolution of 1688.

In the state of nature, Locke argued, certain inconveniences arise because it is difficult to be objective where one's own interests are concerned. In his mind, men have certain rights: life, liberty, and property that are not subject to government intervention. But where conflicts arise, people need government. And he naturally recommended something similar to a limited monarch with a parliament of lords and commons. In addition, he argued citizens have the right, indeed the duty, of rebellion when the sovereign oversteps its bounds. And he suggested England's government was effective because it employed a system of checks and balances, with the executive invested in the king and the legislative and judicial invested in the Parliament. When we get to Thomas Jefferson and the Declaration of Independence, not to mention our Constitution of 1786, you will doubtless notice Locke's influence upon late colonial and early American political thought and policy.

The second new idea to become part of the nation-state system was "reason of state." First articulated in his *The Prince*, Machiavelli, a late-Renaissance Italian, argued a sovereign state should do anything necessary to advance its own well-being, including stealing, lying, or even murder. Ordinary rules of morality, he argued, simply did not apply to states. Clearly it was not wise to do such things all the time. But when the state's vital interests were at stake, it was right to do so. This notion, though rarely openly acknowledged, has been a guiding principle for rulers throughout the modern period down to the present.

The third new political idea to arise out of the nation-state system was "balance of power." States form alliances to protect themselves against other states. The type of government, be it monarchy or some type of republic, was not important. What mattered was size. If you were a small state such as Britain or the Netherlands facing danger from a larger state like France, creating an alliance with other states was the only way to give you enough power to dissuade that larger neighbor from attacking you.

In the seventeenth century, the large state feared the most was France, especially during the reign of Louis XIV. Scholars do not always agree as to how influential balance of power was in shaping political leaders' thinking, but it does serve as a way of understanding some of their actions. Perhaps an example will help. In the War of Spanish Succession, which we will look at in Chapter 2, Austria and England went to war against France to prevent the throne of Spain being passed to Louis's great grandson. The idea of a French ruler in Spain had enormous consequences for the balance of power, and a lengthy war was fought to prevent this occurrence. During the French Revolution, balance of power was replaced by ideology (democracy versus absolute monarchy). But thereafter European states returned to the balance of power pattern, which prevailed throughout the nineteenth century until ideologically based alliances reemerged following World War I, after the rise of communism in the Soviet Union.

One final notion before we look at specific states: most of the states we will be discussing are "dynastic" in character, which means they were defined by the possessions of their family. Parts of an empire could be exchanged as one might sell or swap property today. Such changes did not cause undue consternation in the areas involved, as they had no sense of national identity where their rulers were concerned. This will continue to be true until after the French Revolution and the rise of nationalism.

Divine Right Monarchy in Western Europe

The most popular state form in the seventeenth century was divine right monarchy. It is difficult for American students to comprehend that kings and aristocrats were more often fighting one another than working together to exploit the lower classes. Yet, for European monarchs, the problem had always been how to control the nobility, especially the older families or those who possessed large amounts of land. When the kings were successful, societies were generally peaceful and prosperous. When not, disorder reigned. In the late Middle Ages, the pendulum had swung in the direction of the factious nobility; political stability and social order suffered as a consequence, and the religious dissentions of the Reformation only made things worse. This set of conditions explains why the proponents of divine right monarchy believed giving absolute power to a monarch was the best way to restore order and hold society together. Their intent was to create a system of government that would bring these great lords under royal control. We will look at the reigns of Louis XIII and Louis XIV of France to make the case, but Ferdinand and Isabella of Spain, and the English Tudor, Henry VII, were attempting to do the same thing.

Divine right absolutism should not be confused with the arbitrary power of the sort enjoyed by contemporary Chinese emperors, who could execute offending officials, along with their family members, at will. By contrast, European monarchs understood themselves to be acting on behalf of God; they, perforce, had to take certain religious and moral principles into account. While their religious counselors could not tell them how to govern, they had to give spiritual council for the good of the monarchs' immortal souls, which often came to the same thing.

In practice, creating an absolute government turned on the structure and staffing of the bureaucracy. In the Middle Ages, kings relied mostly upon bishops and great lords. Woe be unto the king who ignored them. By the early modern period, bureaucracies in Western Europe were staffed with men of lesser noble status, or even with legally trained officials, who rose out of the middle class. The great lords and clergy were seldom allowed to occupy the greatest positions of power. They might fulminate against the influence of upstart bureaucrats from classes beneath them, but, unlike their ancestors, were unable to do a lot about the situation.

This is not to say the great nobilities did not continue to be powerful players in society. Until well into the nineteenth century, their control of land and local affairs made them the most powerful, wealthy, and privileged group in Europe. They continued to play important roles in government, in the military, the clergy, and the diplomatic service. But by the end of the seventeenth century, they were no longer able to bring about widespread social disruption or the fall of the reigning sovereign. No monarch wanted to do away with the order; after all, he was its head. He simply wanted to find ways to bring it under control, and for the most part, as we shall see, seventeenth- and eighteenth-century monarchs succeeded in doing so, at least until the end of the eighteenth century and the French Revolution. Somewhat paradoxically, this was an age of aristocratic privilege in which rulers and their bureaucrats, nonetheless, predominated. We will begin with France.

French Absolutism of Louis XIII and Louis XIV

Two conditions in sixteenth-century France help explain how civil war came to that country. First, Protestantism arrived in a Calvinistic form. The Huguenots, as they were called, were located mostly in the south, a region long known for its resistance to rulers from Paris and the north. Second, the monarchs at this time were weak, allowing for conflicts among the nobility who sought to control them. In 1562, the two conditions came together following an altercation between a powerful Catholic nobleman and a group of Huguenots, which resulted in the massacre of the latter and ignited the first of many civil war massacres known as the French Wars of religion. They flared up periodically until 1598 when Henry of Navarre became Henry IV, the first of the Bourbons and initiator of absolute monarchy in France. To do so, he issued the Edict of Nantes, guaranteeing a measure of religious liberty and political independence to the Huguenots, among whom he had formerly worshipped. "Paris is well worth the mass," he is supposed to have said.

To save his life, Henry converted to Catholicism during the most infamous of these wars, the St. Bartholomew's Day Massacre (August 1572), an attempt to execute every Huguenot in France. Perhaps as many as ten thousand people had died by the middle of 1573. Naturally it led to counterattacks and more conflicts. As soon as he was safe, Henry renounced this forced conversion. But after his second in 1598, he remained a Catholic, if only in name, until his assassination in 1610.

It would have been a significant achievement if he had only kept the state together, but he did more. Aided by his advisor, Sully, he not only brought religious peace to France, he created a more streamlined system of tax collection, promoted agriculture, and worked to rejuvenate Paris. In the eighteenth century, he was remembered and praised as the king who did not so much make war (i.e., Louis XIV) as promote peace, and as the king who wanted every French peasant family to have a chicken in his pot every Sunday.

Henry was succeeded by his son, Louis XIII (1610–1642). While Louis himself did not contribute to the development of the absolutist system in France, his chief minister, Cardinal Richelieu, did. This included creating the beginnings of the absolutist system of government that Louis XIV would complete by dividing France into thirty-two administrative districts, *generalités*, each of which was presided over by an intendant, a royal official not from the old nobility. These officials had tremendous power in their districts, including recruiting soldiers, collecting taxes, and seeing to the general state of things there. Everything they did had to be cleared with the king; if they did not, they were replaced.

Henry IV's religious toleration law, the Edict of Nantes, is something one would find hard to attack today. Yet, at the time, Richelieu thought it gave political independence to the Huguenots. They were a state within the state. So, Richelieu sought to undo their political liberties and tear down their walled cities, which the Huguenots had insisted upon to make them feel safe enough to enter into the treaty. La Rochelle, the last Huguenot stronghold, fell in 1628, despite the efforts of Queen Elizabeth of Britain.

Richelieu also sought to weaken the power of the Catholic nobility, destroying some castles deemed too powerful and replacing untrustworthy nobles with those whom he felt he could trust. His spies were thought to be everywhere, and nobles who plotted against the king were executed.

When Richelieu died, the combination of high taxes and noble resentment of the curtailment of their power sparked a popular uprising known as the Fronde (1648–53). The new chief minister, Cardinal

Mazarin, an Italian and later morganatic husband to Louis's widow, Anne of Austria, fled Paris with the thoroughly terrified young future Louis XIV in tow. The latter hated Paris forever thereafter and, once he came to power, settled at Versailles, converting his father's small hunting lodge into the most magnificent palace of the era.

Mazarin did manage to put down the uprising and remained in power until his death in 1661. Louis then assumed control of the state. He was convinced of two things: he did not want to be ruled by a first minister as his father had been, and he knew he needed an all-powerful government to protect himself and France against sedition and insurrection.

Louis XIV (1638–1715)

Louis XIV has become the embodiment of the theory of divine right monarchy and for good reason. When Mazarin died, Louis got rid of ministers who might have become the new first minister and insisted that, henceforth, every ministerial action had to have his prior approval. As the divine right King of France, he sought to control every aspect of life

In government, he continued the administrative system initiated by Richelieu, which by this time had been expanded by subdividing the *generaliés* into "subdelegations," each presided over by a subdelegate who had powers similar to that of the *Intendant* and to whom each was responsible. Below the subdelegations were *communes* (towns), which were answerable to the subdelegates. To assist Louis in making his decisions, there were the *Council of Stat* that dealt with matters of state policy, *Conseil des Dépêches* that dealt with internal affairs, the Council of Finances, and the Privy Council that met in the king's private quarters and was an appeals court. But Louis ultimately made all the decisions.

To understand how the system worked, or was supposed to at least, consider a hypothetical local mayor who had to deal with a flood that washed away a bridge vitally important to the community. He would need financial help for repairs, so he would report the problem and make a request to the subdelegate to whom he answered. This official, in turn, would pass his request up to the Intendant, who would pass it on the Conseil des Dépêches. They would have discussed the matter with the king who would decide whether to honor the request. This information then would make its way back down the chain of command. To be sure, most dispatches originated with the king himself. Louis was a hands-on ruler who devoted long hours to affairs of state.

His officials came from the lesser aristocracy or the legally trained bourgeois. They were loyal and dependable because without Louis's support they had no power or wealth.[2] They were also educated in the law. He rewarded them with land as well as wealth.

Louis did not want the old aristocracy to have real power, but this did not mean he ignored them. On the contrary, he gave them perhaps more attention they might have liked. His rationale seemed to be

---

2   By the next century, the nature of this group changed significantly. Since their descendants acquired land they too became nobles, although these "nobles of the robe" (meaning lawyers, as they were called) enjoyed a lesser social status than aristocrats who could trace their noble roots into the past, the "nobles of the sword." By the eve of the French Revolution, so far from being loyal and reliable servants of the crown, as their ancestors had been for Louis XIV, the robe nobility were at the center of opposition to Louis XVI's government.

that if they were at Versailles, his residence, busy with balls, games, dances, gambling, and other forms of amusement, they would not be present on their country estates to interfere with what his local officials were doing. Versailles became not only the residence of the king, but of his great nobles as well. If you did not spend time at Louis's court, he would profess not to know who you were when you wanted to make a marriage alliance for your children or secure a military commission for your son.

Versailles was also the center of a vibrant cultural life and became one of the most splendid palaces and cities in the whole of Europe (Figure 1.1). A number of imitation palaces sprang up throughout the Holy Roman Empire, suggesting France had replaced Italy as the cultural center of Europe. During Louis's reign, painting, music, and theatre alike came under his scrutiny. Louis was especially interested in classical

Figure 1.1: Chateau de Versailles

ballet, which he promoted from his youth. Consequently, if your art did not please the king, you could not expect to advance. You were advised to make sure that what you said, drew, sang, played, or acted in did not sound critical of Louis and his regime. European recognition of France's accomplishments in the arts redounded to the glory of the king and his nation. Clearly, Louis's interest in the arts was aesthetic, but also political.

Louis also sought to control the religious life of France. Divine right monarchy combines a modern secular understanding of government with a sense of religious duty that is very traditional. It is not surprising Louis felt such a strong sense of responsibility where it was concerned. In particular, he objected to the religious settlement made by his grandfather, the Edict of Nantes, and very much wanted to do away with it. The idea of tolerating a non-Catholic religious body was to him as theologically unacceptable as it was socially unsound.

Louis hoped the time would come when all his Huguenot subjects would have come back into the Catholic fold and he could revoke the offending edict. In 1685, he decided the time had finally arrived. Claiming it was no longer needed as none of his subjects were Protestants any more, he revoked it. Those Huguenots who in fact remained were thereafter subjected to vigorous persecution.

Many of France's most highly skilled manufacturers were Huguenots. Louis needed them for his economy, and there were laws that prevented them from immigrating. His revocation put them in a rather untenable situation. Those who could took their talents elsewhere and fled to Holland, England, and ultimately the English colonies. Some went to Turkey, converted to Islam and became corsairs, pirates who raided the French coast, kidnapping and enslaving French subjects. Some of those who remained converted; others simply tried to be unobtrusive, worshipping in secret and otherwise hiding their religious affiliation. Ultimately, Louis's policy did not succeed, but caused an enormous amount of social and economic harm for France.

Louis also wanted his Catholic subjects to conform to what he regarded as correct Catholic doctrine and practice. In particular, he persecuted the Jansenists, a group of Catholics whose theology espoused an Augustinian predestination. Their arch enemies, the Jesuits, staunchly supported the dominance of the pope in French religious life. Louis also opposed their "Ultramontane" position and insisted on running the French Catholic Church as he saw fit (termed "Gallican"), even in defiance of popes.

Not surprisingly, Louis wanted to control and reform the French military system. Aided by his minister of war, Le Tellier, Marquis of Louvois, Louis created a national army. No longer were soldiers employees of the commanders who recruited them; instead, the state housed, fed, clothed, and disciplined them. Their officers, consisting of both great lords and men of lesser rank, were highly trained and, themselves, under the control of Louis's government.

Louis's reforms worked well for much of his reign. Armies and wars are always costly, and, as the "Sun King" is supposed to have said on his death bed, he did love war too much. But in later years, when it was difficult for his supply lines to keep up with military needs, order and discipline suffered.[3]

An absolute ruler such as Louis would also expect to marshal the economic resources of the nation to support his policies. He followed the dominant economic theory of the seventeenth century: mercantilism, a theory that emphasized state control over the economy, precisely what one would expect in an absolutist state.[4]

Most of the economic reforms Louis instituted were crafted by his minister of finances, Jean-Baptiste Colbert. The several projects cited above suggest the costs of Louis's government were high. Colbert tried to meet them with tax reforms on both property and income. The great lords tried to find ways to evade them, but they were not always successful. He also promoted industry, highly regulated to be sure, and international trade.

By the end of Louis's reign, it was apparent all these reforms were not sufficient. In part, it was a result of the high costs of warfare. Royal expenses associated with Versailles were also exorbitant. And the revocation of the Edict of Nantes had the unintended consequence of driving out of France many of the skilled workmen the realm needed for the success of its economy.

Louis was followed by Louis XV, his great grandson, when the boy was three years old. He would be succeeded by Louis XVI. Neither was suited to run the kind of state Richelieu and Louis XIV had created; nor were the nobility, now accustomed to their political inutility, able to pick up the reins of power.

---

3   We will look at the wars below.
4   We will discuss it in Chapter 2.

Absolutism in Eastern Europe

Louis XIV sought to control all aspects of French life by keeping the highest-ranking nobles firmly under his control, replacing them with lesser lords or legally trained bourgeois. Thereby he sought to be the absolute sovereign in France. Eastern European absolute monarchs (in Russia, Austria, and Prussia) sought to achieve the same objective, but in a rather different manner. In these states, to be noble one must be a servant of the crown; in return, he received lands and serfs to work them. Unlike their French and Spanish counterparts, these aristocrats were a "service nobility." The results were similar in many respects. First, as with Louis, the purpose of these reforms was closely related to military needs. These rulers, like Louis, loved war and spent much of their time engaging in it. And like Louis, these rulers were prepared to introduce modernizing reforms to accomplish their ends. As with France, their reforms provoked a traditionalist reaction that sometimes limited the effects of the changes these rulers had hoped to make, and at others completely overturned them.

During the seventeenth and eighteenth centuries, where serfdom and slavery virtually disappeared from Western European life, in Eastern Europe they became solidly entrenched, thereby creating a symbiotic relationship between the two regions. As the West moved away from servitude, it simultaneously promoted the rise of the middle class, as well as trade, towns, and ultimately empire, all hallmarks of the modern period. But the West could not supply all the raw materials it required; these were supplied by states in the East. Thus, the market for raw materials from the West encouraged the political/social system with its serfdom, which remained a characteristic of life in Eastern Europe until the twentieth century. If you think about a similar nineteenth century American symbiotic relationship that existed between the Southern slave economy and the emerging Northern factory system, you can understand what was going on.

It should also be noted there were other forms of state in Eastern Europe that did not attempt to modernize. The consequences for them were far more destructive. The absolutist states of Russia, Prussia, and Austria—along with England, France, the Netherlands, and for a time Spain—are the nations that will be the primary arbiters of the political events that shaped European history in the seventeenth and eighteenth centuries. Premodern state forms as the Holy Roman Empire or Poland became insignificant, or disappeared completely.

Prussia

Modern Germany arose out of Prussia late in the nineteenth century. In the seventeenth century, this area was part of the Holy Roman Empire, which contained about two hundred fifty territorial units. Prussia's rise to preeminence began modestly in 1640 when Frederick of Hohenzollern, the Great Elector, as he was called, inherited a noncontiguous assemblage of territories that included the Electorate of Brandenburg, the Duchy of Cleves, and the counties of Mark and Ravensberg. Figure 1.2 is a map of Brandenburg-Prussia that helps you see what that meant. He also held the Duchy of Prussia from the king of Poland.

It is difficult to imagine a state that became so powerful could have been fashioned out of territories so widely scattered. Worse still, it was not possessed of an abundance of natural resources and, although

Figure 1.2: Map of Brandenburg-Prussia

mostly Protestant, its people did not all share the same religious persuasion. Frederick William ruled from 1640 to 1688. He was succeeded by his son, Frederick I (who acquired the title King in Prussia in 1701) from 1688 to 1713, who was succeeded by his son, Frederick William I, (1713–1740), and finally by his son, Frederick II, who ruled from 1740 to 1786. Each proved to be capable and, except for the last, produced an heir who was an adult when his father died. Leaving behind a capable adult heir for three generations was no mean accomplishment.

But the most important reason this house became so powerful—initiated by its founder and promoted by each of his successors—was the advancement and cultivation of the military. It was the only institution common to all the original territories, and those added during the next century and a half. The military enjoyed the highest prestige in the society. It came from the aristocrats, or Junkers, who were consistently loyal supporters of the monarchy. Prussian militarism identified this state for as long as it existed, not to mention the German Empire, which grew out of it in 1870. For their service, the Junkers were awarded lands and the serfs to work them. They also assumed important positions in the state bureaucracy these monarchs developed.

Like Louis XIV, the Prussian rulers knew they had to have a strong bureaucracy. But unlike Louis, they came to rely heavily upon these military aristocrats to serve not only in the army but in the government bureaus as well.

The Great Elector first secured control over taxation and used the revenues therefrom to build a strong military. To accomplish this objective, he created the *Genneralkriegskommissarit*, from which grew the state bureaucracy. He recruited a number of foreigners, in particular French Huguenots, refugees from Louis XIV's religious oppression, to staff it.

His son Frederick III, who became Frederick I, King in Prussia[5] for his service to the Hapsburgs in the War of Spanish Succession, was more interested in ostentatious display than the military. As his grandson, the future Frederick II, put it, he tried to make Prussia into the "Athens of the north." He was greatly inspired by Louis XIV's France and spent lavishly on palaces and educational institutions, which had a powerful influence upon his grandson, but his expenditures left his successor, Frederick William I, with enormous debts.

According to that same grandson, when Frederick William I came to power he transformed Prussia into the "Sparta" of the north. Appalled by Frederick I's extravagance and waste, Frederick William sought to build up both the state's finances and strengthen the military, which led him to complete the bureaucracy with four departments headed by the General Directory, assisted by seventeen provincial councils. All were ultimately answerable to the king. These bodies collected taxes, promoted agriculture, and industry. Frederick I's bureaucratic system continued basically unchanged into the early nineteenth century.

The irony of Frederick William's reign is that, for all his love of things military, he did not engage in warfare. Upon his death, he left his son a strong army and a well-filled treasury. In a later chapter, we will see how Frederick the Great, as his son came to be known, made use of that inheritance. The two did not get along. The son found the father's militaristic ways to be oppressive; at one point, the young man became so alienated he plotted to flee to France. The plan was discovered. Frederick's young assistant in the plot was executed in Frederick's presence. Frederick fainted because he thought he was next, but the intervention of the emperor saved him. It was clear the successor to Frederick William I would be made of very different stuff, as we shall see. But Prussia had become an absolutist state reliant upon a service nobility.

The Empire of the Hapsburgs

The second major absolutist state in Eastern Europe was the Hapsburgs of Austria, Hungary, and Bohemia. The Hapsburgs also had holdings in Italy, and they carried the title of the Holy Roman Emperor of the German People.

This is a good point to say something about that title. The Holy Roman Empire was an ancient political institution destined for oblivion. Its origins lie in the medieval period during which time it was a collection of states, loosely held together by the emperor, who, after 1438, was a Hapsburg. It had a legislature of sorts, a Diet, which was unable to collect taxes, raise armies, or do anything that its members did not willingly undertake. By the early modern period, with the rise of the idea of the sovereign state, this form of political association was an anachronism. The Austrians continued to retain the title. But in truth, their real power rested in their dynastic lands, and not in the imperial title. Napoleon abolished it in 1806, replacing it with the Austrian Empire.

---

5   King in Prussia rather than "of" was meant to show he was not also a king in his imperial possessions like Brandenburg. There he was only the elector. But it was a royal title and that was of importance for the future.

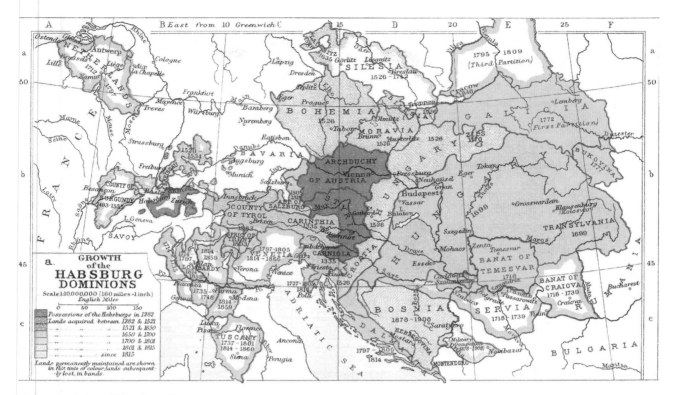

Figure 1.3: Map of Hapsburg Empire

Until 1555, the Hapsburg Empire, under Charles V, had included a Spanish component. But by the seventeenth century there were two Hapsburg branches, the second being in Spain. Its glory days were past to be sure and this line became extinct with the death of Charles II in 1700, resulting in a major European war we see in Figure 1.3.

Here we are concerned about the Austrian branch. To understand its power, we must examine the nature of its dynastic state.

First, its German lands included Upper and Lower Austria, the Tyrol, Carniola, and Carinthia. All these areas were German speaking and mostly Catholic.

Its Hungarian component was mostly in the Ottoman Empire until the end of the seventeenth century. Restored to the Hapsburgs in 1683, following the battle of Mohács, it included several ethnic groups including the Magyars (Hungarians), Slavic Croatians, and the Rumanians in Transylvanian. In religion, the Magyars were a mix of Catholic and Protestant. The Croatians were Catholic, and the Transylvanians a mix of Orthodox Christians, Protestants, and Catholics.

Bohemia, a Slavic state, was Moravian, a precursor of Protestantism and Catholic in religion. The Protestant nobles' attempt to disassociate themselves from the empire led to the Thirty Years War in Germany. It began in 1618 when the Bohemians or Czechs threw a group of Austrian representatives of the emperor out of a third-floor window in Prague (the "Defenestration of Prague") to express their separation as forcefully as they were able. Early in 1619, these same Protestant lords elected Frederick V, the Elector Palatine, a Calvinist, as their new king. The newly elected emperor, also a Frederick, was unwilling to accept this settlement and sent his armies into Bohemia, driving out Frederick the Elector, hereafter known as the

"Winter King." The Protestant lords also lost their lands, and when all was said and done, Bohemia became a land in which the aristocrats were German and Catholic, while the peasants were Protestant and Czech.

The Hapsburgs also had territory in Italy. In all their states there were minorities of Jews and Muslims whose treatment varied from toleration to persecution in both time and place.

Clearly, the Austrian Empire was multi-ethnic in character. That does not explain much about their history in the seventeenth and eighteenth centuries, but by the nineteenth, with the rise of nationalism, it became crucial, and at the end of World War I this empire broke up.

In the seventeenth century, the Hapsburg counterpart to Louis XIV and Frederick William the Great Elector was the Emperor Leopold I (1658–1705). It was he who fashioned a state out of these multi-ethnic provinces along the Danube. It was not as strong or homogenous a state as those of his French and Prussian counterparts. Each region recognized him by a different title: to the Austrians he was the emperor but also the duke, to the Bohemians and Hungarians he was their king.

To hold on to these disparate regions, he was forced to allow degrees of local autonomy his fellow monarchs would not have countenanced. Each region was also controlled by its aristocracy; some continued to have a legislative body and all enjoyed privileges the Hapsburg ruler had to respect. The central government consisted of a series of councils that dealt with war, commerce, trade, and domestic affairs, and made up of aristocrats from all his territories. There were also special councils for each of the provinces making up the state. But Leopold had to be content they paid taxes and provided armies when required, and did not try to rebel and break away. As with all East European absolutist states, the peasants were reduced to serfdom so as to be better controlled by the various aristocratic groups.

Leopold's successors, Joseph I (1705–1711) and Charles VI (1711–1740), sought to make this three-crowned monarchy more secure by making it hereditary in the Hapsburg line. This seemed to be working until the reign of Charles VI, who was unable to produce a son. He tried to guarantee his daughter's succession by persuading his neighboring states and the aristocrats in own empire to agree to "the Pragmatic Sanction of 1713," but when he died Maria Theresa had to fight to hold his kingdom together. Technically the Hapsburg line was extinct. The Austrian Empire itself continued playing an important role in European history until the end of World War I.

The Romanovs of Russia

Russia has always been something of an enigmatic place (See Figure 1.4).

Aside from its size, this map shows the state is north of the hemisphere, and mostly Asian rather than European. Russia originated in Europe early in the Middle Ages, and during the seventeenth and eighteenth centuries expanded eastward toward Siberia, much like the United States began on the East Coast and settled all the way to California. Notice where Moscow, Novgorod, and Saint Petersburg are on the map. They will come up in the discussion below. They are in Europe.

Not surprisingly, geography and climate play an important role in Russian history. To give you an example of what this means, the daily mean temperature for Saint Petersburg from 1971 to 2000 was 21°F

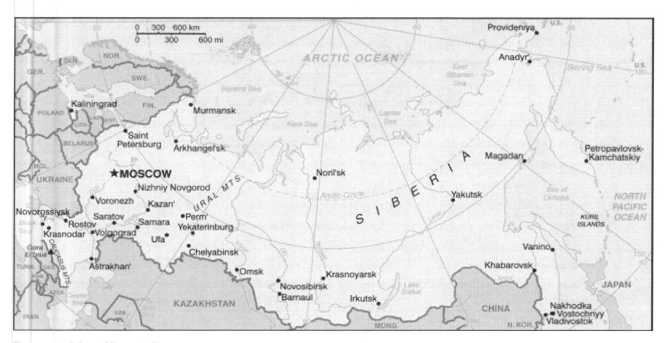

Figure 1.4: Map of Russian Empire

in January to a high of 64°F in July, with a yearly average of 42°F. Now find Yakutsk on the map. It is far to the east. Its averages: January -46°F, July 60°F, with a yearly average of -10°F.[6]

Naturally, Russian civilization reflects both Western and non-Western influences. In the late tenth century, Russia embraced Orthodox Christianity and was significantly influenced by Byzantine religious, political, social, and cultural ideas, rather than Western and Catholic ones. To them, Roman Catholics, and after the Reformation, Protestants, were simply heretics. This certainly separates them from things Western.

In 1453, the Byzantine Empire (the Second Rome, in Russian eyes) came to an end following the fall of Constantinople to the Turks. As there was now no longer any center of Christianity, Russians concluded, that mantle had fallen to them; they began to call themselves the "Third Rome." So at a time when the West was beginning to modernize, to see secular ideas influence their political systems, economy, and intellectual outlooks, Russia, more than ever, wrapped itself in traditional values and beliefs. For some religious leaders, even learning geometry was a sin to be avoided at all costs.

When our course begins, European Russia (not yet having expanded eastward) was just beginning to recover from a series of calamities that had beset the country in the late Middle Ages. In the fourteenth century, it had fallen under the control of the Mongols, whose rulers used Russian princes around Moscow to collect taxes. This political reality is another reason why Russia was isolated from the West.

Muscovite princes thought of themselves as ruling by divine right, much as their counterparts in the West. In reality, they had to share power with an aristocratic military elite, the Boyars, who had come to be independent owners of their estates. Where their mutual military interests came together, the ruler could expect their cooperation, but not otherwise.

---

6   This came from https://en.wikipedia.org/wiki/Climate_of_Russia.

The process of recovery began in the fifteenth century when a Muscovite prince, Ivan III, refused to pay tribute to the Mongols, brought the city of Moscow under his control, and conquered a trading center, Novgorod. His grandson, Ivan IV, the Terrible, continued his work and began the eastward expansion of the state. He was the first Muscovite to be crowned tsar (from the Latin Caesar), rather than prince, in recognition of Russia's now being the Third Rome. He also began looking westward for ideas and people to implement them. Russia's backwardness, he believed, could most effectively be reversed by importing doctors, craftsmen, and technicians. These individuals settled in an area of Moscow known as the German quarter.

As argued in the introduction, a major focus of this course concerns the rise of modernization and how it has affected the world. We have suggested there will be a continuing controversy between those who favor changes in a modernist direction and those representatives of traditional forms of life, who oppose them. This conflict began in Russia during the reign of Ivan IV. When we discuss Russian history in future chapters, we will often have to examine conflicts between "Westernizers" and "Slavophiles." It is a conflict that began in the sixteenth century and continues to this day.

Ivan has been given the sobriquet "the Terrible."[7] He recognized that to become the tsar God intended him to be, he had to overcome any groups standing in his way. The most significant of these was the Boyars, and he did much to break their power. In 1564, he created a new branch of the administrative system, the *oprichnina*, which he used to break the power of the Boyars. Terror and devastation describe the process. By 1572, believing the work was done, he disbanded the body.

Under his direction, the Russian borders grew significantly, stretching from the Artic to the Caspian Sea. With these lands and those he confiscated from the Boyars, which he granted to a new service nobility, he laid the foundations for Russian autocracy. Closely connected was the increase in serfdom this policy required. If peasants had been free to seek their fortunes in unsettled lands, they would have been unable to work on the lands of new nobles.

In his later years, Ivan IV became increasingly unstable, resulting in the execution of his eldest son. He was succeeded by his middle son, who was incapable of ruling and died without issue. The line came to an end, followed by a period of instability, called the "Time of Troubles," that lasted from 1598 to 1613.

In 1613, the national legislature, *Zemskii Sobor*, following a humiliating invasion of Moscow from Poland, convened and created a new line, the Romanovs, by electing Michael as tsar. This line lasted until Nicholas II and his heirs were murdered by the Bolsheviks in 1918.

Michael had many obstacles to overcome. During the previous period, the Boyars had regained much of their independence, peasants gained the ability to move about freely, and Russia's neighbors threatened her borders. Finally, in Ukraine, an area into which the new regime had expanded, there was a restive group of fighters, the Cossacks. This area had been under Polish-Lithuanian control and that did not please the Cossacks (Russian in origin), who had fled to this area originally to escape the Mongols. They were happy enough to be under a Russian ruler so long as he did not do much. When the tsars had other ideas, this region was likely to rebel.

---

7   Many scholars say this is a mistranslation of a word; powerful or awe-inspiring, much as one speaks of the "terrible majesty of God," is a more accurate meaning of the term, they suggest.

Over the seventeenth and eighteenth centuries, the Romanovs renewed and expanded the state system begun by Ivan IV and gradually incorporated the Cossacks into the tsars' military system.

The most successful of the early Romanovs was Alexis, who reasserted his autocratic authority to the disadvantage of the Boyars, encouraged Westerners to settle, and exploited their advanced ideas. He was also the father of Peter the Great.

Alexis encountered three problems that particularly demanded his attention. First, to guarantee the aristocracy that supported him would have workers for their estates, he reinforced the laws that made virtual slaves of the Russian peasantry. Most scholars compare the resultant system to slavery in the Southern United States of the early nineteenth century.

Secondly, he faced a major uprising led by Stenka Razin. To pay for his governmental expenses, Alexis issued a new law code and increased taxation. This provoked a series of uprisings, beginning in 1669, but none was as significant as that of Razin. A Cossack, he attracted a wide-ranging group of discontented people. There was a "Robin Hood" element about the whole affair, and at one point he and his followers controlled the Volga River for eight hundred miles. Many believed he could fly. They certainly expected him to free them from their oppressive burdens, however they defined them. It was all over by 1671; the brutality visited upon the rebels was fearsome.

The third issue to trouble his reign involved reform of the Russian Orthodox Church. A group of theologians at Kiev, led by Archbishop Nikon and influenced by Greek scholars, concluded the Russian Orthodox Church had departed from traditional Greek Orthodox practices and called for reforms, especially in the liturgy, the tonsure, and translation of the Russian Bible.

The "Old Believers," as those traditionalists who opposed these changes were called, viewed the changes as blasphemy. They did not trust the Greek scholars upon whom Nikon and Alexis relied. When the reforms were adopted, some rebelled; about twenty thousand committed suicide by self-immolation. Ultimately the Old Believers were excommunicated (1667) and Nikon was deposed, in part because his ambitions went beyond church reform and clashed with Alexis's autocratic ideas. We are not done with this dispute.

Alexis died in 1676. Peter was only four. His elder brother succeeded Alexis but only reigned until 1682. Following his death, Peter, now ten, was made tsar. But being too young to assume power, Peter came to be controlled by his half-sister Sophia, who acted as regent until her removal from power in 1689.

Peter the Great

Peter was a larger than life figure in many ways. To begin, he stood six feet eight. Raised away from court by his mother Natalia, Alexis's second wife, he was not highly educated; it was said his spelling was never very good, and that his attempt to write German with Russian characters looked absurd. No matter, he preferred activity to scholarship anyway, and his hands were always calloused from physical labor. Unlike most rulers of his day, he was more comfortable among unsophisticated workmen than aristocratic courtiers.

He spent much of his youth among foreigners in the German quarter of Moscow, as the foreign residence near Moscow was called. Here he picked up an appreciation for Western technological innovations, as well as a lifelong fascination with boats and the importance of sea power to a nation. When not drinking and carousing with his friends, he was busy building something. He was practical and utilitarian, rather than theoretical and philosophical.

As Peter approached his majority, he began to maneuver to push Sophia out. Not wanting to give up power and anxious about the accession of this unruly young man, Sophia, in 1689, attempted to have him removed and herself made tsarina, something never occurring before; her attempt failed and she was banished to a convent, where she remained until she died. Peter then made his mother regent until her death in 1694. Afterward, he ruled with this half-brother Ivan until his death two years later. Only then, in 1696, did Peter began his personal rule; he was twenty-four.

Even before he assumed personal power, Peter had built a dockyard at Archangel and launched a military campaign against Turkey, besieging Azov, which he captured in 1696, about the time he assumed full control of the state. He chose this Turkish port city because it was an easy target. But, as he discovered, it was a victory of little use, and led him to reflect upon the weaknesses of his state and its needs for reform. Making Russia powerful and expanding its borders were his lifelong priority. As a result, Peter was at war in all but two years of his reign.[8] Warfare was (and still is) an expensive undertaking and requires state control of men and resources. When a state is relatively backward in comparison with its neighbors, as was the case of Peter's Russia, this meant reforms—reforms that created tension and sometimes provoked outright resistance. Here, in a nutshell, you have Peter's reign: warfare, reform, and resistance.

The next year, 1697, Peter traveled to the West where he worked on gunnery, built a frigate, visited factories and hospitals. He attended anatomy lectures and cast cannon. His trip gave him a lot of knowledge to use in subsequent years, and also enabled him to recruit a number of Dutch craftsmen. Later, Peter would recruit more Westerners, for his armies in particular.

His trip, however, was cut short when, in May 1698, news of a rebellion of the Streltsy Guard aimed at restoring Sophia to power forced him to return to Russia. Once at home, Peter exacted a savage vengeance on those who were involved. He also took advantage of the situation to reform other aspects of Russian life he regarded as backward. Men were forced to wear Western dress and shave their beards (or pay a tax). Women were brought out of seclusion and also began to dress in Western fashion. He introduced a new calendar based upon the Julian, rather than the Catholic Gregorian. Previously, the Russian calendar had been based on the date of creation calculated to have occurred 7,207 years before. To many pious Russians, Peter's new dating system was blasphemous, but it survived until the Bolshevik Revolution changed it to the Gregorian calendar, in 1918.

Peter then turned to building up the Russian military. This included conscription from the peasantry. By 1710, his forces stood at nearly two hundred thousand, plus an additional one hundred thousand Cossacks and others. He built a Baltic fleet and developed his own systems for manufacturing weapons.

Administering such a group was more than the traditional Russian system could manage; Peter reinstated the service nobility of Ivan IV with the concept of *dvorianstvo*: a nobleman's wealth and positon were determined by his service. Late in his reign (1722), Peter regularized the system he had been creating into the "Table of Ranks" with its three columns: civil, military, and court. Theoretically, even a peasant

---

8   We will look at his warfare below.

could rise to the nobility, and a few did, but most peasants remained serfs. After all, Peter was attempting to restore the old practice of nobles being servants of the state in return for lands and serfs to work them. He could hardly have done otherwise.

The government was divided into eight provinces with one hundred twenty-six centers for the army, which served as his tax collectors.

Other sources of income came from encouraging manufacturing based on the widely followed principles of mercantilism. Self-sufficiency being an important idea of this economic doctrine, he promoted industry, in particular iron, but also textiles, china, and glass. To work in these, he imported craftsmen, as we observed in connection with this early trip to the West. To promote the flow of goods he promoted road and canal building. All were valuable also because they could be taxed.

Late in his reign, he experimented with creating a central government based upon the Swedish model of colleges. This allowed him to break down the functions of government by what they were supposed to manage, from foreign affairs to various departments of the military to groups to manage the economy. Each college had ten members, many of whom were foreign. These groups were further subdivided into forty more local units, each directed by a governor appointed by the central authorities.

Peter, not surprisingly, was also interested in reforming education, along the lines of engineering, navigation, mathematics, and medicine. He also sought to create a system of elementary education for the nation.

Peter did not ignore the church, an institution that frequently stood in the way of changes he wanted to make. His reforms enabled him both to reduce its power and also to tap into its revenues. In 1700, when the religious head of the Orthodox Church in Russia, the patriarch, died, Peter simply abolished the position. In 1711, he made the church into what he termed the "Most Holy Directing Synod"—in other words, a department of the state. It remained such until 1917.

Because Peter relied on a number of foreigners who were not Orthodox in religion, he was forced to grant them religious toleration. This is about the same time that Louis XIV drove his religious minorities, the Huguenots with their highly valuable manufacturing skills he could ill afford to lose, out of the country. It puts the two into sharp contrast.

Finally, Peter built the beautiful city of Saint Petersburg, his "window on the West." He labored on it himself. The result was to create a rival to the ancient city of Moscow.

Peter's reforms might have been more permanent if he had had an adult male to succeed him. He did not. His eldest son, Alexei Petrovich Romanov, was accused of treason and executed in 1718. Peter had fourteen children in all. When he died in 1725, only one daughter remained alive, Anna Petrovich, to succeed him, and she died two years later, setting up the renewal of instability not unlike the "Time of Troubles" that had led to the creation of the Romanov dynasty early in the seventeenth century.

How important then was Peter's reign? The most common assessment, by both supporters and detractors alike, is that Peter modernized Russia; he brought the West to the East. It is worth noting that by the nineteenth century, the aristocracy of Russia spoke French among themselves, and only used Russian when talking to their servants. An enormous cultural gap grew up between the two classes, and Peter is to be praised or blamed for it as one wishes.

Some scholars, however, have pointed out that just about everything Peter did had been anticipated by those who came before him. The observation is correct, but earlier reforms were rather tentative, while Peter's were more all invasive and transformative. No matter how the power between the tsar and the nobility shifted in the centuries following Peter's death, Russia was forever altered by the influences coming from the West; Peter made their course irreversible.

GREAT BRITAIN AND LIMITED MONARCHY

Clearly the prevalent state form in the seventeenth century was absolute monarchy, whether in its Western or Eastern form. It is not hard to understand why. Poland, a state that failed to embrace the notion of sovereignty, also failed to develop a strong government. Its aristocracy was free and powerful, but the state itself was weak and, ultimately, destroyed. The wisdom of this age suggested the only way to be safe was to have an absolute ruler.

Britain's story alone belies this wisdom. Some nobles were attracted to the new-fangled idea of divine right monarchy, but most were not. Instead, the English ruling class embraced both the notion of the sovereign state and also, in a modified form, its medieval institution (Parliament) that gave power to the privileged. They did not come to this solution overnight. In fact, Britain's history throughout much of the seventeenth century is characterized by political and religious strife, including a civil war. But by the end of that century, a sovereign state, based on a system of shared power, had triumphed. That system became the structure of government and society that guided this nation until 1832. It is also the system of government that enabled Britain to move from being the minor European player it was during the Tudor dynasty to being a major power, first in Europe and then in the world, a position it would occupy until the end of World War II.

How could this have happened? In particular, how did Britain enjoy the luxury of acute instability for almost a century without being invaded by an outside power? And how did the ruling class build a rather original system of government out of ideas that were in fact very old? That is, how did it transform its medieval constitution into a modern one?

Once upon a time, historians answered these questions by presenting the story of the Stuart Period as a melodrama in which the Stuart kings were cast as the evil oppressors of the people, while the Parliamentarians were seen to be the unselfish champions of freedom. That is no longer the way the story is told. Perhaps tragicomedy comes closer to describing it now. The kings, following their own lights, sought to be rulers over three kingdoms and succeeded rather better than historians once supposed. The Parliamentarians, especially in England, motivated by political and religious considerations reflecting their own class interests and beliefs, challenged and obstructed the kings' efforts, often more successfully than not. Neither was incompetent or evil; both behaved in ways that led to a civil war that neither side wanted, followed by a period of military rule that ended with the restoration of the Crown and Parliament, established on a footing that neither side would have countenanced a half-century earlier. It is often said the British stumble into successful solutions to their problems, rather than walk to them deliberately, with vision and foresight. That certainly fits the story of the seventeenth century.

The question why the British Isles were not invaded is easy to answer. Britain is an island, close enough to Europe to benefit from the association and sufficiently far enough away to develop in its own way. No

TABLE 1-1

Seventeenth Century British Rulers
Stuarts and Civil War

Name	Years
James I	1603–1625
Charles I	1625–1640
Interregnum and Cromwell	1640–1660
Charles II	1660–1685
James II	1685–1688
William and Mary	1688–1702
Anne	1702–1714

successful invasion of England from the continent has occurred since 1066. This is why Britain could be unstable for most of a century and not be attacked from abroad.

The second question requires looking at the events that transpired from the death of Elizabeth I in 1603 until the end of the Stuarts, early in the eighteenth century. See Table 1.1, which is a chart listing the rulers and their dates. Their strengths and weaknesses are an important part of the story. We will discuss each in turn.

We must also notice how England was related to both Scotland and Ireland, since by the end of this period we will be examining the United Kingdom of England, Scotland. Ireland would be added in 1801.

Finally, there were two principle issues behind the controversies of the seventeenth century: religion and power.

First, religion. In England, the Reformation had created the Church of England, but also a number of dissenting groups, including the "Puritans," who believed the Church of England was not sufficiently reformed. There were also some Catholics left. In Scotland, most people had embraced Presbyterianism, a form of non-separatist Puritanism. Some Catholics also remained. In Ireland, the Irish were mostly Catholic, as were the "Old English," descendants of those families who had come to Ireland in the Middle Ages. The Scots, who settled in the north of Ireland, tended to be Presbyterian. Each of these religious persuasions will play a role in our survey of events to follow.

The matter of relative political power is an equally important factor in the shaping of events during the seventeenth century. First, the early Stuart monarchs, James I and Charles I, embraced divine right absolutism, the most advanced thinking of the time on the continent, as we have seen. James himself wrote a treatise on the subject, *On the Trew Law of Free Monarchies*. Kings, he said, are not bound to obey the law, but do so to set an example for their subjects.

James I

Before James became James I of England, he had been and remained James VI of Scotland. His Scottish subjects did not much care for his political ideas and, in practice, he was forced to recognize reality in how he actually governed there. He expected to rule differently in England; however, his English subjects were, for the most part, as opposed to his ideas as were his Scottish ones.

Beyond this, when James came to England he had no understanding of how the English parliamentary system operated. Soon after he arrived, he clashed with members of Parliament, especially those with Puritan religious sensitivities, who, so far from believing in absolute monarchy, wanted to curb the prerogatives of the Crown to the advantage of Parliament. Worse still, whereas Elizabeth had courted and manipulated Parliament to get it to do what she wanted, James, thinking of himself as absolute and above Parliament, ignored it, which allowed the proponents of parliamentary power to gain the upper hand. James and Parliament clashed throughout his reign.

On his way to England, after he became king, James stopped off at Hampton Court, not far from London, to meet with a group of Puritan clergymen who wanted him to do two things. The first he agreed to: a new and authoritative translation of the Bible. It became the King James Version. The second he would not agree to: get rid of bishops. Right off the bat, he was at loggerheads with many clergy as well as Parliamentarians.

James convened Parliament four times. The first met, off and on, from 1604 to 1611. James's fond hope to unite Scotland to England was debated, but rejected. Parliament did gain the right to determine its own membership. It also began the process of creating a system of financing the government through taxation. The systems devised often led to disputes between the king and Parliament over the powers of the king, what was termed his "prerogatives," as opposed to Parliament's privileges where affairs of state were concerned. It was the dispute over such issues that caused James to end his first Parliament.

The most dramatic event of this part of James's reign was the discovery, in 1605, of a massive plot to blow up Parliament by placing gunpowder under both houses. Led by Guy Fawkes, the plan was to kill the king and assembled Parliamentarians at the opening of the session and restore Catholicism to England. Fawkes was caught just as he was about to light the fuses. He was executed, but his name is remembered today in Guy Fawkes Day, celebrated in England on November 5.

There was no obligation on the king's part to convene Parliament, and he went from 1614 to 1621 without calling one. No one thought this especially tyrannical. He only summoned the Parliament in 1621 because of expenses incurred as a result of England's involvement in the Thirty Years War. James would have preferred not to have been involved, but two factors compelled him to do otherwise. First, there was a religious aspect to this conflict: Protestants in Germany were attacked by a resurgent Catholicism. James could hardly ignore the plight of his co-religionists. Second, the conflict was centered on Bohemia, a largely Protestant region that sought to replace its traditional Austrian and Catholic ruler with a Protestant. They offered the crown to Frederick, the Elector Palatine, who happened to be married to James's daughter Elizabeth. The Austrians quickly drove Frederick out of Bohemia, but the war dragged on for thirty years and put a severe strain on England's royal finances.

There were enough anti-Catholic members of Parliament who were only too happy to support the war effort, but they insisted on debating matters the king felt were his prerogative before granting him the money he required. Also, feeling that James's ministers were incompetent bumblers, they revived the practice of impeachment. To protect one of them, George Villiers, the Duke of Buckingham,[9] James was

---

9   There is no doubt James was homosexual and lavished favors upon Buckingham for that reason, but this does not seem to have been particularly significant in parliamentary efforts to impeach him. It was his incompetence that provoked Parliament's ire.

forced to prorogue Parliament without getting the resources he required. His last Parliament met in 1624 and, much to his chagrin, voted money for a war against Spain, favored by his son and heir, Charles.

Charles I

When Charles came to power, there was no reason to suppose his reign would end with his execution at the hands of Parliament. On the contrary, Charles's championing of the anti-Spanish campaign had made him rather popular. But the situation soon began to sour, mostly over problems he inherited from his father. He certainly shared his father's aspirations to be an absolute monarch and to rule over the three kingdoms, and he had to deal with a Parliament that had grown in power and influence during his father's reign.

Charles made his situation worse with his choice of a wife, Henrietta Maria of France, who was Catholic. This made his subjects very uneasy and, given his attachment to the Anglican Church, there were some, especially among the Puritans, who thought he might harbor Catholic sympathies.

His biggest problem was money. English monarchs had always been expected to live off the incomes of their rather vast estates, except under extraordinary circumstances. But Charles spent lavishly on works of art, and England's involvement in the Thirty Years War seemed to Parliamentarians to be a costly failure, for which they blamed Buckingham. The Parliament of 1626 again sought to impeach him, and Charles, like his father before him, was forced to end the session without the resources he required.

To make up for the shortfall, Charles resorted to forced loans. Those who refused to pay were imprisoned. Naturally, the case wound up in court, the so-called "Five Knights Case," and when the justices ruled in the king's favor, many in Parliament took it to be an act of tyranny and felt betrayed by a judiciary no longer concerned with the rights of subjects, but was subservient to the Crown.

Buckingham used some of the money the loans had raised to assist French Huguenots, but his efforts were a costly failure. This required yet another Parliament in which the king was presented with, and accepted, one of the most important constitutional documents of British history, the Petition of Right. By its terms, the king agreed not to raise taxes without the consent of Parliament, not to quarter troops in private homes, not to imprison subjects without due process, and finally, not to declare martial law in peacetime.

The issue of Buckingham was settled in 1628 when he was assassinated, but relations with Parliament in no way improved. In particular, in the Parliament of 1629, some members, mostly Puritan, debated the king's support for Catholicism, as they saw it. When the king learned about the debate, he attempted to end the session. To prevent that from occurring, the speaker was physically restrained from leaving his seat until the members had passed the anti-Catholic measures they were debating by acclamation. The Parliament was then adjourned and, as it turned out, not to be reconvened until 1640.

James I had gone seven years without Parliament and managed to get by until war intervened. Charles would do likewise for a longer period and would make use of the same extra-parliamentary means of raising money his father had employed. The difference is he had agreed to the Petition of Right, which he now ignored. He also came up with a number of new fundraising devices never employed by his father. One especially unpopular levy, the ship money tax, which had previously been imposed only on seaport areas, now was levied on inland towns as well. In something of a replay of the Five Knights Case, a member of Parliament, John Hampton, refused to pay the tax, was arrested, and brought to court. Like the Five Knights before him, he too was convicted, although by a very narrow margin. Still, it seemed to be another example of the judiciary supporting a king who was exceeding the law in asserting his prerogatives.

Charles's religious policies also added to popular resentment against his government. Although not Catholic, and despite popular suspicions to the contrary because of his support for the religious sensitivities of his wife, he was a strong supporter of the Anglican Church and, like his father before him, wanted to impose a religious uniformity on all his realms, including Scotland. To this end, he attempted to force the Scots to use a version of the English Prayer Book. They rebelled; Charles sent troops, who were defeated. The Scots then invaded England. Charles now had no choice but to convene a Parliament. Known as the "Short Parliament," it met for three weeks in April 1640 before being dissolved.

The Scots' invasion continued. By November, Charles had to call Parliament again and, this time, listen to its members' complaints. This body, known as the "Long Parliament," ended Charles's "personal rule," and ultimately led England into civil war.

Civil War

How this came about has been the subject of much historical debate. Suffice to say blame can be apportioned all round. Charles's behavior, both in the past and in the events to follow, was partly to blame, but responsibility must also go to the members of Parliament. Their religious and political differences divided them, leading to creation of a court party that rallied around the beleaguered Charles, and a faction around his parliamentary opponents. Without the divided Parliament, civil war would not have been possible.

At first, members of the Parliament were able to agree on several measures they hoped would prevent a recurrence of the arbitrary policies that had occurred during Charles's years of personal rule. He was forbidden to prorogue Parliament without its consent, and he was required to summon a Parliament at least once every three years. Finally, the "Prerogative Courts" that seemed to be primarily responsible for the king's past abuses of judicial power were abolished.

So far, the Parliamentarians had struck together against the king. After 1640, fissures in this body began to appear, largely over religion. In particular, some Puritans wanted to curb the power of bishops, others to do away with them altogether.

In the midst of this very divisive issue, Ireland intruded itself into the debates with a massacre of some ten thousand English people living there. Lurid stories of roasting English children and eating them circulated in England. In truth, massacres occurred on both sides, adding to the animosity dividing the populace there.

The Crown and Parliament agreed something had to be done, but the problem was who would do it. That is, who would raise the army to invade Ireland and restore order there, since whoever controlled this army, once it had finished its Irish mission, would be in possession of an instrument to settle the matter between the king and Parliament in England.

The situation emboldened the radical Parliamentarians. Issuing the "Grand Remonstrance," they first impeached twelve bishops and then tried to impeach the queen. It passed in the House but not in the Lords. On January 3, 1642, the king responded by invading Parliament to arrest its leaders, who, forewarned, had fled. Once the king withdrew, Parliament passed a militia bill specifying Parliament would raise and, therefore, control the army for Ireland. It also passed bills to end the Anglican Church by doing away with bishops and the established Anglican liturgy. By this point, the Parliamentarians were divided between the Puritans and the Anglicans. The latter began to form a Royalist party in support of the king and in opposition to the radical, mostly Puritan Parliamentarians.

Charles fled London and made his way to York. Both sides now began to raise armies. Several last-minute attempts were made to avert a conflict, but the demands of the radicals, who now controlled Parliament, were too extreme for the king to consider. Officially, the war began August 22, 1642, when Charles ordered his battle standard to be raised at his camp at Nottingham.

Charles had the short-term advantage since his commanders were more experienced; however, Parliament controlled London, which was the wealthiest part of the realm, and also the navy. The long-term advantage was theirs.

The parliamentary side aided its cause by modernizing its forces through the "New Model Army," which included expelling a number of nobles who lacked military skill. This army also included troops from the lower orders, most of whom were separatist Puritans. Parliament was also assisted by troops from Scotland. Not surprisingly, the Scots favored a Presbyterian form of church polity that further complicated the problem of making peace once the war was over.

The new army, with its Presbyterian allies, carried the day, first at the battle of Marston Moor in 1644, and then in June 1645 at the battle of Nasby, where the king's armies were routed. By 1646, Charles, realizing his situation was hopeless, turned himself over to the Scots. In January, after lengthy negotiations, the Scots sold him to the English for one hundred thousand pounds.

Charles had reason to hope all would turn out well because the Parliamentarians were fighting among themselves, particularly over what sort of religion they should have. In particular, a rift had occurred between the Parliament and its New Model Army, which it had sought unsuccessfully to disband after Charles's surrender. In 1647, Charles, hoping to take advantage of this rift, entered into fresh negotiations with the Scots, this time offering to give them what they wanted, a Presbyterian system of church government in England, in return for an army.

The Parliamentarians, now led by Oliver Cromwell, the leader of the New Model Army, defeated the Royalists in what is termed "the Second Civil War." Charles again fled for safety, to the Isle of Wight where he was arrested.

As a result of the king's "perfidy," Cromwell and his fellow radical Parliamentarians concluded the king had to be executed. To accomplish this, they knew Presbyterian votes in Parliament had to be eliminated. In early December, in a classic coup, a contingent of the army expelled them (Prides Purge). The remaining members of Parliament, known as "the Rump," established a special court to try the king, which duly found him guilty of treason. He was executed on January 20, 1649.

Commonwealth

England was now a republic, but what sort? The next several years were extraordinary in the number of political ideas put forward: everything from democracy to communism. Modern economic ideas were also entertained and passed into law. Finally, there was much discussion about religious liberty and the established church. But through it all, finding a workable system of government eluded the victorious Parliamentarians. Ultimately, the military ran things and Cromwell ran the military until his death.

There was a third civil war, from 1649 to 1651, the result of a Scottish invasion of England on behalf of Charles I's son, the future Charles II. There was also a belated response to the Irish uprising that had precipitated the civil war. Cromwell invaded the island, and his forces subdued the Irish with special ferocity (as they were Catholics). The Irish remember the massacre of Drogheda and loath the name Cromwell to this day. This campaign ended by late 1652.

Charles (II) was able to appeal to the fact he was a Scot to attract a royalist following, even among Presbyterians. The English campaign against the Stuarts in Scotland began in 1650 and continued until the Scots surrendered in 1652.

Cromwell, now given the title of Lord Protector, ruled until 1658. Following his death, the days of the Protectorate were limited. Finding someone to take his place proved impossible and in May 1660, Charles I's son returned to his three crowns as Charles II.

Restoration

Technically, it was as though nothing had changed legally from the death of Charles's father, in 1640, until the restoration of the son, in 1660. But, of course, much had changed. After the restoration settlement, almost no one spoke of divine right; it was king and Parliament. The king was not to live on feudal aids, but on a parliamentary subsidy derived from a beer tax. The House of Lords was restored, as was the Anglican Church. The religious settlement, enshrined in the Clarendon Code, severely restricted the religious liberties of "Dissenters," as non-Anglicans were known, and, of course, Catholics.

Everyone who had been part of the rebellion was pardoned except those who had signed Charles I's death sentence, about fifty of whom were still living. These individuals were imprisoned or executed.

Charles also realized he would have to manage Parliament if he wanted things to go his way, so he cultivated a group of men in the Commons, who came to be known as the "court party."

That Charles was secretly Catholic was widely suspected. What was not known or suspected was that, by the Treaty of Dover, he had allied himself with Louis XIV, agreeing to go to war against the Dutch in return for a substantial yearly subsidy. Charles also agreed—"at the right time"—to announce his conversion to Catholicism. To be sure, that time only came on his deathbed, when he asked for last rites from a Catholic priest. He did try to assist his co-religionist in England by issuing a Declaration of Indulgence in 1672, which guaranteed freedom of religion for all. Many Anglicans—and Puritans, for that matter—knew his real purpose. Parliament responded with the "Test Act," which required everyone to take communion in the Church of England once a year to be able to occupy any public post. Those who would not comply were excluded from the military, all government posts, and university positions. This law remained on the books until 1828.

Charles's secret agreement with Louis resulted in three Dutch wars, but England had already been at war with the Dutch because of competition for empire and mercantilist policies that excluded Dutch ships from English commerce. These encounters did not always go well for the English. In 1667, the Dutch carried out a surprise attack, sailing up the English Channel. They burned the entire Royal fleet, except for the Royal Charles, which they hauled away as a trophy. But England did gain New Amsterdam, renamed

New York in honor of Charles's brother, James, Duke of York, and the English began their efforts to expand into the Far East with establishment of the East India Company.

England endured two calamities during Charles II's reign. First, the Great Plague of London, which began in June 1665, killing between seventy thousand and one hundred thousand people. It was the last such plague. And second, in 1666, much of London burned in a fire, the conflagration lasting for a week. It did give Sir Christopher Wren his opportunity to rebuild much of the city, and today Saint Paul's Cathedral and a number of other buildings stand in eloquent testimony to his extraordinary talent.

Charles lacked a legitimate child to be his heir, so, as he aged, the question of who was to succeed him became an important issue. His relationship with Parliament had deteriorated, largely over suspicions about his Catholicism and his pro-French policies. It was well known that his brother James, the next in line in the succession, was Catholic. Some thought he should be excluded from succession for this reason. They came to be known as Whigs. Those who believed, because James was the legitimate heir, he had a God-given right to succeed his brother, came to be known as Tories. Modern-day conservatives are still called Tories. The Whigs' efforts failed and some, including John Locke, had to flee to the Netherlands to avoid arrest. In 1685, James Duke of York peacefully succeeded his brother as James II.

James II

James's reign was rather short. Not surprisingly, his policies offended the Whigs, but he also quickly offended the Tories as well. While they were strong monarchists, they were also staunch Anglicans (i.e., not Catholics like James). Because of the Test Act, they were the people in the most important positions of power in England, dissenters and Catholics being excluded. James offended them by naming Catholics to important positions, as though the Test Act did not exist. He also began to create a Catholic-led military force. Like Charles II before him, he offered a toleration policy. When seven bishops refused to honor the law, James had them prosecuted. They were acquitted by the courts, but James's behavior was reminiscent of earlier Stuart policies the Tories thought had ended as a result of the civil war. Making his situation even more difficult, James insisted that, as king, he was above the law, much as had James I.

The last straw came in 1688: James's new wife bore a son who was baptized a Catholic. If James had not had an heir, doubtless the Tories would have preferred to await James's death in the expectation a Protestant would be named to succeed him. But now there was an heir. In truth, it was the fear of a Catholic dynasty that forced the Whigs and the Tories to make common cause—indeed, to risk a civil war, to replace James. They offered the throne to Mary, his daughter, and to her husband, William of Orange of the Netherlands.

The Glorious Revolution

William's only motive in agreeing to become the king of England was to obtain the land and wealth of his new realm to use in his campaign to protect the Dutch from Louis XIV. An agreement was reached and William invaded England. Everywhere, James's forces disappeared and he fled to the continent, tossing the royal seal in the Thames as he departed; it remains there to this day.

The denouement of this drama came the following year at the battle of the Boyne in Ireland when a collection of Dutch, German, Scot, and French Huguenots (no English) defeated James II and his French and Irish supporters. The issue was settled: England would not have a Catholic monarch.

It is called the Glorious Revolution because no one in England was killed. William and Mary had been invited, by Parliament, to rule England, and this same body defined and limited their powers. A bill of rights specified the king could not arbitrarily suspend laws, detain citizens without due process, raise taxes, or maintain an army without parliamentary consent. In 1701, Parliament enacted the Act of Settlement: no Catholic would be king of England; in particular, this excluded the Catholic Stuarts.

Scotland was not subject to English law, but the English very much wanted the Scottish lords to agree to the exclusion of Catholics, especially Scottish Stuart Catholics. The best way to guarantee this—and, at the same time, end a centuries-old problem of French-allied Scotland attacking England from its "postern gate"—was to unite Scotland with England. It took some persuading, even some bribing with economic opportunities not then available to the Scots, to get the Scottish Parliament to agree, and in 1707 the deal was struck: the two parliaments united, and the United Kingdom of Great Britain with its Union Jack came into existence. It 2015, a vote in Scotland came very close to bringing this union to an end.

The situation for Catholic Ireland was harsher. Fearful of James, and later his son Charles, using Ireland as a staging ground for the invasion of England, the English implemented a series of harsh codes in Ireland. Already the Irish were oppressed by English absentee landlords and the necessity to support the Anglican Church in Ireland, to which none of them belonged, in addition to their own. Now they were subjected to a number of even harsher restrictions. Catholics could not own a horse worth more than five pounds. They could not be members of the Irish Parliament, teach, or lease land for more than thirty-one years, much less buy it. These laws would be relaxed in the future, but the resentments built up in this time could never be erased. Ireland was added to the United Kingdom in 1801, during the Napoleonic Wars.

The England that emerged from this era is sometimes called a "Squirearchy," meaning a land ruled by country squires. It was a state in which the king or queen ruled within well-prescribed limits, and shared power with these squires and their aristocratic betters, as well as a smattering of townsmen who sat in the House of Commons alongside the squires. While Anglicanism was the established church, and so religiously privileged, there was more religious tolerance in England than just about anywhere else in the world. And this state was just beginning to accumulate its empire, which would provide it with the resources to play a role in modern history all out of proportion to its size or indigenous wealth. Looking back at the seventeenth century, it is clear these events laid the foundations for the United Kingdom to be not only safe from foreign intervention, but also to become a major power in Europe and, ultimately, in the world, economically as well as politically.

THE DUTCH REPUBLIC

The Dutch Republic, or United Provinces, came into being as a result of the Reformation. For eighty years, the Protestant Dutch, in the north of the Netherlands, fought against the Catholic South, controlled by Spain, until the former gained its independence in 1648, at the end of the Thirty Years War. In truth, "disunited" provinces would be a more accurate name for the seven states loosely joined into the United Netherlands (Figure 1.5). Each of its provinces enjoyed a good bit of autonomy and preferred it that way. As one historian put it: "Sovereignty lay with the seven provinces separately; in each, the states ruled, and in the states, the representatives of the towns. Action could not be taken without a unanimous vote; it was therefore common for issues to be referred back to the town corporations."[10] This meant it could be difficult to get anything done, even in times of emergency (that is, when England or France invaded), as occurred several times during the period. It was possible to turn to the dominant noble family (the House of Orange) in times of extreme crisis and elect this prince of Orange to be stadtholder (chief executive officer) for each of the seven provinces that made up the state. When they did, the Netherlands, chameleon-like, would change its political colors, as it were, by adopting some of the attributes of a monarchy to deal with the crisis; but when the crisis was over, as quickly as possible, each province would return to its independent state (i.e., becoming an oligarchic republic again). This usually occurred following the death of the stadtholder who had been called upon during the previous crisis.

During this period, the Dutch were at the peak of their economic power through trade in spices in the Far East. The Spice Islands (Indonesia today) was a major area they controlled. They also made a lot of money through banking, the stock market, and hauling generally. As a result, theirs was a rather unique society in the time we are studying. While there were aristocrats, the most powerful class was that of the wealthy merchants. Consequently, the poorer sorts often teamed up with the Orange family and other aristocratic families against these powerful merchant "oligarchs" who, from their urban centers, ran their own individual states, and generally succeeded in excluding both the aristocrats and also the poorer sorts from influence in the society.

The Dutch were unique in another way, too. Theirs was a society in which a large measure of religious freedom was permitted. In a time when people who did not share the same religion or philosophy were unlikely to coexist peacefully, religious and intellectual freedom was the norm here. Within their boundaries lived some of the most significant thinkers of the seventeenth century. Descartes fled there to escape French persecution. The Spanish Jewish philosopher, Spinoza, also lived there, quietly grinding lenses and writing his highly controversial metaphysical treatises. Rembrandt and Vermeer painted; Leeuwenhoek, Swammerdam, and others pioneered use of the microscope. People who wanted to publish a book on a controversial subject came to the Netherlands to publish it. Some books were said to have been printed in the Republic even when they had not. The Puritans, who finally landed upon Plymouth Rock, first stopped off in Amsterdam, but found the place much to open and worldly for their liking. Something of that openness survives to this day.

For all these reasons, the state had lots of enemies. Chief among them was France and, until 1688, Britain. The latter, because the Dutch were commercial rivals and, as we will see in Chapter 2, mercantilism was a "win-lose" economic theory that inevitably led to international wars and rivalries.

As noted above, Dutch conflicts with England go back to the mid-seventeenth century, during the civil war. The Dutch scored some moral victories, but generally the campaigns were indecisive. As already noted, the Dutch did lose New Amsterdam, which became New York.

In 1667, Louis XIV made his move to annex the Spanish Netherlands and the Dutch played the principle role in forming a "balance of power" alliance against him. They even overcame their difficulties with the British, and these two, united with Sweden, forced Louis to back down. This made the French king turn on the Dutch. First, he isolated them diplomatically. Then, in 1672, after bribing Charles II of

---

10   (Treasure, *The Making of Modern Europe*, 1985, p. 478)

Figure 1.5: Map of Dutch Republic

England to join him, Louis invaded the Netherlands. This time, he took the Spanish Netherlands and part of the Dutch Netherlands as well. In fact, only by flooding the country did the Dutch survive.

This was one of those crisis times when the Dutch turned to the House of Orange to save them. They threw the merchant oligarchs out and brought William III, soon to be king of England, to power. Here began his lifelong quest to rid the Dutch of French danger. Indeed, as has been noted already, it was this quest that caused him to take the English throne in the first place. It would guarantee not only peace with a former enemy, but money and people to join in the battle

Once William became king of England, the Dutch inevitably found themselves reduced in importance. In the course of the eighteenth century, they continued to prosper, largely because of the capital they had accumulated during the previous two centuries. They remained an important economic player in Europe and, in comparison with many neighboring states, a relatively wealthy one, but their political influence was a thing of the past.

POLAND

Poland's era of greatest power and prestige occurred before the time we are studying. Then known as Poland-Lithuania, it controlled a sizable empire, including parts of what is Russia today.

The union of the kingdom Poland and the duchy of Lithuania took place in the sixteenth century. It was a powerful state until well into the seventeenth century. It stayed out of the Thirty Years War, which allowed it to avoid the destruction of warfare and to supply the belligerents as well. It even occupied Moscow for a short time (1610–12) during the "Time of Troubles" (Figure 1.6). As this century progressed, however,

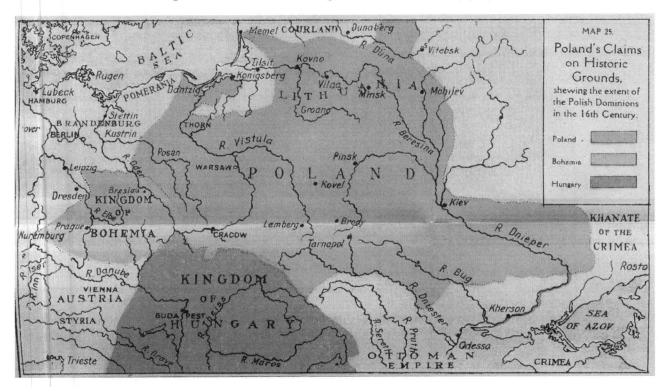

Figure 1.6: Map of Poland

the weakness of this premodern state form became apparent. Poland developed neither an absolutist state, of the sort that arose in France or Austria, nor an effective parliamentary or constitutional system, as in England, nor finally, the chameleon-like system of the Dutch. In short, it refused to embrace the notion of the sovereign state. The liberties of the aristocracy trumped every form of government that would have given it power and, in the late-eighteenth century, it was devoured by its more powerful neighbors.

Technically, Poland was a monarchy. But the king, somewhat like the Holy Roman emperor, had no real power. He could neither raise taxes, nor an army of any size (that might be large enough to control the nobility). Also, by the seventeenth century, the Crown itself had become elective, rather than hereditary, and often the selection of the candidate was a reflection of French or Russian preferences, rather than of the Poles themselves.

The situation would not have been so bad for the state if the legislature could have acted decisively, but it could not. Called the "Diet," every member present at a meeting, in order to accomplish anything, had to agree on the issue under discussion. One person's descent, his "liberum veto," would "blast" the Diet, defeating not only the measure in question but anything else passed previously in the session. No wonder they got nothing done.

As was true of the rest of Eastern Europe, this system did give the nobles complete control over their peasants who were mostly serfs, and discouraged the growth of towns, which the nobles saw as a challenge to their authority. Perhaps you will have noticed their practices were not totally unique in their time. The Netherlands required unanimous consent in its several legislatures to pass laws, and the Austrian monarchy was itself elective. But only in Poland did these features combine in a way so ultimately destructive of the state.

During the course of the eighteenth century, some Poles realized the situation they were in, but found themselves powerless to change things, both because of intransigence from home, and of the desire of neighboring states to keep Poland weak. The ax fell, so to speak, in three phases just before and during the French Revolution (1772, 1793, and 1795). The story of Poland, not to mention the Holy Roman Empire, in the world of modern, sovereign states, is that the price of weakness was destruction!

In this chapter we have sketched the development of the sovereign state. There is more to modern states than this powerful idea, and we will see the remaining part of the formula fall into place in the eighteenth and early nineteenth centuries.

REFERENCES

Derek Beales. *Enlightenment and Reform in 18th Century Europe*. New York: I. B. Tauris, 2005.

William Doyle, *the Old European Order, 1660–1800*. Oxford: Oxford University Press, 1978.

Pierre Goubert. *Louis XIV and Twenty Million Frenchmen*. New York: Vintage Books, 1970.

M. Scott Hamish. *Enlightened Despotism*.

Stanford. E. Lehmberg and Samantha A. Meigs. The Peoples of the British Isles: A New History. Chicago: Lyceum Books, Vols 1 and 2, 2009.

A Lloyd Moore. *The Seventeenth Century: Europe in Ferment*. New York: D. C. Heath, 1970.

Geoffrey Treasure. *The Making of Europe. 1648–1780*. London: Methuen, 1985.

Intellectual Transformation of the 17th and 18th Centuries in Western Europe

INTRODUCTION

In Chapter 1, we explored the transformation of life in Europe in politics and the sovereign state. We examined changes preparatory to the rise of the nation-state, fundamental characteristics of the world in which we live. In this chapter, we will explore the transformation of thinking during the seventeenth and eighteenth centuries, primarily of Western Europeans and their American transplants that resulted in a new, rational, and scientific way of making sense of the world. As with politics and economics, we will have to wait until the nineteenth century to see the full flowering of this intellectual transformation, but it was during the time we are now considering that the foundations were laid.

To qualify as a "world view," people's ideas must offer them explanations for all aspects of existence. This is precisely what occurred. A "scientific" and "rational" approach to solving problems gradually became the norm for every intellectual endeavor of Western people and, by the late nineteenth century, for people around the globe. In due course, every branch of science came to be modernized, and the study of human beings came to be guided by the "social sciences." Even literature, philosophy, and religion did not escape the transformative influences of modernization. Nothing proved to be more corrosive to traditional ways of life than this scientific rationalism that emerged in the late seventeenth and early eighteenth centuries.

This is not to say all vestiges of traditionalism were completely overturned by the new science. Most of the seventeenth-century founders, such as Newton and Kepler, were more interested in protecting traditional social and religious institutions than in uprooting them. By the nineteenth century, when the intellectual changes initiated in the seventeenth and eighteenth centuries seemed to many to have done just that, traditional ideas, especially religious ones, remained powerful. Furthermore, there is no evidence the majority of people, who lived happily in this new world system with its technological and medical advancements, understood a great deal about the new science; nor were they persuaded by it to totally abandon their traditional religious beliefs and social values.

All the same, the thought world that prevailed in nineteenth century Western Europe and its colonial transplants was very different from that which had existed there two centuries earlier. The purpose of this chapter is to show how this crucial intellectual transformation in world history occurred. The chapter will first explore the traditional world view of Europeans that preceded the modern, as a reference point to understand the changes we are describing. This will be followed by an examination of how the new scientific world view came to be and what was so different about it. Finally, we will explore its migration out of the realms of science into those mentioned above, without which it would not truly be a world view.

Not surprisingly, for many these transformations were painful, provoking their opposition. We will be examining the resultant struggle between traditional and the new modern scientific views throughout the rest of the course; it continues to the present.

THE ANCIENT-MEDIEVAL WORLD VIEW

To appreciate the significance of the changes the rise of modern science produced in modern life, we must have some idea about the way people viewed reality before the seventeenth century. Five concepts and a generalized picture of their resulting universe should suffice. The five concepts: authority, tradition, commonsense empiricism, deductive logic, and a holistic outlook. The resultant world picture was a geostatic universe with the earth and man, not to mention hell, squarely in the center of it all.

All societies have **authorities**. In our world, an authority is someone who is recognized as having up-to-date knowledge. We would hardly want someone who was trained in medicine sixty years ago, who has not kept abreast of the changes that have occurred since, to be treating us. It was just the opposite before the rise of modern science. The older the idea the better! Indeed, new ideas were suspect. By the Christian era, the Bible was the foremost authority, followed by the ideas of famous Greeks and Romans. Philosophers and doctors alike were expected to conform their ideas to those of their ancient authorities.

By the nineteenth century, when the new science became influential, this notion had changed completely. The new became reliable and the old suspect. Those who thought otherwise were considered to be out of date and unreliable, though they continued to exist.

By the twentieth century, many Americans became so obsessed with progress and "the new" that they had little or no respect for institutions or ideas from the past.

Currently, this conflict is reflected in the difference between mainstream science and the scientific ideas of many Evangelical Christians. While the former embrace the most recent research in biology, including evolution, Evangelical Christians, even doctors, reject evolution because it is impossible to reconcile this idea with their literal understanding of their leading authority, the Bible. For the same reason, some Evangelicals also reject the theory of relativity.

Closely linked to authority was **tradition**, the propensity to do things in ways they had always been done. The approach Aristotle took to physics, or Galen to medicine, was the way scientists or doctors were expected to work. In particular, this left little place for mathematics, which is central to modern science. It also meant observations were defined in terms of an established tradition, no matter how much they may have seemed to contradict it. As with authority, modern scientists reject past traditions that do not seem to fit observations, and the methods of contemporary science are radically different from those employed by the ancients and medievals.

Commonsense empiricism simply meant people thought what they observed gave a true picture of what was happening. What you see is what you have got! The sun rises in the east in the morning and sets in the west in the evening because we are still, and it is moving. By contrast, modern science increasingly taught Europeans what we think we are seeing is not what is happening at all. We have learned to live with a world view that is anything but commonsense-based. Even the most conservative religious figures today no longer deny the earth moves around the sun, even though we have no way of sensing it. As we shall see, this change was not easily accomplished.

At times, it is difficult to make sense out of what one observes. The movements of the heavenly bodies are quite inexplicable without some sort of theoretical model to unify what we observe. For the ancients and medievals, this required the use of **deduction**. A simple example should explain. If you want to know what sort of fish are in a lake, you could go fishing. That is induction or empiricism. Or you could go to the Internet and read up on what fish are native to the region where you are and not get hot or mosquito-bitten in the process. That is "deduction" and it was the method preferred by the ancients and medievals.

Aristotle largely created this deductive system. Here is his most famous "syllogism."

All men are mortals.

Socrates is a man;

Therefore, Socrates is a mortal.

It is empirically obvious no human being is immortal. Socrates was a human being; therefore, he must also be a mortal.

The ancients and medievals used this approach to string together the bodies of observational information at their disposal. They believed properly constructed syllogisms were absolutely reliable. Modern science also makes use of deductive logic, as you will see, but induction plays a much larger role in both contemporary natural and also social scientific research.

Finally, the ancient-medieval world view was holistic, which means people's ideas worked in such a way as to enable them to make sense out of all aspects of their existence, from cosmology to psychology, theology, and political behavior. It explained why men went to war, or died of disease, why they fell in love, or betrayed those whom they were supposed to love. In short, it was a world view. Now, what did it look like?

This is a picture of their universe (Figure 2.1).

First, notice it was geostatic (not exactly geocentric despite the picture, since the earth was not quite in the center). The entire universe consisted of ten concentric, perfect circles that moved around the heavy and still earth. These heavenly bodies, planets, and stars were composed of something called ether, a rather spiritual and weightless stuff. For the ancients, deities resided there, hence the names of the planets they knew were Jupiter, Saturn, Mars, Venus, and Mercury. Surrounding all these spheres were the "fixed stars." After the Christian era, beyond the fixed stars was heaven. Jesus was understood to have literally ascended

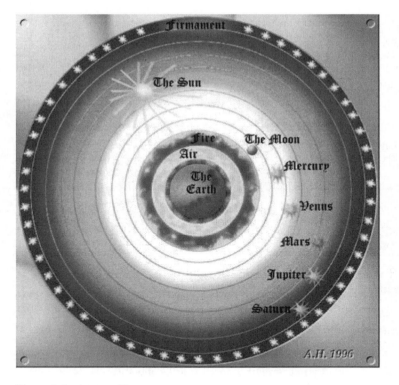

Figure 2.1: picture of heavens

to Heaven. In other words, if you could go high enough, you would get there. And, of course, in the middle of the earth was hell.

Even today, conventional ideas of heaven describe it as a place where there will be no change—not to mention, no unhappiness, no more crying. This concept goes back to the ancients, who believed nothing ever changed in the heavens. If you go outside in the evening, in the fall and winter, and look to the southwest, you will see the constellation Orion, looking exactly as it did thousands of years ago. We still name constellations the way the Greeks did because they look the same as they did when the Greeks named them. To be sure, *we* no longer think the heavens are unchanging, but perhaps you can see why *they* did. It was commonsense empiricism.

Since there was no change in the heavens, all change must happen down here. That, too, was obvious. People are born, grow up, get old, and die. Leaves appear in the spring and die in the fall.

It also followed logically the earth was near the center of the universe and motionless, because, unlike the "ethereal" (virtually weightless) heavens, the earth was composed of four weighty substances: earth, water, air, and fire. It made sense the weighty earth would not move and the almost weightless everything else would swing around it once every twenty-four hours. It is, after all, what we still see.

At the same time, the idea of gravity also added to the certainty that people were not moving. Gravity (the tendency of heavy things to fall to the center) was the quality of earth and water, while air and fire had levity (the tendency of light things to fly upward toward their natural place above earth and water). Again, it was common sense. It you light a fire which way do the flames go? Up. If you burn a log that has moisture in it, what does the water do? It either becomes steam (air) and goes upward, or water and exhibits its gravity by moving downward toward earth.

A number of late-medieval thinkers discussed the idea of the earth's motion, but the notion of gravity made it seem illogical. If gravity means heavy things fall to the center and one assumes the sun to be in the center, when you jump up, you should fall toward the sun. But clearly, you do not; you simply fall to earth again.

Humans were assumed to be composed of the four elements on earth, called "humors." Water was phlegm; fire, yellow bile; earth, black bile; and air was blood. A healthy person had his humors in balance; too much or too little of any one caused the various illnesses to which humans were subject. Moderation was the key. The doctor's job was to diagnose which humor was out of balance and fix the problem, generally by bleeding.

The humeral theory also explained why stars or comets might lead to warfare, famine, rape, murder, and even suicide. It seems rather bizarre to moderns, but it should be recognized it was not magical but biochemical. After all, people take a lot of medicines today to correct their biochemical imbalances that result in depression, ADHD, and suicide.

The ancient-medieval world view made sense of life. The principles that explained medicine and psychology, and how things behaved on earth, explained how things behaved in the heavens. They were also compatible with their religion outlooks, and their social order. Replacing this world view with a new one would not be easy. A few inconsistencies would not be enough to cause people to seek a totally new way to make sense of their existence. The historical question is not why it took so long for modern science to come into being, but rather, why it ever came at all. That is what we turn to now.

THE ORIGINS OF MODERN SCIENCE

You may well be wondering, if the medievals were able to explain so much about their lives so well, why did they give up their old view for these new scientific ideas that are, admittedly, more difficult to understand. Truth to tell, as with all scientific theories, including modern ones, the ancient-medieval world view did not explain everything completely.

Scientific theories, at all times, function to help us understand what we are observing. One theory has always been considered better than another if it is able to explain more phenomena. In the twentieth century, Einstein's general theory of relativity supplanted Newton's theory of gravity because it explained everything Newton's theory did and things Newton's theory did not.

Because a theory does not explain everything does not mean you abandon it. In fact, research generally centers on areas of a theory that don't quite fit. Scientists only abandon a theory when the anomalies in it become so glaring they are forced to seek a new way to explain reality. Then the scientists began to search for a different approach to explain these anomalies. Often a number of approaches are floated before a new one is settled upon, after which scientists abandon the old theory and settle into developing the possibilities and problems of this new one.

All of this is to say there were problems with the fit between theory and reality in the ancient-medieval scientific world view, problems that ultimately forced scientists in the sixteenth and seventeenth centuries to seek a new explanation for reality, which became modern science.

First, consider the planets. Contrary to what one would expect, at times they seemed to reverse course and proceed not from east to west like the sun, but the reverse. After a time, they then began again to move in the expected direction, west to east. A second century AD Greek, Claudius Ptolemy, came up with an explanation for this strange behavior. These "wanderers," which is what planet means, appeared to be going in the wrong direction because they were not traveling directly on a circular orbit about the earth, but on a little orbit, an epicycle, around the planet's main orbit. In effect, it made a looping motion rather than a circular one. When the planet was on the backside of its loop, it seemed to us to be going in the wrong direction. Ptolemy devised other explanations for other anomalies in the earth-centered cosmology, but none quiet solved the problems caused by what astronomers actually saw in the heavens. Clearly something was wrong with Ptolemy's system.

Aristotle's explanation for terrestrial motion was another area in which it was apparent all was not well with the ancient-medieval world view. In the heavens motion was constant, unceasing and natural, and did not need explaining. But on the earth, things move sometimes and at other times are still. Why and how? Using a commonsense approach, Aristotle suggested that on the earth, unlike the heavens, rest is natural and motion forced. A cart moves because a donkey pulls it, but when the donkey stops, the cart also stops. An arrow shot into the air is kept in motion by the air it displaces when it moves, which rushes behind and pushes it along. Aristotle also thought things moved faster in accordance with their size. Medievals had long recognized the inadequacy of Aristotle's ideas. One proposed improvement, impetus theory, suggested that an arrow, for example, receives an "impressed force" when shot into the air. It gradually uses up this force, and when it is dissipated the arrow falls to the ground. But this did not quite explain the motion of projectiles and, as with Ptolemy, here too, by the seventeenth century, many scientists believed new explanations were badly needed.

Finally, everyone who seriously studied the heavens knew the calendar was badly in need of some adjustments. Copernicus, who first proposed the earth might be in motion after all, was in part motivated to undertake his cosmological inquiries because of problems with the calendar.

NICOLAUS COPERNICUS (1473–1543)

Late in the Middle Ages, some scholars had entertained the ancient idea that perhaps the sun, rather than the earth, was in the center of our system, only to reject it as too contrary to common sense to be taken seriously. Yet, it was just such an approach that, late in the sixteenth century, would finally be taken seriously by a Polish monk, Nicolaus Copernicus, who by so doing launched what historians have come to call the "scientific revolution." Copernicus proposed his revolutionary new cosmology both to repair the calendar and also to solve some philosophical problems he had with the old system, in particular Ptolemy's epicycles. He became convinced, contrary to common sense, the earth was moving; his was no mere computational device.

Having studied mathematics in Italy in his youth, Copernicus, who had read the earlier discussions that placed the sun in the center of the universe, decided to try his hand at rearranging the planets in Ptolemy's system to see what he might get. In other words, he did not lose any sleep observing the heavens to develop his new theory; he simply reworked the geometry of the old system. When he had finished, he was able to show, to his own satisfaction, at least, that if you put the earth with its moon in the sun's place, and vice versa, you come out with a much simpler system (mathematically speaking). Furthermore, you saved the circularity of the planets' motions, and did not need any of the Ptolemaic devices that offended his Neoplatonic sensibilities.

You can see this in Figure 2.2. Notice the sun—"sol"—in the center and the earth with its moon where the sun used to be. Also notice the planets move in perfect circles around the sun. Not shown is the region of stars and an empty sphere, making ten spheres, as the Greeks had maintained. Copernicus did not change much; indeed, his revolution was really rather conservative.

Modern scholars have recognized some problems with his calculations. After all, lots of errors had crept into the Ptolemaic corpus over the centuries. Furthermore, Copernicus, like the ancient Greeks,

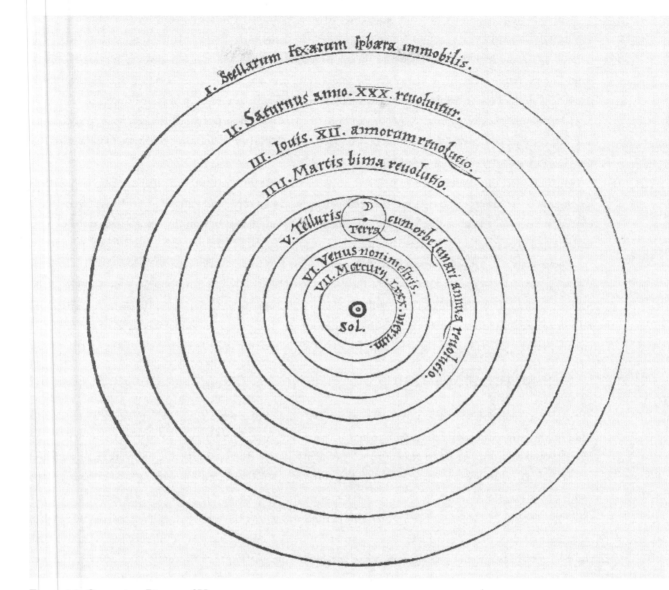

Figure 2.2: Copernicus Picture of Heavens

could not give up the assumption planets move in perfect circles, instead of ellipses, as they actually do. The mathematical formulas for an ellipse and a circle are not the same and attempts to compute one, using the data that fit the other, will necessarily be unsuccessful. But it was a much better fit than the Ptolemaic system could boast, and he was convinced of its basic correctness.

Unfortunately for Copernicus, while his little mathematical alteration might have been convincing from a mathematical point of view, it was harder to imagine as physical reality. If things were as he supposed, the earth was moving in three ways: 1) turning over and over once every twenty-four hours; 2) going around the sun once a year; and 3) spinning like a top, which accounted for what was known as the precession of equinoxes. (It means the pole star has not always been in the northernmost part of our sky.)

It makes you dizzy just to think about it. Do you really feel you are moving in three directions? It should not be hard to understand why Copernicus's contemporaries found his ideas difficult to accept. It seemed to people that a stone thrown in the air would fall behind where it was thrown because the earth would move and leave it. They had observed that a stone thrown in the air on a ship in a strong wind fell into the water behind it. People also asked what about gravity (that tendency of heavy things to fall to the center)? Should not everything thrown up from the earth fall toward the sun if the sun were in the center and not the earth? Copernicus did not feel the need to explain these common-sense type of concerns. But people did want to know.

Furthermore, the Bible spoke as if the earth were the still point in the center of the universe. Joshua commanded the sun to stand still, not the earth! Heaven was up there and hell below. If the sun were in the center, was heaven still above? Also, Copernicus's theory required almost infinite space between the planets and the stars (a phenomenon known as stellar parallax). That too was troubling.

Copernicus did not live to deal with all the trouble he had caused. Tradition has it that, as he lie dying, the printer of his *On the Revolution of the Heavenly Orbs* (1543) brought him the first copy. Others would have to deal with his challenge. The results would be a universe far different from that which Copernicus had imagined. But this rather conservative revolutionary deserves to be remembered as the one whose courage set the process in motion.

TYCHO BRAHE (1546–1601)

The following story takes some interesting twists and some unexpected turns before we arrive at its end. One of the most interesting and unexpected involves the contributions of a Danish astronomer, Tycho Brahe, who was born just three years after Copernicus's death. Brahe became the most accomplished and celebrated observational astronomer of his day, perhaps ever. Recall that Copernicus's work was not the result of observations of the heavens. On the contrary, Brahe unceasingly observed the heavens from a mountaintop in Denmark for twenty years. This in itself was unique; previously, astronomers had only looked from time to time. If a planet had moved from one spot in the heavens to another, they would extrapolate the path the heavenly body must have taken. Brahe and his assistants, however, looked every night they could and, as a result, accumulated the most accurate data ever compiled. He discovered comets orbit the sun and not the earth, as had been believed. This made the older idea of crystalline spheres, upon which the planets and stars were presumed to ride, totally obsolete. While ice fishing one night, he became the first Westerner to notice what we today call a supernova. This, too, was revolutionary because Aristotelian theory maintained all change occurred below the region of the moon. Beyond the moon, nothing ever changed. Wrong again. Clearly, as a result of Brahe's work, the AristotlePtolemy theory was in trouble.

But the supreme irony of Brahe's work is, although he had made the Aristotelian-Ptolemaic system untenable and was thoroughly acquainted with the Copernican hypothesis, he could not accept the latter explanation as an adequate replacement for the former. Recall that Copernicus required immense distances between the planets and the stars. That is what stopped Brahe. He could not imagine God being so wasteful. As with Copernicus, it was a philosophical or theological idea that drove Brahe to seek his solution to the problem of the heavens. He came up with one, and as a result, in the seventeenth century, people were faced with three rival explanations for how this universe operates. (After the efforts of his assistant

Kepler, there would be four. More on that in a minute.)

Brahe's system is a beautiful compromise between Ptolemy and Copernicus. It does away with the need for Ptolemy's devices by having the planets revolve around the sun, just as in Copernicus's system. But unlike Copernicus, he has that planetary system, plus the moon, sun, and stars, all revolve around the earth. That removes the need for infinite spaces between Saturn and the stars. It solves the problem of scripture and common sense at the same time. He thought it was beautiful, and he spent his life trying to prove it. It was a wonderful compromise, but, alas, it was incorrect.

JOHANNES KEPLER (1571–1630)

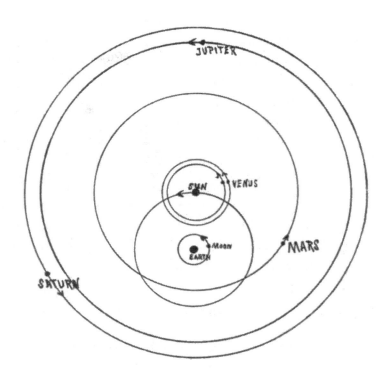

Figure 2.3: Tycho Brahe's picture of heavens

When Tycho Brahe died in 1601, his mantel passed to his young German assistant, Johannes Kepler (1571–1630). Kepler took Brahe's data and used it to prove Copernicus's basic system to be correct (See Figure 2.3). We associate his name with the three laws of planetary motion. Unlike Brahe, Kepler was a mathematician to whom Copernicus seemed to offer a tidier mathematical system. Also like Copernicus, he was a Neoplatonist and a mystic who went into raptures over the sun. In fact, his useful ideas are difficult to find because they lie buried in a lot of speculative material dealing with the regular solids or the intervals of musical scales, which he tried, unsuccessfully, to make the mathematical bases of his system.

But the gold nuggets are there. First, he demonstrated planets do not move with uniform motion. Second, he followed up with the notion planets do not move uniformly because they are moving in ellipses rather than perfect circles. Only Brahe's phenomenal data and Kepler's dogged persistence could have shown him that. No one would have ever guessed it.

Kepler's third law, almost an afterthought, followed again from Brahe's data. It points out that the same mathematical regularity (ratio) exists between each of the planet's distance from the sun and its time of orbit. Mathematically, it is the ratio of the squares of the orbital periods of two planets being equal to the cube of their mean distances from the sun. $(T1/T2)^2 = (R1/R2)^3$ where T is mean time and R is average distance. In other words, there is a single law governing the entire planetary system. This law proved useful to Newton when he was working out the inverse square law central to his theory of gravity.

Kepler crossed over from the ancient and medieval to the modern because he both insisted mathematics is the proper method to use in describing phenomenon (some medievals had already done this), and because he viewed the system as a mechanical operation, not a collection of powers or spiritual forces. Lest we make him too modern, Kepler was a Neoplatonist and something of a mystic, and an astrologer.

Renaissance scientists, including Kepler, were fascinated with all aspects of antiquity, including its magical traditions. As a case in point, Kepler used an incorrect idea derived from an Englishman, Gilbert, who suggested the planets, including the earth, are giant magnets. Magnetism, the "soul" of the earth, moved it along in its orbit around the sun. Using this idea, Kepler was able to imagine the planets going around the sun, mutually attracting one another. Speeds would vary as the planets moved away from the sun; just as magnets lose their attractive power the farther one moves the iron away from the magnetic source. It was wrong by modern standards, part of a way of seeing the world he and his contemporaries would gradually abandon. But it was a step in the direction of replacing magic with mechanism that would characterize the scientific world view of the eighteenth century. Incidentally, this is not the last time we will encounter an error helpful in developing the explanation that later comes to be seen as the correct explanation of a phenomena.

GALILEO GALILEI (1564–1642)

Not everyone who was a devotee of Copernicus was prepared to accept Kepler's conclusions. The most significant of these was Galileo Galilei (1564–1642), and although he was mistaken where he disagreed with Kepler, his contributions to our story are of no less importance. Not only did Galileo help establish the new system in astronomy and the new mechanicalmathematical view of science, he also developed the law of inertia that gave us the modern explanation for motion on the earth, as well as in the heavens. With this law and those of Kepler, and a little help from a few others, Newton had all the raw materials he would need to put the new theory of the heavens together. It is also worth noting Einstein's new theory of gravity assumes Galileo's law of inertia.

Like Kepler, Galileo was a mathematician. And for this reason, his cosmological and mostly Aristotelian academic colleagues thought he had no business sticking his nose into a cosmological problem. Mathematics, as Aristotle had taught, was unable to describe physical reality; Galileo on the other hand was convinced mathematics is the key to understanding nature. He said:

[Natural] Philosophy is written in this grand book, the universe, which stands continually open to our gaze. But the book cannot be understood unless one first learns to comprehend the language and read the letters in which it is composed. It is written in the language of mathematics, and its characters are triangles, circles, and other geometric figures without which it is humanly impossible to understand a single word of it; without these, one wanders about in a dark labyrinth.[1]

He further irritated them by introducing a new technology into the work of astronomy—the telescope. This device was rather like powerful field glasses. He built one and turned it on the heavens. What he saw was extraordinary: the sun had spots, the moon craters, Venus phases (like the moon), Jupiter had moons (like a solar system), and he thought he had found a new star, which turned out to be the planet Neptune when it was identified a century later.

---

1   http://refspace.com/quotes/Galileo_Galilei/mathematics

His machine also demonstrated things in the heavens were corporeal rather than ethereal. Clearly, the old system was untenable, not that everyone rushed to join the Copernican side. After all, what he saw in his telescope could be explained just as easily using Brahe's model, which was far more acceptable to the church.

In 1632, Galileo published his *Dialogues Concerning the Two World Systems*. It was presented as an even-handed discussion of the two leading viewpoints on the questions of terrestrial motion and the nature of the heavens. He was perfectly at liberty to do this, even though he had been ordered by the church not to teach Copernicus's ideas. Yet his book was only a thinly veiled attack on Aristotle, and it completely ignored Brahe's and Kepler's models. Some of his enemies at the papal court whispered to the pope that his imminence was the model for one of the book's protagonists, *Simplicio*, which sounds much like simpleton. There were also rumors that Galileo, like Bruni, was a pantheist. For whatever reasons, Galileo was tried before the Inquisition for teaching Copernican ideas and forced to recant to avoid torture or possibly death. His punishment was to be placed in confinement for the rest of his life, but he did some of his most valuable work on terrestrial motion during that time.

As we indicated, Galileo's cosmology, viewed from our perspective, was not as accurate as Kepler's. All the same, his contributions to the rise of modern physics and astronomy, and indeed to the creation of the scientific world view, are hard to overestimate. His condemned work, written in Italian rather than Latin, was widely read, funny, and easily understood, and did a lot to popularize the heliocentric view. His telescope quite simply revolutionized astronomy. And his solution to the problem of motion on the earth—inertia—is fundamental to modern physics.

Recall that Aristotle's physics had problems explaining not only how things go in the heavens, but also on the earth. Thinking about motion in a new and totally non-Aristotelian way was not easy, and Galileo worked many years completing his theory of inertia. Simply stated it is the assertion a body will remain at rest or in motion unless acted upon by some other body. And inertia is the measure of force (see the mathematics again) required to change that state of motion or rest. For Galileo, the motion was circular, and on this point Descartes had to straighten him out, as it were.

An early biographer of Galileo is responsible for one of the most widely known experiments attributed to Galileo. To disprove Aristotle's idea heavy objects fall faster than lighter ones, Galileo is supposed to have dropped Pisa tower balls of different weights that landed together. If he had, they would not have landed together, as wind resistance would have retarded the heavier one, if only slightly. After all, only in a vacuum chamber does a feather fall as fast as a rock.

We do not know for sure whether he did this experiment. But we do know he did work with incline planes and frequently did "thought experiments," like Einstein after him. Rolling balls down inclined planes and using a water clock to keep time, he worked out a geometric formula for rates of acceleration expressed today in algebraic terms as $s=1/2at^2$. That is more accurate than the legendary experiment in the tower, if less picturesque. It also helped him conceive inertia, for he was able to show Aristotle's idea of a body in motion must be sustained in motion was mistaken. Once in motion, he argued, a body would go on moving were it not for surface tension. Remove that tension and the body would never stop. In fact, a body in motion beyond the reach of the sun's gravity, like Voyager II, will continue moving forever, unless it comes into contact with some other sun's gravitational field.

There is something else less than satisfactory about the tower story. It suggests Galileo thought like a nineteenth-century positivist scientist. Instead, Galileo's writings on experiments and mathematics suggest this picture will not do. He appreciated the value of experimentation, but he valued mathematics more. He once observed to a friend that if an experiment fails and the math is correct, then the experiment is probably wrong. Einstein would think much the same way.

RENÉ DESCARTES (1598–1650)

We will examine René Descartes's philosophical ideas below, but he is also an important player in development of the new science. A contemporary of Galileo, he was primarily a theoretical and mathematical thinker, though he did conduct some experiments in optics. Mathematically, he created coordinate geometry to relate geometry to algebra in describing curves (See Figure 2.4). I bet you will recognize it. It is essential to all applied mathematics today.

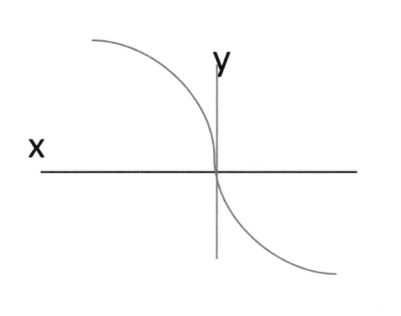

Descartes, like Galileo, wanted to replace the Aristotelian world with one based on mechanical principles. To explain the refraction of light, he used tennis balls and came up with the mathematical formula today known as Snell's law (the sin of the angle of incidence is equal to the sin of the angle of refraction).

His cosmology was the most completely materialistic of all his scientific explanations. It relied upon a system of vortices and the old Aristotelian assumption that

Figure 2.4: picture of heavens

nature abhors a vacuum. God had originally created the universe with a set amount of force that has since been conserved.[2] Objects like the earth were attempting to move off in a straight line (inertia) but were kept in place by the plenum (totally full universe), and so move about the sun in an elliptical fashion. Ironically, Descartes, the great mathematician, did not attempt to present his picture of the universe mathematically. Yet because he seemed to have an explanation for all aspects of motion in the heavens, as well as on the earth, and his work was mechanical, allowing no place for occult powers or action at a distance, it was widely read and very influential.

---

2   i.e., the law of the conservation of matter, which since Einstein's E=MC[2] has become matter/energy.

Because Descartes was such a thorough materialist, he described the heart as a pump, the lungs as bellows, and he further maintained the human soul was itself material: the recently discovered pituitary gland. From this he also deduced that animals, which lack souls, also lack the ability to feel.

CHRISTIAAN HUYGENS (1629–1695)

Christiaan Huygens was a mathematician who taught Leibnitz, one of the inventors of calculus. His work on the pendulum enabled him to develop a reliable pendulum clock, vital for science and travel. This experimentation also led him to deduce the gravitational constant Newton would use in his theory of gravity. Being a convinced mechanist, much as Descartes, he launched the wave theory of light. Finally, he discovered the rings of Saturn.

We are moving toward the conclusion of this discussion, and mention Huygens to alert you to the fact that scientific revolution was not simply the work of one or two men of genius, but of a number of individuals, each making small contributions that enabled one man, Newton, to put them all together into a coherent whole. Without their prior efforts, Newton's synthesis would not have been possible.

When Newton arrived on the scene, the problem troubling these natural philosophers was that Descartes's mechanical philosophy had some problems suggesting his approach was not going to work. Some other way was needed. The earliest suggestion came from another of those seventeenth-century polymaths, Richard Hooke, who suggested perhaps it was a matter of attraction rather than repulsion, in which case the planets would stay in their orbits due to the combined forces of inertia and gravity. Hooke was not a very gifted mathematician, so he was unable to work out what would be needed to prove his insight. Newton was and did.

ISAAC NEWTON (1642–1727)

"Nature and nature's laws lay hid in night.

God said, 'Let Newton be' and all was light."

This rhymed couplet by Alexander Pope reflects the way Isaac Newton came to be viewed, even during his lifetime, and certainly since. Not until Einstein in the twentieth century has a scientist been lionized as much as was Newton. And his accomplishments were extraordinary.

By the nineteenth century, scholars came to present Newton as the chief creator of the mechanical explanation for the nature of reality that dominated science until the last century. It is not accurate since Newton, unlike Descartes, was not a strict mechanist. Indeed, research on Newton in the early twentieth century revealed a person who was as much interested in religion, especially prophesy and biblical chronology, as he was in physics. He was also devoted to alchemy, which may have caused him to suffer from lead poisoning. While many continental scientists, like Leibnitz, could not accept Newton's theory of gravity because it seemed to have readmitted the occult forces scientists had been working so hard to expel, we now recognize the only way Newton could have worked out his theory of universal gravitation was through his attraction to the occult.

The theory of universal gravitation Newton developed, as Hooke had suggested, combined the forces of gravity and inertia and was based, not on Descartes's "repulsion," but on "attraction." Newton invented the term "centripetal force" to explain what he meant. But the mere use of the term "force," not to mention "attraction," was enough to put the materialists off. What after all is a force? How does the sun's gravity "attract" the earth, or the earth's gravity us? And what exactly is an "attraction" if it is not some sort of magic?[3] In fact, Newton never said what it was. He was content to describe the system geometrically in the *Principia Mathematica*, which included his rules of reasoning and methodology.

The universe, he explained, is held together by the force of gravity. The motion of things on the earth, as well as things in the heavens, all obey this single law. How the planets move about the sun, how you stay on the earth, or how apples fall to the ground are all the result of this one principle, which he defined as follows:

Everybody is attracted to every other body with a force that is directly proportional to the two masses, and inversely proportional to the square of the distance that separates them.

In mathematical terms it is: $F = k(m^1 m^2 / r^2)$ where F is force, k a constant, m the masses of the bodies, and d the distance between them. This is a rather simple idea, and he presented it using geometry, which was commonly used in his time. But to work it out, he had to develop a new math, the calculus, or "fluxions" as he called it.[4]

Newton's theory of universal gravitation combined gravity with inertia. As it were, heavenly bodies were held in a state of equilibrium by: 1) a tendency to fly off at a tangent to the curve (inertia) balanced against 2) a mutual attraction of the body and the sun (gravity). In the solar system, for instance, these two forces neatly balance; therefore, a body, say the earth, keeps on circling the sun without either escaping from its grasp or being pulled into it. It is, as it were, constantly falling toward the sun and always missing. By contrast, the space station we sent up a few decades ago was in too low an orbit for the speed at which it was traveling to stay in orbit around the earth. Gradually, with each orbit, it slipped closer and closer to earth until, finally, gravity overcame inertia, and the satellite plunged to its fiery death. The moon, as it turns out, is slowly slipping away from the earth and, in the distant future, inertia will overcome gravity and the moon will break free. But no need to worry; we will have long departed the scene before this happens.

Newton's basic laws, developed in the *Principia,* provided the foundation for modern mechanics, and were not challenged until the twentieth century.

Newton is also remembered for having established optics on a sound (i.e., modern) footing with his famous experiment of splitting a beam of light into the colors of the spectrum and his recognition that, contrary to common-sense expectations, ordinary light, sunlight, or light from a table lamp is composed of all colors. Newton argued light is made up of tiny particles. That part of his idea has an interesting history, as we shall see. Is it any wonder he was lionized in his age as the most extraordinary of geniuses?

SCIENTIFIC WORLD VIEW

We are just about ready to bring this story to its conclusion. With the triumph of the Newtonian system, what do we have? First, the world of the ancients and medievals, with which we began, along with their rules of reasoning, has been completely replaced. Despite Newton's reservations, the new picture that emerged by the mid-eighteenth century was of a universe operating much like a complicated machine: a

---

3   Einstein did not like this concept either.
4   Leibnitz also developed the calculus and an unseemly row developed between the two over priority, each accusing the other of plagiarism. In fact, it seems to have been a case of simultaneous discovery.

clock that ran according to natural laws humans, using reason, could understand. Some people came to see these laws as God's thoughts, as though God were letting us in on a heretofore-secret recess of his mind. Further, the language of God's thoughts and of this universe was mathematics, as Galileo had suggested. Finally, since it was a machine, it was not living but dead, heedless of anything or anyone in it.[5] Over the next two centuries, scientists would use this model to explain increasingly more aspects of science, and even create the social sciences as well.

MODERN PHILOSOPHY

As suggested above, the concept of a world view implies a way of making sense out of *all* aspects of one's existence. Thus far, we have been talking about the new ideas largely in physics and cosmology. Now we turn to examining how this new outlook reformed all aspects of European thought. We will first look at philosophy, since people's scientific ideas are wrapped in philosophy, whether they recognize it or not. This will be followed by a look at the eighteenth-century movement known as the Enlightenment, which resulted in the new science and its methods being applied to the reform of society itself.

It is not surprising people would have questioned their ways of gaining knowledge (epistemology) and of creating authorities during the period leading up to Newton's synthesis. If the things you and everyone you know have believed to be true about nature were proven to be profoundly incorrect, would you not also suspect the way you went about coming to those erroneous conclusions was itself a part of the problem? This certainly occurred in the seventeenth and eighteenth centuries, and for that matter in the twentieth after relativity and quantum mechanics destroyed much of the mechanical world view Newton and others had fashioned in the seventeenth century. In other words, it was not only a problem of mechanics; it was also a problem of epistemology the people of the period had been wrestling with. And when Newton's work had triumphed, it included a new approach to reasoning almost as important as the new views of nature. As the eighteenth century progressed, these new approaches altered the ways in which all educated people reasoned, including the businessmen of that era, and, as recent research has suggested, lower down the social scale as well. Therefore, it behooves us to know something of the nature of this new way of seeking truth.

Let's take a hypothetical case by way of illustration. If you wanted to explain a falling body, say a cannon ball, how would you go about doing it? You might think about the nature of round things and how they fall and then look at one, or you might simply look at one and then make up your mind about how falling bodies behave. In the end, Newton, and modern scientists generally, do some of both, depending on the nature of the problem. The former method is called "deduction" and the latter "induction." Let's look at them briefly. It should be pointed out that ancients and medievals used both induction and deduction, but in different ways than was true by the seventeenth century.

Bacon (1561–1626) and Induction

Induction is a method of discovering information through observation. It was first championed in this period by Francis Bacon. He suggested what was wrong with the ideas from the past was that people did

---

5   That is what Pascal meant when he said, "the silence of the spheres troubles me."

not look enough before drawing conclusions. For him, you keep looking, and eventually a synthesis will arise from all your data. Incidentally, he was not a mathematician, and also not a Copernican. He thought there was not enough data to make a choice. Nor could there ever be! Today the inductive approach is basic to science, but it has gone much beyond Bacon's work through the development of statistics and probabilities that give it the mathematical base Bacon lacked.

Bacon is also important because he argued knowledge is power and that humans should use science to improve human control over nature. He even imagined a future world of plenty and of super transportation, all made possible by science and, of course, technology. And he constructed a new ordering for all human studies and areas of knowledge. This reorganization was especially influential during the Enlightenment.

Finally, Bacon is important for suggesting a *modus vivendi* between science and religion that most scientists have relied upon ever since. Scientists, he suggested, should confine their efforts to explaining the natural world and not make pronouncements about things theological. These should be left to theologians and philosophers. In return, theologians should cease to make pronouncements about the natural world based upon theology.

Descartes (1598–1650) and Deduction

A contemporary of Bacon's, Descartes did not think induction was the answer to the problem of determining what is true or how we know it. He did not think that the way to proceed was by looking, but rather by finding a secure starting point from which you could make a series of mathematically sound deductions, rather like geometry. Following the "Skeptics" of antiquity, he suggested one must be prepared to question everything, the "method of doubt." Unlike the Skeptics, however, he discovered a place from which sure and certain knowledge could be obtained. It was his famous *cogito ergo sum,* "I think therefore *I am.*"

If you are confused at this point, the one thing of which you can be certain is that you do exist. You are thinking, so you must truly exist. From this foundation, Descartes deduced the existence of God and the rest of the world. We have examined his importance to mathematics and the new science above. Suffice to say he is also one of the twin fathers of modern philosophy.

Enlightenment thinkers praised him most for his "method of doubt" and its importance in arriving at truth. His ideas rivaled those of Newton for a time, partly for reasons of national pride, but also because they seemed more mechanical and less magical than Newton's.

Descartes's deductive and geometric approach to constructing his system of the world was followed by several other seventeenth-century philosophers. Like him, they employed geometry as the model of reasoning to follow, and, like him, they attempted to construct a complete system to make sense of reality. We cited Thomas Hobbes for his *Leviathan,* a treatise that supported a secular version of absolute monarchy. It is enough to remind you he was a materialist for whom only matter and motion are real. Geometry provided him with his model for how to explain human behavior.

The Spanish Jewish philosopher Spinoza (1632–1677), following Descartes's geometric approach, reached in his posthumously published work *Ethics* a rather different and certainly shocking conclusion than had Descartes. Often called a pantheist, if not an atheist, Spinoza attempted to reconcile the divine with the new science by suggesting God is indistinguishable from nature; in consequence, there could be no miracles nor incarnation, and prayers were clearly to no avail.

Another rationalist who built all-encompassing systems was Gottfried Leibnitz (1646–1716), a philosopher, scientist, and as noted above, the coinventor of calculus with Newton. Leibnitz was a man with conventional Lutheran religious beliefs. His philosophy was an attempt to reconcile those beliefs with the mechanical implications of the new science that left God with no choice or control over the universe he had created. Leibnitz's approach was to suggest God had created and sustained "monads," the substantive nature of reality. These centers of power (more than atoms) were dynamic rather than static and, as Lloyd Moote noted, anticipatory of the scientific world of the early twentieth century. In the hands of his successor and disciple, Christian Wolff, this system of monads became the basis of a rather simplistic[6] theodicy. God was free to make any sort of world he wished when he made everything, Leibnitz and Wolff maintained. Being good, he created the best of all possible worlds. Any world other than the one we have would be worse. Little fish must be eaten by bigger fish for them to grow bigger for us to eat them. So, individual evil becomes a part of a larger good. This became the doctrine of optimism.

John Locke (1632–1704)

We have already discussed John Locke for his political ideas, and when we get to the American Revolution we will have occasion to mention him again. Our interest in him here is his epistemology. Locke is closer to Bacon than to the rationalists cited above. Newton's work influenced him as well. Without Locke's ideas, the Enlightenment is difficult to imagine.

From antiquity until Locke, Europeans had thought people were born with a head full of ideas. Descartes assumed as much with his approach of establishing sure and certain ideas from which to draw correct deductions. By contrast, Locke in his *An Essay Concerning Human Understanding (1689)* maintained that humans know nothing at birth. He used the term *"tabula rasa,"* or blank tablet. Where then do we get our ideas? From experience and only experience! In other words, your ideas about math are not intuitive, nor are your ideas about God, good, evil, and—above all—politics. His work is important because the Enlightenment was a social reform movement. If humans are born with all their ideas set, they cannot change. If they are blank tablets, you can write and even rewrite upon them. By the eighteenth century, Locke's epistemological idea was largely triumphant, and it went unchallenged until the twentieth century.

Locke's epistemology is also important for another reason. As we noted above, deduction was the primary method of reasoning employed by philosophers. We called them the "rationalist" theorists. They assumed there is a formal reality in everything we recognize because we have an idea of that object or notion from when we were born. Their thinking was said to be *"a priori,"* which meant you did not discover truth by inspection, but by introspection. After Locke, philosophers, who will be called "empiricists," questioned this assumption and, following the ideas first laid down by Francis Bacon, used a more inductive approach to understanding reality. Their approach is referred to as *"a posteriori,"*[7] after the fact. Locke

---

6   A theodicy is a philosophical explanation for the presence of evil when God is understood to be both all powerful and all good.

7   A statement such as "All bachelors are unmarried" is a priori truth and follows from the definition of a bachelor. Whether "all bachelors are happy" can only be discerned by observing bachelors and is therefore a posteriori knowledge.

and his followers insisted we can rely only upon observations to explain how we come to understand our basic truths about science, but also religion, math, and all our social institutions. Their inquiries, as we shall see, led to conclusions far more corrosive of traditional social and religious beliefs than those of the rationalists. Looking ahead, it is fair to say philosophers to this day are divided over the relative merits of these two approaches to understanding reality.

THE ENLIGHTENMENT

Sometimes historians create a name for an historical period. All the people we call Byzantines never called themselves that; they called themselves Romans. This is not the case of the Enlightenment. That term was invented by eighteenth-century reformers who considered themselves to be enlightened. Unfortunately, this does not mean we have a simple definition for the movement all historians accept; however, some notions are generally accepted, and we shall look at these.

First, the movement was principally social. Scientific developments continued to be made in the eighteenth century, especially in chemistry, electricity and magnetism, and biology, but the Enlightenment was primarily a movement of social reform whose methods were inspired by the new science, especially that of Bacon, Newton, and Locke.

The term applied to these reformers in France was *philosophes*, which looks a lot like the word "philosopher." There were a number of formal philosophers, and we will look briefly at the ideas of two of them—David Hume (1711–1776) and Immanuel Kant (1724–1804), as their influence on the future of human thought has been profound. But most *philosophes* were literary figures. They wrote belles letters, and essays, plays, and novels. Many supported themselves from the proceeds of what they published. We will also consider their proposals for reforms.

David Hume

Hume was an important figure in the Scottish Enlightenment, as well as a friend of Adam Smith and Rousseau. He wrote on ethics, economics, and English history, but we will confine ourselves to his empirical philosophy, which is where his most lasting influence has been felt.

Most scholars refer to Hume as the skeptic whose ideas undermined the rational foundations of the Enlightenment by pointing out that neither deductive reasoning, as championed by Descartes and Spinoza, nor inductive reasoning, as championed by Locke and his disciples, was logically sound. Hume accepted the reality of our material world, but he argued, quite persuasively to many, we must accept it only on the basis of experience, and not of rational certainty. You must recognize, he maintained, there is no way to logically prove the chair you sit on will hold you up, but you are prepared to sit on it anyway, because it always has supported you before.

Deductive conclusions, Hume argued, were merely tautological, which means the predicate is the same as the subject; you learn nothing new from them. He also pointed out the "inductive fallacy." In the Enlightenment, induction was the method of reasoning upon which most conclusions reached by the new science had come to be based.

His destruction of inductive certainty was simple and persuasive. If you have seen a thousand cows, all of which had four legs, inductively you should be able to make a causal statement about cows and legs, but you cannot. There are occasionally five-legged cows. Causal certainty is not possible through induction no matter how many observations you make; yet modern science rests upon this foundation. You can say you would be very surprised to find such an unfortunate beast, but no more.

Not surprisingly, Hume's ideas were unpopular in his time. There were many who whispered he was an atheist, and he may have been. He was certainly not attached to any organized religion and was skeptical of all religious ideas. But the same skepticism that kept him from accepting any concept of god also led him to question the assertions of the more robust atheists of his time. Their claims cannot be certain either. Hume's thought came to be very influential in the nineteenth century and continues to be so among philosophers to the present, one of the most important of whom is our second Enlightened era philosopher, Immanuel Kant.

Immanuel Kant

Kant, who was German and raised in a pietist home, was educated in the rationalist tradition of Leibnitz and Woolf until a chance reading of Hume's *Essay on Human Understanding*, as he put it, "woke him from his dogmatic slumbers" and set him on the course of his life's work—attempting to reconcile the contradictory rationalists' and empiricists' approaches to epistemology that had emerged out of the thinking of seventeenth- and eighteenth-century philosophers. Finding both traditions to be erroneous, he launched his own "Copernican Revolution" in thought by suggesting humans create reality in the way their minds act upon the phenomena they experience. He called these "*synthetic a priori* judgments," by which he meant, following the rationalists, that humans have an innate capacity to give meaning to observed reality (the" phenomena" of the empiricists) they encounter. The rationalists had thought reality was out there, independent of us. The empiricists maintained our experiences are all we can know. Kant suggests we are capable of making sense from the phenomena we encounter because of the way our minds are constructed. We synthesize phenomena into causal relationships that are trustworthy. So much for Hume the skeptic! But like Hume, Kant maintained we can only know sensory data, phenomena, so we cannot know what reality is ultimately like, which he called "*noumena*." Locke, Hume, and the empiricists were correct on this point. But if knowledge is what we create out of brute reality, we can make associations and connections with reality, and if all human brains work the same way, as he assumed they did, we can arrive at sure and certain knowledge of what that reality is. There are philosophers to this day who consider themselves to be "Kantians."

Kant reached a surprisingly different conclusion about religion from that of the skeptical Hume. Because one cannot know ultimate reality (*noumena*), he argued, religious claims about rituals, practices, and beliefs cannot be proved logically, nor can we know the nature of God with certainty; therefore, we are justified in having beliefs and following religious practices based upon those claims, precisely because they cannot rest upon empirical certainty.

Kant is also remembered for a pamphlet, *Was Ist Die Aufklurung?* (1784). The Enlightenment, he asserted, is nothing less than the emergence of man from a "self-imposed" inability to make up his own mind about what is truth. We should, he said, quoting Horace, *Sapere aude*, "Dare to know"! In other words, we should have the courage to use our own understanding and not conform to the tutelage of others. This is precisely what the *philosophes* set about doing.

The Philosophes

As a rule, Enlightenment reformers, philosophical or literary, were inclined to apply two tests to existing social institutions. Authority and tradition were not among them. Instead, they tended to value an institution on whether they found it to be "reasonable" and/or useful. An enormous amount of literature from the period was about the nature of "felicity" (happiness) and how to achieve it. If an institution did not contribute to achieving happiness (e.g., was neither reasonable nor useful), the reformers were inclined to replace it with something they thought reasonable and useful that would increase human happiness.

Reason is a tricky word here. The seventeenth-century rationalist philosophers we cited above used reason, deductive reason. The men and women of the Enlightenment were more inclined to work inductively, *a la* Bacon. Locke was also important to them because his ideas suggested reform was actually possible. A good example of this outlook is reflected in one of the works from the period, *Candide*, by Voltaire.

Candide, the hero of the story, goes through one horrific disaster after another. He is accompanied on his journey by a philosopher, Pangloss (really Leibnitz,) who continually assures his young charge that whatever is happening is for the best in the best of all possible worlds. By the end of this witty tale, it is hard to believe in optimism any longer. The protagonists travel to Turkey and settle down to tending their garden (instead of spinning absurd flights of philosophical fancy).

Recent research suggests not only aristocrats and wealthy bourgeois were part of this reform effort, but also many people from the lower orders of society. It is equally true there was no blueprint for society to which all these reformers adhered. They were in opposition to traditional society, but just how much they wanted to upset the apple cart, as it were, varied with the individual. It is also true, as there was no overall goal, some reformers' ideas seem to have been rather supportive of the existing society, while others appear downright revolutionary.

In most treatments on the Enlightenment, the reformers are presented as uniformly anti-religious. While in many instances (especially in France) that was the case, in other areas—e.g., the German states and England—Enlightenment ideas were sometimes extolled from pulpits and used to prop up the existing society. Likewise, many reformers, including Kant, were anxious that reforms not undermine social stability.

The movement is also seen as being primarily French, but it was actually manifested in nations throughout Europe and the world. While many enlightened thinkers were insensitive to women, Jews, or blacks, there were many who were not, and many of these groups made contributions to the moment. Finally, one cannot hope to understand the late-colonial and Federalist periods in United States history without taking the Enlightenment into account.

We will examine this movement by looking at the methods through which its ideas were disseminated, and then at specific areas the reformers wanted to change. Finally, we will evaluate the movement in terms of its consequences, both short term (in relation to the French Revolution) and long term (modern totalitarianism, for example).

To summarize the thesis, the Enlightenment was an eighteenth century social reform movement, inspired by the methods of the new science as reflected in the works of Bacon, Descartes, and, above all, Newton, to bring about reform of the old regime's social order in Europe. John Locke's epistemology was also important, as without his ideas there would have been little incentive to make the effort.

How were their ideas spread?

No Internet, no Twitter, yet the movement grew and spread throughout the century. How? The most important medium was the printing press, because, by the eighteenth century in Europe, literacy was widespread, especially in urban areas. And even when people were illiterate, there were many social occasions in which a literate person read to those who were unable to read for themselves. In other words, reform ideas spread downward in society to the workers, and even to rural peasants; they were not restricted to the upper middle class and aristocrats.

The forms the materials took were varied; some were published legally, while others circulated *sub rosa*, away from the censor's eyes. Some countries, such as the Netherlands, allowed a reasonably free press, and even in France, by the end of the eighteenth century, the censors themselves were part of the reformers and rather lax in enforcing publication censorship laws.

The types of publications included books, a plethora of journals, plays, novels, and scurrilous cheap print works much like today's tabloids. The journals were often connected to a particular occupation or sponsored by a learned society. And of course there were newspapers. It should also be noted there were a number of publications opposed to the ideas of the Enlightenment.

Perhaps the most famous single work of the Enlightenment was the *Encyclopedie,* edited by Diderot, but contributed to by just about everyone of importance in the movement. Published between 1751 and 1772, it numbered twenty-eight volumes, several of which were plates, with more than seventy thousand entries. It included information on all the latest inventions, cosmetics, social systems around the world, and beliefs systems as well. It was editorially slanted toward reform and used indirect ways to attack existing old regime social, political, and religious institutions.

Another important vehicle for transmission of reformist ideas was the "salon," social gatherings sponsored usually by the wives of aristocrats or wealthy bourgeois. These dinner parties provided the occasion to discuss the latest works or ideas among like-minded friends. If you happened to be an aspiring young writer, getting an invitation to one of these gatherings could be vital to your being published, or landing a job in a government agency that needed writing talent. Even the English colonies boasted such groups, especially in Philadelphia and Williamsburg.

What did they want to change?

It would be impossible to discuss all the many proposals for change that circulated as part of the Enlightenment; this is at best a sampling. The areas they wanted to change, however, are easier to identify. We will examine them in the following order: religion, ethics, economics, and political thought. You may be thinking, "What did they *not* want to change?" Well you should! For most, it was their position in society; they were reformers, not revolutionaries.[8]

We will approach all of these by first remembering the tradition they wanted to change, and then by examining the nature of the changes they wanted to make. Finally, we should not expect them to agree on the nature of the changes they wanted implemented.

Religion

We begin with religion because it presented the greatest obstacles to reform, especially in France but in other countries as well. Publicly expressed irreligious ideas could lead to one's death. In Scotland, in 1697, a twenty-year-old student at Edinburgh University, Thomas Aikenhead, was executed for blasphemy. Beyond that, the churches in all European countries were significant bastions of power, with wealth and property to match. Religious leaders tended to be averse to changes that might diminish their influence.

The tradition that Enlightenment thinkers opposed was Christianity, in whatever form it happened to appear. The conflict with religion was greatest where churches were most solidly in control and traditionally conservative. In 1762, in France, a Protestant, Jean Calais, was executed on rather flimsy grounds for supposedly killing his son for converting to Catholicism. The novelist and playwright Voltaire, who was very critical of the church as well as the state,[9] kept a chalet just over the border in Switzerland to which he could escape when things got too hot in his native land. By contrast, the Anglican Church in the eighteenth century was dominated by the "Latitudinarian" outlook, which was more interested in promoting morality than theology. Hell must be preached lest the servants pinch the sliver, but otherwise traditional doctrines, like the virgin birth, were of little concern. It was very common for people to refuse to take communion, including our own George Washington. The idea of the "real presence" was something they could no longer accept.

As the eighteenth century progressed, anti-religious, even atheistic, sentiment increased, especially among the empiricists. Following Locke's idea to its logical conclusion, they presented works that explained all aspects of human existence in strictly materialistic terms. To such individuals, God was no longer needed; indeed, religion was rank superstition, and progress could not be made without it being eliminated from human consciousness.[10] In 1794, even while in hiding during the French Revolution and under sentence of death for being an aristocrat, the Marquis de Condorcet wrote *An Essay on the Progress of the Human Mind,* in which he sketched the future of mankind when religious superstition would be banished and human progress would prevail.

A more popular religious outlook among enlightened thinkers was Deism, which arose in the seventeenth century and continued to be important throughout the Enlightenment. According to this belief, God created the world (through reason, rather than by fiat) and, having made it, was essentially out of a job.

---

8   Robert Darnton in *The Great Cat Massacre* reports that many of the most radical Jacobins of the French Revolution began as hack writers in the last days of the old regime—hack writers who were unsuccessful in breaking into polite society even after it had come to be controlled by the enlightened.

9   His spirited defense of Calais led him to say *"Ecrasez l'infame!"* or "Crush the Infamous thing," meaning the Catholic Church.

10   In particular, Condillac, La Metrie, and the Baron D'Holbach.

Not being a defective universe maker, God simply had nothing left to do. There is a story told about an atheist valet of Ben Franklin, who came into his living room one morning to discover an orrery (mechanical model of the solar system) that had not been there the night before. Surprised, he asked Franklin, a Deist, how it got there. Franklin is supposed to have laughed and replied, "By accident, I suppose." Most Enlightenment thinkers (notice the word most) believed natural laws governed not only the scientific world, but the social world as well. But if there were no God, there could be no laws. No "LAW" then no "laws of nature" either!

Like Franklin, Deists were particularly attracted to the "argument from design" for the existence of God. As presented by Sir William Paley, in his *Natural Theology: or, Evidences of the Existence and Attributes of the Deity, Collected from the Appearances of Nature* (1802), if you found a watch in a field, you would not suppose such a wondrously complex mechanism to have gotten there by accident. Yet, the universe, with all its laws, is ever so much more complex than a watch. It, too, must have had a divine designer.

There were many sorts of Deists. Some were virtually atheists, while others' beliefs were very close to an established religion. There is a lively scholarly debate about whether Thomas Jefferson was or was not a Deist. If your definition requires the believer have no place for divine intervention in life, then Jefferson was not. But if your definition allowed for an occasional intervention, as Jefferson seems to have believed, then he was. But the occasions in which any Deists allowed God to intervene were few and far between.

Most Deists limited their beliefs to ideas common to all religions; particular aspects of creeds—the divinity of Jesus, for example—they happily discarded. Generally, this meant there was a God who created the universe and expected us to behave morally, rewarding or punishing us accordingly. Some believed in an afterlife; others did not. But their basic point was if you had a toothache, you went to a dentist. God had given us the science of dentistry. You should not expect God to alter the structure of the universe (through prayer) because you did not take care of your teeth.

By mid-century, a number of movements arose that challenged the ideas of the Enlightenment. One of them, romanticism, will be discussed in a later chapter, as its greatest influence was felt in the mid-nineteenth century. We will only mention it briefly here.

Simply put, the romantics, also mostly literary thinkers rather than formal philosophers, believed the Enlightenment had overemphasized reason and denigrated the place of emotion in human life. Rather than reason, they stressed feelings and emotions as true guides to truth. Among the earliest of these thinkers was Rousseau whose *Confessions, Emile, and Julie, ou la nouvelle Héloïse*, all works of "sentiment," were very popular and widely read. Equally famous was Johann Wolfgang von Goethe (1749–1832), especially for his *Sorrows of Young Werther*. This sad story of a love-sick young man who finally committed suicide rather than live without his beloved "Clara" moved a generation to tears after it was published in 1775.

Not surprisingly, supporters of traditional religious beliefs continued to oppose the Enlightenment, but so also did new religious reform movements, which, like romanticism, emphasized emotion rather than reason. They found deism in all its forms to be rather cold and altogether too rational; a totally inadequate basis for religion. Methodists, Evangelical Anglicans, Baptists, Pietists, and other such religious movements found meaning in the realization they were sinners who had been forgiven by God. The result was an emotional sense of release and joy, an enthusiasm that Enlightenment thinkers thought dangerous to society.

Lest you get the wrong idea, these reformers—atheists or Deists—were always a minority, albeit an influential one. There is little evidence most people were shaky in their religious beliefs, and the traditional religious authorities were very much a presence in society throughout the period. Furthermore, by the early nineteenth century, the mid-century religious revivals had restored traditional religious beliefs to a central place in Christian thinking in Europe and the new United States as well.

Ethics

Ethics is the philosophy of right conduct. Before the Enlightenment, one's ethics would have been based on one's religious beliefs, what ethicists call "divine command theory." Not surprisingly, Enlightenment reformers were not content to follow a set of religiously inspired dos and don'ts. They wanted an ethic that was reasonable and useful. That, of course, did not mean they agreed on what was reasonable and useful. We will confine our discussion to three rather different but representative thinkers' ideas.

Closest to traditional ethics was the ethic of benevolence. Benevolence is simply doing good to other people. These thinkers sought to transform society using this touchstone as their guide. They introduced reforms in a wide variety of areas ranging from providing bottle milk for babies (to cut down on the widespread practice of abandoning infants at monastery doors so their mothers could be wet nurses for aristocratic women), to providing layettes for poor mothers, or legal advice for people accused of crime. Some sought to reform prisons, particularly the treatment of the insane. Brail systems were devised for the blind, and there was even a theater for the deaf in France.

All of these enterprises were the work of private individuals who paid for them out of their own wealth and gave of their time in their support. In addition, traditional systems of public relief also continued to function.

The rationale behind this movement was those who have been given much had a responsibility to share with those who were less well off. If you did so, you received appreciation that contributed to your happiness. Some of the benevolence reformers suggested it was the reasonable way for a society to be organized, while others spoke of the Golden Rule.

The second approach is that of the Marquis De Sade: sadism. His rationale ran along this line: "Since there is no god, one can do whatever you wish as long as you can get away with it." This included inflicting pain on someone for one's own sexual arousal. This may not sound very ethical, yet it is an ethical theory, and late in the twentieth century it attracted a lot of scholarly interest.

The third ethical theory was that of Immanuel Kant whose epistemology we examined above. Kant's approach to ethics was entirely compatible with organized religions, but totally based on reason rather than divine command. He argued the most reasonable way to treat other people is the way you want to be treated yourself, which he called the "categorical imperative." In practice it meant treating people not as a means to an end, but as an end in themselves. Alternatively, he suggested one can discover the categorical imperative if the question is asked: "Would I want someone to do to me, what I am thinking of doing to them?" If not, don't do it.

Kant's ethics theory is "deontological" rather than utilitarian. An action is not acceptable, he maintained, because it's beneficial to the greatest number, but only if it is right. For this reason, he argued, only execution is a sufficient punishment for murder, as it is the only way to make restitution for having taken a life.

Two conclusions can be drawn from the discussion of these three rather different ethical theories. First, as with religion, most people continued to listen to their priests, pastors, or rabbis when it came to moral behavior. Second, there are many more theories than the three addressed above. When you base your inquiry into human behavior upon reason, rather than tradition, you introduce certain anarchic tendencies into the discussion.

Economics

Mercantilism, which we will look at in the next chapter, is the economic theory based on the idea wealth is specie and limited, and that economic policy should work to maximize a nation's wealth (amount of gold and silver) by regulating the domestic economy with tariffs and monopolies, or by capturing colonial markets. This too came under critical scrutiny during the Enlightenment. The resultant reform may be the most lasting contribution of the movement to the future of the world as it principle idea—*laissez faire*—is very much alive and well today.

The term *laissez faire* (let alone) refers to the government interfering with the market place. It was coined by François Quesnay (1694–1774). In France, his movement, called *physiocracy*, promoted an economy based upon free trade. While his ideas had little influence upon France until after 1789 and the revolution, they were very influential in Europe during the early nineteenth century.

The person most closely associated with *laissez faire*, however, was the Scotsman Adam Smith (1723–1790). As reflected in his *The Wealth of Nations (1776)*, Smith, like Quesnay, argued that leaving the market to run itself would increase the wealth of everyone. In this work, he proposed not only free trade, but also the idea of competition to replace the notion of monopolies, supply and demand instead of prices set by the state, and the invisible hand (by which he meant, if everyone followed his own selfish interests, the best for everyone would be achieved). In short, Smith rejected mercantilism root and branch.

Like Quesnay, Smith's ideas were not particularly influential until early in the nineteenth century when they came to dominate economic life in both Europe and America until well into the century. They recently experienced something of a comeback in the United States among those who call themselves conservatives.

Political Thought

In an earlier chapter we addressed divine right absolutism, the British limited monarchy, the Polish lack of a sovereign state that eventually led to its demise, and the Dutch Republic. Naturally, Enlightened thinkers were interested in political institutions and how they might be improved, and, not surprisingly, their proposals varied.

Enlightened Absolutism

In some cases, absolute rulers sought to reform their societies based on enlightened principles and aided by enlightened thinkers. Voltaire spent some time advising Frederick II of Prussia, and Diderot sought to assist Catherine the Great of Russia. The principle idea was utility must accompany power. Frederick II referred to himself as the "first servant of the state." He introduced reforms that guaranteed religious toleration, abolished torture, and brought about legal reforms. Joseph II of Austria attempted to end serfdom, which led to virtual rebellion in his country. Catherine the Great attempted to introduce legal changes into Russia based on enlightened thinkers' ideas.

In truth, not much came of their efforts. Serfdom was restored to Austria after Joseph's death because of aristocratic and clerical opposition to the change. Catherine II completed the process of making serfs of Russia's peasants begun in the reign of Peter the Great. Physiocratic reforms to introduce free trade into France ended in total defeat.

Montesquieu (1689–1755) and Constitutional Monarchy

One of the most influential political thinkers of the Enlightenment, Montesquieu, a Frenchman, was a champion of limited monarchy, modeled after what he found in England. He argued this case in *De L'esprit des Lois*.

Studying various types of states in the past as well as the present, Montesquieu came to the conclusion that traditions, size, and climate should determine the type of state a people have. Large and/or very cold places such as China and Russia should have a despotism. Very small states, such as the Swiss, should have a democracy (Greek direct democracy, that is). Medium-sized states should have a limited monarchy. Here Montesquieu had England in mind, but he was really interested in his own country. France, as we have seen, had an absolute monarchy. Yet, it was clearly not large enough for such a system, nor small enough for democracy. It should have, he concluded, a limited monarchy, much like that of Great Britain. But (based on French tradition) he suggested the king share power with the *parlements* (French courts, of one of which he was a member), rather than a parliament or legislature, as in England.

Montesquieu also discussed the idea of checks and balances, which he mistakenly thought characterized the British state of his day. Because he was acquainted with a number of America's founding fathers, they were acquainted with his works. It is not only Locke whose ideas helped shape our Constitution.

Rousseau (1712–1778) and Democracy

Perhaps the most original and influential Enlightened political thinker was Jean Jacques Rousseau. Born in Geneva, Switzerland, he settled in France and spent most of his life there. His relationship to the Enlightenment is complicated, since he is also one of the founders of the romantic movement, as discussed above, and had serious reservations about the reliability of reason in human affairs. His first literary success was an essay competition sponsored by the academy of Dijon, in 1750. The subject of this competition was whether Enlightenment had been good for civilization. Rousseau argued it had not and won the prize.

This work was followed by his *Essay on the Origins of Inequality,* in which Rousseau argued inequality was a result of the rise of private property. Part anthropology, part political theory, Rousseau contended humans began in a state of nature (that is, without government) in which everyone was equal, though no one was rich and, of course, everyone was free. When someone says, "This is mine," then inequality in every sense entered human society. Later socialist thinkers, including Karl Marx, were greatly influenced by this work.

In his *Social Contract*, Rousseau carried this analysis further by suggesting the way to have a just society is for everyone to give up all their rights to everyone else. It sounds a bit like having your cake and eating it too. It rested on his idea of "the general will," which meant not what the majority wanted, but what was best for the people. His idea was that people come together in something like a town meeting (*a la* Geneva) and debate what to do about an issue. When a decision is reached, those who disagree must conform. If the process is corrupted, the state may require a "legislator" to "force people to be free."

Rousseau's political ideas had little or no influence on the young United States, but they are very much in evidence in France after the revolution of 1789.

Rousseau's influence extends beyond politics and his critique of the Enlightenment is reflected in his ideas about education, and in his autobiography, *Confessions*. We will examine these when we look at the romantic movement.

ASSESSMENT

Since the eighteenth century, the Enlightenment has had its critics. Contemporaries who opposed the changes these reformers sought to introduce began the process. During the Victorian period in England, they were dismissed as naïve and simplistic thinkers whose ideas were impractical and probably brought on the French Revolution. After World War II, postmodernists, attacking the false assumptions of Western rationalism, naturally singled it out as the origin of all that was wrong with the modern world. Some even blamed it for the rise of totalitarianism.

Other critics have pointed out that some enlightened thinkers were blind to the rights of women, minorities, or non-white races. Their historical understanding, for the most part, was blinded by their assumption all previous times before their own, at least since antiquity, were barbarous and superstition-laden.

While many of these criticisms are true, it is also true the Enlightenment's effort to reform European society in the eighteenth century unleashed a chain of events that has continued to the present. By its challenge to traditional European society, it ushered in the struggle between the modern and the traditional, which is the continual theme in modern history we are following in this course. It continues to this day.

FOR FURTHER READING

Alioto, Anthony. *A History of Western Science.* 2nd ed. New York: Prentice-Hall, 1992.

Butterfield, Herbert. *The Origins of Modern Science.* New York: Macmillan, 1959.

Doyle, William. *The Old European Order. 1660–1800.* New York: Oxford University Press, 1990.

Moote, A. Lloyd. *The Seventeenth Century. Europe in Ferment.* New York: D. C. Heath, 1970.

Morris, Terry. *Organizing the Firm: The Influence of Science on Management, 2006.*

Outram, Dorinda. *The Enlightenment.* New York: Cambridge University Press, 1995.

Treasure, Geoffrey. *The Making of Modern Europe, 1648–1780.* New York: Methuen, 1985.

CHAPTER
THREE

Globalization and War in the Early Modern Period

INTRODUCTION

You are probably aware the world is now undergoing an economic transformation frequently referred to as "globalization." What this has meant for many low-skilled Americans is the loss of their jobs to workers in developing nations who can be paid lower wages than workers in the United States. This phenomenon is recent. For much of the period we are studying, the Western world enjoyed the advantage in jobs and wages and the rest of the world suffered as a consequence. How this occurred and why the tables are now turned is a major consideration for any understanding of modernization and its consequences. And just as the process of developing nation-states began in the seventeenth and eighteenth centuries, so too did this process of globalization, although the connection may initially be difficult to recognize. To begin to understand it, we will discuss what we referred to in the Introduction as the growing "economic interdependence" of the modern period. In particular, we will look at the economic ideas and practices that preceded the seventeenth century, and then at those first appearing in the seventeenth and eighteenth centuries, as precursors of the modern global capitalist system. This will entail an examination of what is usually referred to as the "Age of Exploration," and what is the earliest economic theory to emerge in the modern world, mercantilism.

Another consequence of these economic developments, combined with the rise of sovereign states we examined in Chapter I, was an increase in wars, both among the emerging states in Europe and also between them, and those around the world taken over by the victors. We will also look at these developments in this chapter.

As with the modern state, the completion of this global economic transformation will not occur until late in the twentieth century and, as noted above, it continues to this day. But the foundations for both Western dominance in the world from the nineteenth century until the end of World War II, and also many current controversies between the former dominated states and their former imperial masters, were laid in the seventeenth and eighteenth centuries.

ECONOMIC REALITIES IN THE WEST BEFORE THE MODERN PERIOD

When the Roman Empire came to an end in the fifth century CE, it was supplanted by a series of Germanic and other tribal "successor states" with little respect for cities and, therefore, little appreciation for an economy based on money and market exchange. Medieval scholars refer to the survival method these "barbarian" states devised as "manorial," which links it to the feudalism we discussed early in Chapter I. For our purposes, it suffices to say people survived by being self-sufficient. Every manor-village provided almost everything people needed to live. Very little regional, and almost no wider trade, occurred. Goods and services were exchanged locally, using barter rather than money, and most of the people were unfree tenants or serfs who worked for their aristocratic or clerical lords.

By the eleventh century, this situation had changed considerably. City life had begun to recover. Trade fairs sprang up throughout Europe. Coined money replaced barter as the means of exchange. Also, globalization, in an incipient way, had begun with the Crusades of the late eleventh and twelfth centuries. Europeans became aware of the spices and other luxury goods from the Middle East and Asia, and they wanted them.

Since antiquity, the primary means Europeans had to obtain such goods was through the Mediterranean Sea and overland routes to Asia known as the "Silk Road." It was also possible to secure such goods through trade with Egypt. Such commerce was controlled by Muslim—mostly Arab—merchants. The Muslim world was and is geographically situated between the West on one end and Asia on the other. This placed Muslim traders in an ideal location to bring goods to the Byzantine Empire or Egypt for resale to European merchants, mostly Italians from Genoa and Venice.

Islam had spread into Africa during the Middle Ages largely through its Sufi merchants, which facilitated trade in slaves and gold with the African kingdoms there. Europeans faced a well organized and highly sophisticated system of trade, controlled by Muslim traders who encompassed China, India, and Africa. Additionally, they lacked the navigational skills to directly access the riches of the East. In short, Europeans were totally dependent upon this Muslim-controlled system.

ATLANTIC TRADE REVOLUTION

This situation underwent a significant change when the Byzantine Empire (Orthodox Christian) was taken over by the Ottoman Turkish Empire (Sunni Muslim) in 1453. While the Ottomans did not seek to prevent the Italians from obtaining goods from the East, their duties were much higher than the Byzantines' had been. There were also religious motives for circumventing trading with Muslims. Until well into the sixteenth century, Europeans genuinely feared the Turks might conquer all of Europe for Islam.

On two occasions during the sixteenth and seventeenth centuries, Turkish armies were encamped around Vienna. They had already taken over most of Hungary, as we noted in Chapter I.

Spain and Portugal had been locked in a crusade, the *Reconquista*, to recover their peninsula from the Muslims, which they accomplished in 1492 when Granada, the last Muslim stronghold, fell to Spain. Muslims were forced to leave, convert, or die. But as a result, Spain, in particular, had a number of unemployed crusaders for whom it needed to find employment. A number of incentives came together at this time to encourage Europeans to break out of their economic confinement.

One other factor is significant. By the fifteenth century, new ships (i.e., the caravel)—with rudder and sails, along with a compass for navigation, both Chinese in origin—enabled European sailors to navigate waters they had previously dared not travel. They had also learned about tidal currents and how to sail against the wind (tack) and out of sight of land.

Beginning in the mid-fifteenth century and continuing into the sixteenth and seventeenth centuries, a number of European states sought ways to reach the riches of the East without having to deal with the Ottomans and other Muslim traders. The states along the Atlantic, rather than the Mediterranean, were most advantageously placed to do so: in particular, Portugal, Spain, the Netherlands, Britain, and France. In due course, each learned to sail down either the coast of Africa, or across the Atlantic and down the coast of South America, to reach Asia. They conducted their trade by establishing trading stations along both coasts, and once they reached Asia they established colonies as well. To accomplish their objectives, they fought to overthrow the traditional Muslim trade networks, described above, and replace them with their own, efforts that were only partly successful. They also fought one another. To understand why, we much look briefly at the economic ideas that motivated their actions, what critics such as Adam Smith would call "mercantilism."

MERCANTILISM

On the eve of the modern period, manufacturing, which had earlier been in urban areas dominated by gilds, shifted to rural ones and became part of what is known as the domestic, or putting-out, system. Here an entrepreneur, perhaps a clothier, would buy raw wool from a farmer. He would then take this wool to a fuller and dyer to prepare it to be worked with by a spinner, whose thread then went to a weaver who made cloth. From here the entrepreneur delivered the cloth to a tailor, who made it into clothing the entrepreneur carried to a market to sell. At every point in this process the entrepreneur paid wages. His goal was to sell his finished product for a profit he could use to start the process over again. He was the entrepreneur because he took all the risks. It was a process from which he could accumulate a lot of wealth.

With the rise of sovereign states, the picture began to change. In particular, states began to regulate trade and manufacturing procedures and to tax both for their own benefit. Economic historians disagree as to exactly what mercantilism was, but they do emphasize several aspects of it that state leaders commonly expressed and acted upon during the early modern period. First, it was called "mercantilism" because trading—regionally, but also internationally—was encouraged as a major source of national wealth. The Dutch, for example, prospered in this period by building an extensive empire around the world. Their mercantile industry thrived; there were more Dutch-owned ships selling goods around the world than ships of any other nation. The Dutch had extensive trade networks with the Balkans to supply them with the timber they required, along with networks in Asia and the Americas. The Dutch middle class grew enormously wealthy as a result. Other European states, including France and Great Britain, were not slow to follow in their steps.

Second, trade was promoted by the rulers as a way of increasing their governments' wealth through duties and, therefore, their ability to employ armies to promote their territorial ambitions. As a result, a country's desire to promote its own hauling trade resulted in it trying to restrict the hauling abilities of other states, the Dutch in particular. As we will see below, this led to several wars between the English and the Dutch, and by the late seventeenth century a decline in dominance in the hauling trades for the latter to the advantage of the former.

The nature of wealth itself was another important aspect of mercantilist thinking. Today we speak of a nation's wealth as the measure of its GDP (i.e., the total amount of goods and services produced by the economy in a given period of time). Not so in this period. Instead, most economic thinkers spoke of wealth in terms of specie (gold and silver). The amount of precious metals a nation possessed was the key to its economic fortunes or misfortunes. If specie were leaving a country because that country was buying more from other states than it was selling to them, its economic well-being was thought to be declining. It was getting weaker. Therefore, the governments of the period thought it imperative to promote policies that produced a favorable balance of trade. More specie should be coming into the country than going out. It also became important that a nation's own ships haul the merchandise being brought in from other nations. It was equally important to exclude other nations from enjoying the economic advantages of this trade, and at times wars were fought to decide who would carry goods into a country.

Mercantilist thinking, quite logically, concluded that government should manage the state's economy to guarantee this favorable balance of trade. Mercantilists promoted two policies to accomplish their objective. First, mercantilists encouraged nations to be self-sufficient by buying as little from other nations as possible. To this end, they erected tariff barriers to keep foreign goods out and granted monopolies to domestic suppers to provide those goods, or a substitute. For example, the English discouraged drinking wine from France and promoted drinking sherry that English merchants purchased from Portugal. The government also promoted the consumption of locally manufactured beer. By the eighteenth century, gin was added to the mix as a way of disposing of an excess of grain.

While some states' mercantilist economic policies did not attempt to control all aspects of the manufacturing and exchanges processes in their economies, in particular the Dutch and the English, others, like Louis XIV, Colbert in France, or Peter the Great in Russia, did. In this way, mercantilism was the exact opposite of the *laissez-faire* economy that Smith and his like would propose in the eighteenth century.

The second way to guarantee a favorable balance of trade was to acquire colonies. Here the objective was to obtain raw materials for one's own manufacturers and ready markets for the finished products they produced. If you have ever studied the colonial period in American history, you may recall the British government encouraged its colonies to produce raw materials for the mother country while discouraging their manufacture so the colonials would buy English finished goods. The British also sought to regulate the goods the colonists imported from abroad, in particular tea from India. This favorable balance of trade for England meant currency shortages in the colonies and was one of the grievances that led to the American Revolution.

The Spanish dominated their American colonial ventures even more tightly than the British. Goods could be shipped only from a few select ports, and to take advantage of the shipping centers one had to pay a heavy tax. By the late eighteenth century, Spanish colonials, like their northern neighbors, deeply resented the mercantilist policies coming from Madrid, and these policies were a major reason the Latin Americans broke free of Spain during the Napoleonic Wars.

Sumptuary laws were a third approach governments following mercantilist-oriented policies used to guarantee a favorable balance of trade. These laws restricted the sale to the aristocracy of luxury goods that could only be obtained from another country. England and France restricted the sale of ermine, an expensive fur from Russia, that could not be obtained from traders in the Americas in this manner. This policy helped keep the quantity of such purchases low, but also helped to reinforce social class distinctions at a time when a new class of wealthy people, who were not aristocratic but mercantile, was emerging.

Unlike modern capitalism, mercantilism was a "win-lose" economic theory. It is no wonder warfare played an important role in events of the seventeenth and eighteenth centuries in Europe. If one country were growing stronger by gaining territory and accumulating wealth through its policies (as the Dutch were doing), other countries must necessarily be growing weaker. There was only a limited quantity of specie in the world. Think of it this way: if your nation had 50 percent of the world's wealth, then every other nation would have to divide the 50 percent that remains. You grow strong as you acquire wealth, but it also means other nations are growing weaker. It should come as no surprise these economic polices led to wars all around the globe; it was to be expected in a mercantilist economic system.

It also makes sense the emerging sovereign states along the Atlantic would see the possibilities that expansion into the world economy could mean for them. The question that should arise in your mind is how were a small number of Europeans able to gain control of peoples in Africa and Asia, not to mention the lands of the "New World," when they themselves did not have large populations, sophisticated societies and economic systems, or powerful armies? Europe will come to control the entire world by the nineteenth century, but the "Europe" of the sixteenth and early seventeenth centuries was not in a position to assume such a dominant role in world affairs. Its economic, political, and social situation was more one of disorder and strife than economic and political power and stability, as we saw in the last chapter. If a space alien had chanced to visit Earth in this period, such a traveler would not have thought Europe was where power and influence were to be found on our planet. This alien would have looked to China and other Asian states, or perhaps the Muslim empires, instead. Answering the question why European dominance occurred in the nineteenth century, which is central to understanding modernism and its effects upon the world today, will require that we look not only at the situations in the Asian and the Muslim traditional societies, but also at those in Africa and the Americas on the eve of this period. Because the Asian states (China, Korea, and Japan) and the late-traditional Muslim empires (Mughal, Ottoman, and Safavid) profited from their early encounters with the West rather than suffered from them, we will look at them separately in the two chapters that follow. We will look at the New World and Africa in this chapter. Not only did these two areas contribute significant material and human resources that led to the rise of European power, but they also suffered enormously in the process.

AFRICA BEFORE EUROPEAN INTERVENTION

First, we must keep in mind that when we are talking about Africa, we are dealing with a continent, the second largest on the planet. This continent stretches from the Mediterranean Sea in the north to the Indian Ocean at the fortieth parallel in the south. To the east it is bounded by the Indian Ocean and the Red Sea, and to the west by the Atlantic Ocean. Were it not for the Gaza Strip, it would be an island continent like Australia. Look at this map (Figure 3.1).[1]

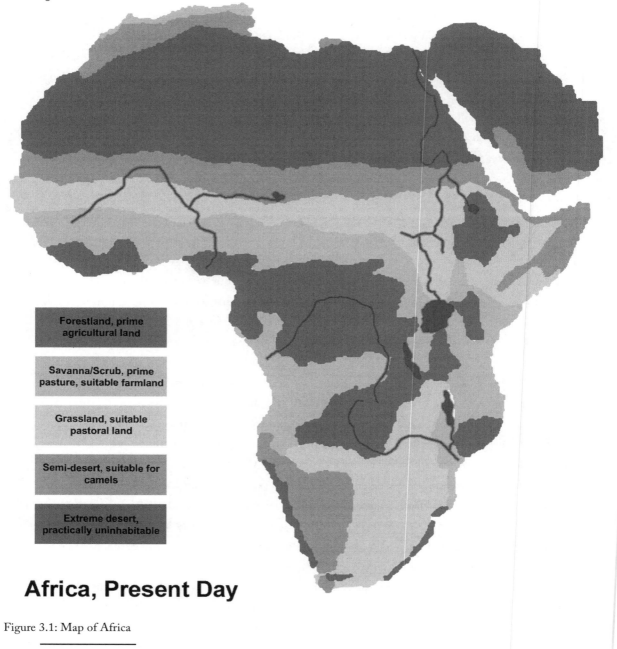

Forestland, prime agricultural land

Savanna/Scrub, prime pasture, suitable farmland

Grassland, suitable pastoral land

Semi-desert, suitable for camels

Extreme desert, practically uninhabitable

Africa, Present Day

Figure 3.1: Map of Africa

1   https://upload.wikimedia.org/wikipedia/commons/9/9d/Africa_Climate_Today.png

The equator is almost in the center of the continent, which means much of its landmass lies outside the temperate zones. In the areas shaded dark green, one finds the rain forest, a region totally unsuited to agriculture. Above, in the light green, is the "savannah," where one finds the herds of large mammals for which Africa is famous, along with farming and grazing lands. Above the savannah lies the Sahel,[2] a semiarid region where most of the great premodern trading empires and civilizations were located. Above the Sahel is the Sahara (Great Desert), and on the coast, one finds lands that are Mediterranean in climate.

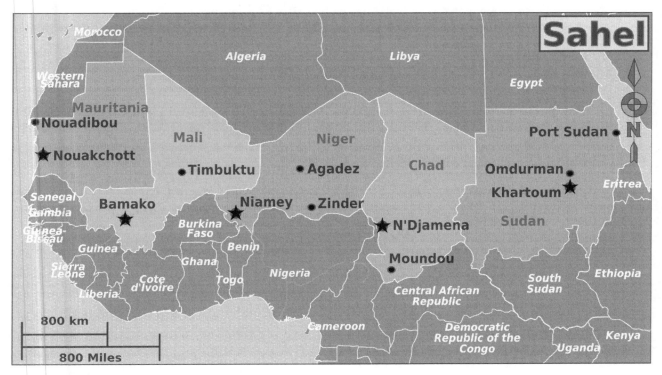

Figure 3.2: Map of Sahel

Because of the centrality of the equator, below it, to a large degree, the regions reverse: going south, one finds rain forests, then savannah, then Sahel, and below the Sahel, desert. Woodland areas are found on the southern coast. In addition, in the east, just below the Horn of Africa, one finds the "Rift Valley," an area of active tectonic plate movement. This is the most mountainous region of the continent, and also the "Great Lakes" region, the largest of which is Lake Victoria, which feeds into the Nile and is the longest river in the world. It is also in the Rift Valley where twentieth-century archeologists found prehuman fossils such as homo habilis, in excess of three millions years old.

Because of its location vis-a-vis the equator, Africa's climate is hot the year around. Indeed, the Sahara is the hottest place on the earth.

Not surprisingly, in a landmass so large, there would be many types of human beings. Arabs and Berbers predominate from the Sahara north, while below this area Bantu-speaking peoples are most widespread,

---

2   See Figure 3.2.

along with Pygmy, and Swahili speakers on the east coast. In the south, one finds small groups of San and Khoikhoi speakers. In modern times, Europeans and Asians have also settled on the continent.

When Europeans took over Africa in the nineteenth century, they perpetuated the idea that Africa, being backward before the Europeans came, had no history, certainly no civilizations to speak of. To the contrary, when the Europeans took over in the nineteenth century, there were a number of highly developed civilizations. Egypt was one of the earliest civilizations in human history and its influence spread south of Sahara in antiquity to Sudan and the Kushite Kingdom.

The culture of Africa north of Sahara was always linked to that of Europe. Yet during the Middle Ages, it became largely Muslim in religion, and its culture reflected this religious transformation. Look at the map marked "Sahel" above and you will notice Mali. This is where the Ghanaian empire was located, as well as the later empires of Mali and Niger. These were powerful trading civilizations that existed from the eighth to the sixteenth centuries. Gold was their most important product, but also slaves, cola nuts, and ostrich feathers. The trade was carried by Arab merchants who crossed the Sahara in caravans heading toward the Mediterranean markets to the north in Morocco and later Tunisia. In 1324, the Malian sultan, Mansa Musa, made a pilgrimage to Mecca, laden with twelve tons of gold, the supply of which he controlled. He distributed his fabulous wealth generously as he progressed; indeed, the amount of gold was so great it produced a temporary decline in the market value of the metal in Cairo, but it did help to cement Africa's reputation as the place to secure gold.

Mali declined in the fifteenth century, and in its place rose the Songhai, which by the reign of Askia Mohammed I (1443–1538) was the largest and most powerful empire in West Africa. A devout Muslim, like Mansa Musa before him, Sakia made a gold-dispersing pilgrimage to Mecca. He also promoted Muslim scholarship in Timbuktu, which boasted universities and more than one hundred fifty madrassas.

South of these Sahelian empires was a forest kingdom, Benin, which was a centrally organized state that carried on trade and diplomatic relations with Portugal. Especially famous for their artwork, Benin merchants also traded in ivory, palm oil, and pepper, not to mention slaves. In 1897, political instability enabled the British to add Benin to its African empire as a part of British Nigeria.

Finally, between the Limpopo and Zambezi rivers from 1100 to the early fifteenth century, was Great Zimbabwe, a highly developed civilization in the southeastern portion of the continent, which was connected by trade to Asia, in particular China and India. This civilization declined, perhaps because of the desiccation of the soil, due in part to an expanding population in a time of reduced water supply. Scholars have also suggested the opportunities presented by the slave trade led the Zimbabweans to relocate. After the British took over this part of Africa, they found it impossible to believe the ruins of the sophisticated stone structures they found could possibly have been built by Africans. First they suggested Phoenicians were responsible, and then that the Africans built them under someone else's directions. It was not until the end of the white Rhodesian government in the mid-twentieth century that the African origins of this ancient civilization were acknowledged, a monumental testimony to the power of bigotry and racism.

In addition to these advanced civilizations, there were areas, especially in the rain forest regions, that have been termed "stateless," often where hunting-gathering still prevailed. These were societies largely organized around clan groups who had—and in some cases still have—little or no desire to live in what we would call a unitary state.

Africa and the Slave Trade

Although Africa was taken over by European states in the nineteenth century, in the period we are concerned about in this chapter, very little loss of territorial integrity occurred. In part it was a matter of not being able to stand the climate with its diseases, especially malaria, that forced Europeans to establish trading posts along the coasts areas of Africa. In the seventeenth century, the Dutch did establish a settlement colony that became Cape Town in South Africa as a resupplying station to facilitate their long journey to the east. Another reason there was no desire to establish colonies in Africa, as Europeans did in the New World, was because they could get what they desired—gold and slaves from African suppliers. But whatever the reasons, as one scholar put it, "If Europeans had had to provide the slaves they needed, the trade would never have gotten off the ground."[3]

It is now recognized these African suppliers had more control over the terms of the trade than we once realized. For example, more male slaves were sold to European slavers than females because the African slave merchants could sell females in the Muslim East, but not the males. While some African rulers would have nothing to do with the trade, others participated in it enthusiastically and, in the eighteenth century, when the campaign against slavery arose in Europe, these rulers opposed the change. The trade was valuable to them as a source of revenue. For the slavers' part, horses, or guns and gunpowder, and brightly colored textiles from Asia were among the trade goods they most prized. And the Europeans introduced a new currency they obtained from India, the cowry shell. It could only be used as jewelry and, as no other country would accept cowry shells as legal tender, had limited value. It was also detrimental to the overall African economy.

Slaves were loaded onto slave ships for the infamous middle passage (Figure 3.3). As the picture below suggests, people were stacked like cord wood and allowed very little time to move about. Olaudah Equiano wrote an account of his slave-ship experience in the mid-eighteenth century. The shackling of two people together, and the stench, he described in vivid detail. Likewise, the horror of what had happened and the fear of what was about to happen drove many to suicide. Many died from disease or suicide, and their bodies were thrown overboard. It was said that sharks routinely followed slave ships.

To be sure, there were some incentives to the slave captains to deliver as many slaves alive as possible. The owners had paid good money for them and the more they were able to sell the more they would earn. Slave captains were given bonuses at the end of the crossing for a low percentage of deaths. To this end, provisions were laid by in the ships and given to the slaves.

Ironically, recent research has suggested those slaves who survived the voyage were often better able to live in the Caribbean than the Europeans who were in charge of them. Still, the life of a slave in both the Caribbean and the Americas, especially in Brazil, was harsh, and there was a need for the colonies to be resupplied constantly with slaves as long as the trade was legal. Those slaves who did reproduce were not recognized as being married, and their children were the property of their owners. It was not uncommon for a woman to be sold and her child left behind, or the reverse.

---

3   John Reader. *Africa*. 1999. 393.

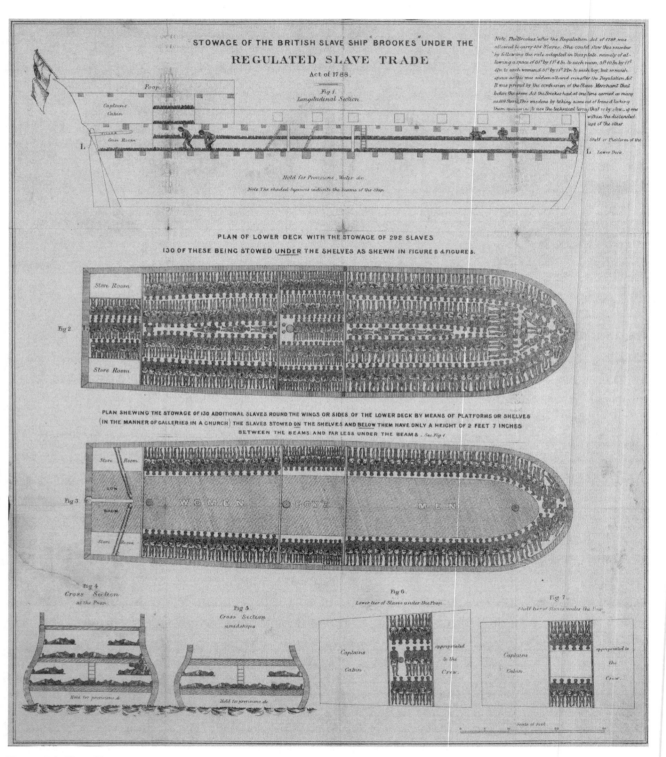

Figure 3.3: Slave Ship

The Influence of the Slave Trade on Africa

Scholars' estimates for the numbers of people taken out of Africa during the four centuries of the European trading, for both the Atlantic trade and trade with the Arab world to the east, runs from nine to thirteen million people. The victims were captured by slavers, mostly other Africans, who raided their villages and hauled the captives away. Some were captured while away from home. Others were sold by family members, and in a few cases they were sold because they were thought to be guilty of sorcery.

Quite apart from the cruelty to the enslaved people themselves, you might have thought these numbers would have had a negative effect upon the human gene pool; however, there is no evidence it did so. In part, this was because the Columbian Exchange brought two new foods into Africa—cassava and maze—that grew well and provided an increase in available food supply, which helped population levels stay at about where they were before the trade began. This completely leaves out what those nine million to thirteen million people would have contributed to their societies and families had they not been taken away, a cost impossible to tally under any circumstance.

No doubt there were psychological and social consequences as well. Equiano noted that, even as a child, he lived with the fear of being taken as a slave. There is also the fact a shortage of women occurred in some parts of Africa, leading to an increase in polygamy, and in others the shortage of men led to an increase in polyandry.

Worse still, the wealth enjoyed by those who profited from the slave trade contributed little to the development of their states overall. Cowry shells are worth very little. The guns and ammunition led to more social disorder, and the wealth rulers received was used to support their opulent lifestyles rather than to develop their states. Finally, Europeans sold many slaves to other Africans, and these numbers seem to have increased once the African slave trade was outlawed in Europe and America. African complicity in this heinous trade in human flesh does nothing to relieve Europeans of the guilt of slavery. It simply helps us better understand how something so plainly evil could have been perpetuated for four centuries by people in no position to have done so on their own without the help of Africans. It is also worth noting much of the wealth that enabled Europeans to take over the world in the nineteenth century was obtained largely because of the profits they made from all aspects of slavery.

Now we shall turn to the Americas, the part of the world to which so many of these Africans were relocated. We should keep in mind they will be part of that story as well.

THE AZTECS AND INCAS ON THE EVE OF SPANISH INVASION

The situation in the Americas on the eve of the Spanish and Portuguese arrivals was different from that of Africa because the Americas had been isolated from the rest of the world since the last ice age. As a result, all the cultural, but especially biological, developments (i.e., diseases) that had occurred in the "Old World" and been experienced by Asians, Africans, and Europeans had not been experienced by Native Americans. As such, when the Europeans arrived in the late fifteenth century, the results were catastrophic. Two advanced civilizations, the Aztecs in Mexico and Central America, and the Incas along the coast of South America, controlled much of the area. What later became Brazil was made up largely of tribal

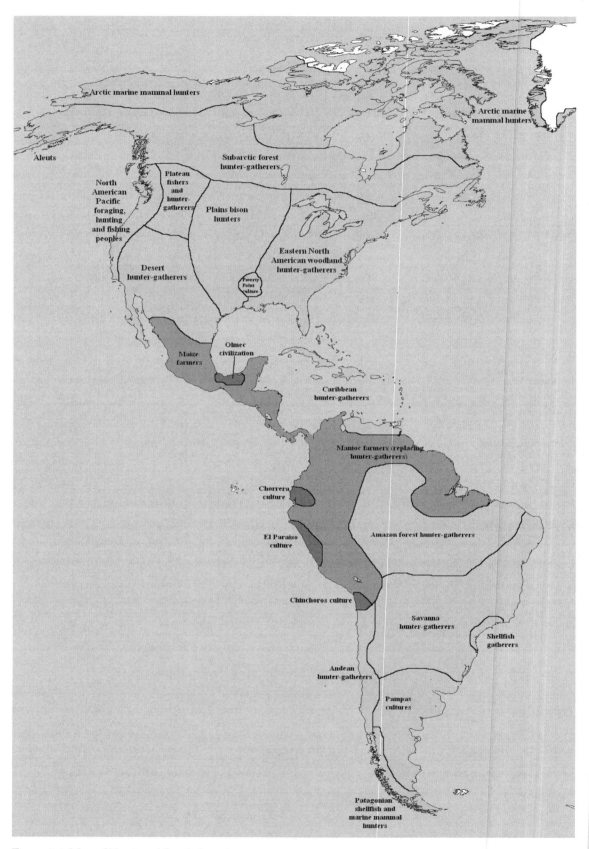

Figure 3.4: Map of North and South America

and stateless societies. All these societies, along with most of their peoples, were quickly destroyed. To understand how this could have occurred, we must briefly sketch what Latin American states were like late in the fifteenth century (Figure 3.4).

Aztecs

The origins of the Aztec Empire can be traced to the early fourteenth century when the Aztecs migrated into the area around what today is Mexico City and established themselves on a small island, Lake Texcoco. Within a century, by developing their military abilities and building alliances with neighboring states, the Aztecs had unified much of Mexico and Central America, which they subjected to a harsh imperial rule.

Their capital, Tenochtitlán, situated in the middle of Lake Texcoco, was the largest city in Mesoamerica, covering three to five square miles. It was the center of commercial life in the empire and contained the palaces of the rulers as well, and also the great markets where tribute goods from throughout the empire were brought.

The tribute they exacted from conquered peoples included precious metals, agricultural products, and fine craft products. According to one scholar, as much as seven thousand tons of maize and two million cotton garments, along with gold and silver vessels and ornaments, were often demanded.[4]

But there were other reasons for resentment against the Aztecs. Bernal Dias, in *The Conquest of New Spain*, which provides a detailed account of Cortes's triumph, recounts the complaints of subject peoples who sided with the Spanish (whose support was the primary reason Cortes prevailed). In particular, they complained to him their wives and daughters were subjected to sexual abuse by the Aztecs and their men were made to work like slaves.[5]

Finally, while human sacrifice was part of Native American religious practices generally, it was especially prominent in Aztec worship and required the sacrifice of large numbers of victims—captives from warfare and subject peoples. The sun god, Huitzilopochtli, their theology taught, did battle every night with the moon and stars and could only return safely the next day if nourished by human blood sacrifices. The ritual included cutting the heart out of the person sacrificed, dismembering the body, and eating the parts. It was a way of paying the debt humans owed the gods for providing the sunshine, water, and food that made life possible. While the number actually sacrificed is in dispute, it is safe to say during certain festivals it would have been in the thousands.

Incas

The Incas in Peru lacked a written language, so information about their origins is difficult to obtain or be certain about. Their empire stretched from modern Columbia to the northern part of Chile, between the Pacific Ocean on one side and the Amazon basin of the other. They seem only to have consolidated their hold on power in the fifteenth century, shortly before the arrival of the Spanish. Unlike the Aztecs,

---

4   Frances F. Berdan. *The Aztecs of Central Mexico: An Imperial Society*, 1982, p. 36.
5   Bernal Diaz. *The Conquest of New Spain*, 1975, p. 210.

the Incas attempted to hold their empire together as much by alliances as by intimidation and conquest. Subject peoples were brought to their capital at Cuzco to live and become acculturated to Inca ways of administration. The Incas also sought to use their language, *Quechua*, as a way of promoting cultural consolidation. Finally, the religion of the Incas did not involve so much human and animal sacrifice.

The Incas' demands upon their subject peoples were not as severe as that of the Aztecs. Lands were divided into parts designated for the support of local people, or the state, or the gods. This system, called the *mita*, would later be adopted by the Spanish. The wealth of the empire was collected in warehouses throughout the empire and used to support the Inca military and elite. If the Incas were not the ruthless oppressors of their subject peoples as the Aztecs were of theirs, they were oppressors all the same, and they had not been in power long enough for the memories and ideas of the peoples they had conquered to be erased.

Finally, whenever the Incas, Aztecs, and Native American societies came into contact with Europeans in the sixteenth century they became highly vulnerable to the diseases the Europeans brought with them. As we look at the story of conquest that follows, disease was a more important factor in explaining the collapse of both these Native American empires than any inherent weakness in these empires themselves or superiority of the Spanish, for that matter.

Now we can turn to the events of European expansion, which led to the beginning of globalization of the world economy. The tiny state, Portugal, led the way.

PORTUGAL

Portugal's leading role in European expansion was largely due to the efforts of one man, Prince Henry the Navigator (1394–1460), who promoted Portuguese exploration along the coast of Africa. Aside from "God" (both in defeating the Muslims and converting the infidels), his original motive was gold, which traditionally had come from Africa through Arab merchants, but he also found that trade in slaves was profitable.

It is not surprising it was the Portuguese who sought an Atlantic route to the riches of Asia, given the country's location in the North Atlantic, but earlier attempts to do so had eluded anyone who had tried. Slowly and patiently, the Portuguese worked their way down the coast of Africa, picking up navigational expertise as they went. By 1487, a Portuguese navigator, Bartolomeo Dias, had rounded the Cape of Good Hope, and by 1498, with the aid of a Muslim navigator, Vasco da Gama had reached Calcutta. Da Gama returned with a ship full of spices, making the trip extremely profitable, and so began the Portuguese empire in the east.

Slaves were valuable, as well. At first, the Portuguese sold most of the slaves to African rulers along the coast. In due course, they began to bring them to Portugal or to their island colonies along the coast of Africa (like the Azores) to work on their sugarcane plantations. In 1500, a Portuguese ship was blown off course and landed in what is today Brazil. Seeing how ideal this area was for cane production, and coffee as well, they established a colony and began to divert slaves to labor there.

The overall Portuguese objective was to replace Muslim merchants in the Asian spice trade centered at the city of Malacca in modern Indonesia. In 1511, Admiral Afonso de Albuquerque took over the city, killed all the Muslims there, and established it as a Portuguese "factory," or trading station. The Portuguese also established "factories" along the West African coast to facilitate their trade in slaves and gold.

Portugal, a very small state, prospered greatly as a result of it being the first European state to exploit the possibilities of Atlantic trade. But such wealth was bound to attract the attention of other nations and, try as they may, the Portuguese were simply not large or powerful enough to both fight off the Muslim traders who resisted their encroachments and to also keep their European rivals out. By the end of the seventeenth century, Portuguese dominance was at an end. But their contribution, whether one blames or praises them, was to be the nation that established the basic systems of exploitation and commerce in the Atlantic—including the commerce in slaves—that prompted other European states to join the scramble for wealth and empire that followed in the eighteenth and nineteenth centuries.

Additionally, this shift in trade to the Atlantic route from the Mediterranean-Silk Road route, which had prevailed since antiquity, also shifted the relative prosperity and power of nations for the future. Areas that had been backwater posts when trade was centered on the Mediterranean (e.g., Britain and Spain) were now in the center of world commerce, and grew in power and prestige accordingly. Those centered on the Mediterranean (e.g., Italy and the Ottoman Turks) by contrast found themselves in a less advantageous position, and their power slowly declined. Furthermore, the volume of world trade, as opposed to local and regional, began its steady increase, which by the twentieth century gave us the globalized world economy.[6]

SPAIN

The Spanish were the first to challenge Portuguese dominance. Instead of contesting with the Portuguese, who had already obtained papal recognition for their African route, the Spanish decided to seek another way, one that might even be shorter. An Italian seaman, Christopher Columbus, persuaded Queen Isabella this idea was worth investing in. He was basing his calculation on Claudius Ptolemy's map that under-estimated the size of the earth by at least a third. Sailing west to reach the east did not seem like the vast undertaking that it is. As you are no doubt aware, on October 12, 1492, Columbus reached what he thought was his objective: India. He named the indigenous peoples he found there "Indians" for that reason. In fact, he had landed, most likely, on Watling Island in the Bahamas. He returned to Spain in triumph and made several more voyages, never realizing he had not discovered India, but new lands no one in Europe knew existed.[7]

The Spanish success did, however, create a potential problem between the two nations over who should control which parts of the lands they had found. To be sure, they were not yet fully aware they were dealing with new lands rather than the lands in Asia they were seeking. To avert a conflict, the pope, Alexander

---

6   Recent scholarship, it should be noted, suggests something like a global economy already existed, albeit it centered around China rather than the West. See Andre Gunter Frank, *ReOrient: Global Economy in the Asian Age* (Berkeley: University of California Press, 1998).

7   The first navigator to argue that in fact it was a "new world" Columbus had discovered was Amerigo Vespucci (1454–1512). As a result, the mapmaker Martin Waldseemüller, in his *Cosmographiae Introductio* (1507), named the new land mass "America" after Vespucci's first name, and it stuck!

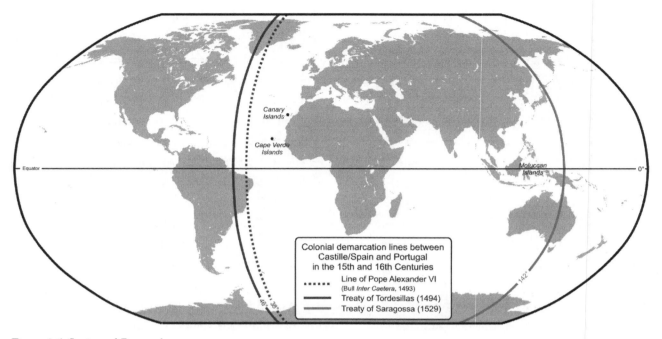

Colonial demarcation lines between
Castille/Spain and Portugal
in the 15th and 16th Centuries

Line of Pope Alexander VI
(Bull *Inter Caetera*, 1493)
Treaty of Tordesillas (1494)
Treaty of Saragossa (1529)

Figure 3.5: Spain and Portugal

VI, in 1492 decreed the two nations would divide the world along a line that ran along the Tordesillas meridian (Figure 3.5).

This treaty made no provision for any other nation and after the Reformation was generally ignored. You can see that what will become Brazil was already largely a part of the Portuguese half.

Once they did realize they were dealing with new land and a lot of it, both the Spanish and the Portuguese were not slow to exploit the economic possibilities these lands offered. One consequence was the destruction of the two civilizations that dominated Latin America in the fifteenth century, the Aztecs and the Incas. A second was a massive die-off of the indigenous peoples in these lands. Another was the creation of a new civilization fashioned out of the Spanish or Portuguese, Native American, and African peoples, and their respective cultural traits.

The conquest of the Aztecs did not take much time. In 1519, a Spanish expedition from Cuba, led by Hernan Cortes and consisting of only five hundred fifty men, a few horses, and ten canons, destroyed the Aztec civilization in about a year. You will recall the Aztecs had many enemies who were only too happy to join the Spanish in overthrowing their hated masters. Finally, European diseases began to take their toll on the Aztec population and so played a part in the Spanish victory.

The Aztec ruler, Moctezuma, according to tradition, first thought Cortes was the god Quetzalcoatl. Realizing his mistake, he sought to buy him off with offers of wealth, which only whetted Cortes's appetite. Once welcomed into the capital, the Spanish conquistador took the Aztec king captive. Shortly thereafter, Moctezuma died. The Aztecs, now thoroughly alarmed, sought to destroy the invaders, but the Spanish were able to withstand their attacks, in part because of their weaponry, but more important because of the support of Aztec enemies and European diseases such as smallpox. By 1521, the battle was over, the Aztec capital city, Tenochtitlán, had been razed to the ground.

Incas in the Spanish Empire

The story of the Incas in Peru is similar to that of the Aztecs. In 1526, Francisco Pizarro, the counterpart to Cortes in Mexico, exploring near what is today Panama, happened upon the Inca empire, the existence of which he was unaware. It was clearly a place of great wealth and well worth conquering, so Pizarro returned to Spain to secure a commission from the government, which he received in 1529. He began his conquest in 1532 with 168 men, two canons, and 27 horses. But like Cortes, Pizarro had a number of forces operating in his favor that offset his numerical disadvantage.

First, smallpox had arrived in the Inca Empire shortly before Pizarro, killing both the emperor and also large numbers of his subjects. Furthermore, as a consequence of the emperor's death, a succession dispute had arisen between his two sons, Huáscar and Atahualpa. Finally, as with the Aztecs, there were thousands of subject peoples only too happy to assist the Spanish in defeating their hated Inca masters.

Perhaps overconfidence on the part of Atahualpa played a role in his defeat. Having an army of eighty thousand that had just defeated his brother in a contest for the throne, he agreed to meet with Pizarro. At the meeting, he was informed he must embrace Christianity and acknowledge the superiority of the Emperor Charles V. Atahualpa was not prepared to do this and instead offered Pizarro an enormous bribe of gold. Pizarro, who enjoyed a temporary advantage at the meeting, had another plan in mind; following Cortes's example, he took Atahualpa prisoner, tried and executed him.

Pizarro then placed another brother of Atahualpa, Manco Inca Yupanqui, on the Inca throne as a sort of Spanish puppet. Quarrels among the Spanish conquerors over how to exploit the wealth of their newly acquired lands quickly alienated Manco, who joined other Incas in attempting to drive the Spanish out. By this point the Spanish were too strong, and by 1572 the Incas' resistance was at an end. A combination of tactics employed by the Spanish, which included canons and mounted cavalrymen, neither of which were known to the Incas, the Incas' own internal disagreements, the effects of smallpox on their people, and the resentment against them by their subject peoples, all help to explain how this conquest by so few Spaniards occurred. It is worth repeating it was not because of some supposed superiority of the conquerors.

Once the conquests were completed, the Spanish and Portuguese began to construct a colonial empire to exploit the lands they had taken over. The result was a new civilization fashioned out of Iberian, Native American, and also African elements. We call it "Latin America" today. Look at the map below (Figure 3.6). It will suggest something of the extent of the Spanish claims. You will also notice the area of Brazil. As we have noted, it was Portuguese.

The extent of the die-off of Native Americans who first came into contact with European diseases as a result of the "Age of Explorations" is staggering. It is impossible to say exactly how many died, as we do not know how many there were to start with. But estimates suggest within a century of the Europeans' arrival, Native American populations had declined by 90 percent, and in some areas even more.[8]

These massive die-offs forced the Spanish to seek laborers from outside the continent; African slaves proved to be an available and reliable source. As noted above, the Portuguese had begun using them for their colonies off the coast of Africa, and once they began growing sugarcane in Brazil, large numbers of

---

8   Similar die-offs affected the Maori of New Zealand, the Aborigines of Australia, and other indigenous populations in Micronesia from European diseases during the next several centuries.

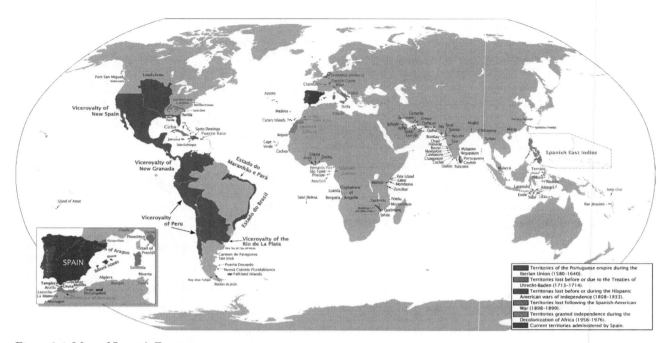

Figure 3.6: Map of Spanish Empire

Africans were imported to work there. The Spanish—and ultimately every other colonial power—would simply follow the Portuguese lead.

As a result, in both Spain's and Portugal's colonies in the New World, a multi-racial society quite unlike anything in Europe had emerged. Early on, the Spanish authorities allowed men from Spain to marry Native American women, as there were very few Spanish-born women for them to wed. Their offspring formed a new class, the *mestizos*. With the influx of slaves from Africa, there arose another mixed group, mulattos, and the mixing of Native Americans and Africans created yet a third group, *zambaigos*.[9] Above all these stood the *peninsulares*, those of pure Spanish descent who were born in Spain, and just beneath them were the *Creoles*, people of pure Spanish descent born in the colonies. Not surprisingly, at the bottom of the social ladder were the peoples of pure Native American stock.

Administering the New World from Spain or Portugal was clearly impossible, given the distance between them and the resultant slowness with which information could be conveyed. The Spanish created a "Council of the Indies" in Madrid, which was responsible for overseeing the entire operation, but the day-to-day work was primarily entrusted to officials in the colonies themselves, the viceroys and captaincies.

At first, the primary interest of the Spanish in their new lands was obtaining precious metals, gold and silver. As the *conquistadores* were ill-suited to running such operations, a new system was devised called "*encomienda*," which involved indigenous people being given to the new landowners, generally from the peninsular or Creole classes, to work their lands. They were not slaves, but were exploited ruthlessly and many were simply worked to death in the mines.

By the mid-sixteenth century, as the number of Native Americans declined and the Spanish and mixed-race peoples multiplied, pressure was brought upon the authorities in Madrid to reform the labor

9   In Mexico, *zambaigo* now refers to someone of mixed Chinese and Native American ancestry.

system to make it possible for the new landowners to obtain workers. It was called *repartimiento*. This system closely resembled the mita of the Incas. In part, the change reflected the concern of some Roman Catholic clergy over the treatment of American natives whom they were trying to convert.

Ultimately, both these systems gave way to the hacienda. This was a system that centered around the central estate of the landowner and was more likely to be devoted to agriculture than the extraction of precious metals, crops such as wheat, maize, dye-stuffs, cacaco, vanilla, and cotton that could be sold in the developing cities. It is this latter system that came to prevail throughout much of Latin America by the nineteenth century.

In some coastal areas, a plantation system also grew up that involved the exploitation of African slave laborers.

THE COLUMBIAN EXCHANGE

One of the most significant consequences of the era of explorations we are examining is known as the "Columbian Exchange." We have already noted the devastating effects of disease, but disease was not the

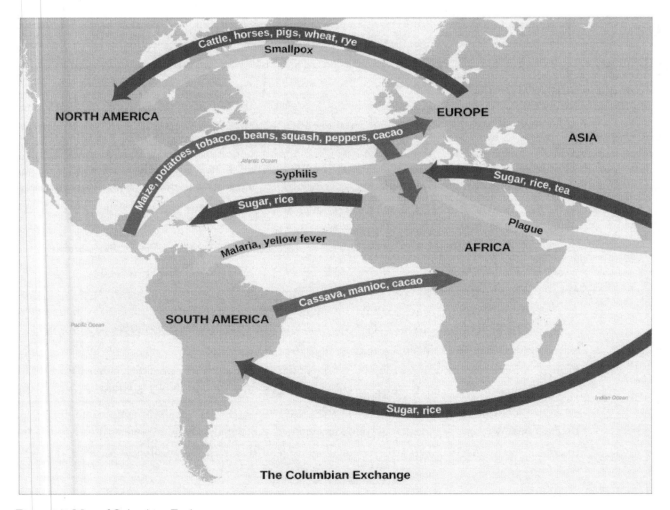

Figure 3.7: Map of Columbian Exchange

only exchange that took place between the New World and the Old in this period. The chart below shows what else was involved (Figure 3.7). Notice the range of plants and animals introduced between the two worlds. As we shall see, Asia was also significantly affected. Finally, notice that one disease did make its way from the New World to the Old: syphilis. Likewise, malaria and yellow fever came to Latin America from Africa, probably carried by infected slaves.

The new food products are particularly significant. While horses, pigs, and cattle made their way to the New World, maize, potatoes, beans, squash, and tobacco moved across the Atlantic to Europe. Chocolate from Mexico was also introduced. Native Americans did not drink it with milk or sugar, but mixed it with corn. It was the Spanish who transformed it into the beverage we customarily consume. Peanuts seem to have originated in the Americas, made their way to Africa (where they are called "ground nuts") and, much improved, made their way back to the Americas. Rice came from Asia to Africa and then on to the Americas. I trust you can see there was a globalization of food consumption as important as any increase in worldwide commerce resulting from the explorations of the world in this period.

NETHERLANDS

The third state to enter the contest for empire in the late sixteenth and early seventeenth centuries was the Netherlands. It is no surprise that this small state should have sought wealth and power through an Atlantic-based trading empire, given its location and its past experiences as a mercantile state. In particular, the Dutch gained an economic advantage in the previous century after developing a fishing boat enabling them to dominate North Sea fisheries. They also developed superior technologies for their limited agricultural possibilities, as well as industrial goods, especially textiles, which they were able to trade, in great part because of their superior dying industries. They also led the rest of Europe in shipbuilding. The source of timber for ships came largely from the Baltic Sea area, and here the Dutch preeminence in the cloth trade gave them a product to exchange for the much-needed timber. When Peter the Great traveled to the West late in the seventeenth century, he spent four months in Amsterdam studying Dutch shipbuilding techniques.

The Dutch also developed their production of paper, brick, tobacco and pipe-making, brewing, and munitions. As Immanuel Wallerstein observed, "no other country showed such a coherent, cohesive, and integrated agro-industrial production complex in the 16th and especially the 17th century."[10]

Not surprisingly, the second half of the seventeenth century is generally recognized as being the Dutch "Golden Age." Indeed, Wallerstein suggests the Dutch were the hegemonic power in Europe at this time for all the reasons listed above. In any event, economic power helps explain their overlarge role in the establishment of European expansion occurring at this time. This map suggests the extent of their empire (Figure 3.8).

Unlike the Spanish and Portuguese, but very like the British, the Dutch established their world empire through two chartered private companies. The more important of the two was the Dutch East India Company (the VOC), which, in 1602, was granted a monopoly—in good mercantilist fashion—for twenty-one years, just two years after the founding of the British East India Company. In 1621, the VOC

---

10   Immanuel Wallerstein. *Mercantilism and the Consolidation of the European World-Economy*, 2011.

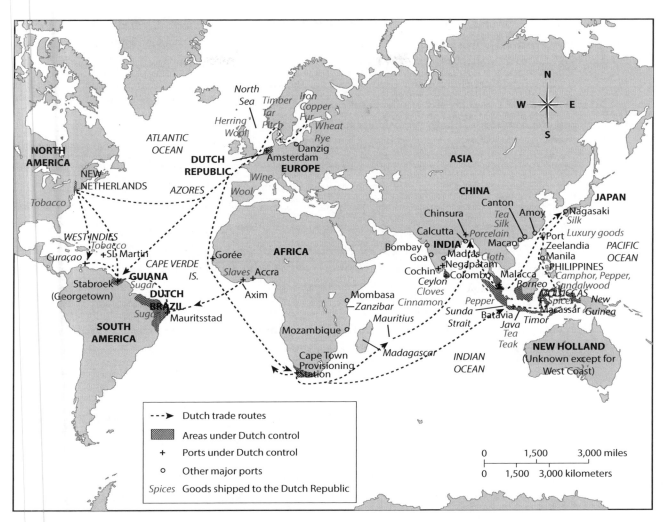

Figure 3.8: Map of Dutch trade

was followed by the Dutch West India Company, another private company given monopoly rights to trade in the Americas for twenty-five years.

During much of this time, the Dutch were fighting with the Spanish (the Eighty Years War, which began in 1566), and later the English and French. The war with Spain was for independence, and as much as anything, was part of the Reformation because the Dutch were Calvinists (Reformed), a situation not acceptable to Counter-Reformation Spain. In 1580, the king of Spain, Philip II, added Portugal and its colonial empire to the empire of Spain. Previously, the main source of spices from Asia had been in Lisbon, and the Dutch had gained them through this source along with everyone else. After Philip's annexation, however, this source of supply was closed to the Dutch, which forced them to seek to supply their own needs and to enter the world trading market at the same time. If you recall the somewhat piratical behavior of the British during this era, you will not be surprised the behavior of the Dutch was rather similar. In addition, they sought to and succeeded in acquiring colonial outposts of their own, as the above map makes clear. Doing so meant pushing the Portuguese out of their previously held monopolistic trading position. At one point, the Dutch even managed to wrest part of Brazil from the Portuguese, but that proved to be overreach.

The Dutch did gain control of Goa and eventually replaced the Portuguese traders in Japan, because the Dutch were less interested in converting the Japanese at a time when the Japanese rulers were implementing a policy of isolating Japan from European, especially Christian, influence.

Dutch colonial efforts were not always successful. We noted their failed attempt to control Brazil. In addition, they tried, unsuccessfully, to take over the Philippines, which the Spanish had colonized as a result of Magellan's famous trip around the globe in 1521.

The West India Company sought to push the Spanish and Portuguese out of the American sugar trade and to replace them as slavers between Africa and the Americas. This also led to the short-lived colony in North America, the fortified town of New Amsterdam, which eventually fell to the British and became New York.

Wallerstein points out that no hegemonic power remains dominant for very long. Their success invites the envy and opposition of other states seeking to rise in power and prestige. In any event, such rivals did appear by the end of the seventeenth century, in particular the British and French, the last Western powers to enter the quest for World Empire. Once they did, Dutch dominance, and indeed the Dutch "Golden Age," began to come to an end.

Dutch economic power and influence would last long after its military power had declined. A part of being a hegemon is acquiring some control over world finance, which the Dutch did through their stock markets, insurance companies on which other nations relied, and banking system. These continued to be prosperous long after the Dutch had become only minor players in the new European world trade.

ENGLAND, AND FRANCE ENTER THE QUEST FOR WORLD MARKETS

Domestic as well as European continental conflicts caused England and France to be latecomers where new world trade was concerned. We will look at their wars later in the chapter, but for the moment we are interested in how these powers came to challenge the three states that had gotten there before them. In the case of England (by the eighteenth century, Great Britain), it becomes a question of how it replaced all its competitor nations and emerged as the dominant colonial power and remained so until the end of imperialism following World War II. In other words, to use Wallerstein's phrase, to see how Britain replaced the Dutch as the hegemon in world trade.

Since the Spanish and Portuguese were thoroughly ensconced in their own trade routes by the sixteenth century, England and France began by attempting to find a northern route to reach the riches of the East. While that is increasingly becoming a real possibility in the twenty-first century, due to global warming, it was not an option in the seventeenth century, as all those who made the attempt discovered, since they died in their attempts. It did, however, see these two states establish colonies in the northern hemisphere of the New World.

Early in the seventeenth century, both the English and the French also established colonies in the Caribbean, which inevitably led to the importation of large numbers of slaves to work the sugar plantations, the primary motive for these colonies. Moving onto the mainland of the Americas was a more challenging proposition. The French developed a lucrative fur trade in what would become Canada, and some made their way down the Mississippi River, establishing New Orleans in 1718.

The English, utilizing several private models of colonization closer to that of the Dutch than the Spanish and Portuguese, made a significant departure in the early seventeenth century by sending significant numbers of their own citizens to settle on lands from which the indigenous peoples had been or were removed, often as much by disease as by warfare. This process began during the reign of Queen Elizabeth I with the ill-fated colony of Roanoke Island, set up by Sir Walter Raleigh in 1585. In 1607, the Jamestown colony in Virginia became the first permanent English settlement in North America, which was followed by a series of such settlements culminating in the colony of Georgia, established early in the eighteenth century. While the Spanish sought to evict the English from these settlements, they were unsuccessful, and a new and permanent English presence was established in North America.

At first, the North American colonies were hardly profitable. The riches the Portuguese had made out of their Eastern colonies were not forthcoming. There were no spices, very little gold, and no silver in North America. Furs, naval stores, and timber, as well as fish and meat, were about all that they could boast. The conversion of the natives was reason for the venture, at least among some of the Anglicans, and settling peoples in the New World was looked upon as being good for society in the Old World. Remember that colonies were an important component of the mercantilist thinking of the era. But as these were profit-making concerns, the results were hardly inspiring until the discovery of tobacco.

The craze for tobacco was taking off, just as the craze for sugar had a century earlier. But Native Americans did not prove themselves to be any more serviceable as workers on tobacco plantations than they had been for sugarcane, nor were there enough white settlers from England, indentured servants, to do the job, either. The solution was obvious: slavery. Beginning about 1640, the English followed the Spanish, Portuguese, and Dutch by importing slaves from Africa to work on the sugar plantations of the Caribbean and later to work on the tobacco plantations of the Southern colonies. Large numbers of slaves did not begin to arrive there until early in the eighteenth century. By then, the supply of indentured servants was no longer available.

In the eighteenth century, in South Carolina, plantation owners began to cultivate rice and indigo for export. These crops increased the demand for slaves, but the greatest increase came with the introduction of cotton early in the nineteenth century as a result of Eli Whitney's cotton gin (1791), which made Southern cotton easier to produce and cheaper to sell. Slavery was solidly entrenched in American society from this point on, until the defeat of the Confederacy in the American Civil War brought it to an end.

CHINA AND THE ATLANTIC REVOLUTION

Much has been written about the Atlantic World in connection with the expansion of Europe we have been examining. In particular, scholars have stressed the importance of the economic interdependence of the slave trade in Africa and the settlements in the New World of the Spanish, Portuguese, Dutch, English, and French, and the Swedes and Norwegians as well. All these states got involved in the slave trade and the triangular trade system that linked Africa, the continent of Europe, and America. But there is another dimension equally important, and that was Asia. After all, what started the Portuguese, and ultimately every other exploration venture, was the desire to gain the riches of the East without having to employ Arab and Muslim middlemen in the process. In short, where did the Portuguese and the Spanish take all the silver they mined in the New World, and what did they want to exchange it for? They were headed to India and China, and they wanted spices, silks, porcelains, and various china goods. During the sixteenth and seventeenth centuries, the end destination of the silver from Japan, but also Latin America, was China because the Ming dynasty, in the sixteenth century, switched from paper currency to silver. Not having much of the white metal, the Ming had to find sources of silver outside China to mint into coins. At about the same time, two enormous silver deposit sites became available, one in Japan and the other, the Potosi mines, in Peru. As a result, a lot of silver came to be available all at once. Two monetary historians, Dennis Flynn and Arturo Giráldez, suggest this situation contributed significantly to the emergence of a truly global economy, compete with arbitrage speculation in silver.

Arbitrage is an economic term for "buying low and selling high." Because there was so much silver, and the cost of mining it, largely done by Native American or slave laborers, was very low, the price of silver in Europe fell. By buying it up cheaply and taking it to China, where the demand at times seemed insatiable, it was possible for European traders to exchange the silver for Chinese goods at a very advantageous rate for the Europeans. Even the exchange rate of gold to silver was lower in China than in Europe, since the Chinese did not value gold as highly as they did silver.

The argument is further supported by the suggestion all the world's major currencies, including cowry shells from India to be used as currency in Africa, were in play as a result of China's demands for silver. For example, huge amounts of copper were also shipped to Europe via Japan because of China's almost insatiable demand for silver.

Finally, as the authors point out, food exchanges also were part of the trade. In particular, maize from the Americas became a major food product in China, resulting in significant growth in China's population. Because corn could be grown in the areas unsuitable for the production, it brought about shifts in where people lived. In short, there were ecological consequences of opening the world to trade in addition to human ones.[11] We will look at China in greater detail in the following chapter, but it was important to make you aware of the interconnections between the world's four major continents that the European age of discovery produced.

One point Flynn and Giráldez are making is that it was the Chinese who were the instigators of all this economic activity, and not the Europeans as is usually suggested. It was, of course, very advantageous for Europeans, but had the Chinese not had such a great need of silver for currency purposes, they would hardly have been prepared to part with so much gold, porcelains, and silks as they did. But their most important conclusion point is that we are truly dealing with a global economy, one in which the Chinese are dominant and not the Europeans.

EUROPEAN WARS IN THE EARLY MODERN PERIOD

Now that we have examined the early modern state system (Chapter 2) and the beginnings of the global economy (Age of Explorations for Europeans), we are in a position to look at the wars that accompanied these developments in the sixteenth to eighteenth centuries, for they were the product of both these developments. Accordingly, the wars themselves were fought in Europe for control of territory in the continent and in the colonies for the riches these brought to Europe. At times the consequences of the interaction between the two were more important than the conflict in either one itself. We will begin with

---

11   Dennis Flynn and Arturo Giráldez, "Cycles of Silver: Global Economic Unity through the Mid-Eighteenth Century," *Journal of World History*, Vol. 13, No. 2 (Fall 2002, pp. 391–427).

a continental conflict, the Eighty Years War that the Dutch fought to gain their independence from the Hapsburgs.

Eighty Years War

In the sixteenth century, the Dutch Netherlands were part of the Spanish Hapsburgs' empire. As we have seen, they were early participants in the Atlantic trade system from which they profited mightily. We have also seen the Dutch were Calvinist in religion. In 1564, Philip II, king of Spain and ruler of the Netherlands, decided to enforce Catholicism upon all his subjects, pursuant to the decrees of the Council of Trent.[12] This led the Dutch to found a union of the Protestant provinces, mostly in the north, and form the Union of Utrecht. By 1581, all possibilities of a compromise seemed hopeless so the Dutch, in July, deposed Philip as their ruler. Naturally, the Spanish fought back, but other conflicts Philip had with both the English and the French divided his forces and enabled the Dutch to drive the Spanish out. A twelve-year truce was agreed to in 1609, but a final peace was not settled upon until after the Thirty Years Wars (1648).

Thirty Years War (1618–1648)

It is easy to see this conflict as a continuation of the Dutch-Spanish War, but it involved the Austrian branch of the Hapsburgs (the Holy Roman emperors) as well. And like the Dutch–Spanish conflict, it was driven by religious, economic, and political considerations.

You need to recall that Germany as a state did not exist. Instead, in the Holy Roman Empire there were a number of territories ranging from monarchies to free cities. There were also areas that were Catholic in religious faith, but also Lutheran and Calvinist. And always nearby were neighboring states looking to advance their own national interests at the expense of the Hapsburgs, in particular France, Sweden, and England.

It is this lethal combination of motives by different players that turned this conflict into a thirty-year, blood-letting experience for the peoples of what today we call Germany.

It began in Bohemia, today the Czech Republic. The Czech version of Protestantism was actually older than the Lutheran's, going back to the fourteenth century, when an uprising of the Moravian Brethren, followers of Jon Hus, had forced the Austrian rulers of that era to grant the Moravians a certain measure of religious freedom. But, somewhat like Philip II in his dealings with the Dutch, the Austrian ruler and future emperor, Ferdinand, was determined to force these heretics back into the Catholic fold. To this end, he revoked their right to religious freedom that had existed since 1575. They responded by rejecting him as their ruler, which entailed unceremoniously ejecting his representatives from the third-story window of the royal palace in Prague. Catholics insisted angels had guided the men to safety, while Protestants pointed to

---

12   This council, which met from 1545–1563, defined Roman Catholicism as a result of the Protestant Reformation. It basically reaffirmed traditional Catholic doctrines and left little ground for compromise with Protestants, especially Protestant subjects of the Hapsburg rulers in both Spain and the Holy Roman Empire, with significant consequences, as this narrative will relate.

a pile of animal dung below that broke their thirty-foot fall and saved their lives. To replace the deposed emperor, the Bohemians selected a Calvinist, the Elector Palatine Frederick V (1616–1623), to be their new king. As it happened, his wife was a daughter of James I of England.

Frederick came to be known as the "Winter King" as he lost his bid to be king in Bohemia and lost his lands in the Palatinate to Catholic armies, partly from Spain, as well. The war also spread into the more Protestant sectors of the empire in the north. But the motives for being involved were not just religious. Territorial ambition played a part as well. The situation was further complicated by the fact that Lutheran and Calvinist Protestants were no less intolerant of one another than they were of Catholics, and so did not present a united opposition to this "Counter-Reformation" effort.

Protestant rulers and their subjects were now thoroughly alarmed. James I, who had no interest in war as much because of its costs as anything else, was forced to get involved because of his daughter, but the real leadership of the Protestant side was taken up by Christian IV, the king of Denmark (1577–1648), a Lutheran. His invasion of Germany (in which he held territory) inaugurated the Danish phase of the war.

As before, God seemed to be favoring the Catholics because the Danish were soundly defeated by the superior military skill of a Catholic mercenary, Albrecht of Wallenstein. By 1629, the emperor was in a position to attempt to reverse all the gains Protestants had made since the original religious settlement of 1555, the Peace of Augsburg. This would have meant an end to toleration of Calvinists and the restitution of Catholic rule over cities and towns, not to mention bishoprics, with their substantial territories that had gone over to the Protestants since that time. Even some of the Catholic princes became alarmed. These victories represented a substantial expansion of the emperor's power, unwelcomed by independent-minded German princes no matter what their religious persuasion.

The Protestant cause was now taken up by a perhaps strange combination: Sweden and France. The Dutch also joined, not unmindful of the threat that Catholic Spain represented to them. At first, things seemed to go well for the Protestants. The ruler of Sweden, Gustavus Adolphus II (1594–1632), was a man of extraordinary military talent who made a number of tactical innovations that enabled his armies to defeat those of Wallenstein, until Adolphus was killed at the battle of Lützen, in 1632. Shortly thereafter, Wallenstein himself was assassinated at the behest of the emperor, who feared his growing power. With the two major military players out of the way, it seemed possible peace might at last be restored to Germany, but the French and Dutch were unwilling to see it end for reasons of their own, having nothing to do with the situation in Germany. This led to the final and perhaps most destructive phase of the war when the armies of France, Spain, and the Swedes waged war throughout the empire, looting and plundering as they marched. Entire villages were depopulated; lurid tales of cannibalism circulated due to the famine that stalked the land as a result of the protracted warfare. It has been estimated the population in the empire had been reduced by perhaps a quarter—or more—when this war finally ended.[13]

The major powers of the day finally agreed to terms in the Treaty of Westphalia, in 1648. It is often said to have been the first modern treaty because it reflected the advent of the nation-state system. It is worth noting the pope was not represented and that the conference was conducted in French, rather than Latin. It is also true that, while Austria and Brandenburg-Prussia were prominent German powers at the

---

13   Treasure, p 41

conference, the territorial divisions that had prevailed in the Holy Roman Empire—and would soon lead to its demise as a state—a holdover from the medieval period, were carefully preserved, as much by France as by the German princes themselves. The Dutch did at last gain official recognition from Spain for their existence as a state.

Geoffrey Treasure has noted that in the seventeenth and eighteenth centuries in Europe, times of peace were rare and warfare was the norm. There were only seven calendar years in the seventeenth century without a war somewhere. While there was some peace early in the eighteenth century, after 1740, the conflicts picked up with even greater fury, running into the nineteenth century with the wars of Napoleon.[14] But these were not the only places Europeans were in conflict. The mercantilist policies of the period inevitably also led to wars around the world. Before we return to the continental wars from 1648 on, we should take a look at conflicts away from Europe, contemporaneous with the Thirty Years War.

As we noted above, the aim of the Portuguese was to replace the traditional Arab/Muslim traders, not only where European markets were concerned, but also in intra-African slave markets. This meant sending soldiers alongside merchants to blast the competition out of the water and turn Asian/Muslim settlements into Portuguese ones. Indeed, by the mid-sixteenth century, they had created a string of factory/forts from Lisbon to Tanegashima in Japan and were growing quite wealthy from the trade. Nor were they willing to share the water routes they had discovered with fellow Europeans. The Spanish, after all, made the decision to try their luck sailing west to get to the east because of the Portuguese prior claims on the Atlantic route. But once the Dutch, English, and French entered the imperial quest, military encounters among all these powers, along with rulers in the regions to which the Europeans were moving, became inevitable. Nor is it correct to imagine these other European powers were any less rapacious than the Portuguese. Human greed and contemporary economic theory (mercantilism) guaranteed they were not.

The first European power to challenge the dominance of the Portuguese was the Dutch through the Dutch East India Company, or VOC, as noted earlier in the chapter. The conflict between them lasted from 1602 to 1663. While the VOC was not completely successful in driving the Portuguese out of Asia, the Dutch did succeed in creating for themselves a place in this lucrative market. In 1619, they took control of Jakarta, which they renamed Batavia. Thereafter they seized Malacca in 1641, Colombo in 1656, Ceylon in 1658, and Cochin in 1662.

The Dutch also challenged Portugal's place in the sugar/slave economy by creating the Dutch West India Company, which attempted to take control of Brazil. Their efforts here were not especially successful and although they gained control in Brazil on two occasions, they were unable to hold this possession and abandoned the quest after their treaty with Portugal in 1661. All the same, by mid-century, the Dutch dominated the spice trade in the east and, to facilitate that trade in 1652, they established a colony on the southern tip of Africa that today is the Union of South Africa.

The Dutch also established a presence for themselves in the New World. In 1609, Henry Hudson explored the waterway that now bears his name. The first Dutch colony, New Netherlands, was established in 1624. Close proximity and mercantile rivalry with the newly emerging British caused relations between

---

14 | Treasure, 201

these two Protestant countries to deteriorate. In 1623, the Dutch executed a group of British merchants in Amboyna, whom they feared were plotting against them. The British maintained the charges were baseless, and bad feelings over this matter lasted for most of the rest of the century. The Dutch, for their part, resented the English coming to terms with Spain earlier in the century, but their greatest objection was to the British passage of the Navigation Act of 1650, which required all goods bound for English markets be carried in English ships. This would lock the Dutch out of the lucrative hauling trade their merchant marine superiority had guaranteed them. The first Dutch War, 1652, did not work out well for the Dutch, and Cromwell imposed harsh terms of settlement.

In 1664, the British forced the Dutch to surrender New Amsterdam, which was renamed New York. The affair provoked a second war with Britain in which the Dutch fared better, although England's control of New York was recognized by the treaty that brought it to a close. But it was already clear the Dutch, like the Portuguese, would have trouble maintaining control over all the territories that were part of their worldwide empire.

By the eighteenth century, the connection between the European continental and the world colonial aspects of warfare were more clearly recognizable. Most of these were instigated by France under Louis XIV, who was seeking to expand France to what he deemed its "natural borders." France also attempted to expand its navy under the direction of Louis's finance minister, Colbert.

In 1667, Louis laid claim to the Spanish Netherlands and the Franche-Comté in the "War of Devolution," ostensibly because his Spanish wife was supposed to have inherited the Spanish Netherlands, but did not. His swift military victories frightened his neighbors, in particular the Spanish and the Dutch, and the latter organized the "Triple Alliance" with themselves, England, and Sweden. By 1668, Louis was forced to seek peace, resulting in the Treaty of Aix-la-Chapelle, under the terms of which Louis only received a few towns bordering the Spanish Netherlands.

The Dutch motives for forming this alliance against France seem to have been a combination of worry over the aggressive behavior of the French toward their neighbors to the south, and in Germany to the north of them, and the growing competition France represented in the colonial world as a result of the expansion of its navy. If the Netherlands had not intended its actions to have alienated Louis, it very much miscalculated, because he held it responsible for the outcome of his military campaign and set about preparing to invade the Netherlands for revenge.

To accomplish this end, he carefully isolated the Dutch. He negotiated the secret "Treaty of Dover" with England, under the terms of which Charles II would bring England into a war against the Dutch. Recall the latter were trade rivals who had already fought two wars. In return, Louis paid thee million pounds annually, which greatly aided Charles II's financial situation vis-à-vis Parliament. Louis also made an alliance with the Swedes, who not only agreed not to join a coalition against France but also to threaten Brandenburg-Prussia in the event this state acted like it might become involved against France. By 1672, Louis was ready to strike. It is known as "the year of disaster" in Dutch history. The nation survived by flooding the country and so depriving the French of the means to overrun it. As a result, the Dutch did unite around William of Orange, who would become William III of England in 1688. William formed another coalition against France that succeeded in preventing Louis from achieving his objectives and saved the Dutch.

The third major conflict from Louis's reign resulted from a royal death. In November of 1701, Charles II of Spain (1661–1700) died without issue. His throne was awarded to Louis's grandson, Philip of Anjou. To many at the time, this was a rather terrible turn of events. They feared, as one Spanish official is supposed to have said, "There is no longer any Pyrenees." An alliance to undo the Spanish king's bequest, the "War of Spanish Succession" (1701–1714), was the result. This alliance against France consisted of England, the Netherlands, and the Holy Roman Empire. The Treaty of Utrecht late in 1713 with Britain, and the Treaty of Rastatt with the empire and the Netherlands early the following year, brought this conflict to its conclusion. When it was over, France was economically and politically exhausted.

Philip remained king of Spain but England gained control of Gibraltar, giving it access to the Mediterranean. Britain still maintained control of this important piece of rock, to the everlasting annoyance of Spain. Also, by the end of this war, a new ruling family had come to Britain, the Hanovers of Germany. Their right to inherit (over that of a Catholic Stuart) was affirmed by France also.

Financially important, and a significant sign of Spain's increasing weakness in this time, was the clause in the Utrecht treaty that allowed the English an *asiento*, or contract, to supply forty-eight hundred slaves a year and five hundred tons of goods to Spanish colonies for thirty years. The British looked upon this clause as more or less a cart blanche for trade, but the Bourbons, once they took over Spain, looked at it otherwise and began to enforce its terms strictly. The result was the next war, the first of the eighteenth century, the "War of Jenkins's Ear."

There had been something of a respite in conflicts between England and France early in the century because of the mutual exhaustion from their previous military adventures. But, in 1731, the Spanish caught an overly aggressive English slave merchant, Captain Robert Jenkins, trading illegally. Pursuant to the usual way of dealing with such offenders, the Spanish cut off his ear. Jenkins returned to England, seeking a pension for services rendered to the state and breathing fire for revenge against Spain. He even testified before Parliament. Public indignation rose and, along with it, war fever, which began in 1739. It would not have been a major affair, however, if something else, rather more significant had not just occurred. Charles VI, the Holy Roman emperor, had died without a male heir.

Throughout his reign, Charles VI had sought to guarantee that his daughter, Maria Theresa, would be recognized as his heir upon his death. It was the "Pragmatic Sanction" of 1713. But when Charles died, Frederick II of Prussia invaded Silesia. Maria Theresa had only recently given birth to her first son and heir, Joseph. Going before the assembled noblemen, both Austrian and Hungarian, she appealed to their sense of honor and they dutifully came to her aid and accepted her father's arrangement. But in the end, Silesia was lost. This war lasted from 1740 to 1748, and Jenkins's conflict was subsumed within it.

There may not seem to be any connection between a conflict over English trading rights and the succession to the Austrian/imperial throne, but there was: it was France, which supported Prussia against its old enemy, Austria. It is worth noting that throughout this period, when balance of power was a major factor in the making of alliances, it was always true that England was opposed to France and Austria to Prussia, but also true was the opposition of Austria to France. At this juncture in history, as a result of this alignment of states, the resultant conflict had a lasting influence on Europe and, ultimately, the world. France, by siding with Prussia, brought England into the conflict that spilled over into the colonial world as "King George's War. "Having to fight a war on two fronts proved to be more financially taxing than the

French could afford and aided the British in solidifying control over their colonies throughout the world. Furthermore, the war ended indecisively and foretold a quick renewal of hostilities, which in fact occurred.

This brings us to the last war of the eighteenth century until the American and French revolutions. It is known as the "Seven Years War" (or "French and Indian War" in American history) because it spanned the years 1756–1763. It was fully as important for its colonial consequences as for its continental ones. And it was, as suggested, a continuation of unsettled issues from the previous war.

But before we can examine this, we must take note of a major shift in diplomatic alignment occurring just before the war broke out. Now that George of Hanover was king of England, Britain had a greater interest in continental affairs than in the past. Or at least, George did. In particular, George was concerned France might attack his beloved Hanover because of the French colonial rivalry with England. The result was an unprecedented switch in alliances: England now allied itself with Prussia (instead of with Austria, as it always had). This forced Austria and France to seek an accommodation that was completed by May 1756. It was truly a "Diplomatic Revolution"!

In the ensuring war, the cards now seemed stacked against Frederick II of Prussia. Knowing that Saxony, France, and Austria were allied against him with the intention of breaking up his polyglot state, he decided to strike first, invading Saxony in August 1756. At one point he faced the combined forces of the three above cited states along with Sweden and Russia and some lesser German states. All he had to rely upon from his ally Britain was money. His superior leadership was important for his survival, but a fortuitous event helped him out, as well. In 1762, the Empress Elizabeth of Russia died and was succeeded by Tsar Peter III; a great admirer of Frederick's, Peter promptly changed sides. This was all the advantage Frederick needed to hold off the French and Austrians; the war ended in 1763 with a treaty that left the Prussian state intact and occupying the borders it had occupied from the beginning of the conflict. The most important point for the future is that Prussia survived.

There is also a significant colonial aspect to this war. When it began, England and France were both major contenders for control of empire in both the Americas and India.[15] When the war ended with the Treaty of Paris in 1763, France had lost its empire in both areas, and England, while financially devastated by the conflict, was now the unrivaled master of both the colonial empires it and the other European powers had been struggling over since the fifteenth century. During the course of the nineteenth century, England would become the major power in the world, the true hegemon, both because of its empire and its process of industrialization; and Prussia would go on to become the unifier of what is today modern Germany, and Britain's primary rival. This conflict was one of genuinely momentous consequences for the history of mankind.

In this chapter, we have been looking at the beginnings of our present global world order. In particular, we looked at the ways Europe's economy developed around world trade and commerce, and how power shifted to those states along the Atlantic that were in the best position to take advantage of their geographic location. There is more to this story of globalization than we could tell in this chapter. But now

---

15   In was during this conflict that the infamous "Black hole of Calcutta" incident occurred. On June 20, 1756, a local Indian nawab imprisoned 146 mostly British colonials in a small cell with only two windows and left them overnight, more by accident than design. Only twenty-three remained alive the next morning. It became quite a cause celebre in England once it became known.

we must turn to the rest of that story. In particular, we must examine areas of the world that were affected rather differently by the arrival of Europeans traders and soldiers. In Chapter 4, we will look at East Asian traditional states, and then in Chapter 5 we will look at the three Muslim empires, all of which survived well and even prospered in this period.

FOR FURTHER READING

Jorge Cañizares-Esguerra, Eric R. Seeman, eds. *The Atlantic in Global History, 1500–2000*. New Jerrsey: Pearson Publishing, 2007.

E. Ray Canterbury. *Brief History of Economics*. New Jersey: World Scientific Publishing, 2001.

Alfred W. Crosby, Jr. *The Columbian Exchange*. Connecticut: Greenwood Press, 1972.

William Doyle. *The Old European Order 1660–1800*. New York: Oxford University Press, 1978.

Charles A Desnoyers. *Patterns of Modern Chinese History*. New York: Oxford University Press, 2017.

Bernal Diaz. *The Conquest of New Spain, 1975*. (available online).

Dennis Flynn and Arturo Giráldez. "Cycles of Silver: Global Economic Unity through the Mid-Eighteenth Century, *Journal of World History,* Vol. 13, No. 2 (Fall 2002, pp. 391–427).

Andre Gunder Frank. *ReOrient: Global Economy in the Asian Age.* Berkeley: University of California Press, 1998.

A Lloyd Moote. *The Seventeenth Century. Europe in Ferment.* Massachusetts: D. C. Heath, 1970.

John Reader. *A Biography of the Continent Africa*. New York: Vintage Book, 1999.

Geoffrey Treasure. *The Making of Modern Europe, 1648–1780*. London: Methuen and Company, 1985.

Immanuel Wallerstein. *Mercantilism and the Consolidation of the European World-Economy.* Berkeley: University of California Press, 2011.

CHAPTER FOUR

Traditional States in East Asia

"You, O King, live beyond the confines of many seas, nevertheless, impelled by your humble desire to partake of the benefits of our civilization, you have dispatched a mission respectfully bearing your memorial. Your Envoy has crossed the seas and paid his respects at my Court on the anniversary of my birthday. To show your devotion, you have also sent offerings of your country's produce."[1]

THE EMPEROR QIANLONG TO KING GEORGE III, 1793

When Europeans came into contact with Chinese emperors during the Ming and later the Qing dynasties, they were received as people of decidedly inferior status, offering gifts in recognition thereof, as the above quote suggests. Indeed, anyone visiting Chinese emperors in the early modern period was so received. Just how inferior one was depended upon how far his state was from China, the center of civilization in the world.

Western historians used to tell this story to illustrate just how naïve and out of touch the Chinese had become. Already, these historians opined, the handwriting was on the wall; it was only a matter of time until the inevitable fall of China into Western hands would occur, as in fact, it did early in the nineteenth century. You will not, however, encounter historians expressing this interpretation today. On the contrary, what you are likely to encounter is the opinion that China's position in the world of the sixteenth through eighteenth centuries more than earned it its sense of superiority. You will not read the West was already the center of culture and civilization for the world that it was to become in the nineteenth century. "Eurocentrism" has become a cardinal sin historians commit at their peril. At times, the

---

1   https://legacy.fordham.edu/halsall/mod/1793qianlong.asp

correction of focus becomes an overcorrection of "Sinocentrism" that is no more accurate than the biased Eurocentrism that preceded it.

The trick is striking a balance. The judgment that China was the fulcrum of world trade and commerce in the early modern period seems quite correct. As we noted in the precious chapter, China's need for silver with which to mint its coinage gave ample opportunities for Western powers to provide the needed white metal in return for valuable spices, silks, tea, and porcelains. This arrangement benefitted everyone involved so long as the silver held out. But later, when it did run out and the British turned to using opium to pay for their purchases, the Chinese economy began to suffer. And, when the Chinese tried to do something to end this nefarious trade, they found the barbarous Westerners had, in fact, developed sophisticated weaponry the Chinese military was incapable of defeating. That they failed to recognize the danger their trade with the West represented, or what the dangers Western technological advancements forebode, is precisely what you would expect of such a state with its highly successful political, economic, and social system. As the old adage has it, "If it ain't broke, don't fix it."

In this chapter, we will examine China's evolution during the early modern period, in particular with an eye to how well it worked. In other words, we will not let our knowledge of how things turned out in the end shape how we explain the events that made most of the Ming and Qing periods highly successful ones in China's long history.

We will also look at other Asian empires during this time frame: Japan, Korea, and the smaller states of Southeast Asia. Each of these has its own individual story to tell, but all are to some degree influenced by their neighboring colossus. As with China, we will avoid asking the question, "Why did they not see it coming?" and look at just how well late-imperial civilizations worked in these nations, as it did in China.

THE MING DYNASTY (1368–1644)

China was among the earliest places on the planet to develop a civilization. About the time of the Roman Empire, during the Han dynasty, that civilization became imperial in form. In subsequent centuries, dynasties fell and disorder followed, but always a new Chinese dynasty arose to restore the empire much as it had been before the previous dynasty had fallen. In 1271, when the Song dynasty was destroyed, China fell under the control of the Mongols, led by Kublai Khan. This was different in that the Kublai Kahn was not Chinese but Mongolian. Claiming the "mandate of heaven" had passed to him, Kublai gave a Chinese name to his dynasty, the Yuan. He and his successors ruled China successfully until twin troubles arose undermining that claim. First, the late-Yuan ruler, Kublai Kahn, near the end of the thirteenth century, made two disastrous attempts to conquer Japan, both of which were defeated, the Japanese claimed, by divine winds (kamikaze). This was soon followed by an even more serious disaster, the bubonic plague, which reduced the Chinese population by at least a third before it subsided.[2] It was true then, and seems true today that when disaster strikes, the Chinese take it to be a sign that heaven is no longer happy with those ruling over them. In 1368, having reached this conclusion, an orphaned young

---

2   It now seems that the Mongol army was the vector of transmission for the plague into Europe.

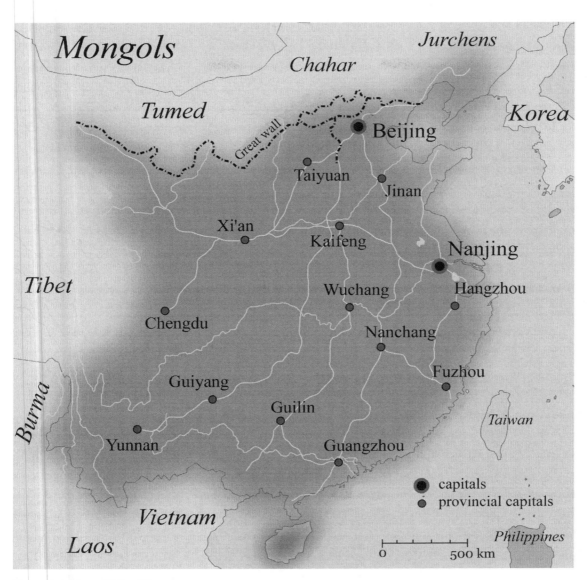

Figure 4.1: Map of Ming Dynasty

man, Zhu Yuanzhand,[3] led an army against the decaying Yuan, captured Beijing, reunified China, and proclaimed himself the founder of a new dynasty, the Ming (bright; See Figure 4.1 for location of Ming dynasty shaded in brown.), which would last until 1644.

Zhu Yuanzhand's reign lasted until 1398, during which time he strove to restore China to it pre-Yuan state, especially seeking to bring back Confucian virtues such as filial piety and loyally to the emperor, restore stability to the state, and reduce the costs of government. He clearly saw himself as driving out foreign barbarians (Mongols), although it took a while for some of the scholar-bureaucrats who had accepted Yuan claims to power to come around to his way of thinking. Also, he seems to have been genuinely

---

3   It was common for Chinese emperors to be given a posthumous name. In Zhu's case, it was Ming Taizu. You may see him called by this name in some works.

interested in the plight of poor peasants. He had grown up in poverty himself. He owed his education to a Buddhist monastery that had taken him in after members of his family perished in the plague.

There is a negative associated with Zhu Yuanzhand's thirty-year rule. As he aged and the ideal of China that had inspired him did not materialize, he came to blame the failure on the dishonesty and disloyalty of his officials, and set about purging the government of such individuals. On one occasion, a bureaucratic shortcut that involved no graft led to the deaths of thousands of officials who had employed it. By his death in 1398, the emperor had executed perhaps as many as one hundred thousand officials and their family members.

Despite his excesses, Zhu Yuanzhand left a strong and unified state that, after a brief struggle, passed to his son, the Yongle emperor, whose twenty-two-year reign cemented the work of his father. The dynasty would last until the middle of the seventeenth century, although none of the successors was equal in statue to these two founders. The Confucian bureaucracy, as well as eunuchs who served the later, less-capable emperors at court and in the country, account for the length of this dynasty.

Under the Yongle emperor's direction, scholars prepared a series of books for use in civil service exams; furthermore, he commissioned an encyclopedia of all known Chinese works, which had twenty-two thousand chapters and more than fifty million words.[4]

Additionally, the Yongle emperor led five military campaigns against the Mongols who threatened China again, rebuilt the Grand Canal to promote commerce and trade, and built a new capital in what is today Beijing, along with the magnificent Imperial Palace that included the royal residence (Forbidden City), where subsequent Chinese emperors resided until the end of the empire in 1911.[5]

To display the power of the new dynasty, the Yongle emperor sent out the largest naval fleet ever recorded in history, at least for the next five hundred years. The seaman behind these ambitious voyages was the Muslim eunuch and friend of the emperor, Zhen He (1371–1433), who, beginning in 1403, made seven voyages that took him all the way to the southern end of Africa and some have claimed even farther. On this first trip, his fleet included sixty-two ships, some more than one hundred feet in length, and carrying more than twenty-seven thousand people. It was loaded not only with military equipment but also gifts to distribute to these lesser peoples with whom the Chinese came into contact. In return, rulers sent representatives to China seeking permission to come and trade and bearing "tribute," including a number of animals in a menagerie of exotic beasts, including giraffes. Zhen was neither exploring new territories nor attempting to establish trade relations as the Portuguese a half-century later, would do. As much as anything, the emperor was "trooping the color" through this series of explorations. In any event, the Chinese were well ahead of the Portuguese in reaching these areas. Zhen died on the return trip of his seventh voyage, and not long thereafter the enterprise was terminated and the navy allowed to decay.

Government

Western scholars, in hindsight, have suggested the Chinese made a fatal error by allowing their fleet to decay and instead relying on Westerners to come to them. But if what you need can be obtained by others bringing

---

4   Paul Ropp, *China in World History*.
5   If you go to this website you can take a virtual tour of this magnificent structure: http://www.kinabaloo.com/forbidden_city.html

it to you, and if you see yourself at the center of civilization, as the Chinese did, you would hardly see any reason to go to much trouble and expense merely to display your superiority to distant and inferior peoples.

More than that, as Andre Gunter Frank has pointed out, recent research, especially by Asian scholars, has demonstrated the Chinese tribute system functioned as a system of world trade, not only with the Europeans but also with the Japanese, Indians, and other Asians. Merchants created essentially false "tribute" documents to entitle them to engage in this trade. Clearly, China benefited greatly from its position.

By the nineteenth century, when the West became technologically and military advanced, this policy of relying on the world to come to China proved to be disadvantageous and even destructive to China's independence. But the future has always been difficult to foresee, and what might be has never been the basis of a nation's contemporary policies, especially when they are so profitable.

Ming emperors also have been criticized by Westerners for their supposed isolationism. Recent scholarship suggests just how incorrect this judgment is. As Andre Gunter Frank has observed, China was the center of world trade and not Europe. Not only did this lead to a huge influx of silver, but also of new foods imported from the West, including, maize, which led to a rapid expansion of China's population in the Ming and the Qing period that followed.

Beyond that, Ming emperors were prepared to learn from Westerners such information as they found valuable. They embraced new astronomical ideas once they began to appear and promoted innovations in medicine as well. One emperor hung a Western-style world map, appropriately adjusted to reflect China's position of centrality, in the royal palace in Beijing. The Ming leadership entertained Jesuit Christians for their knowledge and tolerated Christianity, until it began efforts to push other religions out. Restricting the movements of Europeans to specified areas such as Canton was a practical way to benefit from what the Europeans had to offer without giving them an opportunity to undermine the society. Just how prescient that idea was will become apparent when we examine the fate of China in the age of imperialism in the nineteenth century.

The Ming emperors' objective was to restore China to its former glory, in particular by restoring things to the way they were before the Yuan period. Their power was absolute. Their displeasure, as we saw in the case of the first emperor, Zhu Yuanzhand, could mean death, not only to the official but to members of his family as well.[6] They were served by scholar-bureaucrats who staffed the extensive Chinese bureaucracy, and by eunuchs who served them personally. Conflict between these two groups was continuous throughout the dynasty and beyond. By the end of the dynasty, the number of eunuchs was something of a drain upon the regime's resources.

The Confucian-trained scholar-bureaucrats staffed the major government positions, in Beijing and throughout the country. To recruit such officials, the Ming restored the local, regional, and national level examinations in traditional Confucian classics, which had been the standard for acceptance into the bureaucracy at least since the Tang period (ninth century CE), but had fallen into disarray during the Yuan

---

6   In the mid-sixteenth century, an official, Hai Rui, had the temerity to criticize an emperor for his behavior. The emperor, Shih-tsung, flew into a rage and ordered his execution. A nearby eunuch assured him that Hai Rui was prepared to die. Hai had said goodbye to his family, and his coffin was outside the palace awaiting him. This shocked the emperor so much that he spared Hai and forgave him for his impertinence. He might well have killed him and all his family members as well! See C. O. Hucker, *China's Imperial Past. California: Stanford University Press, 1975, p.206.*

period. To prepare, applicants could obtain books and formal instruction, even at local levels. To gain an appointment, one had to pass exams at three levels, ultimately being tested in the presence of the emperor himself. Successful examinees were given jobs in the civil service for life, until retirement, but they never served in the province from which they came. This basic system remained in place, even after the Qing dynasty (made up of Mongols rather than Chinese) replaced the Ming, and only came to an end when the republic replaced the empire in 1911.

At the top of the administrative structure itself was the emperor, who literally sat on a dais above his chief officials, who bowed down in his presence. How much power any emperor actually exercised depended upon how prepared he was to rule. Some were more interested in pleasure than government. One devoted his entire reign to mechanical constructions. In such cases a wife, dowager empress, or favorite eunuch might actually be the one making decisions. But decisions were made all the same.

No ruler can carry out his own orders. He requires an effective administrative system. The Chinese had this as well. At the top were three departments (chancellery, department of state affairs, and secretariat). The second of these three was further subdivided into six ministries, each with a specific function. Again, following ancient precedent, the nation was divided into fifteen provinces, which were subdivided into prefectures, and below there were the districts and cantons. The Manchus added additional territories to China and so added districts to the administrative system, but the system itself did not change under them. Until the nineteenth century, China was a well-administered society.

Economy and Society

We examined the importance of China in the world economy in the previous chapter. Suffice to say the agricultural, industrial, and commercial sectors of China's economy all prospered during the Ming period as a result of their expanded role in world trade. As Frank and others have pointed out, the Western expansion of the sixteenth century was really only a small part of the global economy centered in China during this period. But how much did all this economic expansion filter down to the Chinese people?

A good way to measure a society's well-being is to examine what is happening to its overall population numbers. In the Yuan period, population had fallen, as much a result of the plague as anything else. Throughout much of the Ming dynasty, the numbers rose steadily, largely through government-led efforts to expand economic well-being. There is evidence of female infanticide in rural areas, and there were periodic outbreaks of disease, but the overall trend was upward. No doubt the introduction of foreign foods contributed to this expansion, as did the overall economic expansion of the economy of China during the period.

The living standards of the Chinese people also grew throughout the period; the rising population suggested as much. But other developments also speak to this development. Urbanization expanded rapidly as did repopulation of rural areas abandoned during the Yuan. But also the overall direction of what today we would call GDP was upward. So also was life expectancy.[7] By the end of the period, the numbers had risen to the point of becoming a problem as the Chinese had reached what ecologists refer to as the carrying

---

7   See http://afe.easia.columbia.edu/special/china_1950_population.htm

capacity of the land, given their agricultural technology. That the population expanded steadily throughout the Ming dynasty is still a testament to this dynasty's ability to increase food production sufficiently to feed its growing population.

The government attempted to make taxation less of a burden on the people by implementing what it called the "single-whip tax system," payable in silver, rather than goods, and in installments throughout the year.

Cultural Developments

We have already referred to the vast number of goods China exported to the West. These manufactures not only enriched the government, but the people as well. And they added considerably to the quality of life of these Chinese. In fact, fashion consciousness appeared by the sixteenth century, and the literacy rate among men rose to between 40 and 50 percent by the seventeenth century. Wealthy merchants emulated the scholar bureaucrats by adorning their luxurious houses with calligraphic artworks, musical instruments, and exquisite gardens—all fashionable collectors' items. The increase in wealth created a local market for such goods. They were not all being shipped to Europe, India, or Japan.

Not surprisingly, the Ming restored traditional Chinese religious and philosophical preferences to the dominance they had enjoyed in the past. This meant Christianity lost out to a resurgence of traditional Chinese folk religious practices, along with Confucianism, Daoism, and Buddhism. It was during this period that the last Nestorian Christian groups, which had been in China since the fifth century CE, were absorbed into Daoism.

There were some Confucian reformers who sought to challenge the dominance of the aristocratic classes in scholar-bureaucratic offices by suggesting even peasants who possessed knowledge were worthy of such offices. Some proposed women should be educated equally along with men, but most scholar-bureaucrats, especially those in the highest levels of government, opposed such radical notions.

Figure 4.2: Ming Painting[44]

8   https://en.wikipedia.org/wiki/Ming_dynasty

Figure 4.3: Ming Vase[9]

The Ming period was also a highly creative one in the arts and literature. As the commercial class grew through the economic expansion China enjoyed from trading with the West, with Japan, and other nations in the region, the market for literature and art grew as well, culminating in the production of a variety of works from fiction to how-to books in business. Much art was produced to adorn urban dwellings.

Consider Figure 4.2, an example of painting on silk. Lord Cecil, Queen Elizabeth I of Britain's leading minister, had an obsession with Ming vases, such as those shown in Figure 4.3.

Interest in and appreciation of Chinese opera grew in popularity as well.

End of the Ming Dynasty

The Ming dynasty came to an end for many of the same reasons as the Yuan had before it. In 1556, a severe earthquake took the lives of more than eight hundred thousand people. About this time a cooling of the climate (the "little ice age" in evidence in Europe and also in the Americas at this time) reduced the food supply and led to famine. In 1641, an onset of plague throughout China killed large numbers of people. Finally, wars in Europe diminished the supply of silver transported to China for trade goods, making it harder to obtain and driving up its price. This curtailed the government's revenue at a time when China was called upon but failed to defend Korea, one of its most important tributary states, from an invasion from Japan (1597–98). All these disasters contributed to a growing feeling the dynasty had lost "the mandate of heaven," as had the Yuan before it. Rebellions started, and ultimately a new dynasty took the place of the Ming. They were non-Chinese (Manchus) and would be the last dynasty in China's two-millennium imperial history.

Yet as we have seen, although many of the emperors themselves were not competent rulers, the Ming system itself gave China a sustained period of growth, prosperity, and economic well-being. It was a period in history when the Chinese were the best-fed people in the entire world.[9] Clearly, China had developed an immanently workable system of government under the Ming. Now we turn to how the Manchu would make use of it.

---

9   Upshur, et. al. *World History. Vol. II, Cengage Advantage books*, p. 543.

THE QING OR MANCHU (1644–1912)

The last dynasty to reign in Imperial China was the Qing. They were not native Chinese, but Manchu. Who were they? In particular, what difference did it make that they were not Chinese? To understand how they ruled over China from 1644 to 1911, we must begin by answering these questions.

Notice in particular the area in light blue that runs across the lower section of the upper-third of the map (See Figure 4.4). This is the "Eurasian Steppe." A "steppe" is a semiarid plateau of grasslands without trees. You know it in the United States as the "prairie" that extends from northern Oklahoma, across the Midwest and northward up into western Canada. Because the area is semi-arid, its inhabitants usually are more occupied with raising livestock than food crops. In our case it was the buffalo, until the farmers of the nineteenth century discovered how to make corn grow there.

As with Native Americans, the peoples who have lived in the "Great Steppe," as the area in Eurasia

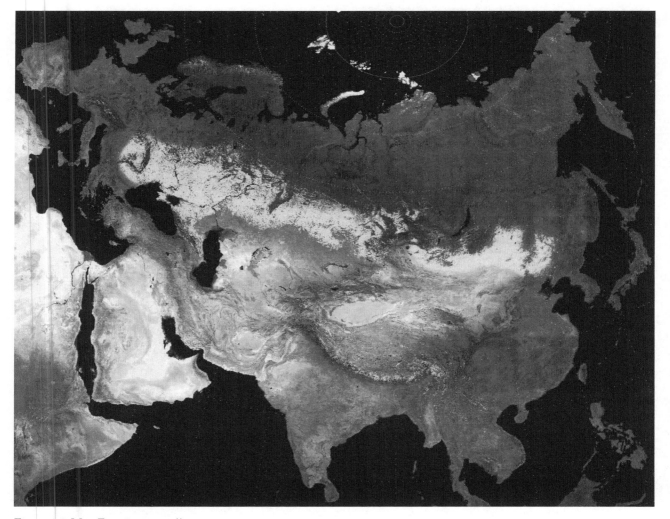

Figure 4.4: Map Eurasian steppe[11]

is known, lived in tribal, seminomadic groups. Some were hunters and fishermen, and a few, including the Manchu, were farmers. In this area, political unity was tenuous and generally of short duration. Periodically, various groups, temporarily unified, swooped down upon the more advanced and prosperous peoples south of them in China and elsewhere, wreaking havoc, and sometimes reigning over them, before breaking up and disappearing back into the area from where they came. Kublai Kahn, a Mongol, was one such conqueror. His Yuan dynasty governed China from 1271 to 1368, until overthrown by the Ming, as we discussed above. The fourteenth-century conqueror, Tamerlane, is another, especially bloodthirsty example.

A number of such groups played an important role in China's history, including being the stimulus for the building of the Great Wall. One in particular, the Xiongnu, repulsed by the Han Chinese in the fourth century CE, redirected their attacks to Rome, resulting in the collapse of its western half that we call the "Fall of the Roman Empire." We know them as the Huns.[10] Simply put, throughout recorded history peoples from this part of the world have periodically exploded out of their upland-planes homeland and visited death and destruction on all with whom they came into contact. They have also forced changes and adaptations. The Manchus are another example of such people.

Before the seventeenth century, the Manchu as a unified group did not exist. They emerged at this time, unifying various peoples in the areas north of China's Great Wall. They themselves seem to have been descendants of the Jurchens, who conquered Northern Song China in the thirteenth century, forming the Jin dynasty that ruled until the Mongols under the Yuan replaced them. Their language is Tungusic, part of the Altaic family of languages that includes Turkic, Mongolic, and some say even Korean and Japanese. At first, both the Ming Chinese and the Chosŏn dynasty in Korea employed them as a counterweight to the Mongols. The idea was to ally with one barbarian to control another you fear more.

The founder of the dynasty, "Nurgaci" (1559–1626), began with only a small group of followers and accepted a tributary relationship with China. He also introduced the "banner system" characteristic of the Manchu throughout their history. Both a military and a social organizing system, it enabled the Manchu to unite the disparate tribal groups around them. Each unit had its own color scheme and its members were rewarded for service with land. In this manner, the Manchu created a "state" that transcended the narrowly defined tribal organizations so characteristic of the region. Banner groups consisted not only of Jurchens but Chinese, Korean, Mongolic, Tibetan, and Turkic groups. There were even some of Russian origins.

No matter what their ethnicity, the "bannermen" were required to learn to speak and later to read Manchu, and to adopt the Manchu style of dress, i.e., cutting the front of their hair and allowing the back to grow long, the "queue." In so doing they created a sense of Manchu identity out of these rather disparate ethnicities and tribes.

In 1635, Hong Jaiji, son of Nurgaci, adopted the name Manchu. At the same time, he took a Chinese dynastic name, Qing, the exact meaning of which is unclear. What is clear is he wanted to erect a state along Chinese imperial lines.

The Manchu were not themselves steppe nomads, but interacted closely and intermarried frequently with them. Their writing system was adopted from the Mongols rather than the Chinese, which may help explain why their extensive historical materials were exploited by scholars only recently. By 1635,

---

10   Today, the Uighurs are the descendants of such people who are resisting being absorbed into China. They are not murderous attackers but they are part of this tradition.

Manchu emperors began to claim direct descent from Genghis Khan. And before the conquest of China, the Manchu, or perhaps we should say the Qing, had acquired control over the Mongols, Uighurs, and the Tibetans, all of whom were incorporated into the Manchu banner system. As the Ming declined, the Manchu rose: thus, it is not surprising that, finally, the former were overthrown by the latter.

As we noted above, during the late Ming period, because of a number of adversities, this last native Chinese dynasty was beset by a number of uprisings and rebellions. In 1644, a desperate Chinese Ming loyalist general invited a Manchu army to enter the empire to defend the Ming against a rebel army. It did so, defeated the rebel army handily, but went on to conquer Beijing. While treating the last and now dead Ming emperor with respect, the Manchu claimed the "mandate of heaven" had passed to them. What followed was a period of conquest that did not end until the last Ming holdouts were subdued on the island of Taiwan, in 1683. One scholar notes that more than eight hundred thousand bodies were cremated in Yangzhou alone. The resistance must have been fierce. Indeed, the Manchu were always fearful of uprisings, and the Chinese never forgot the Qing were foreign conquerors. Still, many, if not most, accommodated themselves to their new rulers. Until the end of the eighteenth century, Qing China was a powerful and prosperous nation, as much the leading force in world trade as the Ming before had been.[11]

Whenever the numbers of a people taken over are vastly superior to those who conquered them, the biggest challenge to the conqueror is to hold the areas taken without being absorbed into the group you have conquered. Just how the Manchu accomplished this, and how they reigned, has become the subject of much scholarly debate in the last quarter century. The basic interpretation that prevailed until that time suggested the Manchu survived by becoming Han Chinese in their way of governing and thinking. There can be no doubt this is the way the Manchu presented themselves to their Chinese subjects. Even before coming to power, they had adopted "Qing," a Chinese name for their dynasty. Yet, they also required Chinese to adopt the Manchu hairstyle as a sign of subjugation. Clearly, the explanation is more complicated.

Ironically, after 1978 and the reforms of Deng Xiaoping, Western scholars gained access to materials they had never exploited before. In particular, they began to study Manchu language documents, which are extensive. Native Chinese historians had never bothered to learn the barbarian language of the conqueror and figured they were simply translations of information contained in the Chinese version. Western scholars concluded otherwise.

The new interpretation at first presented a picture of the Manchu that was almost a mirror image of the earlier view. From this perspective the Manchu looked more like the Yuan, another earlier Steppe-nomad conquering power. Recently, however, there has been a move toward a middle ground. This view suggests the Manchu created a multiethnic state that consisted of Han Chinese, Manchu, Mongols, Tibetans, and Uighurs. In other words, they tried to be Han to the Chinese, but Mongol or Tibetan or Uighur to these other ethnic communities. They spoke much of ruling over one people but the unity involved was their rule, not Han ethnicity.

---

11   For this discussion, see Charles Holcombe, *A History of East Asia. New York*: Cambridge University Press, 2011. P. 170 ff.

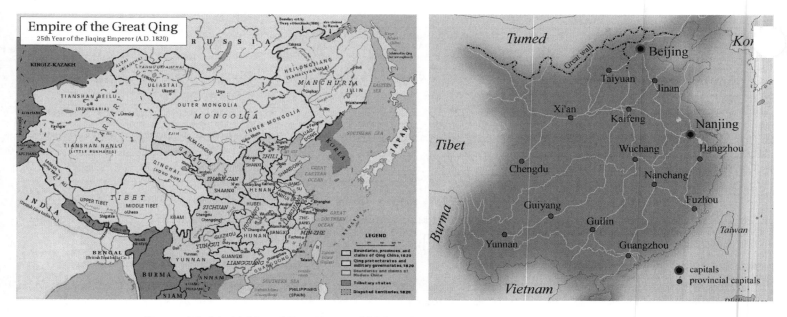

Figures 4.5a &b: (a) Map of Qing Empire; (b) Map of Ming Empire

There is no disagreement among those involved in a debate that Qing China was the most extensive empire in Chinese history (See Figure 4-5). By subduing all of the "barbarian" peoples north of China, the Manchu ended the problem of barbarian invasions from the north, something that had never been accomplished before. It is also true that China today includes all the areas controlled by the Qing, including Tibet[12] and Zingiang, an autonomous region in southwestern China made up of Uighur-speakers who are Turkic Muslims, both of which very much want to be independent of China. Look at the maps below. On the left is the Qing and the right the Ming. It should make the difference clear.

The Manchu approach to empire included preventing Han Chinese from migrating into Manchuria, forbidding intermarriage between the two groups, and forbidding Manchu and other non-Chinese women from the Chinese practice of foot-binding. They even tried to end the practice in China, but to no avail.

Inside China, the Manchu established themselves as a separate ruling class. Bannermen were stationed throughout the empire in garrisons to protect against uprisings. While not all bannermen were Manchu, those who were, even those who were Han Chinese, were loyal to the Qing dynasty. All the same, most of the top government officials were Manchu. The Manchu continued to utilize their national language rather than Chinese with their subject peoples. All bannerman, for example, were required both to write and speak Manchu. Imperial decrees were issued in both Han and Manchu.

On top of the bannermen system, the Manchu continued the Ming bureaucratic structure. But the steppe areas they took over were largely governed in accordance with their local traditions. They did try

---

12   In the fourteenth century, the current sect of Buddhism came to Tibet, which included rule by the Dali Lama, a Bodhisattva whose current incarnation, Tenzin Gyatso, is in self-imposed exile in India. Like all the peoples north of China, Tibet has been both attracted to and repulsed by its stronger neighbor to the south. The Qing subjugation of the area, even though it allowed the Tibetans a large degree of autonomy, is part of contemporary China's justification for holding on to this area.

to control them politically and, as noted above, often spoke of the Qing as ruling over one people, by which they did not mean one Han Chinese people.

Interestingly, most scholars suggest that by the mid-nineteenth century, despite their best efforts, the Qing rulers and almost all the Manchu were almost indistinguishable in language and culture from Han Chinese. The Manchu language was hardly spoken anymore.[14]

The Manchu were fortunate in that their first three rulers' reigns lasted more than a century, and that all three were highly capable individuals. During this period, the population of China doubled. The standard of living was as high as that of any region in Europe at the time, and frequently higher. Life expectancy increased as the government was capable of responding to disasters and famines, both because of food reserves and adequate transportation facilities. On four occasions, owing to the well-filled nature of the national treasure, the annual land tax was cancelled.

The first emperor, Kangxi (ruled 1661–1722), a contemporary of Louis XIV of France, had the task of securing the dynasty. This he did not only by putting down opponents inside China, but also by securing the northern borders, as we addressed above. One end product of this northward expansion of China was an encounter with another famous contemporary, Peter the Great of Russia. The result was the Treaty of Nerchinsk (1689)—written in Manchu, Russian, Chinese, and Latin—that settled border issues as well as trade.

Kangxi took a personal interest in Western ideas, first brought to his attention by Jesuit missionaries who served at his court as cartographers and astronomers. Some Christianization among Chinese followed, until Dominicans and Franciscans arrived and insisted Chinese Christians could not honor their ancestors. As a result, the emperor expelled all Christians except his Jesuit scientists whom he allowed to remain.

Yinzheng, the Yongzheng emperor, succeeded Kangxi in 1723 at the age of forty-five. He ruled until 1735 when he died unexpectedly, some said murdered by a family member of a writer he had executed. An able ruler, he tightened central control over the government and rationalized the tax structure.

Yongzheng was succeeded by his son, Hongli, whose reign name was "Qianlong." As his grandfather before him, Qianlong's reign was long, from 1735 to 1795. It was the Qianlong emperor who expanded China to its farthest extent and pacified the areas he ruled by allowing the populace to follow local customs and not requiring they cut their hair in Manchu style.

Qianlong was a patron of culture of the peoples he ruled. He even dabbled in being a scholar himself, appending poetry to his edicts. He spoke not only Manchu and Chinese but also Mongol, Tibetan, Uighur, and Tangit. He strove very hard to fit the model of the Confucian "sage emperor" by working very long hours in the day and devoting his evenings to working in reading, painting, and calligraphy.[15]

---

14   This debate is ongoing. The presentation above is therefore tentative at best. Ironically, the current government of China has even joined with an official denunciation of the direction of the new scholarship. It prefers the older view that the Qing became Han Chinese. It also uses the conquests of the Qing to justify it controlling Tibet and Zingiang, both of which would very much like to become independent of China. From an historiographical point of view, this discussion provides two insights. First, changing outlooks and political interests influence the shape history takes. And second, an historical interpretation of an event can be significantly affected if new and previously unused data become available, as is definitely the driving force here.

15   See Patricia Ebry, et. al. *East Asia*. New York: Houghton-Mifflin, 2006, 321.

As he grew older his judgments were sometimes clouded, and in an extraordinary act of filial piety, in 1795, he abdicated to prevent himself from ruling longer than his grandfather, the Kangxi emperor, had ruled. His influence at court persisted until he died in 1799, at the age of eighty-nine.

By the end of the Qianlong emperor's reign, forces were beginning to work against the Manchu system. In particular, a more insistent group of Western powers were pressing China to open its doors more to trade. This group was particularly chafed under the restrictions the emperor placed upon them. By the eighteenth century, tea was the most highly sought trading commodity China had to offer, even over silk. As the foreign merchants were confined to Guangzhou (Canton) and the source of tea was nowhere near this port, the cost of procuring this item was significantly higher than what it would have been with closer access. The emperors were rather indifferent to their concerns. They certainly saw no reason why they should be interested in barbarians so very far from the center of civilization nor their desire for more favorable trade relations. That those barbarians would soon be coming to call with weaponry far superior to anything the Chinese could muster, they could not have imagined. As we shall see in a later chapter, that is precisely what did occur and the Manchus were ill-prepared to deal with it.

Manchu China enjoyed one of the highest standards of living in the world in the eighteenth century. By the next century, all this would change.

TOKUGAWA JAPAN (1603–1867)—THE UNIFICATION OF JAPAN

Earlier History

Before we address the Tokugawa period in Japanese history, we must have a little background information on geography and climate, and a bit of history leading up to this period. Look at Figure 4.6.

First, notice that Japan is an archipelago along the eastern coast of Asia, stretching from Korea in the south to Russia in the north. To its west is the Sea of Japan, also referred to as the "inland sea" by the Japanese. A relatively placid body of water, it has always facilitated trade and cultural exchange with the more sophisticated Chinese mainland, while providing protection therefrom against a threat to Japan's independence. [17]

The climate varies as you move from south to north. Look at the chart above.[18]

Japan's northern-most extent approaches Russia and lies on approximately the same latitude as Boston, giving it a New England-like climate (See Figure 4.7).[19] In the south, Japan approaches Korea and lies on the same latitude as Miami. Accordingly, the climate there is warmer. Not surprisingly, rice is a major agricultural product in the south. Some areas will even allow double-cropping. As you travel north, dry

---

16   https://commons.wikimedia.org/wiki/File:Map_of_East_Asia.png

17   In fact, only the Yuan (Mongol) emperors of the late thirteen century ever tried, and their efforts ended in disaster, as we noted above in our discussion on the rise of the Ming.

18   https://www.google.com/url?sa=i&rct=j&q=&esrc=s&source=images&cd=&cad=rja&uact=8&ved=0ahUKEw iO9sq2h7fLAhVHWCYKHaLZCVsQjB0IBg&url=https%3A%2F%2Fwww.japanmeetings.org%2Fwhy-japan%2Ffacts-about-japan.php&psig=AFQjCNElx0nJzOiB8jb7GtOKLdtPTVpeFA&ust=1457731541255154

19   The average temperature in Tokyo varies from 10° C in January to 25° C in August.

farming prevails; the major crops include cotton, maize, wheat, sweet potatoes, soy beans, and tobacco. Some of these did not appear until after the arrival of the Portuguese in the sixteenth century, others even later.

For much of its history, Japan enjoyed a certain geographical isolation. Other than crossing the Inland Sea, the only routes of contact, before the Europeans came over the Pacific in the early modern period, were either from Russia south, via the Kurile Islands to Hokkaido, or by crossing the Tsushima Strait from Korea to Chugoku and proceeding northward. Western historians have often noted Japan's similarity to Great Britain vis-a-vis the European mainland, where location and relative isolation are concerned.

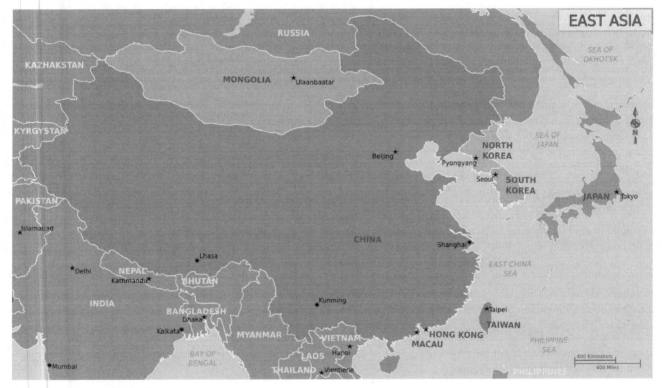

Figure 4.6: Map of Eurasia[18]

Most scholars believe the Japanese migrated to their islands from the mainland, via Korea, about eleven thousand years ago. They further point out that the Japanese language is in the Ural-Altaic family, which includes Korean, Manchu, Mongolic, Turkic, and possible Finnish.[20] The Chinese language, by contrast, is part of the Sino-Tibetan group.

The earliest civilization to arise in Japan was heavily influenced by China, in particular the Tang dynasty (ninth century CE), with its imperial form of government. China was also an important source of cultural and religious ideas, in particular Confucianism and Buddhism, both of which play a prominent role in

---

20   See Charles Holcombe, *A History of East Asia*. New York: Cambridge University Press, 2011. There is some controversy about this entire group and whether the languages are truly related.

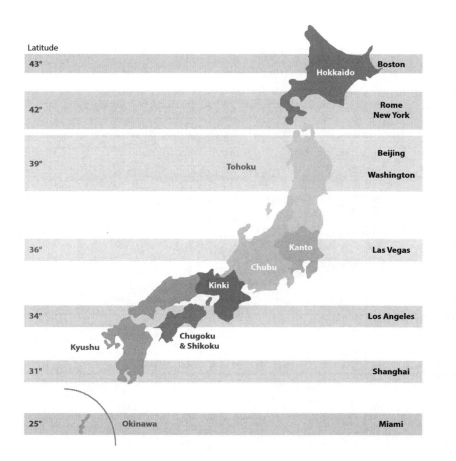

Figure 4.7: Climate Map of Japan

Japan's history. Finally, the earliest Japanese script, *kanji*, was adapted from Chinese.[21] In all three cases, the route of transmission was indirect, through Korea.

Although long recognized as being among the world's most talented cultural borrowers, the Japanese are also innovators and, in the late twelfth century, replaced the Chinese imperial tradition of government for a system of their own making. It is known as the "shogunate." Before the Tokugawa period there were two dynasties of shoguns, the Kamakura (1185–1333), who invented the system, and the Ashikaga (1338–1603), who followed them and lasted until replaced by the Tokugawa.

Historians often compare the shogunate to European feudalism because, despite its differences, it is the easiest way for Westerners to understand the system. The shogun presided over the state (technically on behalf of the emperor) from his *bakufu*, or "tent government," aided by loyal nobility, soldiers like himself, the daimyo, who, in return for their loyalty and military service, received grants of land and control of the peasants to work them.

Unlike the European feudal system, there were also warrior bands of Buddhist monks who controlled large areas of land in return for military service, similar to the secular daimyo.

Also rather similar to European feudalism, the daimyo subdivided their lands and placed a class of warriors over them, the *samurai*.[22] These heavily armored knights, with their two swords, became a resident garrison whose job it was to keep the peasants under control and working the land, and when necessary to put down uprisings among them. The samurai were also the soldiers upon whom the *daimyo* relied to fight their personal battles. As in Europe under feudalism, the samurai's loyalty was to his daimyo and not the shogun. At times the system brought relative security to Japan, but, as in Europe, it also often led to

---

21   By the early modern period, the Japanese had developed two additional scripts that are phonetic, *hiragana* and *katakana*.

22   See images of these warriors at https://www.google.com/webhp?sourceid=chrome-instant&ion=1&espv=2&ie=UTF-8#q=samurai.

civil war, as ambitious or ruthless daimyo sought to increase their power at the expense of other daimyo, or even the shogun himself.

Also important to the system was a strict code of behavior for the warrior that came to be known as bushido. A warrior was expected to follow this military code scrupulously. It combined not only martial arts training, but also the responsibility to be loyal and do one's duty in accordance with Confucian principles of service. In some ways, it resembled the late-feudal European code of chivalry. There was one major difference: when a samurai failed to live up to his duty, he was honor bound to take his own life. That was what his short sword was for.

The daimyo lived in grand fortified castles that, as in Europe, could be a fortress of defense against attackers, or a basis from which to launch one's own attacks. Yet, they, along with an emerging middle class during the Ashikaga period, stimulated not only the economy but also an impressive growth of cultural by-products, including novels, theatre, and artworks, to decorate their homes in the towns. It is often recognized as having been a golden age of Japanese art.[23]

The peasants were still armed and, at times, a poor daimyo would unify with them against a greater lord. The late Ashikaga was especially plagued with such instability, which brings us to the Tokugawa and their unification of Japan.

THE THREE UNIFIERS

Bringing order out of chaos was a challenge all states faced in the early modern period. In China, when emperors were strong, the system took care of things, and sometimes it did so even when they were not, as we saw above. In France, the wars of religion led to the creation of an absolute monarchy based upon the theory of divine right monarchy, as we saw in an earlier chapter. In Japan, the shogun system also led to civil war, disruption, and disorder, not unlike how England suffered in its almost contemporaneous civil war. What we want to understand is how the Tokugawa succeeded in creating a unified society without adopting either a Chinese imperial or French absolutist model to do it. In short, how did the Japanese make their feudal system work?

To be sure, much that occurred in the Ashikaga period, prior to the Tokugawa, prepared the way for Japan's unification in the seventeenth century. But it was three strong individuals, building on these preconditions, who actually brought about the unification of Japan, culminating in the Tokugawa shogunate, which would rule Japan until 1867.

First, during the Ashikaga period, no matter the conflicts between the ruling classes, Japan saw a notable increase in foreign trade. We have already examined the importance of Japanese silver in Portuguese trade with China. Additionally, the rise of commercial towns and the improvements in agriculture, in part aided by the introduction of new crops from the Americas, led to a sustained growth in the wealth of the society. It is also true the growth of cities had weakened the dominance of the rural daimyo, and class lines between the aristocracy and peasantry were weakening.

All these changes created an increase in wealth that enabled the great daimyo to build more strongly fortified castles and to field larger armies. At the same time, a change in warfare led to an improved

---

23   See W. Scott Morton and J. Kenneth Olentik. *Japan: Its History and Culture*. New York: McGraw Hill, 2005. 95.

situation for commoners in Japan. Armies employed a new gun-centered warfare, replacing the mounted, armor-clad warrior of the past. It happened quite by chance when a Portuguese shipwreck allowed smoothbore muskets to fall into Japanese hands. The superiority of this weapon over traditional ones was recognized at once, and soon the Japanese began making similar weapons for their peasant soldiers to use. Since merchants supplied these new weapons, the daimyo realized how vital this previously despised group was to their interests, and began to treat them with more respect.

Japan experienced other influences from Europeans as well. In 1549, Father Francis Xavier landed in Japan, followed by a number of other Jesuits.[24] The Jesuits' efforts were successful because they did not insult Japanese traditions, nor did they seem to be attempting to create a new Christian-based religious political order. Additionally, they were conversant with the astronomical and mathematical ideas coming from Europe and with Western engineering applications the Japanese found useful.

Christianity grew significantly, and many samurai converted. They took Christian names and carried rosaries and crucifixes into battle on behalf of their shoguns. In 1582, according to Jesuit sources, there were 150,000 Christians and 200 churches in Japan. Japanese admired the Jesuits because they reminded them of Zen Buddhist monks in the disciplined way they led their lives.

In short, much was happening in late sixteenth-century Japan that helps to explains how the country was ready to be unified, but making it happen (that is, overcoming the anarchistic tendencies of the shogunate system) was the work of three men: Oda Nobunaga (1534–1582), Toyotami Hideyoshi (1536–1598), and Tokugawa Ieyasu (1534–1616). An old Japanese anecdote has it that Nobunaga quarried the stones, Hideyoshi shaped them, and Ieyasu laid them in place. To be sure, having three strong and powerful men to succeed one after the other gave the continuity that such an enterprise would have required. And the final product would last until the mid-nineteenth century without substantial alteration. While many historians fault the resultant state as one totally unprepared to survive in the modern world, some historians suggest, on the contrary, it was the Tokugawa who laid the foundations for a Japan that would be able to survive in the tumultuous world of nineteenth-century imperialism, when almost all other nations succumbed to European domination.[25]

Oda Nobunaga

Nobunaga began the process that led to unification in the 1560s with a series of campaigns, initially begun at the request of the Ashikaga shogun. In the process, Nobunaga and the other two unifiers came to see it was to their advantage to cooperate rather than fight one another, and also to see no advantage in keeping up the fiction of serving the interests of the shogun. By 1573, the last Ashikaga had been removed, and no new one put in his place. For a time, the position of shogun was allowed to lapse.

A ten-year campaign to remove their chief rival, a Buddhist military monastery, the True Pure Land League, was completed by 1580, accompanied by great loss of life. This victory was followed by the defeat

---

24   Dominicans and Benedictines arrived later. Their efforts were not so successful since they suggested all Japanese traditional ideas were incompatible with Christianity, a price most Japanese were unwilling to pay to embrace this foreign religion.

25   Morton, 105

of rival military clans in the north. It was Nobunaga's adoption of the use of firearms that made the difference. The day of the mounted warrior was at an end. And when this campaign was over, Nobunaga's personally controlled about one-third of the lands of Japan.

Nobunaga's work was cut short in 1582. He was taking tea in a castle he had built on the grounds of the Buddhist monastery he had recently defeated, when a surprise attack by one of his own generals led him to commit suicide, rather than be taken captive. His new castle was burned to the ground with his body inside. At this point, Japan could have easily descended into chaos once more. It did not.

Toyotami Hideyoshi

Toyotami Hideyoshi, Nobunaga's chief lieutenant, acted quickly to avenge his compatriot's death and to seize control of his territories as well. He awarded some estates to his supporters, but most he kept for himself. As a result, Tokugawa Ieyasu became alarmed at Hideyoshi's increasing power and challenged him in several campaigns, before Hideyoshi persuaded him that cooperating was better than fighting. They fought rival daimyo for eight more years before the unification of Japan was complete, but Hideyoshi died of old age, rather than at the hand of an assassin or in combat. How he accomplished this is worth noting, given the continual struggles between the great daimyo families throughout much of the Ashikaga period.

First, much of the work had been done by Nobunaga. Second, more than Nobunaga, Hideyoshi was prepared to conquer by turning former enemies into new vassals. Tokugawa Ieyashu, for example, ultimately received more territory than Hideyoshi had himself. His 2,402,000 koku[26] made Ieyasu the largest landholder in Japan. There was a certain amount of danger for Hideyoshi in this approach. Yet the lands held by Tokugawa Ieyasu were distant from the highly developed lands Hideyoshi held west of Japan, near the imperial capital, and Ieyasu, initially at least, was kept busy gaining control over these areas that had belonged to rival daimyo whose samurai by no means accepted the changing situation.

There is a story that one day the two unifiers dismissed their followers and rode out alone to Edo Bay. When they arrived, Hideyoshi unleashed his sword and gave it to his companion, a sign of trust, and then, waving his arm around, suggested Ieyasu make his capital there. We cannot be sure of the veracity of the story, but it was there that Ieyasu's capital was built, and it proved to be a good choice. Surrounded by excellent agricultural lands, it was geographically central enough to be a good point of control over the area. Neither man knew just how important Hideyoshi's suggestion would be, but today this area is at the heart of Japan: it is the city of Tokyo.[27].

Hideyoshi's lineage was too humble to claim the title of shogun. The emperor did recognize him as his regent. Hideyoshi conducted a land survey some have compared to the survey of William the Conqueror. This secured his tax base and his income. In addition, he published regulations for the behavior of daimyo and began rounding up swords. "Taiko's Sword Hunt," as it is known in Japanese history, deprived everyone below the samurai class of weapons. This included Buddhist warrior monks, gentlemen farmers, and peasants. In so doing, Hideyoshi created a clear class distinction between the samurai and the farmer classes, which in former times the samurai were supposed to manage and with whom they had frequently united in

---

26   A *koku* was a measure of land said to grow five bushels of rice, enough to feed a man for a year.
27   See Morton 109.

their attempts to gain power. In other words, it ended armed rebellions among the samurai for the future. Finally, in 1591, he issued an edict designed to set the Japanese class structure in perpetuity.

Christianity had continued to grow during the period of unification. By 1596, according to one source,[28] there were at least three hundred thousand Japanese converts, including one of Hideyoshi's generals and a few women high up at his court. The youth were observed to be wearing Portuguese clothing and carrying rosaries and crucifixes. Portuguese words and games made their way into the culture. One such "Japanese" food dish survives today. It arose out of the fact that on ember days, *"quattuor tempor,"* Portuguese monks ate fish rather than meat. To prepare it, they dipped their shrimp, for example, in batter and fried it. We call it "tempura." Nagasaki was run by the Portuguese and Japan's trade with them and China was increasing. But in 1587, everything changed when, quite unexpectedly, Hideyoshi decreed a ban on Christians and Christianity.

Several possible motives help explain this sudden change of attitude. Some scholars point to Buddhist opposition. One of the reasons given in the decree was the destruction of Buddhist shrines by overly enthusiastic Japanese Christian converts. The decree also charged the Portuguese were selling Japanese into slavery. One scholar points out that absolute allegiance to one god seemed to Hideyoshi and his successors to detract from a man's allegiance to his lord. In other words, Christianity would be socially disruptive.[29] Whatever the reasons in half a century, this new policy would lead to the deaths of most Japanese-Christians, and the Dutch would replace the Portuguese as Japan's only European contact. The Dutch were far more interested in making money than they were in saving souls.

Hideyoshi had had a long and eventful career without a slipup, but his good fortune ran out when he conceived the grandiose scheme of conquering China, which required invading Korea. He launched his invasion in April 1592.

At first it was a glorious success. One almost hears him reporting to his loyal supporters at court, "Mission accomplished!" Seoul, the capital, fell quickly and Hideyoshi's armies advanced, all the way to the Manchurian border without encountering resistance. Then things began to go awry. The Koreans recovered and began to launch guerilla counterattacks and successful naval campaigns. A severe winter caught the Japanese totally unprepared. By the next year, at least a third of the occupiers had died in the campaign.

China, which claimed suzerainty over Korea, had some responsibility for its welfare. You may recall the Ming dynasty was near collapse by this point, but it did eventually respond. The worsening situation made Hideyoshi amenable to negotiations, but the manner in which the Chinese addressed the Japanese, their inferiors (as they saw all non-Chinese), was offensive to Hideyoshi, leading him to renew the war effort with a second invasion. This time the Chinese sent a more vigorous military response, and the war turned into a stalemate. When Hideyoshi died in 1598, the war was quickly brought to an end.

Hideyoshi was a long time in dying; he was sick for two years and spent much of that time trying to guarantee that his son Hideyori, then a child, would ascend to his position when of age. Tokugawa Ieyasu swore he would honor his old companion's wish, but it was not to be.

---

28   Morton 110
29   Ebry, p. 311

Tokugawa Ieyasu

It was the third of the unifiers whose family name is attached to this era. Have we not been trying to explain how the Tokugawa shogunate, which would last until 1868, reunified Japan? Early on, Ieyasu faced challenges from ambitious daimyo hoping to replace him. In 1600, he defeated his most formidable rival, Ishida Mitsunari, at the battle of Shimabara. Most scholars pronounce this to be the end of the period of civil wars that had raged in Japan throughout the Ashikaga period.

Because Ieyasu, unlike Hideyoshi, was descended from the Minamoto clan,[30] in a distant cousin sort of way, he was worthy of the title of shogun, which the emperor revived and bestowed upon him in 1603 (the same year in which James Stuart of Scotland became James I of England).

At first, Ieyasu honored his vow to Hideyoshi to protect his son and heir. By 1615, however, Ieyasu decided his old ally's son had to be removed if the Tokugawa dynasty were going to be founded. In 1616, using trumped-up charges of disloyalty, he laid siege to Mitsunari's castle at Osaka. When it finally fell, Ieyasu forced both Hideyori and his mother to commit suicide.

Some scholars cite one other conflict as part of the process of Tokugawa unification. It did not occur until 1637, during the third shogun's reign, and involved Japanese-Christians who rose in rebellion because of the persecution and harsh economic conditions they suffered under at the time. The Shimabara Christian Rebellion took a year to put down; about ten thousand people were killed as a result,[31] but for two centuries thereafter Japan would enjoy internal peace. If indeed, Ieyasu "laid the stones" quarried and shaped by his predecessors, just what shape did the Tokugawa shogunate take?

TOKUGAWA SHOGUNATE

Peace does have its benefits. In the case of Tokugawa Japan, they included economic expansion along with population growth; urbanization on a scale heretofore unknown in Japan; and cultural developments, largely based on Confucian ideas with which one still associates Japan. Indeed, this period is known as the "Golden Age of Confucianism" in Japanese history.

Another distinguishing characteristic of this era was the isolation of Japan. We have already seen the important role Japan had played in the silver exchange between Portugal and China in the sixteenth century. Many other items of trade were also involved to the economic advantage of the daimyo houses. All this came to an end now. Furthermore, Ieyasu, following the example of Hideyoshi, sought to rid Japan of all foreign, Western influences. To this end, as we noted above, he expelled all alien Christians, and all Japanese were required to register with a Buddhist temple to affirm they were not Christians, or face death. Some chose martyrdom; others simply disappeared from sight. Additionally, Japanese who had gone abroad to study were not allowed to return. No Japanese were permitted to go abroad, and all contacts with the outside world were forbidden to all but a few Japanese merchants who traded with the Dutch, confined as they were to Nagasaki. Trade with Korea and China continued, but under the shogun's exclusive control

---

30   That is, he was a descendant of a cadet branch of the imperial family.
31   Somewhat ironically, Dutch naval bombardment of the rebels was important to the shogun's victory over the Christians.

and to his benefit. This meant, that at the time when the West was beginning to develop industrially, Japan was largely unaware of these changes. It was a trade-off, to be sure.

Christianity, but also modernizing Western ideas, tended to be disruptive to traditional societies, as we have seen and will see in the next chapter. Not allowing them to have a lot of influence was probably helpful where maintaining stability was concerned. In addition, Japan was never totally isolated from the West with its new ideas; indeed, by the early eighteenth century, the eighth shogun, Yoshimune, allowed the importation of all foreign books, except those that taught Christianity, which led to a flood of foreign scientific, medical, mathematical, and even economic literature into the country. Near the end of the century, a bureau to oversee the translation of "barbarian literature" was begun. It even resulted in the introduction of the sweet potato as a food source. More than China or Korea, Japan, on the eve of Western imperialism, began to open itself to foreign ideas on its own terms, which may help explain its more successful response to that threat. All of this is to say, the isolation of Japan should not be viewed simply as a backward and reactionary policy; instead, the isolation should be viewed as one part of the shoguns' policies designed to achieve their primary concern throughout this period: the maintenance of order. Perhaps several centuries of disorder had taught them something. In any event, everything they did was aimed at this objective.

You will not be surprised that a second and equally important obstacle to stable rule in Japan came from the great feudal families themselves, the daimyo. This was not a problem unique to Japan in the seventeenth century. Indeed, at this time, in France, Richelieu and Louis XIV were addressing the problem of a disorderly feudal aristocracy by introducing royal absolutism. It worked also, but it did not bring two hundred years of peace.

For Japan, such an approach would have meant returning to the Chinese system of government it had abandoned a thousand years earlier; Ieyasu did not consider it. The daimyo houses were too powerful, anyway. Instead, he devised ways to turn feudalism into a system of social order and stability by freezing it. Never again would these honored and powerful men be in a position to rebel against the state or his family.

The god-emperor remained high and lifted up, but powerless; real power was in the hands of the shoguns. They, in turn, entrusted the control of large sections of the country to three types of daimyo: family members, vassals, and "outside daimyo," the descendants of the great lords who first opposed them but made peace with Ieyasu during the settlement period. The Tokugawa relied most heavily on the vassal daimyo and never fully trusted the others. These powerful and wealthy families did continue to run their own regions almost as independent states, and the shoguns were careful to treat them respectfully. The system also had the added advantage that the Tokugawa did not have to be concerned with, or pay for, local affairs.

One way the Tokugawa kept the daimyo under control was through the introduction of primogeniture into Japan as the norm for the military ruling classes. This brought an end to sibling rivalries that had often led to civil conflicts. But the most important innovation made was the system of *sankin kōtai*. After 1635, all daimyo were required to spend part of the year away from their home estates, at the shogun's court in Edo. Furthermore, when he was at home, the daimyo was required to leave hostages (a wife or son) behind as a guarantee of loyalty. Not only could the shogun keep the potential rebels closer at hand and divided at the same time, but this policy required they maintain two households, leaving them a lot less money for planning insurrections.

A valuable but perhaps unintended consequence of this policy was economic in nature. The necessity to transport large numbers of retainers to and from Edo throughout the year resulted in the development of road and communication networks centering on Edo, and aided in the creation of a national economy. Merchants were also attracted to the area to satisfy the needs of this wealthy class and its retainers.

The shoguns also taxed the daimyo heavily, especially those they did not trust, and restricted their ability to expand their own castles, while requiring them to spend on public works, even on Tokugawa castles. Finally, no daimyo was allowed to enter into any direct communication with the emperor. There was an official at the shoguns' court for that purpose.

On average, the great lords enjoyed an income of at least fifty thousand koku, while some were wealthier. One could not aspire to this status with less than ten thousand koku. The shoguns themselves controlled the most landed wealth, about twenty-five percent.

The warrior gentry, the samurai, who often held less than ten thousand koku, were classified as hata-moto, *"bannermen."* As their land holdings were insufficient to sustain their lifestyle, they were often paid a stipend, and settled in cities away from the peasants. In time, the presence of a somewhat poverty-stricken class of warriors, without a function, created social disruption. Some found work in government positions, while others ran military schools. Many of these traditional knights with their two swords simply survived in poverty.

Although the organization of the government at the national level grew throughout the two centuries of the Tokugawa state's existence, it acquired its settled form under the third shogun, Iemitsu (1623–1651). Advising the shogun on matters of policy was a group of three, later reduced to one, the Tairo or "Great Elders." A Roju, or "Council of Elders," between two and four individuals, looked after the shoguns' affairs with the Imperial Court, public works, and money. This included the shogun's vast territorial holdings.

Judicial affairs were also part of the responsibilities of the Roju, although it was assisted by commissioners from the various departments of the shogun's government.

While the central government did not have to concern itself with the affairs of local daimyo, it was interested in controlling the affairs of all large cities. In other words, the daimyo did not enjoy the wealth or control of these increasingly important parts of Japanese life. Also, the shogun appointed commissioners to run the cities almost exclusively from the ranks of the feudal daimyo, that is, confederates-in-arms, and not from either his family daimyo or certainly the "outside daimyo." The result was a military-run system that some scholars have described as being very much like a police state.[32]

Peace also led to economic expansion throughout much of the Tokugawa period. New lands were opened to rice cultivation, but also new crops from the West were added: wheat, maize, tobacco, the sweet potato, and cotton. Careful attention to soil types and climate conditions led to improved yields, as did improved seed varieties. Rapeseed production increased to provide fuel for lighting, as a rapidly expanded literacy rate promoted the growth of the book trade. By the mid-eighteenth century, Japanese farmers were making and selling their own silk products and producing sugar. Some of these developments were

---

32 | Morton 121

instigated by the shoguns, and others by merchants, but some were inspired by the need of the daimyo to finance their trips to Edo. Japan did not undergo an industrial revolution as did Europe; instead, most of these innovations occurred in cottage industries scattered throughout the country. Yet, these changes did prepare the way for that innovation once it appeared in the Meiji Restoration later in the nineteenth century.

Until the late eighteenth century, most wealth was concentrated in cities. Daimyo sold their rice to merchants who, when needed, advanced them credit against future harvests. At times this led to poverty among the poorer daimyo. It also led to bills of exchange that became a kind of paper currency. In short, while Japan's economy was not totally modernized before the Meiji Restoration, it was developed in such a way as to be prepared to do so when that time arrived.

The Tokugawa period was also a time of significant cultural development. We have already noted the decline of Christianity during this period. Buddhism declined, as well, while Neo-Confucianism thrived. It began early in the period, in 1615, when Ieyasu decreed all *samurai* should devote themselves to the practice of arms and the "pursuit of polite learning." This latter meant, in practice, Neo-Confucianism because of its stress on loyalty vital to the support of the regime.

One of the most important proponents of this philosophy was a confidant of Ieyasu who helped him develop his anti-Western policies. Hayashi Razan (1583–1657) drew large crowds to his lectures on Neo-Confucianism, as often members of the emerging middle class as samurai warriors. A highly renowned scholar, Razan taught history, literature, and Shinto studies, along with Confucianism. In fact, Shinto and Confucianism were seen to be mutually compatible. All in his audience were encouraged to apply Confucian principles to their work. Unlike Confucianism in China, in Japan the philosophy stressed loyalty to the shogun above even family.

Other cultural areas blossomed in the Tokugawa period, in part because of the growth of cities, which resulted from the forced residence of the daimyo at Edo for part of the year. They needed not only to be housed and fed, but entertained as well. One result was a somewhat flashy *kabuki* theatre. Because women were forbidden to be actors (as in Shakespeare's England), men had to take on those roles. The result was a group of specialized professionals who mimicked the behaviors of women.

Also popular was *bunraku,* puppet theatre, a serious rival to kabuki. Some puppets were large, requiring several people to operate them. Bunraku too provided opportunities for writers to specialize in producing literature for this genre.

Traditional *No* drama continued in Japan, but was almost exclusively attended by great daimyo houses.

The Tokugawa era also saw an expanded interest in poetry, especially haiku, which consisted of only seventeen syllables in a 5-7-5 pattern. The most famous of these poets was Matsuo Basho (1644–1694). Here is an example of his work:

> *The summer grasses—*
>
> *Of brave warriors' dreams*
>
> *all that remains.* [33]

---

33   Morton, 131

The book trade flourished during this period. Most were written in Japanese and ranged in subject matter from novels to popular guides in household management. In 1692, publishers in Kyoto produced seven thousand titles.

There was also a "floating world," as it was called, made up of entertainers whose reputations were less reputable. The "*geisha*" were at the center of these enterprises. These women were skilled dancers as well as conversationalists. They were often also musicians and artists. Their training was rigorous and most were not involved in the sex trade. There were, of course, many people who were.

Finally, the Tokugawa continued the artistic developments begun in the Ashikaga. Wood-block prints were especially popular. One popular artist, Katsushika Hokusai (1760–1849), is supposed to have produced thirty-five thousand designs over his career. Many of these artists drew their subjects from the members of the "floating world" and from landscapes.

The Tokugawa period gave Japan a long period of stability in which very little social change or, seemingly, any change at all occurred. We have noted some things were changing all along. We have also noted the classes that dominated in Japan increasingly found it difficult to remain wealthy and prosperous, especially a number of lesser daimyo and samurai who found their social situations difficult to maintain by the early nineteenth century when change would be forced upon Japan. Yet, Japan was better prepared to withstand the onslaught of imperialism soon to come than all the other powerful late-traditional-era states we have examined (and will be examining), in no small measure because of the stability the Tokugawa shogunate gave it, and the capacity for change in the regime, despite its best efforts to prevent change from occurring.

KOREA

Humans have been living in Korea for about thirty thousand years. Modern genetic research, along with linguistic studies, suggest Koreans are linked to Mongolia rather than to China and therefore are ethnically close to the Japanese. Some linguists have noticed similarities between Japanese and Korean. They classify early Korean as being among the Altaic family group, a claim many others reject, suggesting instead Korean is an "isolate," with no connections to this purported family. Whatever the origins, the culture of Koreans, like the Japanese, developed under the shadow of China. Their first script was derived from Chinese, and the Koreans made a virtual religion of Confucianism. The relationship between the two peoples was generally cordial, as Chinese emperors rarely sought to control Korea directly, viewing it, instead, as a loyal tributary kingdom. The Koreans, for their part, looked upon China more as a benevolent big brother than a dangerous and powerful neighbor.

The climate on the peninsula is cold in winter, with heavy snowfall in the north, to warm and humid in the summer. Monsoon winds move south to north with heavy rain in July and August. The best agricultural lands are in the south, where double-cropping of rice is possible. Dry farming crops are more common in the north: barley, millet, and ramie (a fiber plant). The presence of rugged mountains in the north limits the amount of arable lands. In modern times, maize and potatoes are also grown. Korea does suffer from

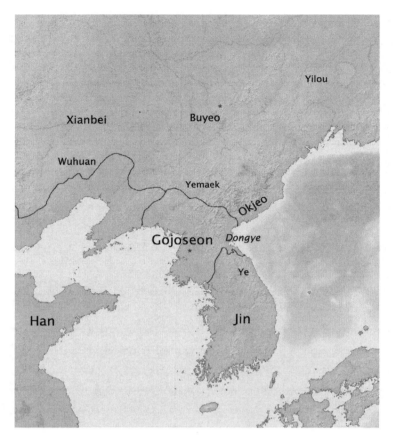

Figure 4.8: Map of Korea[36]

a lack of rivers large enough to be useful for navigation.

Westerners get the name Korea from the Koryŏ dynasty (889–1259) that, while heavily influenced by China, adapted Confucian ideas and institutions to Korean ideas and needs. The most notable difference was in staffing the bureaucracy. In China, something of a meritocracy existed; in Korea, only members of the aristocracy were eligible to study Confucian classics to take the exam for government and military service. Collectively, these aristocrats, known as the *"Yangban,"* dominated Korean society well into the modern period.

Korean marriage customs are another example of the differences between China and Korea. In the former, for example, marriage between people with the same sir name was forbidden, whereas in Korea, marriage to cousins was common, and occasionally even half-brothers and half-sisters. Unlike China, Korean women were entitled to equal shares of the family inheritance with their brothers.

The Koryŏ dynasty was weakened by the coming of the Yuan to China, replaced in 1392 by the Chosŏn dynasty that lasted until 1910. During the reign of King Sejong (1418–1450), Korea's northern boundary was established permanently along the Yalu and Tumen rivers.

Remembered as King Sejong the Great, he also is credited, in 1442, with introducing *han'gŭl*, a completely alphabetic script of twenty-eight characters not derived from the Chinese and used throughout Korea today.

Through the study of Chinese classics, Sejong and his successors went further than anyone in Asia, including the Chinese, in attempting to emulate the earliest forms of Chinese Confucianism, the so-called Neo-Confucian movement. Writing into law requirements for patrilineal descent, ancestor veneration, and mourning obligations, they attempted to create what they perceived to be a universal Confucian moral order.

In the late sixteenth century, Chosŏn Korea suffered a series of calamities, prompting it to introduce an isolation policy more rigid even than that of Tokugawa Japan. The term "Hermit Kingdom" is often used

34   http://www.topicsinkoreanhistory.com/wp-content/uploads/2012/07/korea14192.jpg

to describe Korea during the early modern period. We have already noted the Japanese invasion late in the sixteenth century. In response, the Koreans can lay claim to having developed the first ironclad "turtle" ships, which they used to ram Japanese vessels. They also developed a multiple rocket launcher, the *hwacha*, used against the Japanese forces with maximum effectiveness. At the battle of Haengju (1593), 3,400 Koreans defeated 30,000 Japanese samurai with the aid of forty hwachas.[35]

Even so, the conflict was devastating for Korea. About two million people lost their lives and agricultural production did not return to preinvasion levels for at least a century. In response, the monarchy attempted to protect the state by isolating it from its neighbors.

Relations with China also contributed to the isolationistic trend. When the Manchus took over in the early seventeenth century, Korea remained faithful to the Ming, which led to a Manchu invasion in 1627, followed by a second ten years later. As a result, Korea was restored to its tributary relationship with the Qing much as had been the case under the Ming, but, like many Han Chinese, the Koreans considered the Qing as barbarians and even came to see themselves as the last bastion of true Confucianism in the world. Also, they kept the Ming calendar and refused to adopt the Manchu style of dress and hairstyle.

Part of the reason Korea remained isolated was a lack of navigable rivers, which made commerce difficult (See Figure 4.8). The Koreans' Neo-Confucian positions, with its disdain for merchants and commerce, encouraged these tendencies as well.

Yet, Chosŏn Korean was not totally cut off from the outside world. In the seventeenth century, tobacco from the New World was introduced, and it is impossible to think of Korean cuisine today without thinking of chili peppers, also introduced from the West. In addition, from China came clocks and telescopes. And eventually, also via China, came converts to Christianity, which spread rapidly throughout the peninsula.

Late in the nineteenth century, Korea began to feel pressure from Europeans and Americans to open its doors to trade. Unlike the Japanese and even the Chinese, the Koreans were successful in keeping the unwelcomed foreigners out until late in the nineteenth century. There were some calls for reform (the school of "practical learning," as it was called) but they were to no avail. The Yangban were convinced their Confucian-based society could withstand all outside pressures and remain unchanged into the future. In a later chapter we will see how Korea was finally forced to make changes.

VIETNAM

The attitude of the Vietnamese toward China was radically different from that of the Koreans. As there is no natural border between China and Vietnam, for nearly a millennium (from the Han dynasty until the early Song) the two were effectively one state. It is not that the Vietnamese happily accepted this situation, but not until the second Song emperor decided that the costs were too great were the Vietnamese allowed to become an independent, if tributary, state.

---

35   See an interesting article at https://en.wikipedia.org/wiki/Hwacha.

All the same, the Vietnamese found national unity very difficult to achieve, partly because it was divided into three regions: Tonkin, around what is today Hanoi; Annam, around Hue; and Cochin China, around Saigon. The problem was made more difficult because as the Vietnamese moved into Annam and Cochin China, they encountered ethnically different peoples from themselves, in particular Khmers, Chams, and Malays, some of whom were Muslims. While a more or less powerless monarch resided in Hanoi, the princes who ruled over Annam and Tonkin were the effective rulers of these areas.

In the 1770s, a peasant uprising ultimately led to national unity under the Nguyen family that was Annamese, aided by French Catholic missionaries. The unified state resembled Qing China more than Chosŏn Korea. Chinese-style Confucian bureaucrats (mandarins) who successfully completed the civil service exams were selected for bureaucratic positions. This strong emphasis of Confucian principles created some discord, especially among the Christians and Buddhists. And, as we will see in a later chapter, Vietnam was easily absorbed into the expanding French empire in the nineteenth century.

BUDDHIST KINGDOMS

The last area we need to cite in this chapter is generally referred to, along with Vietnam, as "Southeast Asia," to distinguish it not only from China and Japan, which we have examined, but also India, which we will look at in the next chapter (Figure 4.9). The descriptor "Buddhist" is useful because these areas are not as heavily indebted to China (not Confucian, in other words) as those we have discussed above, and their dominant religion is Theravada Buddhism.[36] The particular states involved here include: Cambodia, Laos, Thailand, and Burma. It also includes the islands of the Malay Peninsula, some of which are Muslim and Christian. These states include Malesia, Indonesia, and the Philippines (See Figure 4.10).

To the Vietnamese, because their southern neighbors failed to embrace Confucian principles in their government and life, they were semi-civilized. In the early modern period, before Europeans took them over, the two dominant states were Vietnam and Thailand, both of which vied for control of their Khmer and Laotian neighbors who maintained a semi-independent status by playing one off against the other.

Burma was a similar state that survived primarily on military expansion against its neighbors. By the early modern period, having failed to expand in the direction of Thailand, it redirected its efforts toward India, in particular British-ruled Bengal. None of these states was sophisticated enough to withstand the onslaught of Western powers that it faced in the nineteenth century, as we shall see in a later chapter.

Most of these produced rice as their primary agricultural product. Some practiced slash-and-burn agricultural technologies. Settlements were small, and towns were few.

Also part of Southeast Asia is the area encompassing Malesia, Indonesia, and the Philippines.

We had occasion to mention these areas when we examined European expansion in the previous chapter. The Portuguese, followed by the Spanish and then the Dutch, sought to control areas to allow them access to the spice trade. The Dutch, who were interested in trade and not conversion, and so did not attempt to interfere in the ways of life of the peoples in these areas with whom they traded,

---

36   This sect of Buddhism sees itself as true to the original, non-theistic version of the religion. It accepts only the Pali scriptures. To learn more see: http://www.accesstoinsight.org/theravada.html.
37   https://en.wikipedia.org/wiki/Ayutthaya_Kingdom

emerged victorious in this contest, until later expelled by the British. Nor were Chinese junks totally driven from these waters by the superior armed ships of the Europeans. The strongest impact in the area was in the Philippines, which the Spanish conquered, colonized, and in time largely Christianized. In truth, as the number of Spanish was small, the degree of conversion and social transformation went slowly.

We have also noted the tendency of Western scholars to incorrectly suggest that, by the early modern period, Europeans were in the driver's seat of world trade. European traders were welcomed as they paid for what they bought with precious metals, especially silver. And until the nineteenth century, Europeans had accepted their subordinate status, which gave local rulers no reason to suspect their states might be in danger from these foreign businessmen.

This chapter has looked at a number of what are generally termed "late-traditional states." They clearly are not heavily influenced by the tendencies we have

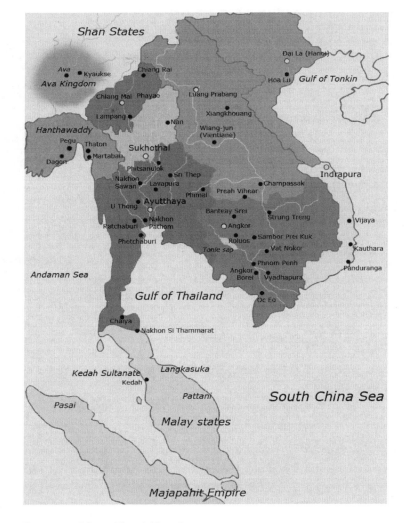

Figure 4.9: Map of South East Asia

described in earlier chapters as "modern." They also do not seem to have suffered for not being such. On the contrary, there are many things about their ways of life that are appealing to many of these peoples in the twenty-first century. Throughout the chapter, we have also tried to convey something of a sense of foreboding since by the nineteenth century these states will fall under European and American domination, their living standards will decline, and their life expectancies will be reduced. We will see how this transpired in later chapters. The purpose of this chapter was to describe just how functional these peoples, with their various ways of life and social and religious systems, were. It does not change the degree of the tragedy that will befall them. But it does make the process through which it occurred all the more interesting.

We have to look at another group of late-traditional societies before we can move on to the nineteenth century and that question. They are Muslim empires and we will look at them in Chapter 5.

38   https://en.wikipedia.org/wiki/Geography_of_Indonesia

Figure 4.10: Map of South East Asia[40]

FOR FURTHER READING

Charles A. Desnoyers. *Patterns of Modern Chinese History*. New York: Oxford University Press, 2017.

Patricia Ebrey, Anne Walthall and James B. Palais. *East Asia: A Cultural, Social, and Political History*. New York: Houghton Mifflin Company, 2006.

Andre Gunder Frank. *ReOrient. Global Economy in the Asian Age*. Berkley: University of California Press, 1998.

Charles Holcombe. *A History of East Asia*. New York: Cambridge University Press, 2011.

John H. Miller. *Modern East Asia: An Introductory History*. New York: Routledge, 2015.

W. Scott Morton and J. Kenneth Olenik. *Japan: Its History and Culture*. New York: McGraw Hill, 2005.

Paul S. Ropp. *China in World History*. New York: Oxford University Press, 2010.

Immanuel Wallerstein. *The Modern World-System II*. Berkeley: University of California Press, 1980.

COPYRIGHTED MATERIAL — DO NOT DUPLICATE, DISTRIBUTE, OR POST

CHAPTER
FIVE

Three Muslim Empires in the Early Modern Period

INTRODUCTION

Chapter 5 continues our examination of traditional states in the early modern period. As in the previous chapter, our objective will not be to explain how these empires were ultimately taken over by the West; instead, we want to understand how they worked well for as long as they did. No sociopolitical system in history has proven to be immortal. Judged against the record of past world empires, these three enjoyed pretty good runs.

The empires under consideration in this chapter—the Ottoman Turks, the Mughals in India, and the Safavids in Iran—had one thing in common: they were Muslim. Accordingly, we will begin with a discussion of Islam, followed by a brief sketch of its history from its beginnings to the early modern period. Just as you cannot hope to understand modern European history without some knowledge of Christianity and the Middle Ages, you cannot hope to understand these empires without some knowledge of Islam and its role in shaping their pasts. With this background in mind, we will examine the developments in each empire in the early modern period. We will conclude the chapter with a preliminary examination of why these, and most of the East Asian societies we discussed in Chapter 4, fell under European control in the nineteenth century.

ISLAM AS A BELIEF SYSTEM

Islam is the youngest of the world's major religions. It burst upon the world stage in the early seventh century in Mecca. A forty-year-old Arab merchant and mystic, Muhammad Ibn Abdullah, began preaching the simple message "There is no God but God." Mecca, a bustling center of commerce,

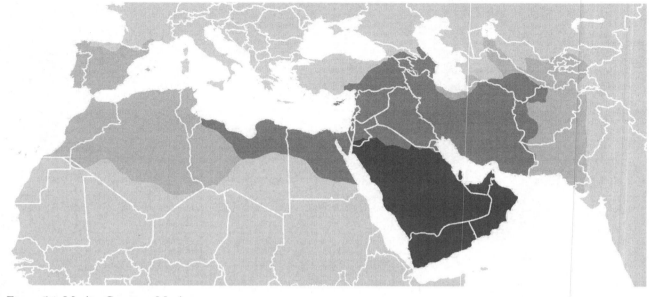

Figure 5.1: Muslim Conquest Map[1]

was also a major religious hub of polytheistic worship centered around the Ka'aba, or "black stone," a meteorite. Muhammad's monotheism, which he saw as the restoration of the beliefs of Abraham, led him to attack the city's existing political and religious leaders, the Quraysh, for teaching false religion. In 622, they responded by attempting to kill him. He and some of his followers fled to *Yathrib*, which quickly came to be called Medina. This flight, the *Hijra*, as it is known, marks the beginning of the Muslim calendar and, therefore, of the establishment of the new religion.

From Medina, Muhammad built up a following, and in 630, following a series of battles with the Quraysh, he returned to Mecca in triumph, destroyed the idols in the Ka'aba, and made this city the center of the new religion, although he remained in Medina for the rest of his life.

Thereafter, Islam spread rapidly, as the map that covers the period 622–750, suggests (See Figure 5.1).

The areas listed include the Levant, Mesopotamia, Persia, North Africa, Iberia, Transoxiana, the Sindh (in northern India), and the Caucasus. Not everyone in these regions became a follower, nor were they required to by their conquerors. In fact, a major reason Islam spread so far so quickly was that Muslims were quite prepared to leave such peoples to follow whatever religious views they wished so long as they paid the *jizya*, a poll tax levied on nonbelievers, while Christians persecuted fellow Christians with different religious viewpoints (heretics) and all non-Christians. Over the next several centuries, most of the people in these areas embraced Islam; in part because it seemed to be the true religion, since it kept on expanding; in part because the tax on Muslims was lower than the tax on non-Muslims; and also because non-Muslims enjoyed a lower social status than Muslims in their societies. It was not, however, a matter of convert or die, as was true of Christianity at this time.

Islam is not a complex religion. First, the word "Islam" means "submission"—submission to the will of God (*Allah* in Arabic). A Muslim is someone who submits and follows the will of God as explained in the *Qur'an*, the Muslim sacred text, which Muslims believed to have been given by God to Muhammad

---

1   https://en.wikipedia.org/wiki/Early_Muslim_conquests

through the angel Gabriel. Christians were prepared to create a written language for converts who lacked one—the Cyrillic alphabet, for example—but Muslims were, and still are, expected to learn to read—or better still, to memorize—this seventh-century Arabic document. No translation is considered to be equal to the Arabic text. This is because, for Muslims, the Qur'an is the exact word of God, and Arabic presumably is the language of heaven. To be sure, Jews of that day assumed it was Hebrew, while Christians thought it was either Greek or Latin.

Five Pillars of Islam

The basic beliefs you find in the Qur'an, the "Five Pillars" as they are called, are not theologically complex. Indeed, they are more about how to practice religion than what religion means.

Sahada is first. It is simply the assertion that "There is no god but God and Muhammad is his prophet." One who makes this assertion in a public place is considered to be a Muslim.

In addition, the faithful are to practice *salat*, praying five times daily and attending congregational prayers on Friday.

As Muhammad had been an orphan and knew the hand of poverty growing up, he was always sympathetic to the plight of the poor, widows, and orphans; therefore, zakat, giving alms to the poor, was a necessity if one expected to make it to paradise. How much one gave was a function of his means.

Jews and Christians alike practice fasting at certain times of the year. The Qur'an designated the month of Ramadan, the ninth month of the Muslim lunar calendar, as a period of daylight-to-dawn abstention from eating or drinking for Muslims. After dark, one can break the fast, and the end of Ramadan is celebrated with a major feast, the *Eid*.

Finally, there is the *hajj*, an injunction if at all possible to make a pilgrimage to Mecca during the second week of *Dhu'l-Hijja*, the twelfth month of the Muslim calendar, at least once in one's lifetime. If one simply is too poor, that relieves him of the obligation. Devout Muslims, from the beginning to the present, want to make this journey, which goes a long way toward promoting a sense of community among believers who come speaking many languages and following many variations of the basic religious system.

Certain dietary restrictions were also enjoined by the Qur'an, including the abstention from consuming alcoholic beverages and pork.

The Qur'an reflects the influence of Judaism and, to a lesser extent, Christianity on Muhammad. The Qur'an includes a number of stories from the *Torah* familiar to Christians and Jews. Abraham is the common father to all three religions. It was he who built the Kaaba, remembrance of which is the reason for the hajj. Muhammad also honored a number of Jewish prophets, along with Arab ones not part of the Judeo-Christian tradition. Jesus is also a prophet, second only to Muhammad. The Qur'an accepts his Virgin Birth to Mary (also a highly honored figure), while insisting Jesus was not, nor did he claim to be, God. "God has no sons" is repeated a number of times in the text.

For Muslims, God had sent prophets to all peoples—Abraham and Moses to the Jews, and Jesus to the Gentiles. Muhammad was the special prophet God had sent to the Arabs. Although Muhammad was the greatest and the last of the prophets, according to Muslims, he was only a prophet.

The Qur'an suggests there will be a judgment when all are held accountable to God for their lives and actions. Those who are faithful will go to paradise, which is a rather sensual place, while those who are not faithful will go to a hell of fire and brimstone.

Although not one of the Pillars of Islam, the obligation to *jihad* has played an important role in its history and continues to do so today. It is often translated "holy war" but more accurately means "struggle." It is used in three ways. First, a personal struggle to live up to the demands of the Qur'an to lead a moral and righteous life is a jihad and applies to all Muslims.

Second, it is an obligation on some Muslims to expand the areas in the world under Muslim control through conquest. The Qur'an divides the world into two regions, the *Dar-al-Islam* (house of Islam) where the Qur'an is honored through law (*Sharia*) and peace is possible, and the *Dar-al-Harb* (house of war) where no peace is possible since the Qur'an is not honored.

Like Christianity at this time, Islam was an evangelistic religion. At the same time, the Qur'an forbade forced conversions. In particular, monotheists, Christians, and Jews, who were the "people of the book," were only required to submit to the rule of Islam and pay the jizya, a poll tax somewhat higher than the *zakat* required of Muslims to live peacefully in the Dar-al-Islam.

Muslims were less sympathetic where polytheists, "idolaters," as the Qur'an called them, were concerned. Here Muslims read the Qur'an as requiring such peoples must either convert or die. Not all Muslims followed this interpretation, as we shall see when we discuss the Mughals of India whose subject people were mostly Hindus.

A third meaning of jihad has to do with maintaining the purity of the Dar-al-Islam. If, for example, a ruler does not live up to the requirements of the faith, a jihad against him was possible. Anwar Sadat, the president of Egypt, was murdered because he made peace with Israel, which seemed to those who murdered him to be called for by the Qur'an as Sadat had diminished the house of Islam. Also, if non-Muslims attempt to take over part of the House of Islam, Muslims are expected to rise up in defense of these areas. Our recent invasion of Iraq was widely seen as requiring jihad for that reason.

Some, like ISIS or al-Qaeda today, regard jihad as a "Sixth Pillar" of Islam. That interpretation goes back to the earliest days of Islam and the Kharijis, of whom more is addressed below. All people, they say, are called upon to take up the sword. Other Muslims believe only certain religious leaders may declare a jihad, and everyone is not expected to take up the sword, only to support those who do. Osama bin Laden, because of his piety, was selected by his father, who had more than fifty sons, to be the member of his family to assume that obligation. The rest continued with their secular and commercially profitable lives.

Who may declare a jihad is a matter of some dispute. Over time, different answers have been advanced. Some maintain only religious leaders are qualified to do so; others allow anyone who is righteous to do it.

One other Islamic practice should be mentioned: the *fatwa*. This is a legal opinion regarding correct and incorrect behavior. It is generally issued by a recognized religious leader or imam, and once pronounced can only be rescinded by the one who pronounced it. The influence a fatwa carries is wholly dependent upon the reputation of the person announcing it. As with jihad, who can pronounce a fatwa is unclear.

Finally, if someone who is Muslim renounces his faith, he or she becomes an apostate. This is taken very seriously and many Muslims believe such a person is worthy of death.

Islam is often said to be a theocracy. The Qur'an is certainly the basis of law in traditional Muslim states today, as well as all Muslim states before the modern period. Rule through the Qur'an, in practice, led to the development of Sharia law (meaning "way" or "path"), which is interpreted through four schools of law. What this means in practice is that being Muslim involves more than having a particular set of religious beliefs. It also means living in a particular type of community structured around those beliefs, and conforming one's behavior to them. In short, family life, society, and societal obligations are part and parcel of living in a Muslim religious community. The modern notion of separation of church and state has no meaning in a traditional Muslim state.

Christianity is a complex religion, and controversies over theology have divided its adherents since its foundation. Islam is far less complicated; you might have thought it would have been spared the kind of interfaith controversies and bloodshed that have plagued Christianity. But such was not to be the case. While not mainly theological in nature, divisions in Islam have been quite as harmful to Muhammad's desire for a sense of religious community—*ummah*, among Muslims—as any controversies that have plagued Christianity. These divisions began when he died in 732, and resulted in the three-way split in Islam that is with us still.

BRIEF HISTORY OF ISLAM

Muhammad died after a short illness. As a result, his followers were ill-prepared to deal with who should be his successor *(caliph)*. Four early followers were especially close to the prophet. The youngest of the four, Ali, was also Muhammed's nephew and son-in-law.[2] These four became the earliest leaders. Many Muslims refer to them as "the rightly guided ones," and regard this as the golden age of Islam. They became the *Sunni*, "followers of tradition." There was a minority, however, who thought only Ali, the blood-relation of the prophet, could be Muhammad's rightful successor. These supporters of Ali come to be known as the *Shi'i* (also *Shi'a* and *Shi'tes*), meaning Ali's party.

This dispute over who should succeed Muhammad led to a civil war and the beginning of the Sunni-Shi'i division we know today. It began after Ali became caliph in 656. The relatives of his predecessor, Uthman, who had been murdered, and fearing they would lose power and influence now that Ali was in control, rose in rebellion. After several bloody encounters, Ali was persuaded to negotiate with the leader of the rebellion, Mu'awiya, further dividing the community. A small group of Ali's supporters regarded negotiating with such an unworthy man to be a betrayal of true religion. They therefore disassociated themselves from Ali and became the *Kharijis*, "the ones who went out." To them, only the most religiously pure should be the successor. Nothing else mattered, and by negotiating with Mu'awiya instead of killing him, Ali had forfeited his right to be caliph, as well. One of their number subsequently murdered Ali. The mind-set of the Kharijis is the third division in Islam. Anyone who does not adhere to strict Islamic practices as they construe them is an "apostate" and should be executed. Never a very large group, the Kharijis reappear throughout Islamic history up to the present.[3]

---

2   Ali was married to Muhammad's daughter Fatimah. She became important to Egyptian history later.
3   Some scholars have noted a similarity between them and the current ISIS movement, struggling to reestablish the caliphate in Syria.

There is one other group that should be mentioned at this point. All of the groups cited thus far have one thing in common, which reflects the Jewish influence upon Muhammad. Right religion is a matter of following a prescribed set of rules found in scripture. God is the source of these rules and the judge of men where they are concerned. But God is not a being one could feel especially close to. After all, God is totally "other" (i.e., in no way human). There were Christians who viewed the Trinity in a similar fashion. But for some this rather impersonal God is unsatisfactory. One thinks of the Kabbalah in Jewish thought and of Christian mystics such as Saint Bernard of Clairveaux, or Saint Francis of Assisi in Christianity. In Islam, these people are known as *Sufi,* from the Arabic for "wool," from which many made their clothes. Sufis appear early in the eighth century and are a vital part of Muslim life today. While their practices and rituals are varied,[4] the underlying uniformity is their insistence that one should encounter God personally. Unlike Christian mystics who tended to be ascetics insisting upon chastity and poverty, Sufis worked in the world, married, and had families. At times, their personal quest for God put them at odds with established religious authorities, and when it caused them to stray too far from orthodoxy, they were persecuted, and even put to death.

Many Sufis traveled about the world as merchants, spreading their teaching to non-Muslims whose existing religious ideas they sought to accommodate to this personal God they worshipped. As with Christian monks, Sufi mystics did more to spread Islam than any other group of Muslims.

We have addressed four distinct religious expressions of Islam. This does not begin to exhaust the list, but does give you some idea of the diversity within the religion in the past, as well as in the present. As we proceed, we will encounter other groups.

The Umayyad Dynasty

Following Ali's death, Mu'awiya quickly established himself as the caliph and went a step further than his predecessors by establishing the first Muslim dynasty, the Umayyads, by naming his son to be his successor. He also moved the capital to Damascus in Syria, which had the effect of emphasizing the Arab nature of the religion. Mu'awiya's dynasty, which lasted until 737, continued the military expansion and institutional development of Islam. But to Shi'is and Kharijies, the days of a pure Islam were at an end. Neither group would accept the legitimacy of the dynasty and resisted it wherever possible.

The Abbasid Dynasty

The Umayyad dynasty was overthrown by the Abbasids. Islam as a religion proclaimed that all Muslims are part of the same umma, or "family." When Islam conquered the Persian world, the tendency to promote Arab over non-Arab Muslims produced resentment, especially among the Persian aristocrats whose civilization was far more ancient than that of the Arabs. Their resentments dovetailed nicely with those of the Shi'is. Taking up the mantle of Shi'ism, claiming their founder Abu Muslim descended

---

4   The most celebrated in the Western imagination are the "whirling dervishes," who arose in fourteenth-century Turkey.

from an uncle of Muhammad's, they succeeded in rallying support from around the Muslim world and overthrew the Umayyads, all but one of whom were killed. The Abbasids quickly became Sunni, since the great majority of their subjects followed this sect. But once the transfer of power was accomplished, Persian influences began to enter the Muslim world and, at least until the twelfth century, this caliphate was strong. Islam was at its zenith during the first several hundred years of the caliphate's reign. Europe, by contrast, was reeling from new invasions, not only from Islam, but also from the Vikings and Magyars. Islam was going from strength to strength. It was never defeated. Clearly, in the view of Muslims, God was on their side. Along with China, the Abbasid dynasty was the economic center of the world. Today, Muslims look back on this era as their golden age and sometimes ask, "What went wrong afterward?"

The Abbasid era was also a time of intellectual vigor. The caliphs promoted learning and established schools, especially in Baghdad. A number of philosophers, whose ideas were very influential in Europe during the High Middle Ages, lived and worked under the aegis of the Abbasid court. Also, because Islam was centrally situated between east and west, Muslim merchants and missionaries traveled not only to Africa, but also to India and China, picking up ideas from these areas and disseminating them in other regions where they traveled. Our numbers are called "Arabic numerals." Muslim merchants learned them from traveling to India, where they were invented, and spread their use, along with algebra, eventually even to the West. Additionally, scientific studies in astronomy, chemistry, and medicine flourished. Literature and art also flourished as well, as did Greek philosophical ideas, especially those of Aristotle.

But the Abbasids were never the unrivaled successors to the prophet among all Muslims. From the beginning, there was one area not under Abbasid control: Spain (*Al-Andalus*). Established in 750 by the Emir (prince) Abd al-Raman (the Umayyad who got away), this emirate would survive until Isabella of Spain drove the last Muslims out in 1492. It was, for much of this time, a remarkable center of culture and learning, art, and literature. The Muslim court at Cordoba, its capital, influenced the cultural life of Western Europe far more than did the court at Baghdad.

The Fatimids of Egypt

The Fatimids, a Shi'i rival caliphate, arose in Egypt in the tenth century. They founded the city of Cairo, which became the center of an international trade network that ranged from India and China to the Byzantine Empire and Italian city-states. Most of the Egyptian people remained Sunni, and, until the early eleventh century, the Fatimids tolerated not only this rival Islamic sect, but Christians and Jews as well. In 1010, however, a brutal caliph, Al-Hakim, reversed these policies and even destroyed the Church of the Holy Sepulcher in Jerusalem, one of the reasons for the Crusades later in the century. One night in February 1021, al-Hakim went out for a walk and disappeared, never to be seen again. Presumably he was murdered, but to many of his contemporaries, he was "occulting"—i.e., he became a divine being who would reappear at some future point. This belief system survives today in the Druze religious communities in Syria, Israel, and Lebanon.

The Muslim World Disrupted

In short, the dream of a unitary Islamic world gave way to three rather secular states each claiming the prophet's mantle. As this reality set in, an additional series of setbacks beset the Muslim world. The first, the Crusades, was more an annoyance than anything else. The second, the Mongol invasions begun by Genghis Kahn in 1219, were devastating. Both were upsetting because they played havoc with Muslims' understanding of their world. Since their faith had begun, they had been victorious in battle. Islam had been expanding, and even if the long-sought unity eluded them, the expansion of their numbers had been steady and unceasing. Now that too seemed to be slipping away from them.

Crusades

The Crusades were a result of many factors in Europe and the Muslim world. In particular, a new power, the Seljuk Turks, had intruded itself into both the Abbasid and Byzantine areas of influence. They took over Baghdad in 1055 and defeated the Byzantines at the Battle of Manzikert in 1071. Thoroughly alarmed, the Byzantine emperor appealed to the West for assistance. In 1095, Pope Urban II responded by calling for what became the first of nine Crusades against Muslims in the Holy Land. While the Second Crusade succeeded in taking over Jerusalem and establishing a series of Crusader states in the Middle East, a Muslim counterattack led by Saladin, late in the twelfth century, brought much of the area, including Jerusalem, back under Muslim control. Saladin also ended the Shi'i Fatimid rule in Egypt.

Mongol Invasions

The Mongol invasion was far more disruptive. An Arab historian, Ibn al-Athir (1160–1233), described it as "the greatest calamity that had befallen mankind."[5] The Muslim world did not feel the full effect of the Mongol conquerors until 1255 when Hulegu Khan, a grandson of Genghis, was dispatched by his brother to add Muslim lands to their empire. The effort was successful and, by 1258, Baghdad was taken over with the accompanying loss of eighty thousand lives, including the caliph's. Afterward, Hulegu established his empire in Azerbaijan before moving on to conquer Syria and then southern Palestine. He was headed for Egypt when news his brother had died forced him to go home to secure his succession. He never returned.

At this point, help came from an unexpected quarter, the Mamluks, slave soldiers recruited from throughout the region, converted to Islam when necessary and trained as elite forces. In the midst of the disorder that resulted from Hulegu's invasion following his return to Mongolia, one of these Mamluks, Baybar (1223–1277), defeated the Mongol army and reestablished the Abbasid caliphate in Cairo under the uncle of the murdered caliph. In truth, the caliph and his successors became figureheads, answerable to the Baybar sultans who ruled Egypt for two hundred fifty years.

In the fourteenth century, the Asian Steppe disgorged yet another world conqueror, Timur the Lame, or Tamerlane as he is known in the West. At its height it stretched from southern Russia across Persia and

---

5   Hill and Awde, p. 99

what is today Afghanistan all the way to China. Along the way, he invaded India and sacked Delhi. He is perhaps best remembered for his pyramid of skulls and the smoking ruins of cities he destroyed. His death prevented his armies from invading China and his empire collapsed, almost as quickly as it had risen. His heirs, the Timurids, became scholars, patrons of artists, and manuscript collectors. Indeed, among them is Babur, whom, as we shall see next, founded the Mughal dynasty in India.

With this brief survey of Islamic beliefs and history before the early modern period, we should be in a position to understand the three late-traditional empires that shaped the Muslim world from the fifteenth to the nineteenth centuries.

THE OTTOMAN TURKS

The Ottoman Turkish Empire was erected out of the ruins of the Byzantine Empire it conquered in 1453. It was a "gunpowder empire." The walls of Constantinople, which had previously been impenetrable, were destroyed by Ottoman canons.

The Ottoman use of firearms and cannons largely accounts for its military invincibility for the next several centuries thereafter; indeed, the Ottomans continued to expand, almost without ceasing, for three hundred years. In the early modern period, Europeans feared them as the most imminent threat from a resurgent Islam. Christians, whose territory bordered on the Ottoman Empire, came to fear that they too might share the fate of their fellow believers in the Balkans and Greece, not to mention Hungary. On two occasions (1529 and 1683), the Turks besieged Vienna; it seemed all of Austria might be lost to them. The Safavids of Persia, Shia Muslims, also learned, to their dismay, that swords and cavalry men were no match for well-armed Turkish infantry with their rifles and canons.

Like all empires, the Ottomans ruled over many ethnic groups with different, languages, customs, and religions. The Ottomans were Sunni Muslims and considered their sultan worthy of the title of caliph, although the other Muslim empires we are considering in this chapter did not agree. The peoples they ruled over were not only Turks, but also Kurds, Arabs, Serbs, Greeks, Egyptians, and various groups from North Africa. Many of their subjects were Orthodox Christians, Jews, and other varieties of Muslims, along with a few Roman Catholics and, after the Protestant Reformation, Protestant Christians.

For most of Ottoman history, these subject peoples were not seething with discontent, seeking to gain their independence from their Turkish masters, as came to be true from the nineteenth century on. For four centuries, in fact, the Ottomans brought peace and order to these culturally and religiously diverse areas. Ironically, the Middle East has known very little peace and stability since the Ottoman Empire came to its end after World War I. How did such an empire arise? How did it manage these diverse peoples for so many centuries, and what finally led to its decline and ultimate demise are the questions we want to answer.

Origins

"Turks" first appear in history in Chinese sources from the sixth century BCE, and later in Greek sources. Herodotus mentions them. They were tribal, stateless, nomadic horsemen living in the Asian Steppe, much like the Mongols and other such groups. Originally, their religion was shamanistic, with

Figure 5.2: Map Ottooman Empire[7]

some embracing Manichaeism[6] and some Nestorian Christianity. After the coming of Islam, most became Sunni Muslims. From time to time, these tribal groups would coalesce around a leader, leave their steppe homeland to invade surrounding, more advanced and wealthy areas, and form empires. We have already seen how the emergence of the Seljuk Turks in the eleventh century led to the Crusades. Also recall the Mamluks who came to rule Egypt, and the Uyghurs, who periodically raided China's northern border area, were also Turkic peoples. Later in the chapter, we will look at the Safavids of Iran and the Mughals of India, both of whom have Turkic connections. But for now, we are concerned with the Ottomans.

---

6   Manichaeism is a third-century BCE dualistic religion that grew up in Persia. Life is a struggle between good and bad, light and dark. It is similar to Zoroastrianism. Nestorian Christianity was an early Christian teaching that came to be regarded as heresy because of its idea that Jesus had both a divine and human nature that were distinct and separate (i.e., not coequal and co-eternal). Both religions exist today.

7   https://commons.wikimedia.org/wiki/File:Ottoman_empire.svg

Ottoman legendary history suggests that in the thirteenth century a group of Turks, fleeing the advancing Mongols, migrated out of the Russian steppe region of Khurasan and settled in Anatolia. There, they allied themselves with the Seljuks fighting the Byzantines. In return for their assistance, the Seljuks rewarded them with territory (*iqta'*, rather like a feudal overlordship) in Sogut, in central Turkey. Their name "Ottoman" derives from Osman (r 1280–1326), the leader of this band. Subsequent rulers (sultans) expanded their territory until, by 1453, during the sultanate of Mehmed II (1421–1451), they were able to breach the walls of Constantinople and bring the Byzantine Empire to an end.

Early in the sixteenth century, Selim I (r 1512–1520) conquered Mamluk Egypt, which not only enabled him to end this Shi'i dynasty, but also to add a rich territory to Ottoman control. He further enhanced his prestige by relocating the caliph, a descendant of the Abbasids, from Cairo to Istanbul, along with a casket of holy relics, including Muhammad's mantle and military banner. Finally, their empire now included all the Muslim holy places, including Mecca, Medina, and Jerusalem.

The Ottomans reached the apex of their expansion during the sultanate of Suleiman the Magnificent (r 1520–1566; see Figure 5.2). His conquests included Rhodes and territories in the Balkans that had previously eluded Ottoman control, including Hungary and Belgrade. His siege of Vienna sent shock waves throughout Europe.[8] Twice he defeated the Shi'i Safavids of Iran.

Suleiman's unsuccessful attempt to add Vienna to his empire was not his only sally into European affairs. Very much aware of the danger a unified Europe represented to his empire, the sultan intervened in the religious controversy we know as the "Protestant Reformation" on behalf of the Protestants, to whom he provided financial assistance. The idea was to promote strife and weaken the area. In addition, it was his policy to assist any Muslim state facing European expansion, which, as you may recall, was beginning at this time. For this reason, he resisted Russian expansion into Central Asia and drove the Portuguese navy out of the Red Sea. To someone who believed he had the right to be called the caliph, this was only natural.

The Ottomans called Suleiman *Kanuni*, "law giver." While he could not countermand Sharia law, he did have control of *kanun*, which covered secular legal areas such as criminal law, land tenure, and taxation. After studying the past practices of former sultans, he introduced a unified law code that remained in force until the nineteenth century. In addition, he sought to provide protections for his Christian and Jewish subjects. Serfs from Christian states were known to flee to Ottoman territory because life was better for them there.

Suleiman was also associated with educational reforms, establishing libraries, soup kitchens, and public hospitals.

Late in his life, Suleiman made a decision that brought great harm to his empire. Under the influence of his favorite wife, Hürem, he executed one son and exiled another, both of whom were capable but not her sons. Thereafter, he was succeeded by Hürem's son, Selim II, "the Sot," who, as his sobriquet suggests, was completely incompetent. Almost prophetically, few subsequent sultans were as capable as Suleiman and his nine predecessors had been.

---

8   It seems Vienna was fortunate that cold weather came since the Janissaries, who insisted upon returning to the barracks when the weather turned cold, would no longer fight.

Ottoman Government at its Height

It is unusual for a dynasty to produce ten capable rulers in succession. In part, this phenomenon can be explained by the fact the Sultan's eldest son was not automatically his successor. All worked alongside their father as they grew up, giving him many opportunities to observe what sort of rulers they might make. Unlike Suleiman, the sultans generally chose the most talented son as his successor. To avoid the power struggles that could arise from multiple claimants to the throne, once a new sultan was proclaimed, frequently all his siblings would be executed, strangled with a silken cord. In the cases where the brothers were not executed, they were exiled to distant parts of the empire. Later, the sultan's potential rivals were simply confined for life to the royal residence, Topkapi, with their wives and concubines, in a velvet prison, as it were.

Unlike contemporary Christian rulers who were expelling both Jews and Muslims from Europe, Turkish sultans were only too happy to welcome Christians and Jews into their service. Protestant refugees, in particular, found a welcoming and religiously tolerant place of refuge in Turkey. A number of Jews obtained important positions in the sultans' diplomatic service, in banking, and in finance.

Political and Social Systems

The Ottoman successes during the sixteenth and seventeenth centuries were the result of the political and social systems they put together. All power was given by god to the sultan, but one cannot govern effectively without assistants. His government was, therefore, divided into four branches: the administration, military, a scribal division, and a cultural one. The administration included the palace where the sultan's wives and children resided, along with their servants, and the *divan* or cabinet, which supervised all branches of the Ottoman government and made the day-to-day decisions. The chief administrator over this division was the "grand vizier," who was able to stand in for the sultan himself, either in the divan or on the battlefield.

The bulk of the sultan's army, when the Ottomans came to power, consisted of Turkish warriors, *sipahis*. These were mounted archers who fought with lances, bows and arrows, and who were expected to be ready to serve on a moment's notice. Technically, the sultan's god-given power made him owner of all the lands the Turks conquered. To support these knights, sultans granted them "*timars*," lands as payment for their military services, somewhat like European feudal tenure. At first the sipahis collected goods in kind from the peasants who worked their lands. The sipahis were also expected to use these revenues to support additional knights whom the sultan required. In due course, the in-kind payments were transformed into money. If a sipahi failed to provide the required military service or allowed the peasants under his control to leave their lands, the timar would be taken away from him. Also, at his death, his eldest son only had an expectation to succeed his father. He was not guaranteed the position because of his father's past service, but had to prove himself worthy to succeed upon his father's death.

In the late fourteenth century, the sultan Bayezid I implemented a new way to recruit his soldiers and administrators, the *devshirme* program, or "boy levy." Young Christian boys were levied and taken to Istanbul to be raised as Muslims and trained to serve, either in the sultan's administration, or in the military.

Much like the Mamluk system in Egypt, these boys were well trained and, for a time, thoroughly loyal supporters of the sultan. The soldiers (*Janissaries*) were trained rigorously, using firearms the traditional sipahis would have no part of. The Janissaries lived in barracks and were forbidden to marry until after their training was completed, and then could only marry non-Turkish women who had undergone a similar training. Their children were not eligible to become Janissaries after them.

Janissaries were totally dependent on the sultan for their livelihood, and they were well paid. Indeed, on such occasions, the sultan donned a Janissary uniform and took his place among them to receive his salary. In any event, they had no choice but to be loyal. They could not return to the place of their birth, nor could they integrate into traditional Turkish society. While many Christians resented this levying of their children, some were happy for them to have what they saw as an opportunity for advancement. In some cases, Turks would entrust their children to Christians, in the hope they would be taken into the corps.

Bayezid's objective in creating this slave soldier corps was to provide a counterweight to the aristocratic and potentially divisive sipahi soldiers. In due course, the devshirme corps came to control most of the important administrative and military posts in the Turkish government. By the sixteenth century, the increasing sophistication of firearms, including siege cannons and field artillery, which the Janissaries employed, made the traditional Turkish lancer-mounted-knight tactics of the sipahis obsolete and their numbers slowly declined.

The Ottoman scribal branch was responsible for raising and dispensing the funds necessary to run both the administration and also the military. By the sixteenth century, the timar system, which was not based on the new gunpowder weapons, began to decline. The slaves from the devshirme became more numerous and important in administration and the military, and costlier. To meet those needs, these officials introduced a system of tax farming, the *multezim*. A tax farmer would buy the right to collect taxes in an area of the empire. The right was put out to bid, and the person offering the government the most money got the contract for a set number of years, usually only one or two. He paid these costs to the government in advance or in installments, and then sought to collect that money and more as his profit. Often the multezim had to borrow the money to enter into the enterprise. There were no restrictions on how much he could extract from the peasants. All the same, it was a tricky system for the multezim and the peasants alike. It could lead the tax farmer to gouge the peasants. But peasants could appeal against them in religious courts, or move to other places that offered better terms (they were not serfs or slaves). If for this or any reason the multezim failed to make his payments to the state treasury, he would lose his concession and at times, even face imprisonment.

The empire's revenue also came from other sources. First, a capitation tax was paid by the non-Muslim subject population. Tribute was paid by states such as Wallachia, Moldavia, and the Republic of Ragusa. But most of the state's revenues came from commercial sources, customs duties, harbor taxes, tolls, ferries, and various state-held monopolies on needed products, including salt, soap, and candle wax. The government also generated revenue by leasing the rights to the mining of silver, copper, and lead concessions.

Not surprisingly, the empire continued to exploit its position in the overland trade routes with Asia taken over from the Byzantines. They increased the duties they collected from the Christian merchants, mostly Italians. Over time, more of this trade passed to Christians, especially Greeks and Armenians, and from Jews within the empire rather than to merchants from outside.

Beyond the capital area, the empire was divided into two districts, Anatolia and Rumeli. The first was administered by a governor-general or *beylerbey*, and the second by a "pasha of two tails." Both districts were further subdivided into *sanjaks*, subdistricts under military governors (*beys*), "a pasha of one tail." Their job was to command the sultan's forces, collect taxes, and generally keep order in their districts. At the time of the conquest, there were twenty-six sanjaks in Asia and twenty-eight in Europe. As the empire expanded, these numbers increased.[9]

As noted above, the estates awarded to the sipahis were not generally controlled by the sanjaks, nor did the state benefit from their taxes. Over time, the government let the timars lapse when its holder died, and entered that land into the multezim system.

Administrators in more distant provinces, such as Algeria and Egypt, enjoyed more liberty in how they governed, but were ultimately responsible to the sultan. Janissaries were also stationed in these areas to insure their loyalty.

The *ulema*, Muslim scholars and judges, made up the cultural branch of the Ottoman system. It administered justice and the Islamic charities that supported schools and hospitals, the waqfs. It was also responsible for the education of the young.

Turkish society divided people into the ruling class and those whom they ruled, the *rayah* class. Because of the multiethnic and multireligious nature of the empire, in particular where the rayah class was concerned, it was vital to the success of the state to find a way to exploit these peoples without provoking them into rebellion. The Turks used a system they called the *millet*. Every ethnic/religious group within the empire was treated as a political/religious unit, and governed by members of its own faith in accordance with its own laws and beliefs. The patriarch headed the millet of the Orthodox Christians, while a chief rabbi appointed by the Ottomans looked after Jewish interests. Even Turkish rayah considered themselves to be in a millet. What makes this system unusual is that the sultans allowed their non-Turkish subjects to live in according with their own laws and religious practices, even when in violation of Turkish laws and practices, or the Qur'an. In short, if conquered people paid their taxes and remained peaceful, they were free to live their lives as they wished.

Roman Catholics, and later Protestants, who worked in the empire as resident aliens were not in the millet system but were granted "capitulations" or autonomy from Turkish laws just as if they were. Turkish merchants living in Europe were awarded the same privilege there. The easiest way to understand the system today is to compare it to diplomatic immunity.

OTTOMAN CULTURE

Being an empire of many peoples, languages, and cultures, Turkish culture was influenced by many sources. Turkish poetry was heavily influenced by Persian styles. The "divan" style is a good example. Lyric in nature, it followed carefully prescribed meters and forms inspired by the Persian. The subject matter was often romance.

The Ottoman script is calligraphic in nature and derived from Arabic (See Figure 5.3). It reached the height of its complexity during the reign of Suleiman I.

---

9   Lord Kinross. *The Ottoman Centuries*. New York: Morrow-Quill, 1977, 150ff.

Figure 5.3: Ottoman Caligraphy[10]

The Ottomans also excelled in miniatures, which were unusual in the Muslim world because they depicted human figures (Figure 5.4).

Weaving and tapestry were areas in which Turkish artists excelled. As it was a custom to remove one's shoes when entering a home, carpets to walk on were one outlet for their craft; but in addition, tapestries were popular as wall hangings, which added insulation (Figure 5.5).

Figure 5.4: Miniature[11]

10   http://iosminaret.org/vol-8/issue21/Hasan_Celebi.php

Figure 5.5: Ottoman Tent[12]

The Turks also developed their own distinctive styles in jewelry making, music, and dance.

Ottoman Decline

Late in the seventeenth century, the Ottomans once again besieged Vienna. Very cold weather had saved the city from Suleiman's earlier attack, but this time the superior arms and military tactics of the defenders drove the Turks out, even though the sultan's army greatly outnumbered the defenders.[12] By the end of the conflict, under the terms of the Treaty of Karlowitz, Hungary was ceded to the Hapsburg Empire and the Aegean coast to the Venetians. In 1774, the Russians gained control of the Crimea and, also, the right to represent the interests of Turkish Orthodox Christians. By the eighteenth century, fears of the Turkish menace were replaced by concern over what to do about Turkey, the "sick man of Europe." Western powers such as Austria and Russia, but also France and England, began to pick away at its outlying territories. Non-Turkish subjects, under the influence of nationalism, began seeking to establish their own nations independent of the Turks. Indeed, as we shall see, Turkish weakness led to acute international instability, the "Eastern Question," as it was called, and even played a role in causing what became World War I. How do we explain this extraordinary change of circumstances?

---

11   http://www.hali.com/news/an-ottoman-tent-from-the-wawel-collection-cracow/
12   There is a well-established tradition in Vienna that among the things the Turks left behind when they retreated were coffee beans. A Viennese who had lived among the Turks as a spy knew what to do with them, and as the story goes, all of Austria was soon drinking coffee.

Scholars point to a number of changing conditions, both within and without the empire, to explain the Ottoman's decline. Many point to weakness at the top. The sultans of later centuries generally were not equal to those first ten. The sultans insisting on commanding the army personally were concerned that if they were attacked from two directions at the same time, it would be difficult to mount a coordinated and effective defense.

While a new sultan no longer strangled his siblings upon assuming office, he and they did grow up in a confined, stultifying atmosphere around the harem, which did not prepare the one who actually became sultan to rule. The Janissaries, until they were eliminated, conspired to keep them in that state. Those who sought to reform the system faced a strong opposition within both the military and also the administration from this quarter. Indeed, one sultan was assassinated to prevent reform from occurring.

As the Janissaries became the *de facto* army, their power and influence increased while their effectiveness as a fighting force decreased. They acquired the right to place their own sons into the system, which led to a relaxation of discipline and a weakening of loyalty to the sultan. Positions in the military came to be based upon family ties and favoritism rather than merit. When the weather turned cold, the Janissaries returned to their barracks until spring! They even gained the right to engage in nonmilitary trades, which distracted them from their training. Late in the empire, it seemed the Janissaries were no longer the sultan's slaves, but he theirs. At a time then when the Ottomans were facing the rise of serious threats, especially from Russia, the Janissaries were no longer the crack defenders of the empire they had been in the past.[13]

By the late sixteenth century, the Ottoman's weapons and tactics were falling behind those being developed in Europe. The officers were accustomed to the old ways of doing things and did not wish to learn new ones, nor risk the effects such changes might have on their power. Earlier, the Turks had overwhelmed their enemies because of the superiority of weaponry and tactics; now they were themselves overwhelmed.

The changing economic situation also played a role. Competition for trade with China from the water routes to the East discovered by the Europeans reduced the volume of trade coming via the "Silk Road," and therefore the Ottoman share of that trade. The flood of cheap silver that was part of this transformation of the world's economy produced inflation in the Middle East, further worsening the Ottoman economic well-being. As the empire's revenues diminished, its taxation system that had been at times vexing, became extortionate and, since the rural population continued to expand, many peasants were too poor to remain on the land and became vagabonds and thieves to survive, making the situation worse.

Faced with these changing circumstances, the ulama became increasingly conservative and resisted, on traditional religious grounds, innovations that might have helped the society, including introduction of the printing press.

The empire's slow decay in the nineteenth century, culminating in its demise following World War I, will be addressed in a later chapter. Yet throughout much of its history, the Ottoman Turkish Empire inspired both respect and fear not only among Europeans but also among the other Muslim empires we are looking at in this chapter. It was a traditional sociopolitical system that worked effectively for an extended period.

---

13   The system came to a violent end in June 1826 when the sultan dissolved it, killing about thirty thousand Janissaries along with their wives and children in the process.

THE SAFAVIDS (1501–1736)

Blocking Ottoman expansion to its east was another Muslim "gunpowder empire," the Safaris (Figure 5.6). Unlike most Muslim states, then and today, the Safavids were Shi'i Muslims. They were also different from their Ottoman neighbors because the Safavids, although Turkic in origin, ruled over subjects who were ethnically mostly Persian, a civilization that underwent a significant revival during the time this dynasty reigned.

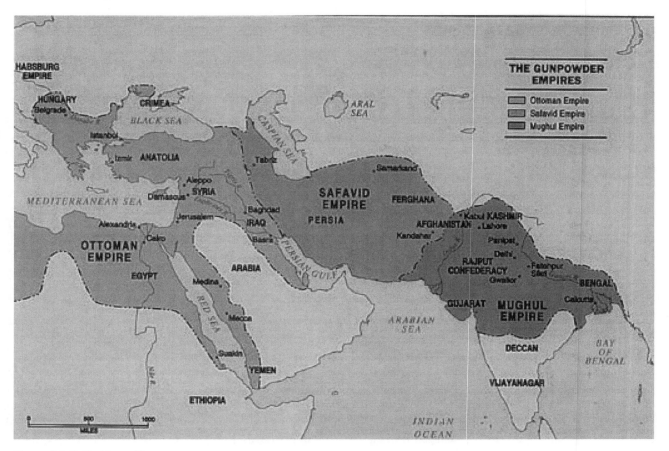

Figure 5.6: Saffavid map[15]

There were also economic reasons for the rivalry between the Ottomans and Safavids. Just as the Ottomans profited from trade coming from the old "Silk Road" in the east, so too did the Safavids. Indeed, the Safavids actively promoted it by encouraging Christians to live and work inside their empire. As the European states became increasingly powerful, the Safavids also sought to build alliances with them, both economic and political, against their common enemy, the Sunni Ottomans. For all these reasons, the Safavids were bitter rivals of the Ottomans and fought with them on a number of occasions in the sixteenth and seventeenth centuries.

ORIGINS

The dynasty gets its name from *Safi al-Din* (1252–1334), a highly revered Sufi mystic, reputed to be able to prophesy and work miracles, who founded an ascetic order of Turkic people. Over time, the followers of the order he founded grew in numbers and power and became militant, fighting "holy wars" against their Christian neighbors in the Caucasus. In the fifteenth century, they underwent their most important transformation by becoming "Twelver Shi'is." What that means and why it is important requires a little explanation.

Twelvers

Perhaps you will recall that shortly after Muhammad died, his movement split into three factions: Sunni, Shi'i, and Kharijies. The "Twelvers" are a branch of the Shi'i faction. To Shi'i generally, the first three caliphs were not legitimate successors of the prophet because they were not descended from him, as was Ali, the fourth, whom they consider the first true caliph, or as they say "imam." They further believe there is always only one imam present on earth to guide people in the way they should go. So, they selected imams just as the Sunnis selected caliphs. Their first split occurred in the mid-eighth century when the fourth imam died, leaving two sons. One, Zaid ibn Ali, was leading a rebellion against the Ummayds, whom he regarded as spiritually unworthy. All the same, it was the other son who became the accepted imam to most Shi'i of the time. The group that supported Zid, unwilling to accept this decision, split off and became the "Fivers." The next split occurred when the sixth imam died and the "Seveners," or *Ismaili* sect, was born. Both these groups survive to this day, although as a tiny minority among the minority Shi'is. The group we are concerned about are the Twelvers, the majority sect among Shi'i. The first appeared in 874, after the eleventh imam died, and was followed by his third son, a child who disappeared, in all likelihood murdered. To Twelver Shi'is, however, he is still very much alive, in a state of "occultation." Only Shi'is believe in occultation, which means the twelfth is invisible to ordinary mortals. You can appreciate why such a concept would make Sunni Muslims uneasy. It certainly seems to weaken the basic monotheism of Islam. Twelvers also believe the "Hidden Imam" will reveal himself again at the end of time when the judgment comes. For this reason he is also called the *Mahdi* or "expected one."

This is the version of Shi'i Islam the Safavids embraced and, to visually express their beliefs, the mystic Safavid soldiers took to wearing a red hat folded into twelve segments, as a result of which they came to be known as the *Qizilbash*, Turkish for "the redheads." Each of the twelve folds symbolized one of the twelve imams they recognized.

Ismail

By the end of the fifteenth century, the Safavids had become a powerful force in western Persia and eastern Turkey. Tamerlane's empire had collapsed and there was political chaos in both areas. Both areas were ruled by Turkish chieftains who were Sunni. Shi'ism had long been identified with resistance to non-Persian foreigners. It was only natural the militant Safavids would link up with the Persians. This led one of the Sunni Turkish groups to attempt to wipe out the Safavids. In 1488, they killed the leader of the group along with his son. His remaining son, Ismail, then only two, was spirited away by his Qizilbash supporters, only a few steps ahead of the would-be assassins. For the next ten years the boy lived in hiding. When he was twelve, he came out of hiding and killed the Turkic Sunnis who had killed his father. At this point a rush of Shi'i supporters joined his cause.

By 1502, when he was fifteen, he declared himself *Shahanshah* of Iran, the "king of kings." This was the title previous Persian kings had given themselves, and by taking it, he was identifying himself not as Turkish, which was his background, but rather as Persian. Furthermore, he claimed to be descended from not only a Sassanid Persian, but from Muhammad's nephew Ali as well. He also proclaimed Twelver Shi'ism to be the official religion of his state. It is worth noting this remains the dominant religion in Iran today.

Ismail suffered a severe setback in 1514 at the hands of the Ottomans. Once he had conquered Iran, he began to propagandize among the Turkish tribes on behalf of his Shi'ism, which enjoyed some support among them. Naturally this did not suit the Turkish sultan, Selim I (1470–1520), and so he invaded and at the battle of Chaldiran, handed the Persian king, who must have thought of himself as invincible by this point, a severe defeat. The Qizilbash thought it very unmanly to fight with guns on horseback. They also looked upon their ruler as a god-protected chosen ruler. Given his history, that should not be hard to understand. But you already know how important guns and cannons were to the Turks; the battle decidedly went in their favor. The Turks occupied Tabriz but left after a week. Fortunately for Ismail, the weather was turning cold and the Janissaries had to return to winter quarter!

The Safavids learned from this experience; by the next year they were prepared to resist by a scorched-earth policy that left the Turks nothing to subsist on. The current border between Turkey and Iran was established as a result. In due course, the Safavids also adopted the use of firearms.

Ismail never recovered from this shattering experience. Many of his wives were captured by Selim and taken away to become consorts of Turkish commanders. Some sources say Ismail spent the rest of his life hunting and drinking, others say writing religious poetry. Whatever, his state gave up trying to export Twelver Shi'ism and turned to becoming prosperous and safe instead.

Shah Abbas I

The high point of the Safavid era came in the reign of Shah Abbas I (1587–1629). Abbas increased the power of the central state, expanded trade and commerce, and promoted culture. Indeed, a genuine Persian cultural renaissance occurred during this period.

GOVERNMENT

Technically, the shah was an absolute ruler. His central government included a number of officials who answered to him directly, e.g., the grand vizier, the finance minister, and the minister of justice. The royal court included other ministers who looked after his wealth, and also his family. These included the *nazir*, or court minister, a "grand steward," and a "minister of the stables." In addition, the shah was advised by a group of physicians and astrologers.

Local government was divided into public lands, and lands of the shah. The public lands were administered by *khans,* the most of whom were Qizilbash. These were given estates on which to live and through which to support the soldiers the shah might require. Over time, especially after Abbas I, the government attempted to convert the system into state-run lands whenever a Qizilbash line ran out.

Not unlike the Turkish Janissaries, Abbas introduced the practice of conscripting Christians to be administrators and soldiers, the *Ghulams.* Unlike the Janissaries, however, not all the Ghulams converted to Islam. The idea was to create competition between the Qizilbash aristocracy and the slave Ghulams, which the shah could use to his advantage in controlling both. Ultimately, as with the Janissaries, the Ghulams came to control the state, especially when it was in decline in the eighteenth century. Also, the autocratic tendencies in the government were at times harmful. Shah Abbas is a good example. Suspicious of everyone, he had his sons either blinded or executed, and was succeeded by a weak grandson, whom, of course, he had not feared.

ECONOMY

Economically, the Safavids were in a location to profit from trade passing between Asia and the West; indeed, the Silk Road enjoyed something of a revival in the sixteenth century. Persian goods moved not only to the West but also to China, and Chinese and Indian goods moved through Persia to the West. Because the Ottomans had taken over most of the traditional overland routes, the Safavids developed a route of their own that took them through the Caspian Sea to Russia, and with the assistance of the Muscovy Company, on to Europe via Poland.

As part of this effort, Abbas also saw that good roads were built thought the empire, along with *caravanserai,* roadside inns where merchants and travelers could rest. These were located at strategic points to ensure the safety and comfort of the merchants and to promote trade. Tolls for their maintenance were collected.

As a part of the expanding trade, especially in silks, the Safavids came to rely upon their Armenian Christian subjects. Shah Abbas's religious tolerance policy was in part promoted for this reason.

CULTURE

The largest centers of Persian culture in Safavid Iran were at Tabriz, Quazin, and Isfahan.[15] The latter became Abbas I's capital in 1598. It was a city of about 600,000 people with 162 mosques, 48 madrasas, hundreds of caravanserai, and 273 public baths.[16]

---

15   Check the city out on the Internet. http://wikitravel.org/en/Isfahan.
16   See Fred James and Nicholas Awde. *A History of the Islamic World. Hippocrene Books, 2003, p149.*

Figure 5.7: Safavid Fresco[18]

Safavid artists excelled in weaving, but also ceramics and textiles (See Figures 5.8 and 5.9). Like the Ottomans, calligraphy was itself an art form, and unlike most Islamic art included excellently executed human figures. Figure 5-7 is an example of a fresco from Shah Abbas palace at Chehel Sotoun.

SAFAVID DECLINE

By the eighteenth century, the Safavid dynasty was in decline and invited invasion. In this case it came from Afghanistan, whose invaders seized Isfahan. Turkey counterattacked to assist, but instead settled for a treaty that gave the Afghan invaders much of northern Persia. This so infuriated the Iranians that they rose in rebellion against both the Afghans and the Turks and eventually drove both out. The leader was perhaps the last great Persian ruler, Nader Afshar Shah, who is 1736 was proclaimed Nadir Shah. His career might have been more long lasting had he not been a Sunni Muslim who tried to convert the Persians to his version of

---

17   https://en.wikipedia.org/wiki/Safavid_art#/media/File:Fresque_chehel_sotoun_esfahan.jpg

Islam. He was assassinated in 1747 and thereafter Iran entered into a protracted period of instability.

MUGHAL INDIA

The third Muslim dynasty we are considering in this chapter is the Mughal. In today's terms, the Mughals ruled over India, Pakistan, Burma, Bangladesh, and Afghanistan, about 20 percent of the world's population at the time. It, too, was a gunpowder empire, and its rulers were Sunni Muslim. India was by far the largest and wealthiest portion of the empire, but its population was mostly Hindu. In the other two Islamic empires we have examined, their non-Muslim subjects were considered "peoples of the book," meaning monotheists. As we have seen, if they accepted Muslim rule and paid the jizya, they could worship as they pleased and both conqueror and conquered could live in peace. But idolaters were another matter. The Qur'an was rather clear idolatry should not be tolerated; idolaters must renounce their idols or be killed. But when the vast majority of the subject peoples were Hindus, as in India, that option clearly presented problems. This factor alone will make the story of the Mughal Empire different from the other two.

Muslim Rule in India before the Mughals

You may recall that by 712 the early expansion of Islam extended to the region of the Sind (in today's Pakistan). No further incursions into India occurred until the tenth century when a Turkic ruler from Afghanistan, Mahmud of Ghazna (971–1030), raided northern India, primarily for plunder. He

Figure 5.8: Safavid Door[19]

Figure 5.9: Ceramic[20]

18   95https://en.wikipedia.org/wiki/Safavid_art#/media/File:D%C3%A9tail_porte_madreseh-echahar_bagh_esfahan.jpg

19   https://en.wikipedia.org/wiki/Safavid_art#/media/File:Plate_pomegranates_Louvre_MAO868.jpg

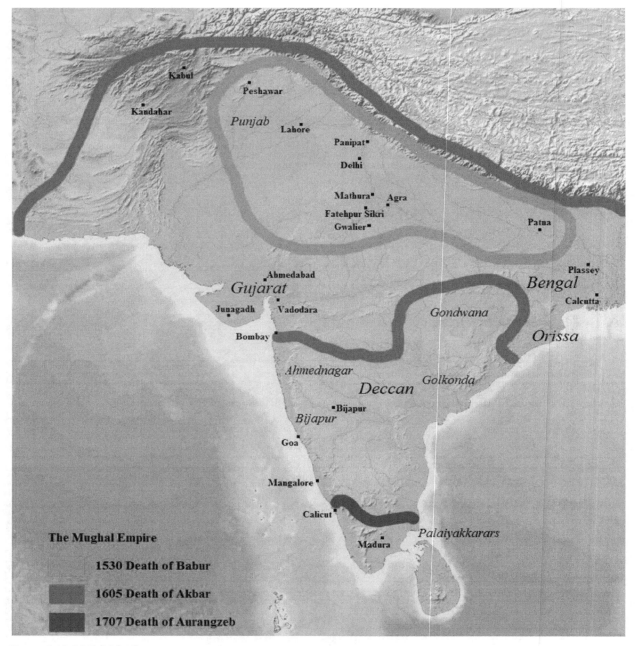

Figure 5.10: Muhal Map[21]

delighted in destroying the cities and slaughtering the people, as they were idolaters. The wealth he took from India enabled him to build Ghazna into a powerful city from which he ruled over part of Iran and in India as far as the Punjab region. Like most Muslim leaders, he patronized the arts, in particular a poet, Firdawsi (940–1020), whose *Book of Kings*, an epic of sixty thousand verses, recounted the history of Persian kings. A great work of art, it was very influential on future Muslim rulers. But Ghazna's empire did not last, and by 1186 it came to an end.

---

20   https://commons.wikimedia.org/wiki/File:Mughal_Historical_Map.png

From this point until the coming of the Mughals, northern India was an unstable area. Successive Turkish rulers, known collectively as the "sultanate of Delhi," rose and fell in rapid succession. We know something about one of these sultans, Muhammad Tughluq (r 1325–1351), because an intrepid traveler and scholar/judge, Ibn Battuta (1304–1368), made his way to Deli where he served as a judge at Tughluq's court. Ibn Battuta described Delhi in these words:

. . . a metropolis of India, a vast and magnificent city, uniting beauty with strength. It is surrounded by a wall that has no equal in the world, and is the largest city in India, nay rather the largest city in the entire Muslim Orient.[21]

Naturally this made the city an attractive target for would-be conquerors and, in 1398, Tamerlane appeared. Like Ghazna before him, he delighted in raping the women, slaughtering the idolaters of both sexes, and burning and looting their cities. As he died soon thereafter, he made no further depredations into India. He did, however, create a dynasty, the Timurids, that would enable his descendant, the Mughal conqueror, Babur (1483–1530), to establish the Mughal Empire.

MUGHAL DYNASTY ESTABLISHED

Babur I (1485–1530)

Babur's father ruled over a small kingdom, Fergana, in modern Uzbekistan. When he died, the throne passed to his twelve-year-old son Babur. Not surprisingly, Babur soon lost Fergana but quickly regrouped, gathering about him loyal supporters of his father and, over the next several years, won and lost Samarqand and Fergana on two occasions. He claimed ancestry from Genghis Khan on his mother's side and Tamerlane on his father's, which ancestral heritage assured him he was destined to rule somewhere. Just where was the question. He finally decided to try his luck in Afghanistan, in particular Kabul. Here he was more successful and this area became his base of operations. In 1504, he was crowned king of Kabul. According to Afghan scholar Tamim Ansary, who grew up in the area, there has always been a fondness for Babur in Afghanistan. His grave in Kabul is a popular shrine.[22]

Giving up returning to the land of his birth, Babur decided to turn south, following in the footsteps of Tamerlane, and try his luck in northern India. In 1526, he invaded India with ten thousand men. His opponent was a Deli sultan with ten times as many soldiers, but Babur had the guns and cannons his opponent lacked. Babur routed the sultan, took possession of Delhi, and declared himself to be the sultan of Delhi and Agra. The Mughal dynasty was established.

Able Successors

For the next two hundred years, six long-lived and mostly capable men would lead the empire. Babur, which means "the tiger," would be succeeded by Humayun (1508–1556), who died of a fall from his

---

21   Hill and Awde, p.155
22   Tamim Ansary. *Destiny Disrupted. A History of the World through Islamic Eyes.* Public Affairs, 2009.

astronomical observatory. (He had a fondness for opium, it seems.) Happily for the empire, his thirteen-year-old son, Akbar (1556–1605), succeeded him. "Akbar" in Arabic means "the Greatest," and he truly lived up to that epithet. He was succeeded by his son, Jahangir, which in Persian means "Conqueror of the World." He was not a very good administrator, but his twentieth and favorite wife, Nur Jahan, was, and between the two of them his reign was successful. He was succeeded by Shah Jahan (1628–58), who in turn was succeeded by his son Aurangzeb (1618–1707). While highly capable militarily and otherwise, it is with Aurangzeb that the decline of the dynasty set in. See Figure 5-10 for map of succession in the Mughal Empire.

While there were succession struggles among rival sibling claimants to the throne between almost every reign, the Mughals did not practice fratricide, as did the Ottomans.

Government and Religion

At first, the Mughals governed as they had done before they came to India. It resembled the Turkish and Safavid practice of granting lands to loyal supporters in return for military service. As we saw in both Iran and Turkey, to counteract the power of these aristocrats, the rulers turned to slave soldiers and administrators. We also saw that over time these, too, came to rival the ruler's authority, quite as seriously as their ethnic nobility. Akbar departed from this tradition. First, he ended the practice of rewarding the aristocracy with land. Instead, salaried officials from the aristocracy were appointed to offices on a yearly basis and moved to another place the following year, if he wished.

Akbar also departed from tradition by turning to Hindu Rajputs, land-holding warriors, for his soldiers as the counterweight to the traditional aristocracy. Most were from pre-conquest families who ruled over regional areas. It was a clever move, politically as well as militarily. As we have seen, earlier conquests of India had been accompanied by the slaughter of idol-worshiping Hindus. With Akbar, this approach changed. He realized he could never have a peaceful rule without religious tolerance. His Muslim soldiers were required to protect all religious shrines, not just Muslim ones. He appointed local upper-caste Rajputs to be his governors and administrators. His revenue minister was a Hindu who was expected to ensure the tax system treated Hindus fairly. Many lower administrative positions were staffed by Hindus. Defeated Rajput chiefs were made local governors or were granted the same privileges granted to Muslim nobles. The overall effect was to create competition between the two groups for Akbar's favor and to create loyalty.

Akbar also ended the jizya tax, forbad the slaughtering of cows in deference to Hindu sensibilities, opposed slavery, and did away with the death penalty for apostasy. Hindu women who married Muslims were allowed to keep their own religion. He even replaced the Muslim lunar calendar with a solar one.

Clearly much that Akbar did ran contrary to the Qur'an. The ulama, "the learned ones," whose job it was to guarantee that society was faithful of its teaching, were especially uncomfortable with many of the changes Akbar introduced. Yet, they did not rebel against him.

Why Akbar made these changes has been explained in several ways. First, it was an expedient move. Only with a policy of toleration could the minority Mughal Muslims expect to govern the overwhelming numbers of their Hindu subjects. Some have pointed to his Hindu wife. But there was more. Akbar had a deep interest in religious questions. He wanted to learn as much about as many religions as he could;

therefore, along with Muslims and Hindus, he brought together Jains[23] and Christians. His basic idea was there was some religious truth in all religions, but no one religion contained it all.

Some of Akbar's religious ideas resemble a movement that began in India shortly before he was born, the Sikhs. In 1499 a mystic, Nanak (1469–1539), announced his new religion, Sikhism, which combined Muslim and Hindu ideas. First, it espoused monotheism, yet neither followed the Qur'an, nor accepted that Muhammad was the final prophet. Nanak also rejected the caste system and religious rituals in both Islam and Hinduism. In some ways, he resembled a Sufi. He was eventually executed, but his movement survived and grew in the Punjab region.

Akbar's religious reform suggested God was one and all-powerful. No one should do harm to anyone, and should follow the example of people who had led exemplary lives, like Muhammad. And, modestly, he suggested himself.

His religion did not cause people to rise up against him. They also did not rush to embrace it; it died with him. It was, after all, neither really Islam nor Hinduism.

Economy

We have already noted that much silver from the New World made its way to China in the early modern period. A lot made its way to India as well. Indian textiles, indigo, and sugar were among the products sold. Since India, like China, has little natural silver, this trade was the major source of metal for its currency.

The most important driver in the Mughal economy was agriculture. The Indian subcontinent had more acres of arable soil than any other landmass of comparable size in the world, and the Mughals controlled almost all of it. Their policies promoted large-scale population growth and urbanization. As a late sixteenth century Mughal administrator put it:

At present there are three thousand and two hundred towns; and one or two or five hundred or a thousand villages appertain to each of these towns … Out of these there are one hundred and twenty great cities, which are now well populated and flourishing.

India was a regional economic giant. It was able to feed its own population and export food as well. Part of the prosperity grew out of the peace that came to India under the Mughals. Roads were built to facilitate commerce as well. In fact, the economic integration included not just Mughal territories but also Ottoman and Safavid ones.

Culture

Muslim rulers, throughout the history of Islam, have felt it a duty to promote culture. They have been interested in the arts, literature, and science. The Mughals, with the exception of Aurangzeb, were no exceptions.

---

23   Jains are a minority religion whose primary practice is avoiding violence to living things. They are never warriors or butchers but often businessmen. Many, in order to get rid of what remains of karma at the end of their lives, starve themselves to death.

Architecture

Because the Mughals were wealthy, their rulers build a number of structures around the north of India. Most of these were tombs that combined Muslim (Turkic and Persian) elements with Indian and Timurid ones. One of the earliest was Humayun's tomb (Figure 5.11).

Originally surrounded by gardens, as time passed those spaces were given over to tombs for later rulers. The architect was Persian and a number of Persian influences are evident.

Figure 5.11: Humayun's tomb[25]

Perhaps the most celebrated architectural work of the Mughals is the Taj Mahal (Figure 5.12), a tomb for Shah Jahan's favorite wife, Mumtaz Mahal, who died after giving birth to her twentieth child! The original plan called for her husband to be buried opposite her, with a reflecting pool in between, but his successor, Aurangzeb, not oriented toward art works, was content to instead bury his father alongside this wife, in the same mausoleum.

---

24   https://commons.wikimedia.org/wiki/File:Humayuns_Tomb_Delhi_31-05-2005_pic2.jpg

Figure 5.12: Taj Mahal[26]

The Taj Mahal was sixteen years in the building. Situated on the banks of the Jumna River, it includes eight formal gardens and a reflecting pool. Shah Jahan himself oversaw its construction.

Poetry

Persian was the literary language of the Mughal elite, as it was of the elite in the other two Muslim empires we have been discussing. Royal patronage encouraged a steady stream of Iranian poets to settle in India, with the result that more Persian poetry was written at the Mughal court than in Safavid Iran itself. Humayun, himself an accomplished poet, used it in preference to his native Turkic. This had the effect of encouraging others to do the same.

One especially popular form, the *ghazal*, was an ode from between four and fourteen couplets written in a variety of rhyme schemes. Its themes were courtly love among the aristocracy, who lamented their

25   https://en.wikipedia.org/wiki/Taj_Mahal

unrequited loves or infatuations, and encounters with their indifferent beloveds. The poet describes the agony of separation and closed with expression of fatalistic resignation. Here is an example:

I wonder what was the place where I was last night,

All around me were half-slaughtered victims of love, tossing about in agony.

There was a nymph-like beloved with cypress-like form and tulip-like face,

Ruthlessly playing havoc with the hearts of the lovers.[26]

A second popular form, the *qasidas*, was panegyric in nature, generally intended to win the support of the aristocratic family to whom the flattery was directed. Western scholars have often referred to the court of England's Elizabeth I as a "nest of singing birds." The same can certainly be said of the Mughal period in Indian history.

Painting

Just as poets drew much inspiration from Persian sources, so did the miniaturists. Geometrical harmony characterizes these paintings. To establish a Mughal atelier, Humayun invited two Safavid artists to work at his court. His son Akbar continued this patronage following his father's death. One example of the resulting style, combining Persian and Indian influences, was "Princes of the House of Temür" (Figure 5.13).

The Mughal conquerors of India never lost their fondness for their ancestral homeland in Afghanistan, nor did they forget their Timurid ancestry. This painting reflects that longing and demonstrates the fusion of two rather different cultures.

Many of the miniatures were used as illustrations in histories of Mughal reigns, and often included figures in distinctive Indian dress or scenes that are recognizably Indian. The resultant tradition combined Iranian technical training with distinctive Mughal themes.

The golden age of Mughal art stretched over seventy-five years from the last two decades of Akbar's reign until Shah Jahan's deposition by his son Aurangzeb, in 1658. In part, it was inspired by competition with the other Muslim courts for prestige; and in part, it grew out of these Mughal

Figure 5.13: House of Timur

26   https://en.wikipedia.org/wiki/Ghazal

rulers' genuine interests and cultural sophistication. There were even Christian symbols in some of Shah Jahangir's commissioned works, as he included among his entourage some Jesuit missionaries. Western art seemed exotic and therefore fascinating.

When Aurangzeb seized his father's throne in 1658, the golden age came to an end. As he took an orthodox Islamic view of painting, royal patronage declined, which encouraged the now unemployed artists to seek work in aristocratic houses throughout the realm. Appropriately, the only work of art left by Aurangzeb was a Sunni legal text he had written.

DECLINE OF THE MUGHALS

In 1739, the Safavid ruler Nadir Shah invaded India, sacked Delhi, looted its treasury, and even hauled away the symbol of Mughal sovereignty, Shah Jahan's peacock throne. How did it happen that this dynasty had fallen so rapidly in the eighty years since Aurangzeb had seized the throne and imprisoned his father, Shah Jahan?

Most scholars place the blame on Aurangzeb. His counterparts in Ottoman Turkey and Safavid Iran, during their nations' declines, fell victim either to the dissolute life of the haram, or to wine and drugs, respectively. He, by contrast, was a vigorous ruler who personally led his armies into battle throughout his reign and added substantial territories to his control. It does not seem to fit the usual explanation for why a state declines. Instead, the main reason for the decline in Aurangzeb's reign was his religious devotion. He followed a strict interpretation of the Qur'an. Not surprisingly, he found many policies and practices of his father, not to mention his earlier ancestors, to be unacceptably un-Islamic. As a result, he revoked many of the measures his predecessors had implemented, which enabled them, although Muslim, to rule over a nation largely composed of Hindus. He reinstated the jizya, and had his forces destroy all new Hindu shrines. All Hindu officials in government were dismissed. He also reinstated the Muslim lunar calendar.

Ultimately, his religious intolerance toward his Hindu subjects led to war with the Rajputs, those semi-autonomous Hindu rulers in the south of India upon whom his predecessors had come to rely as a check against the power of the Mughal aristocracy. The relationship between the Rajputs and the Mughal rulers had always been based upon mutual advantage, and these Hindu princes enjoyed significant power in the regions where they resided. The change in the situation led them to rethink this imperial relationship and, in many cases, simply to withdraw support for the central state and form local areas under their own control and authority. By the eighteenth century, when Mughal power began to decay, many Rajputs openly opposed taxation, raided caravans, and even defeated Mughal commanders.

Aurangzeb's Islamic conservatism was also reflected in his dealings with the Sikhs. Their efforts to create a religious blend of Hinduism and Islam led to the creation of a distinct social order in the Punjab, one of the richest regions in the Mughal India. Akbar had supported their movement. But as early as 1605, hostility between the Mughals and the Sikhs had begun when Jahangir executed the Sikh leader (*guru*) for converting Hindus and Muslims to their new religion. His concern seems to have been more social than religious. But for Aurangzeb, converting Muslims was intolerable on religious grounds. In 1670, he executed the guru for blasphemy. Previously, this religious community had been pacifists. After Aurangzeb's persecution they became a warrior sect in a distinct community, one the Mughals could not control. Even one of Aurangzeb's sons, Akbar, joined them in rebellion against his father for his religious intolerance. Aurangzeb did not create the Sikh problem, but his way of dealing with them clearly acerbated it.

The Rajputs and the Sikhs were not the only challenges to royal authority that Aurangzeb and his successors had to deal with. Equally important were the Marathas, a Hindu subcaste in the mountainous regions of the east-southeast, in the Deccan Peninsula, near what became Bombay under the British.

Spreading into the Deccan Peninsula had been a goal of Mughal rulers since Akbar's reign, a century earlier. During his father's reign, Aurangzeb had brought several local rulers under Mughal control. His efforts in this area were interrupted by the struggle with his father, which led to Shah Jahan's imprisonment and to Aurangzeb's assumption of power. In 1681, he returned to the region, moved the entire court, harem and all, to the area, and never returned to Delhi again.

Subduing the Marathas was the reason for this relocation. They were a politico/religious community not under his control, and they became increasingly stronger during his reign. His principle opponent in the area was Shivaji, a Maratha prince who in 1674 was crowned as an independent Hindu raja, using traditional Hindu rituals. At times, Aurangzeb seemed to bring them under control, but when he died they were still a source of instability in the region and would remain so until the final end of the Mughals.

The Mughal Collapse

Aurangzeb was succeeded by Bahadur Shah (1643–1712), the last of the capable Mughal rulers. While he was capable and had gained experience serving his father before coming to power, he faced the same three major sources of instability his father had faced, and like him was unable to find a way to bring these areas totally under his control. He also continued his father's religiously intolerant and alienating policies. It should also be noted he was sixty-four when his reign began and that he died in 1712, at age seventy. He hardly had time to solve the complex issues he faced.

After Bahadur Shah's death, the situation continued to deteriorate. Subsequent rulers were incapable and usually pawns in the hands of other powers. It was this decayed Mughal state that Nadir Afshar Shah invaded in 1739. From this point on, the situation was irreversible. Increasingly, while still professing their Mughal loyalty, Rajput, Sikh, and Maratha rulers more and more ran their own regions independently.

Political weakness often encourages outsiders to seek their fortunes in such places, and in this case it was not only Nadir Shah who invaded, but after him a series of Afghan princes who wound up fighting with the Marathas, ironically now titular supporters of the Mughal emperors. But the greatest opportunists of them all were the British, in the form of the British East India Company that gradually took over large sections of India in the eighteenth century, until the British government assumed direct control in 1858 as a result of the Sepoy Mutiny and made India "the jewel in the crown."

CONCLUSIONS AND AN HISTORIOGRAPHICAL NOTE

At the end of World War II, all the nations of the world that had been under imperial domination since the nineteenth century, largely the subjects of the last three chapters of this text, regained their independence. The influence on the writing of history was tremendous. History, after all, is an important tool for political control. "Who controls the past controls the future. Who controls the present controls the past," is the way George Orwell expressed it in his novel *1984*. Those assuming power in recently freed states felt the story that had been told about their past by their imperial masters had been falsified to justify imperial rule. Indigenous historians, joined by sympathetic Western ones, set about revising the history to free it from these Eurocentric biases. Consequently, significant changes have occurred, and are continuing to occur. First, increasingly more students are now being exposed to "World Civilization" rather than to "Western Civilization." Even American history is being taught in a less Western-centered manner. This textbook is itself a reflection of that change.

Of more importance, the way history is presented has also changed. In particular, the Eurocentric focus of earlier historical interpretations is being replaced. World historians do not seek to define past civilizations in terms of Western values and beliefs, but in terms of those of the civilizations and cultures they are examining. They recognize, as we have noted in the past three chapters, that non-Western civilizations were viable ways of life; indeed, often far more advanced economically and culturally than were their Western counterparts at the time. They also point out it was access to a cheap and ready source of silver, extracted by forced labor as a result of Western nations' conquests of Latin America in the sixteenth century, rather than any innate superiority in the Western way of life, that gave the West the means to get into the world trade system, at that time dominated by China and, to a lesser degree, India.

But transformation does not stop there. Many world historians seek to bring the West down a bit. They are inclined to suggest that terms such as "traditional," which we are continuing to use, are a holdover from the Eurocentric past. "Modernization" is merely a way to glorify European ways of life, they say, and that most of the modernizing traits attributed to the West were in fact begun in the so-called traditional areas of the world.

The problem with these revisions is there is no getting around the fact that in the nineteenth century, modernized Western nations took over almost the entire world. Japan escaped this fate by becoming modern and joining in the conquests. Somehow, modern states such as England, Spain, Portugal, and France arrived at a place where they were able to impose themselves on the peoples of Africa, Asia, and Latin American, what historians refer to as "imperialism," which we will examine in due course. If the rest of the world, the "traditional" world, was the creator of everything modern and not the West, why were they taken over? Clearly, somehow, the West went from being behind to catching up, to taking over, beginning about the mid-eighteenth century and culminating in the mid-nineteenth century.

By contrast, in this text, we use "traditional" to characterize civilizations all over the world before modernization occurs. Modernization came first to Western Europe, beginning in the seventeenth century, which we have traced in earlier chapters of this text. We are claiming it was becoming modern that gave the West the edge enabling it to conquer the world in the nineteenth century. We are decidedly not claiming any sort of innate superiority for Europeans or Americans. Furthermore, we recognize there long existed many modernist-looking components in traditionalist societies around the world before all the elements came together in Western Europe, including the civilizations in medieval Europe itself.

There are also elements of capitalism in China, and Chinese scientists made sophisticated scientific and technological discoveries well ahead of their Western counterparts. But China did not become a modern capitalist state. Its scientists did not center the sun in our solar system, nor did they create scientific, political, or economic systems based on the notion that, like the universe, these studies must be examined in materialistic terms. The modern nation-state, which defines most states today, is itself a Western invention that only came to fruition in the late eighteenth century. There were no precursors in any of the states we have discussed in the last three chapters, just as there are none in Europe.

Some historians have attempted to explain the West's taking over the world in the nineteenth century by suggesting actions they engaged in while they were still weak were responsible. Others suggest history moves in long, centuries-long cycles, and the West was fortunate to be ready to take over when the rest of the world was in a down part of a cycle. These areas, such as China and India and the Muslim World, had been up the centuries before, when the West was backward. This is certainly an intriguing concept, but it leaves unanswered why the cycles wax and wane, which is surely the important question that needs to be answered if cycles are to explain anything significant about the past.

Most of these historians who are seeking to diminish the importance of the West in the history of the last two hundred years are inclined to think only economic considerations are important. Accordingly, they think all they need do to prove the West played only a minor—and mostly negative—role in the events of the modern period is to show that the West was economically backward by comparison with China in the fifteenth and sixteenth centuries (which it clearly was); that, by obtaining large amounts of silver by exploiting forced labor in Latin America, it gained the leverage it needed to get into world economic trade (which it did). But we think more than economic considerations must be examined to understand what humans have done and why they have done it, certainly in the past three hundred to four hundred years.

In particular, we argue the ideas and beliefs people held is as important as their economic practices for any understanding of the past. It was not for economic reasons that Suleiman passed over his two capable sons to leave his throne to a less worthy candidate. Nor was Aurangzeb acting out of economic considerations when he departed from the conciliation policies of his Hindu subjects that had worked so well for the Mughal emperors for over a century. Suleiman was persuaded by a favorite wife to make his ill-conceived choice, and Aurangzeb was influenced by his conservative religious beliefs. Both these men's choices had absolutely nothing to do with the West. In fact, neither had any particular reason to be concerned about the West because the area, as these contemporary world historians have pointed out, was not strong enough at this point to cause them any trouble.

In the following chapters we will explain how the West did, in fact, become strong enough to give every nation on the globe lots of trouble. Economic considerations are clearly important. Latin American silver is certainly a significant factor, and so were the cycles referred to above. As we have seen in the previous three chapters, while the states in Asia, and Africa for that matter, were viable sociopolitical entities until the eighteenth century, thereafter each showed signs of decay that occurred just as the West was beginning to develop ideas and institutions it would use to conquer them. But the ideas are just as important as the economic developments in explaining what transpired.

In our next chapter, we will begin to explore the coming to maturity in the West of the modern idea of the nation-state, when we discuss the "Democratic Revolutions" of the late eighteenth and early nineteenth centuries.

FOR FURTHER READING

Ali, Omar H. *Islam in the Indian Ocean World*. New York: St. Martin's Press, 2016.

Ansary, Tamm. *Destiny Disrupted*. New York: Public Affairs Books, 2009.

Dale, Stephen Frederic. *The Muslim Empires of the Ottomans, Safavids, and Mughals*. New York: Cambridge University Press, 2010.

Frank, Andre Gunder. *Reorient: Global Economy in the Asian Age*. Berkeley: University of California Press, 1998.

Goldschmidt, Arthur Jr. and Lawrence Davidson. *A Concise History of the Middle East*. 8th ed. Boulder: Westview Press, 2006.

Hill, Fred James and Nichlas Awde. *A History of the Islamic World*. New York: Hippocrene Books, 2003.

Hunt, Margaret and Philip J. Stern. *The English East India Company at the Height of Mughal Expansion*. New York: St. Martin's Press, 2016

Kinross, Lord. *The Ottoman Centuries*. New York: Morrow Quill Publishers, 1977.

Lewis, Bernard. *What Went Wrong?* New York: Oxford University Press, 2002.

CHAPTER
SIX

The Emergence of the Nation-State System

INTRODUCTION

In this chapter, we turn our attention back to Europe, focusing on the events of the half century between the last decades of the eighteenth century and the early part of the nineteenth century, often called the "Age of Democratic Revolutions." During these momentous decades, revolutionaries created new political systems they labeled "democratic." They also created new social systems appropriate to their new political structures. Both have come to characterize life in Europe, in the Americas, and indeed in much of the rest of the world today.

To make sense of these transformations, we will begin by examining the economic changes leading up to them, and the social system that characterized Europe shortly before them. With this information we will turn to the major events of this era, beginning with the political developments in Britain that culminated in the American Revolution, followed by the French Revolution and the reign of Napoleon. Finally, we will look at reform efforts in Britain, and at uprisings in Ireland and in Haiti, which although unsuccessful were nonetheless inspired by the economic and social transformations occurring in Europe and America at the time.

In subsequent chapters, we will see how these "Democratic Revolutions" spread from America and France to the rest of Europe and throughout the world. As the nineteenth century progressed, the ideas behind revolutions will change, but everywhere the cry for liberty, enunciated first by the reformers and revolutionaries in this period, will continue to be heard, as indeed they are heard up to the present. It is hard to overstate the importance for the modern world of the events that occurred in this half-century.

The expansion of Europeans around the world, which we looked at in the previous three chapters, is partly responsible for these sociopolitical transformations, as is the beginning in Britain of what some historians call the "Industrial Revolution." Both produced significant social and economic pressures the political structure of Old Regime Europe could not contain. Equally important were the new ideas about humans' abilities to regulate their own lives that guided the reformers and revolutionaries of this half century. As we observed in Chapter 5, ideas and beliefs are as important in understanding human behavior as are economic forces or interests.

A word about terminology is in order before we proceed. So far in this text, we have suggested that "modernism," which has had such a profound influence in the shaping of contemporary life, arose in the seventeenth century in Europe. We began by suggesting what that term meant and examining some of its earliest manifestations. Societies that did not undergo this process we called "traditional." Perhaps it has already dawned upon you that before the seventeenth century, everyone was traditional, although the forms the traditions took varied. As we proceed, we will point out how modernization came to define more and more aspects of life, in more and more places around the world, always replacing traditional ones as modernization develops. This is a useful distinction for you to keep in mind as you proceed through the text.

We also need to introduce a second terminological distinction, somewhat akin to the "traditional vs. modern" one. Historians routinely refer to the sociopolitical order that prevailed in Europe before the French Revolution as the "Old Regime." Such a distinction did not exist until after the French Revolution and arose from the fact the French word *ancien* can mean "old," but also "former." In our case it means "former." The "new" regime came after the French Revolution. It is a very handy distinction provided you understand what it means, and we shall use it.

ECONOMY

In the eighteenth century, just as in other parts of the world, population in Europe gradually rose. There were several reasons for this upward demographic. First, during the seventeenth century, the earth's climate underwent what has been termed "a little ice age." Slightly cooler temperatures resulted in longer, wetter winters, and subsequently smaller yields of food. Naturally this led to famine. But during the eighteenth century, the earth's temperature gradually rose, which meant more food to feed an expanding population.

In addition, new foods from the Americas (corn, squashes,[1] and potatoes) were added to the European diet. Just as we saw in our examination of China and other Asian states, increasing the foods from the "New World" that were available to people increased life expectancy and therefore overall population growth.

The available food supply also expanded because of a number of improvements in agricultural practices. The changes were not experienced evenly across the continent, with the Netherlands and Britain undergoing the most change. But everywhere, "enlightened" monarchs or aristocratic farmers sought to apply the ideas of agricultural reformers to improve their crop and animal yields. The results were improved planting techniques. Jethro Tull (1674–1741), for example, introduced the "seed drill" that resulted in seed being planted in rows instead of being scattered willy-nilly around the field.

---

1   Tobacco should also be mentioned.

Charles "Turnip" Townshend (1674–1738) introduced the practice of planting nitrogen-fixing plants—crops that not only put nutrients back into the soil, but provide "fodder" that could be fed to animals during the winter. Before these changes, it had been necessary to slaughter most of a farmer's herd every fall, as there was no grass to keep them alive over the winter. But with fodder crops, they could be kept alive. The next year one began with a larger herd, and each year the size expanded. With more meat in the market, its costs became less, and more people ate more meat.

Robert Bakewell (1725–1795) introduced the practice of selective breading of livestock, in particular sheep, horses, and cattle. His idea was to use selective breeding to produce sheep with longer wool, cows with better meat or more milk, etc. His work was especially influential upon Charles Darwin, whose "natural selection" mechanism for evolution was a logical outgrowth of Bakewell's sexual selection.

The advent of journals devoted to farming and agricultural practices made a wider dissemination of the new ideas possible, as did the books of reformers such as Andrew Young (1741–1820), who traveled about Europe and Britain publicizing innovations in agriculture. His works were read by King George III, George Washington, Lafayette, and Catherine the Great of Russia.

The overall effect of these changes was to bring about an increase in the amount of meat protein available to Europeans in the eighteenth century.

Infectious diseases that had killed so many in the seventeenth century were less virulent by the eighteenth century, progressing from epidemic to endemic. Finally, in Europe, people in the eighteenth century suffered less from warfare than they had in the previous century.

The changes were not universal. In many parts of Europe, fallow cropping was still practiced. Well into the nineteenth century, in some parts of France, the use of wooden plows rather than iron ones was preferred because peasants feared the iron would harm the soil and make it less fruitful. Whereas in England, because of primogeniture and entail, the enclosure of fields that had begun under the Tudors continued, resulting in a few larger but more prosperous farms. In France, the system of small farms persisted, many of which were too small to afford to make the changes the "improving landlords" in other nations were making. Yet, the famines, which had been one of the pestilences humans had had to deal with in the past, came to be an uncommon occurrence of short duration in Europe during this century. All these changes combined help to explain the steady rise in population.

Commerce and finance also underwent significant developments in the eighteenth century. The steady growth of maritime trade led to the advent of insurance companies and to the stock exchange. In England, the first is represented by Lloyds of London, and the second by the coffeehouses around which they grew up. Greenwich Mean Time was developed in England, and because of the invention of the "chronometer," a clock to use on board ships, one could calculate longitude and sail safely out of sight of land all over the globe.

Following the mercantilist practices of the times, governments promoted trade and commerce. In Eastern Europe it was called "cameralism": government agencies that promoted trade and improved tax collection. Other governments, especially the Dutch and British, relied on private businesses like their "East India" companies to conduct most of the trade and even government functions in their colonies, as we saw in an earlier chapter.

England and France experimented with paper money with less than successful results. In France, the scheme promoted by the Scottish financier John Law resulted in the "Mississippi Bubble," and in England a similar one led to the "South Sea Bubble." Both linked foreign trade to the governments' monies through state-owned banks. The idea was to use the wealth from the colonies to diminish the governments' debts. People were encouraged to buy stocks in the company, including exchanging state debt for shares. The "bubble" arose when people began to speculate on the shares. Inevitably, the share prices rose all out of proportion to their worth; some investors grew wary and sold their overpriced shares for specie, which eventually emptied the state banks, causing them to fail. The French bubble burst in 1721, and Law fled to the Netherlands for safety. Following similar practices, not long thereafter the South Sea Company collapsed. Both were subsequently reconstituted as profitable companies.

The difference in government responses to the crises is instructive. In England, as a result of the crisis, the statesman Walpole came to be the king's chief minister, pledging to create a "national debt" and a "sinking fund" to deal with the losses. Those who lost money were eventually repaid. In so doing, Walpole created not only a permanent national debt, but also a system that would enable the British government to borrow successfully to fight its wars against France during the French Revolution and age of Napoleon. This included building the empire that would catapult Britain to the status of a world power in the nineteenth century. The French government simply allowed those who had lost money to suffer their losses and its credit took a hit as well. Ultimately, the French government was forced to use the Catholic Church to back up its debts and, although a much larger country, France never had the finances its English adversaries enjoyed.

As we have already seen, the slave trade and resultant expansion of the Atlantic states in Europe played a significant role in the expanding prosperity of both governments and businessmen in these countries. These new sources of revenue contributed to the growing prosperity and power of Europe in the eighteenth century.

Finally, the eighteenth century witnessed the beginning of what is sometimes called the Industrial Revolution. The full effects of this economic and social phenomenon will occur in the nineteenth century, which will be discussed more fully in a subsequent chapter. Still, it is worth mentioning that it originated in England during the late eighteenth century.

It began in the textile business. Increasing demand for cloth in England led to a shortage of skilled workmen in this area. They were mostly French, but not permitted by the French state to emigrate to work in England.[2] Shortage generally promotes innovation and in this case it led a group of entrepreneurs to develop machinery, including the "spinning jenny" and the "mule" that could do the work of unavailable workers and of others as well.

At first, water was the power source but it is unreliable. This difficulty led to the development of a new source of power, the steam engine, which itself led to the need for a new source of fuel, coal, to use in these engines.

A large amount of capital was not necessary to develop this equipment and was generally raised by the entrepreneurs themselves who appealed to friends and family members for support. These changes met with resistance from workers—Luddites, as they were called—who attempted to break up the equipment that was destroying their livelihoods. But in due course, a new kind of worker, the factory hand, replaced

---

2   Many Huguenots had fled to England in the previous century, bringing their industrial skills with them.

the handloom weaver in his cottage. By 1789, England had more than one hundred fifty cotton mills. The putting-out system of the past was still responsible for the greatest quantity of manufactured goods in England. But the handwriting for hand production was clearly on the wall.

These economic changes also helped to produce a new political and social life in Europe. But before we discuss how these came about, we need to have some understanding of the social structure of Europe the postrevolutionary world would replace.

SOCIETY IN OLD REGIME EUROPE

Four principles explain the social structure of Old Regime Europe: authority, tradition, privilege, and estates. We have already discussed the first two. You may recall the best authority was the oldest, in particular, ancient Greeks and Romans, and the Bible. In our earlier context it had to do with scientific ideas. Social orders, however, would work the same way. The more ancient the family the more prestige it enjoyed. Tradition too is the same as before and meant doing what you have done in the past. So in this case, prestigious families have pride of place because they have always had it. Or, at least, they seemed always to have had it. The other two traits require a bit of explanation.

Privilege and Estates

A privilege is generally a right one individual or group enjoys that another does not. When you were a senior in high school, you enjoyed "Senior Privileges," which might even have included leaving school in the afternoon to go to a job. This was not an option for your younger peers.

Privilege in Old Regime Europe was a bit more complicated. To understand why, it would be helpful to introduce the fourth term, "estates," into the explanation. An estate was a legally recognized community. Everyone belonged to one of them and his or her status was determined by the one to which he or she belonged, frequently the one into which that person was born. In France, there were three. The First Estate were the clergy, the Second the nobility. It began with the king and included everyone down to the poorest aristocrat. The Third Estate comprised everyone else. On the eve of the French Revolution, that encompassed more than 90 percent of the population of France. The First and Second estates enjoyed the privilege of not paying taxes, at least not on a regular basis. That burden was reserved for the Third Estate.

Aristocrats were allowed to wear certain types of clothes forbidden to everyone else (ermine, for example). They could sit in certain reserved seats in theatres that wealthy Third Estate members were unable to purchase. Members of the Third Estate were expected to show proper respect when they were in the presence of members of the other two. In Prussia, the military aristocracy, the *Junkers,* owned the lands that were worked by serfs. If a Junker were walking down a street, everyone else was to move over to make room for him to pass, or they could be knocked out of the way with impunity.

There were other sorts of privileges. In France, some pieces of property, not necessarily owned by the aristocracy, were exempted from taxation because the holder of these properties had been given this privilege by a monarch in return for some favor or service the family had rendered at some time. Even when the estate was sold, the privilege went with it. Towns on the French border with Switzerland were exempted from providing soldiers for the military and paid a monetary fee instead. This was because young men on the border towns had but to pop over into Switzerland when the recruiters came, and wait until they left before returning.

The easiest way for you to understand what privilege meant is simply to recognize that in the United States we are all, in theory, supposed to be equal before the law. It should both punish and protect us the same, regardless of our family name or fortune. That the rich are more likely to escape the legal consequences of their actions because of the quality of their legal counsel, we know to be true, but we also think it something that should not be so. In the Old Regime, it was the way that things were supposed to be. On one occasion, attending a party in Paris, Voltaire insulted a nobleman, the Duc de Rohan. Not long thereafter, someone called for Voltaire. When he went out to inquiry, he was attacked and left in a bloody heap on the ground. The other guests thought this appropriate, as someone with the status of a duke should not be insulted by someone as insignificant socially as Voltaire. Privilege in the Old Regime meant people were not equal before the law; instead, each enjoyed a set of special relations with the state that grew out of the estate they were a member of, or the awards the government had granted to their family. It made for a complex and increasingly more unworkable system.

THE THREE ESTATES

This is a good point to warn you of another difference between their world and ours. We are inclined to think riches and social status always go together, since they do in our society. Instead, hierarchy in Old Regime society was within the orders more than between them. All clergymen enjoyed the privileges of the First Estate, but most clergy were not much wealthier than the peasants to whom they administered the sacraments. Many members of the Third Estate were wealthier than some members of the Second and most members of the First, yet their social status was decidedly inferior to members of either.

First Estate

The First Estate in France, the clergy, came in two varieties: monks (regular clergy) who were supposed to lead a secluded existence centered on prayer, and priests (secular clergy) who worked in the cities and towns, giving sermons, hearing confession, marrying couples, baptizing their children, and burying the dead. These same duties fell to the Protestant pastors in and outside of France as well.

England had done away with monastic orders and confiscated their estates during the Tudor period. The remaining clergy were supposed to be working with people in parishes and towns. Many had embraced a rather "enlightened" outlook toward religion by the eighteenth century. They tended to be an educated class, many attending Oxford or Cambridge. This gave them a social status higher than perhaps the one into which they were born. By the eighteenth century, the Church of England, under the influence of the Enlightenment, frequently espoused what were termed "latitudinarian" ideas. They were less concerned with doctrinal purity and more with moral behavior. Basic Christian doctrines seemed a bit old-fashioned as did notions of heaven and hell, though they were careful not to discuss such matters around the servants.

During the course of the eighteenth century, a religious revival, "the Great Awakening," along with a new religious community, the Methodists, brought about the revitalization of traditional Christianity in England that by the next century transformed the state into the more theologically orthodox and morally pietistic community that we call "Victorian."

The First Estate in Eastern Europe was likewise closely attached to the privileged social world and enjoyed luxurious lifestyles for the upper clergy and penury for those who worked with rural populations. In Germany, a religious revival "pietism," which closely resembled the "Great Awakening" in England, occurred mid-century.

It is also important to realize that individuals who were not comfortable with Christianity were advised to keep their opinions to themselves, or else they might suffer at the hands of the law. As the Enlightenment progressed, this rule of thumb became less true in France, England, and Scotland; however, in most of the Catholic world, and in all of the Orthodox Christian states, the political power of religious authorities did not abate, and you challenged it with irreligious statements at your peril. The era of revolutions that follows will change this situation. And, as we proceed into the nineteenth century, Christian dominance of life in European states will gradually subside, being replaced by secular ideas associated with citizenship.

Second Estate

The Second Estate in France was the aristocracy. At the apex of this hierarchy stood the king and just beneath him his family members. They were the wealthiest members of this order, to be sure. Beneath the king and his kin were the "Nobles of the Sword," members of families whose ancestry could, at times, be traced back centuries.[3] Their wealth, while not usually equal to that of the "royals," was substantial by comparison with everyone else in the realm.

Beneath the "Sword Nobility" was the "Nobility of the Robe," nobles to be sure, but of decidedly recent venue, as most of them were descendants of middle-class lawyers who served Louis XIV in his government when he was establishing the absolute monarchy in France during the seventeenth century. Now they had become landowners in their own right and had acquired titles.

Beneath them were a group of decidedly poor nobles, the "*hobereaux,*" which translates "sparrow hawk," a small predator bird that had to be vicious to survive. They, too, were vicious to the peasants who worked their lands as tenants. While serfdom was gone, the indignities they could visit on these unfortunates were real. But when the revolution came, it was this group of nobles whose estates were most particularly singled out to be put to the torch, and whose dovecotes were feasted upon with the greatest joy by their former tenants.

There is one other group of nobles of sorts late in the Old Regime. One of the ways a person could advance socially in this society was to buy one's way into the nobility. In return for a sizable sum of money, the king would sell a member of the bourgeois a "patent of nobility." It did not make him a high member of the First Estate and, on the eve of the revolution, some of these found their patents revoked. The recently ennobled bourgeois were willing to enter into such agreements because it did advance their social status, but of even more importance, it enabled them to avoid paying taxes in the future.

---

3   This author had the experience, in 1972, on a plane returning from England to the United States, of sitting next to an English M.P. who could trace his family heritage back to Rollo, a tenth-century count of Rouen.

Nobles in Eastern Europe remained tied into the serf labor system. In return for their service to the state, they enjoyed the labors of peasants.

Aristocracy in Britain is the most difficult to explain. Technically, only the eldest son of a nobleman would inherit the family title and with it noble status. All other sons were "commoners," yet they were clearly aristocratic in background. England also practiced "entail," which meant the son who inherited the title also inherited all the estates of the family. Younger sons had to find another way to gain admittance into the world of privilege in England. Some did so by going into the clergy and becoming wealthy and privileged in that manner. Recall that unlike Catholic France, English clergy regularly married.

Another avenue for advancement was the military, which would give one the wealth to buy property and acquire a seat in the House of Commons. Or else, one could marry the daughter of a wealthy merchant and use her money to acquire property and status. The House of Commons in the eighteenth century, its critics pointed out, was really only a secondary branch for the aristocracy, as most of its members were younger sons of nobility.

One thing is clear. The eighteenth century was the last great era for the aristocracy in Europe. The French foreign minister to Napoleon, Talleyrand, himself an archbishop before the French Revolution, lamented, "Those who have not lived in the eighteenth century before the Revolution do not know the sweetness of living."[4] As you will see in subsequent chapters, new political systems and ideas about life arose in the decades following Napoleon.

Third Estate

The French Third Estate was mostly composed of peasants who were themselves arranged hierarchically. A few owned their own land and even rented lands, hiring laborers to work on them. They were rather similar to the Yeomen farmers of Britain.[5] Most peasants, however, rented the lands they lived on from either the aristocrats, the clergy, or some of the middle class who had bought rural lands. Beneath this group were the "cotters," who did not have enough land to survive on and eked out a precarious existence selling their labor to those better off than themselves. It was they who in very hard times—due to weather, for instance—were most likely to perish. At the bottom of this estate were, again, the homeless who were at times roving bands of thieves.

In Eastern Europe, most of these peasants were un-free tenants. While serfdom was disappearing in Western Europe, it was growing in Eastern Europe. In Germany, Austria, Prussia, and Russia, the aristocracy exchanged service to the government for lands and the peasants to work them. Even in Poland, where there was only a very weak central government, the peasantry was subjugated to the aristocracy. No matter whether free or serf, the peasants lived hard and uncertain lives, and if periodic famines became less a factor of eighteenth-century life than they had been in the previous century, a peasant's life was harsh and, at times, perilous.

---

4   *Celui qui n'a pas vécu au dix-huitième siècle avant la Révolution ne connaît pas la douceur de vivre.* https://en.wikipedia.org/wiki/Ancien_R%C3%A9gime

5   In Jane Austin's *Emma*, Mr. Martin is a good example.

Also part of the Third Estate was the middle class (*bourgeois*). This group enjoyed the greatest prosperity of any member of the estate. The bourgeois resided in towns and led a life rather different from that of the aristocracy, as they were the owners of banks, factories, or were merchants who traded nationally and internationally. Some among them bought land and tried to become aristocrats, at times even abandoning the trade that had been the source of their wealth to live as country gentlemen. Others invested in rural land for the economic benefit it represented.

In the towns, the most powerful people were the merchants or masters. Beneath them were their journeymen and below them were apprentices. The apprenticeship system was the primary way one learned a trade. Beneath theses classes were people who had no skill, or were old or weak, or otherwise unemployable. Their situation was generally desperate, and they relied upon the charity of the church as there were no state-sponsored relief agencies. Alternatively, they became vagabonds or thieves.

Shortly before the convening of the Estates General in 1789, local French communities in all three estates elected their delegates and prepared lists of concerns (cahiers) they wanted the delegates from their region to address when they arrived at Versailles. Not all of these cahiers survive, but those that do have been studied and the results suggest that when they were prepared, the people of France were not seething with anger and anxious to destroy their society root and branch as they soon would. It is also true in the months leading up to the American Declaration of Independence, the colonials who were most anxious to separate from England were not the loudest voices in the land. Yet, in both cases, the existing political system was soon destroyed and in France that included the Old Regime social order as well. Just how this could have occurred is what we turn to now.

AMERICAN REVOLUTION

> When in the Course of human events, it becomes necessary for one people to dissolve the political bands which have connected them with another, and to assume among the powers of the earth, the separate and equal station to which the Laws of Nature and of Nature's God entitle them, a decent respect to the opinions of mankind requires that they should declare the causes which impel them to the separation.

Declaration of Independence, 1776.

No doubt you recognize this as the opening paragraph of Jefferson's Declaration of Independence, adopted by the First Continental Congress on July 4, 1776. If you read it carefully, you will realize it is an apology for the delegates' decision to separate politically from Britain, an apology addressed not to the people of the colonies, but to the world at large. After all, the British Empire began establishing these colonies late in the sixteenth century. Jamestown became a permanent English settlement in 1607. Massachusetts Bay Colony was established in 1628. The others followed until 1732 when Georgia, the thirteenth and last colony, was founded. That is a long time to be part of Britain. So the apology seems to be saying: these are the reasons we are taking this extraordinary step. How this came about is the first question we want to answer. Then we will try to explain how these puny and greatly disorganized colonies took on the greatest empire in the world (at that time) and won. Finally, we will want to address the consequences of our Founding Fathers' actions on the rest of the world.

Unlike the Spanish colonists in South America and Mexico, or Englishmen at home for that matter, these English colonials, at least the white males among them, enjoyed an unprecedented degree of self-government from the beginning. Representative assemblies were created for Virginia and Bermuda in the seventeenth century, and, as subsequent colonies were established, they too set up such institutions. In them, the qualifications for voting were more generous than in England. In other words, English settlers getting used to having a say in their everyday lives was unique in the world.

During the course of the eighteenth century, the English government attempted to bring the colonies more under central control, making them royal where they had been proprietary, and subjecting them to the oversight of royal governors. But for the most part, the colonials decided what the rules and conditions of their own lives would be. Andrew Burnaby, an English clergyman and travel writer, made the following observation in his *Travels through the Middle Settlements in North-America* (1775).

> The public or political character of the Virginians, corresponds with their private one: they are haughty and jealous of their liberties, impatient of restraint, and can scarcely bear the thought of being controuled [sic] by any superior power. Many of them consider the colonies as independent states, unconnected with Great Britain, otherwise than by having the same common king, and being bound to her with natural affection.

Most scholars suggest the policy of "salutary neglect"—followed by the British in the eighteenth century, largely because of their wars with France—so accustomed the colonials to their more independent lifestyle that attempting to rein them in after 1764 ultimately led to the "separation" that we call the American Revolution.

This chain of events began in the years following the Seven Years War. As we noted in an earlier chapter, Britain emerged triumphant over France in both the continental and also colonial theaters of this war, but it had been an enormously expensive victory to achieve. To the dismay of the Crown during that conflict, the colonials had proven themselves incapable of providing for their own defense, forcing the British government to hire German mercenaries, the Hessians, to help out. The situation was made worse since the Crown had to bear that cost. From the Crown's perspective, in the future the colonials were going to have to assume more responsibility for their own defense, and that meant paying the costs. To be sure, the colonials had other ideas.

Another source of tension between the Crown and the colonials was itself a by-product of England's victory over France in the Americas. The British had gained a vast territory, north and west of the American colonies in what is today Canada and the lands west of the Allegheny Mountains in the northwestern part of the United States. In an attempt to manage these areas, which were largely inhabited by Native Americans, the British government issued "The Royal Proclamation of 1763." This greatly angered the colonials because it forbade them to settle in these rich areas.

THE CROWN

The Crown's first effort to increase colonial taxation was the Sugar Act of 1764. This law, which provided for the collection of a tax on sugar and molasses, alarmed merchants on the Eastern Seaboard, as it reduced the supply of currency available to them.[6] The Stamp Act of 1765 had the same effect. It covered paper, liquor, playing cards, dice, newspapers, calendars, and even academic degrees!

The colonials responded by boycotting English goods and, in October 1765, convened the Stamp Act Congress in New York City. Delegates from nine colonies were present. From their perspective, the Crown did not have a right to tax them because they were not represented in the British Parliament. The "No taxation without representation" argument made its first, but certainly not its last, appearance.

The British did back down, largely because London merchants were suffering from the American boycott, but Parliament maintained it did indeed have the right to tax the colonies (Declaratory Act of 1766), whom, they claimed, were in fact "virtually represented." These two irreconcilable positions would be solemnly adhered to by both sides, until the revolution settled the issue ten years later.

The government of George III returned to the matter in 1767 with passage of the Townshend duties on colonial imports of tea, paper, paint, and lead. Naturally this led to the same colonial response and was followed by a British surrender, except for a three-penny-a-pound tax on tea. Three years later, the government actually made the retail price of tea lower than that the colonial smugglers bringing in Dutch tea were asking. This threat to the tea merchants' livelihood resulted in the "Boston Tea Party." On December 16, 1773, about ten thousand pounds of tea were dumped into Boston Harbor by the "Sons of Liberty," disguised as Native Americans.

The British responded to what to them was hooliganism and vandalism by closing the port of Boston and suspending elections in Massachusetts, the "Intolerable Acts," as the colonials called them. In that same year, Parliament also passed "The Quebec Act" (1774), incorporating all the lands west of the Alleghenies into Quebec, and guaranteeing the free exercise of Catholicism there. To the government, both measures seemed eminently reasonable. The area could be more easily administered from Canada, and the majority Catholic subjects in Quebec had to be placated if Britain hoped to hold on to this newly acquired territory. But the colonials saw it quite another way. They resented the concession to Catholics almost as much as statute's clauses that blocked their way to expand westward. Catholics were certainly not tolerated in England, why should they be tolerated in the colonies? Furthermore, to the colonials, the British were trying to use their former French enemies (the Seven Years War had not long been over) to help force the colonies into submission.

The war was not far off now. In September 1744, all the colonies but Georgia sent representatives to the First Continental Congress to discuss resistance. Not everyone at this meeting was committed to separation, but many were. The point of no return came April 7, 1775, in Massachusetts, at Lexington and Concord, when a group of British regulars sought to capture a colonial arms cache. This was the night of Paul Revere's famous ride. The roused colonials removed the arms to another place and, temporarily at least, had the British general in Boston, General Gage, bottled up. British assistance soon arrived and moved straight away to dislodge the colonials at Breeds and Bunker hills on June 17. While technically the

---

6   Recall that the principle idea of mercantilism is that more gold and silver must be brought into the country than go out of it for it to be strong. When the reverse occurs, the country becomes weak, much like hemorrhaging blood does to a human body.

British won the battle, it is was a "Pyrrhic victory"[7] at best; half of Gage's forces were killed in the battle. But unmistakably, the war had begun.

In the near term, the British had the advantages. The irregulars of the colonials were never a match for the regulars or "British Red Coats," as they were called. The British also had more resources at their disposal. In the long term, however, the advantages were all with the colonials. They were defending hearth and home and did not have to travel thousands of miles to be resupplied. As the war dragged on, London merchants and Whig landlords in England began to question whether holding on to the colonies was worth it.

The turning point came in 1777, as a result of the battle of Saratoga when British forces, under the command of General John Burgoyne (1722–1792), were forced to surrender. More important, the French who had been supporting the colonials surreptitiously, now decided the American cause was worth supporting openly. In particular, the French Navy would play a vital part in the eventual American victory. At this point, Britain's war with its colony became a world war.

Up to this this point, the colonials and their commander in chief, George Washington, had done little to cover themselves in military glory. Almost surely faced with defeat, on Christmas Day, 1776, Washington ferried his armies across the Delaware River and was able to capture the Hessian garrison offguard at Trenton; however, he was forced to retreat into New Jersey in early January. Things only got worse from there. But he held on, and in the end he prevailed.

The British, realizing their greatest support was in the South, sought to move their forces into this region. By May 1780, the campaigns had shifted to South Carolina, and by the spring of 1781, the British, led by General Cornwallis, were setting their sights on Virginia. This in effect split British forces into three parts: one in Manhattan, a second in South Carolina, and the third in Virginia at Yorktown. Washington, with the aid of the French under Rochambeau, decided to attack at Yorktown. Nathanael Greene defeated the British in South Carolina, while the French Navy prevented the British from coming to Cornwallis's assistance in Yorktown. By October 19, 1781, Cornwallis had realized surrender was his only option and, while the war could have gone on, there was little heart in England to continue. A peace was signed at Paris in 1783, recognizing the colonies' independence from Britain and returning Florida to Spain.

THE NEW NATION

Appearing just under the title of the Declaration of Independence is this phrase: "The unanimous Declaration of the thirteen united States of America." Notice that "united" is in lowercase. Becoming the United States of America would take some time, as we shall see. The first governmental system of these former British colonies, The Articles of Confederation, was such a weak instrument that by 1787, somewhat surreptitiously, a new federal constitution was agreed upon by enough states to replace this first effort. The Constitution of 1787 gave more power to the central government, but divided it among three branches: an executive, a legislative, and a judicial. This system of "checks and balances," as political

---

7   From the name of a Hellenistic general, Pyrrhus of Epirus, who fought with the Romans in southern Italy in the early Republic. While he won all the battles, he lost so many of his men in doing so that he was forced to give up and return to Greece. So he won the battles but lost the war.

scientists call it today, was inspired by Montesquieu's understanding of the English government of his day. Shortly after the adoption of the Constitution of 1787, ten amendments known as the Bill of Rights were quickly ratified. These included freedom of religion, speech, press, and assembly, the right to bear arms for the purpose of guaranteeing a militia, and a number of amendments to protect against arbitrary government. The tenth stated that anything not forbidden by the Constitution was allowed.

There were many who doubted this new republic would last. There were also many in Europe and around the globe who found its ideals inspiring. We will see in the remainder of this chapter how our experiment in self-government influenced others seeking more freedom for their lives in France, England, Ireland, and Haiti. But the influence will not stop there. In 1989, on July 4, a group of Chinese students were run down by tanks or arrested and imprisoned for seeking to bring about an American-style democracy to their country. From a contemporary perspective, the Founding Fathers' democratic credentials need a lot of burnishing; yet, their ideas were pregnant with the future and they continue to inspire people today as they have since our republic began.

THE FRENCH REVOLUTION AND NAPOLEON

It was the best of times, it was the worst of times, it was the age of wisdom, it was the age of foolishness, it was the epoch of belief, it was the epoch of incredulity, it was the season of Light, it was the season of Darkness, it was the spring of hope, it was the winter of despair.

Charles Dickens, *A Tale of Two Cities*.

For more than two hundred years, historians, as well as novelists such as Dickens, have been trying to make sense of the events that transpired in France and Europe between 1789 and 1815. In 1889, to celebrate the centenary of the French Revolution, France erected the Eifel Tower. The French celebrated the revolution for having created the rational political order that had become modern France. Fast-forward another century and the celebration was marred by serious reservations about what had transpired two hundred years earlier. Many thought France would have been better off if it had not occurred. The quest for understanding and evaluation continues to the present day.

We will focus on answering the same three questions we asked about the American Revolution: How did it happen, what course of events did it follow, and what were its lasting consequences? Given that the French Revolution has been subjected to such a variety of interpretations, we may assume a more complicated set of historical events characterize it than its American counterpart. Unlike the American Revolution, which drove out the British but did not change power relationships in the nation, the French Revolution was primarily a civil war that sought to oust the existing ruling classes and replace them with another, often termed "the people." While the Americans only had to fight the British, during the French Revolution France found itself arraigned against all the major European powers of the time. The French Revolution, unlike the American, became decidedly anti-religious, certainly anti-Christian. It was also significantly more violent than was the American event. Indeed, the main reason there is so much discomfort with the French Revolution today is because of the resultant bloodletting, most of it in French lives.

Intellectually, the two revolutions were rather similar. Both believed all that was required to create a just society was a political transformation. A new political vocabulary arose in both states. The revolutionaries claimed to be acting on behalf of "the people," for "freedom" and "equality," or to be defending the rights of "citizens" and the well-being of "the nation." Even the forms both new political systems would take were not different enough to explain the disparate experiences of the two nations. Finally, there was only one American Revolution. In France, there were five or three, depending on one's ideological perspective.

How the French Revolution Began[8]

Historians recognize some of the causes of the French Revolution were political in nature, while others were economic and social. For much of the twentieth century, the economic/social interpretation dominated. Recently, the political one has become more important. But both must be taken into consideration.

Like the rest of Europe, France experienced population growth throughout the eighteenth century. By the eve of the revolution, land had become scarce and many peasants were unable to obtain enough to live comfortably. Vagabondage was on the rise. In a nutshell, life for the peasantry had become difficult and, at times, precarious. This was the class that bore most of the burden of taxation. The cartoon depicted in Figure 6.1, from the period, captures the situation from the perspective of this group. Notice that the First and Second estates are riding on the back of the Third.

Secondly, during the eighteenth century, the middle class had grown stronger, economically and socially, and more educated. In rural areas, most of the literature people read or had read to them remained devotional in nature, but among the bourgeois, the literature of the Enlightenment was prevalent. Conservative historians, from Edmund Burke on, have tried to blame the revolution on this movement by suggesting enlightened thinkers were the source for the destructive ideas that came in the wake of the revolution. That the Enlightenment did cause people to question Old Regime society is not in doubt, but the likes of Voltaire and Diderot were rather more reformers than revolutionaries.

The American Revolution also played a role in the events leading up to the French Revolution. Its literature was

A FAUT ESPERER Q'EU JEU LA FINIRA BENTOT

Figure 6.1: Troisordres[8]

---

8   https://en.wikipedia.org/wiki/Estates_General_(France)#/media/File:Troisordres.jpg Figure 6-1

similar in tone to that of the revolutionaries in France, and the fact that a place presumed to be so wild and ungovernable could create its own instruments of self-government was inspiring to those seeking to improve the political situation in France.

In the decades that followed the French defeat in the Seven Years War, France's international status had fallen significantly. The Dutch and Austrian Netherlands, traditional enemies of France, had undergone revolutionary upheavals that were in France's interests to support. When the Prussians and English crushed them, the French could do nothing because they did not have the money to mount any action. In 1772, Poland, an ally of France, was partitioned by Austria, Prussia, and Russia, the first of three that would see the state disappear completely during the French Revolution. France did nothing for the same reason. French weakness was also made plain in 1787 when Turkey, another old ally, was attacked by Austria and Russia. Once again, France was in no financial position to become involved.

Louis XVI was an indecisive monarch. Inevitably these diplomatic reversals were laid at his door. Furthermore, his Austrian wife, Marie-Antoinette (1755–1793), was never popular and frequently blamed for the reversal of fortunes France was undergoing. When they married, a physical problem of the king's that prevented them from consummating their union led to talk of the king's impotency and her infidelity. Such claims grew viler with the passage of time.

Discontent with the current state of affairs led to complaints about "despotism" and calls for reform. Central to much of this agitation were the *parlements,* the thirteen regional courts in France, whose power included the right to register a decree by the king for it to become binding in the area under each one's jurisdiction. The king could force them to register his decrees, change the location of the courts, or even dissolve them, as Louis XV did in 1771, shortly before he died. It was risky to do so and when Louis XVI assumed the throne in 1774, he quickly reinstated them. Yet, the parlements would remain at the center of opposition to the Crown, almost until the eve of the revolution.

Taking all these factors into account, it remains true the fundamental and ultimately insolvable problem that led to the breakdown of Old Regime France was financial. France was a rich country with a poor government. In part, the problem was that the king, with all his kith and kin, lived extravagantly. But a greater problem grew out of the fact it was difficult for the government to tax the people who had money, in particular the members of the First and Second estates.

Ironically, the French decision to aid the Americans only made the king's financial situation worse, as it added a billion *livres* to a debt that already exceeded two billion. Debt-servicing was an enormous strain on state finances. The diplomatic embarrassments mentioned above made everyone aware that something had to be done, but *what* exactly was the question. Several approaches were tried to deal with the government's insolvency, all to no avail, and the final expedient, reconvening the Estates General, which had not met since 1617, led to the outbreak of revolution.

The first unsuccessful attempt, made in 1774, sought to increase royal revenues by expanding the economy. François Turgot (1721–1789) trumpeted the virtues of unrestrained trade, but his policies led to shortages in the economy. A frightened king quickly abandoned Turgot and his reforms.

Louis next turned to a Swiss financier, Jacques Necker, whose ability to borrow money paid for France's involvement in the American Revolution. Necker, a vain man, naturally acquired enemies at court, which resulted in his disgrace and resignation. Just before his departure, however, he published the first complete accounting of state finances, the Compte Rendu of 1781, which purported, largely with the aid of some fancy accounting tricks, to show a small profit for the government. People were not fooled but it did give them a look at how money was actually spent in the government by the royal family, which only reinforced the perception the state was corrupt and in need of reform.

Necker was succeeded by two ministers, Calonne (1734–1802) and then de Brienne (1724–1794), who attempted to save the state by bringing together a group of carefully chosen aristocrats, the "Assembly of Notables," whom they hoped to persuade to agree to reforms. The Notables would have none of it and were dissolved, having accomplished nothing.

The only remaining avenue was to appeal to the parlements, who had come to fancy themselves the protectors of France against a governmental tyranny, although in truth they were only the guardians of aristocratic privilege. They of course refused to countenance de Brienne's reform measures. But to deal with matters this severe, they suggested it would be necessary to resurrect the medieval legislature, the Estates General, which had not met since 1617.

At first, Louis would not even consider doing so. He even abolished the parlements and established new courts, but these "acts of tyranny" caused such a national outcry that he was forced to recant. By this time, the government was almost bankrupt. In August 1788, Louis fired de Brienne, recalled Necker, and agreed to the convening of the Estates General, to take place in 1789. The response to the news was overwhelmingly positive throughout France.

When the Estates General had last met, it had assembled and voted "by order." Each estate met separately and voted as an estate. For a measure to pass, all three had to agree. Those who penned their hopes on reconvening this body recognized that if they voted in the old way, nothing was going to be accomplished, as the Second Estate would never agree to being taxed. Reformers, mostly in the Third Estate but a few from the other two, wanted to see the three estates meet together and vote as individuals, "by head. This was the only way they could hope to force changes on the aristocracy. In September, the parlements revealed their true colors by supporting meeting by order. Their alliance with the Third Estate collapsed immediately.

The First Estate tended to be divided in accordance with whether delegates were bishops or lesser churchmen, with the former supporting meeting by order and the latter meeting in a single body. One member of this estate, who would play an important role in the revolution down to the assumption of power by Napoleon, the Abbé Sieyès (1749–1836), produced a truly revolutionary pamphlet that had a powerful influence upon this debate. Titled *What is the Third Estate?*, Sieyès concluded the Third Estate was the "Nation," as it represented the vast majority of the citizens. Giving in to public pressure, Louis agreed to double the representation of the Third Estate, but he did not say anything on the crucial question of how the Estates General would vote.

It was an exciting period for France. For the first time in at least two centuries, people throughout the country were electing representatives to the estate to which they belonged. This was also the time when the Cahiers we cited earlier were drawn up.

The months leading up to the opening sessions of the Estates General, set for May 5, 1789, did not bode well for the outcome. The winter was especially severe, and a poor harvest caused bread to consume nearly 88 percent of a workman's income. Bread riots broke out in Paris a month before the opening session.

As soon as the Estates General began to meet, things began to go wrong. The government had no proposals for the delegates to consider, nor was it prepared to rule on the question of how the orders should meet and vote. Frustration in the Third Estate mounted until, on June 17, this body declared itself (a la Sieyès) to be the "National Assembly" and invited members of the other two estates to join them. Members from the other two gradually began to do so.

On June 20, when the delegates to the National Assembly arrived at their meeting place, they found the doors locked and guards posted outside. The king was planning to give an address and this was the only place large enough to accommodate everyone. Of course, he did not explain his actions, so the members of the new National Assembly, assuming he was trying to prevent them from meeting, relocated to an indoor tennis court and took an oath they would not disband until France had a new constitution. Seven days later, the king relented and ordered the holdouts in the first two estates to meet with the National Assembly. The revolution had begun; how it would progress was another matter.

REAPING THE WHIRLWIND

As you move through this course, you will become aware that it is one thing to overthrow a government, but quite another to establish a workable one in its place. This can certainly be said of the French revolutionaries. Indeed, events seemed to spiral out of control almost from the outset. The National Assembly had barely gotten down to work, when new waves of disorder swept the country, in part a result of the economic hardships people were suffering, but also because of rumors the king was planning a counterrevolution. When the king dismissed Necker, these suspicions were only confirmed in the public's mind.

The revolutionaries in Paris responded to this news by creating a new municipal government and a new militia (National Guard), both of whom swore allegiance to the National Assembly and not the king. Crowds roamed the streets looking for ammunition. They found some in *Les Invalides,* a military hospital at the time, but their main object of interest was an old fortress on the outskirts of Paris, the Bastille.

The Bastille had once been used as a political prison. When it was stormed by the revolutionaries seeking arms on July 14, 1789, it housed only seven inmates, none of whom was a political prisoner. A few of the defenders of the castle were killed by the attacking crowds, and the stores of gunpowder were triumphantly removed. By the end of the first year of the revolution, this day had become memorialized and has been celebrated since as France's national holiday.

Perhaps even more disturbing to the delegates at the National Assembly was news from outside Paris. Known as the "Great Fear," it was a series of uprisings in rural areas in response to rumors that brigands had been hired by the king or the aristocrats to loot and plunder the countryside in an effort to force the National Assembly to disband. Local nobility were especially at the mercy of the mobs at these events, and some were murdered as a result of altercations. While they were about it, the peasants destroyed manor rolls, ending all written records of any legal obligations the peasants traditionally owed their landlords.

Responding to these pressures, the National Assembly passed a number of transforming pieces of legislation. First, on the night of August 4, the delegates agreed that all should pay taxes in accordance with their wealth, that the clergy would give up its titles, and that all remnants of serfdom would be abolished. Finally, on August 26, the National Assembly passed the "Declaration of the Rights of Man and the Citizen." This document, which reflected both the American Declaration of Independence, and Constitution of 1787, now declared France to be a nation of citizens who all stand equally before the law. Privilege still existed, but henceforth it would be based on a man's worth to society, rather than his birth status. While in many particulars you can see the American influence, in one way it was uniquely French. Law was a manifestation of what Rousseau termed the "general will." But there can be no doubt: the Old Regime was well and truly dead.

By October, a good harvest had been gathered, but a drought prevented its being shipped to Paris. The hungry crowds in the city there were suspicious that a "pact of famine" to break the revolution was at work here. Worse still, rumors began to circulate in the city that the queen, hearing of the misery of her subjects, had callously remarked, "Let them eat cake." On October 5, a group of Parisian women of all classes walked from Paris to Versailles. When they arrived, they invaded the National Assembly, demanding bread. The next day, they returned to Paris, bringing the Royal Family with them. The National Assembly soon followed.

Once the National Assembly set up shop in Paris, it was under more radical influences than it had been at Versailles. Political organizations sprang up in Paris and around France to debate the issues of the day, to keep an eye out for suspicious individuals who were presumed to be everywhere, and to seek to influence the decisions of the National Assembly, as well as regional governments. The most influential among these groups were the Jacobins, named for their meeting place in Paris. The members, originally deputies to the Estates General from Brittany, were soon joined by other radicals. Most were wealthy businessmen; all were republicans. Their chapters spread rapidly and, by 1791, they numbered more than four hundred throughout France. Another radical group, the Cordeliers, from a working-class district of Paris, gave the revolution its most famous motto: "Liberty, Equality and Fraternity." In addition, women's groups and an anti-slavery group emerged. All these groups were influential on the course of events until the end of the Terror. None more so than the Jacobins.

Since the middle of the twentieth century, historians have been particularly interested in one group of radicals known as *sans-culottes* and their role in the course of the revolution. Called sans-culottes because they did not wear knee britches, but long, baggy pants, they were artisans from Paris who were republicans, mostly atheists, and generally in opposition to people with wealth and power, all of whom they regarded as aristocrats. To better influence the course of the revolution, the sans-culottes organized the working-class sections of Paris into pressure groups and were not above rioting or demonstrating to get their way in the Assembly. It is they who mainly stormed the Bastille, and it is they who will bring down the Constitutional Monarchy and establish the First Republic. Their influence only began to wane at the end of the Terror. The picture below is a representation of one of them (Figure 6.2).

Because censorship had completely vanished, a number of radical publications also helped shape political events in the early years of the revolution. Perhaps the most influential of them was *Père Duchesne*, a newspaper published by Jacques Hèbert (1757–1794), until he was executed during the Terror. Hèbert mixed a colorful, somewhat workman-like language with a fiery defense of republican virtues. His venom was aimed at anyone whom he regarded as an enemy of the new state and, in particular, he vilified Marie Antoinette, playing up a number of sexual perversions of which she was popularly judged to be guilty. It was in this atmosphere that the National Assembly attempted to create a new system of government.

The new difficulties seemed almost insurmountable. In particular, the government had no money and no credit either. In November, a solution emerged. The state would confiscate the lands of the church, along with those of fleeing nobility and use these to pay the "nation's" debts.

Assignats were issued in denominations (like currency) to be held for periods of time before redemption (like bonds).[10] All would have gone well if, when the bonds matured and were exchanged for land, the assignats behind them had been destroyed. But by this time, as they were also functioning as currency, they were returned to circulation, causing inflation. By 1795, the assignats were worth only about 5 percent of their original value and had to be removed from circulation.

This solution to the financial crisis was not without negative consequences from another quarter, the church. In June 1790, as the church had now lost all means of support (having given up tithes and lost its lands), the Assembly tried to address the situation by passing the "Civil Constitution of the Clergy." This

Figure 6.2: Sans-cullotes[9]

effectively made the clergy employees of the state, Protestants and Catholics. To further streamline the new system, the number of bishops was reduced to one for each of the new administrative districts, the *départements.* Perhaps most troublesome of all, clergy were required to swear an oath of allegiance to the nation. Not surprisingly, at the pope's urging, most French clergy rejected the law, thereby losing their livelihoods. Worse still, this legislation created a fissure in the new state: Frenchmen were now forced to choose between their God and their nation.

Largely because of this law, in June 1791, shortly before the new constitution the National Assembly had been working on was adopted, the king and his family were stopped on the Austrian border while attempting to flee the country. They returned to the Tuileries, virtually as prisoners. The official story was that the king had been kidnapped and rescued, but no one really believed it.

Despite the attempted flight of the king, the Assembly went ahead with creation of a new constitution for France, which was adopted September 3, 1791, with "The Declaration of the Rights of Man and the

---

9   https://en.wikipedia.org/wiki/Sans-culottes Figure 6-3
10   So much land released into the market all at once would have made the land virtually worthless.

Citizen" attached as its preamble.[11] This constitution provided for a limited monarchy. The executive power was in the king's hands, aided by his cabinet. Yet, his powers were severely limited in that his cabinet had to agree to anything he proposed, and the king was given only a suspensory veto of four years over laws passed in the legislature.

In the Old Regime, France had had a bewilderingly complex set of administrative and church divisions, reflecting the higgledy-piggledy way the state had grown up. To create a more rational political system, the new constitution divided France into eighty-three provinces, *départements,* all about the same size. The départements were divided into *arrondissements,* or districts, which were divided into *communes* or municipalities. Officials in these areas enjoyed a lot of power. Unlike France before the revolution, where the king was absolute, under the new constitution little power was given to the central government. It would not be improper to compare the results to the American Articles of Confederation. Each capital city was near the center of the department, easily accessible to the people. Also, all functions of government, including religious ones, were to be conducted there. Recall that the number of bishops was reduced to one for each département. The legislative power was to be in the hands of a single house. The constitution also gave France a uniform law code. As in the United States, marriage became a civil ceremony, not a religious one.

For all of their talk about freedom and equality, the new constitution did not consider all men equally capable of either serving in government, or electing those who did. Citizens were divided into two groups: active and passive. Only active citizens could vote. To be active you had to pay a tax equal to roughly three-days' pay for a workman (1.5 to 3 livres). Voting was indirect. Those who qualified as active citizens voted for electors who were wealthier still (paying a tax worth about ten-days' labor), and they elected the delegates. Jacobins bitterly assailed this provision, pointing out that the real active citizens were the people who stormed the Bastille, many of whom were not wealthy enough to vote under this constitution. To be sure, the resulting legislature was composed of men of substance.

The new legislature met October 1, 1791. While its membership was mostly young, relatively prosperous, and mostly lawyers, it was divided into three ideological groups. The most conservative and royalist delegates happened to be seated on the right, while the most radical sat on the left. Those in between, who could be swayed one way or the other, sat in the center. This is where the modern designation of left, right, and center in politics arose.

The most important faction on the left at this time, a group known as Girondins, was convinced that only by spreading the revolution throughout Europe would it succeed. They, therefore, agitated for war with Austria, where most of the French émigrés had fled. Some members of Louis XVI's court also favored war. France would be defeated and the restoration of the Old Regime would follow, they reasoned, incorrectly as it turned out. On August 20, the legislature declared war on Austria. The French could not have imagined that they would remain at war for most of the next twenty-three years.

Not surprisingly, the war did not go well for France. Most of its military leaders were in exile, and the new government was weak at the top, which made organizing for war difficult. Prussia and Austria invaded France in July. On July 30, the Duke of Brunswick (1735–1806) issued a "Manifesto" threatening to burn Paris to the ground if the royal family was harmed in any way. The duke's manifesto helped galvanized the radicals.

---

11   It has been the preamble to every constitution since.

On the night of August 10, a group of Jacobins, supported by national guardsmen assembled to go to the front, attacked the Tuileries, and took possession of the king and royal family. They declared Louis deposed and the legislature dissolved. The nation was to have a new constitution. France, now a republic, entered the second phase of its revolution. Included among the national guardsmen who thronged Paris at this time was a group from Marseilles who marched into town singing a new song that became, and remains, the French National Anthem.[12] As befitted the situation, its tune was rousing, its lyrics were bloody, and it was prophetic of what lay ahead.

THE SECOND REVOLUTION

The leaders of the coup decided a new government should be created by a body elected by universal male suffrage, to be called the National Convention. To manage until a new government could be formed, a committee of those who had seized power, mostly Girondins led by George Danton (1759–1794), took control.

The assignats did not regain their value, nor did bread magically appear in Paris because France had undergone a second revolution. And the situation on the battlefield seemed to worsen by the day. There was an almost universal fear of traitors in their midst. All these pressures led to an outbreak of revolutionary violence known as the "September Massacres." Mobs went from prison to prison, executing those whom they deemed enemies of the state. This anarchic situation went on for four days; thousands were summarily executed before it subsided.

The anarchic situation in Paris and the dismal news from the battlefield encouraged the revolutionaries to move quickly. Elections for the Convention occurred in early September, and the body assembled on September 20. It lasted until the Terror ended in late 1795. Although supposedly elected by universal male suffrage, only about 12 percent of the eligible voters actually voted. The body that was elected was rather like the one that had preceded it.

To be sure, there were no monarchists. The right in the Convention was now occupied by the Gironde, with a new group on the left called the Mountain because its members sat high up in the meeting hall. As before, the dominant group numerically was the center, or Plain.

On September 21, 1792, all sides did agree to declare France a Republic. Beyond that, agreement was difficult to find. The Gironde wanted to continue the federal constitution that kept most power in local hands. The Mountain, led by a flamboyant lawyer, Maximillian Robespierre (1758–1794), insisted on creation of a more powerful central government. If the state were to survive, he maintained, it must become a republic of virtue through terror. As Robespierre explained: "terror was nothing but justice, swift, severe, and inflexible; it is an emanation of virtue. . . . It has been said that terror is the mainstay of a despotic government. . . . The government of the revolution is the despotism of liberty against tyranny."[13]

The Mountain ultimately prevailed, and the slide into "The Reign of Terror" followed swiftly. First, Louis XVI was sentenced to die by the newly instituted guillotine on January 21, 1793. A month later, the Convention rejected the Gironde's proposed constitution and a life-or-death struggle between the two factions ensued.

---

12   You can hear it and read an English translation of the text: https://www.youtube.com/watch?v=laWljgWDesE.
13   Winks and Kaiser, p. 160

Shortly thereafter, the French armies suffered a series of defeats in the Netherlands, as well as several defections from generals associated with the Gironde, including Lafayette and his subordinate, Dumouriez (1739–1823), both of whom deserted to the Austrians. In July, one of the leaders of the Mountain, Jean-Paul Marat, was killed in his bath by a young woman, Charlotte Corday, which added to the difficulties the Girondists faced.

Living conditions in Paris steadily worsened with shortages of food and even soap and the accompanying high prices. On June 2, 1793, a group of sans-culottes invaded the hall where the Convention was meeting, demanding the arrest of twenty-nine Girondin deputies as traitors. The Plain was cowed by the mob and the Mountain into giving in to their demands, and the right of the Convention was sentenced to be guillotined.

THE REIGN OF TERROR

Saving the revolution was now the problem of the Mountain. Having rejected the Girondin constitution, the Convention quickly approved a proposal to create a unicameral legislature, to be elected by universal male suffrage. While overwhelmingly approved, the "Constitution of the Year I" never saw the light of day. Instead, it was set aside until the end of the war, with France governed by the Convention itself through three committees. The most important was the Committee of Public Safety, often referred to as the "Twelve who Ruled," among whom the most prominent was Robespierre. It was responsible for the conducting of the war, dealing with opposition outside of Paris and seeing that shortages were addressed. Technically answerable to the Convention, this committee, in effect, ruled France until overthrown. It functioned like a committee in that no one member always dominated, including Robespierre.

The second governing body was the "Committee of General Security." It was charged with police functions and those who fell into its grasp were turned over to a third group, the "Revolutionary Tribunal," for trial.

This judicial body consisted of five judges and twelve jurors. In time it expanded to four courts to expedite matters. As it progressed, it became increasingly arbitrary. The accused were not allowed to have defense council and, if convicted, the only sentence to be given was death. While many of its victims were famous—Marie Antoinette, but also Danton who proposed that it be created—most were clergy, or people who were caught smuggling. In Paris alone, nearly three thousand people were executed, and in the rest of France, it was closer to fifteen thousand.

The problems the leaders of the Terror faced were not limited to foreign armies; in addition, they had to deal with internal insurrection from two additional sources. First, there were many in France who did not approve the growing centralization of power from Paris that the Convention had introduced. These "federalist areas," as they were called, much preferred the decentralized power structure of the Constitution of 1791. Secondly, there were parts of France where Catholicism was strong, and these areas were virtually outside of government control. There was also the fear they would collaborate with foreign enemies.

The Convention sent out "representatives on mission" to bring these regional areas under control. Local Jacobin clubs were purged of those whose loyalty was suspect, and revolutionary tribunals were set up to administer swift justice.

The *Vendée* was a strong center of Catholic opposition. Nantes, a city in this department, experienced the mass drowning of clergy, at least one hundred fifty on two occasions. Estimates are that about a quarter-million people in this region were guillotined, drowned, shot, or died from imprisonment during the Terror.

The Convention adopted other measures to insure the revolution. All bachelors or widowers between the ages of eighteen and twenty-five were drafted (*levée en masse*). Because of the problems of inflation, the regime also experimented with wage and price controls (the maximum). The Convention even regulated the way bread could be made, insisting only whole wheat be used. Finally, any remaining *émigrés* properties were confiscated to be distributed among landless French citizens.

Among the more interesting areas of new research into the French Revolution in the last half century or so has been a growing appreciation for the emergence of what is often termed a new "political culture" stemming from the revolution. In part, it was reflected in a new set of festivals to replace those of Christianity and the Old Regime. These occurred throughout the revolutionary era and changed character as the revolution itself underwent changes. Their primary purpose, however, was the same: to create a new culture that would "transfer sacrality onto political and social values ... thus defining a new legitimacy ... in which the cult of mankind and the religion of the social bond, the bounty of industry and the future of France would co-exist," to quote Monica Ozouf.[14] Old celebrations were abandoned and replaced by new ones designed to promote a new social solidarity. Even the look of municipalities changed. Throughout France, in place of statues of Mary were erected statues of "Marianne," a young defender of reason and liberty.[15] The names of streets and squares were changed, and houses were numbered to give the community coherence. The festivals, Ozouf points out, were celebrated not on the town greens but out in the open air. Newspapers, plays, and music were recast to deliver a revolutionary and nationalistic message. People came to be known not as Mr. and Mrs., but as "Citizen" and "Citizeness."

Inspired by the Enlightenment, the Convention introduced the metric system, and even passed a bill to mark time by a revolutionary clock based on one hundred minutes to the hour. It never saw the light of day. A new calendar, however, was created. In place of the seven-day week, France introduced a ten-day week. The new days of the week were simply the First, the Second, etc. In place of the traditional months, they introduced a new set, dating from the beginning of the republic (September 22, 1792), which became the first day of the "Year I of Freedom." The name of each month matched the season in which it occurred: *Venédemaire,* the first month, from September 22 to near the end of October (old calendar), referred to the grape harvest. The month corresponding to late January and most of February was called *Nivôse,* or "the snowy" month. *Thermidor,* which began in late July and went until late August, meant the "hot" month.[16]

All these measures were part of a concerted effort on the part of the republic to rid France of Christian influences. Churches were closed and most priests had either fled, were in hiding, or were executed. A ten-day week obscured when Sunday would come. Since the Catholic Church had attached saints' names to all the days of the year, an effort was made to replace them with the names of common plants.

While some of the revolutionaries were atheists, most were not. They simply wanted a religion appropriate for their new state. Robespierre attempted to provide this by introducing 20 *Prairial,* Year II (June 8, 1794), the first celebration of the "Worship of the Supreme Being." By all accounts, most Parisians enjoyed

---

14   Monica Ozouf, 282
15   Quite by accident, this author happened upon one in a remote city in Pyrenees.
16   Napoleon reverted back to the traditional calendar in 1805.

the festival, but a new religion is hard to decree, and this one died when its creator died. The free exercise of religion, however, would not return to France until Napoleon.

By 1794, France's military situation had changed dramatically. French armies had not only driven their enemies out of France, but they had also taken over Belgium. The Austrian armies retreated across the Rhine, and the British into the Netherlands, to defend Holland. Federalist opposition in France had been broken, and a supply of grain had been secured for Paris. Many in the Convention began to wonder if it were not time to relax the Terror. Yet the Committee of Public Safety, convinced more strenuous efforts should be enacted to protect the revolution, insisted on passage of the Law of 22 *Prairial*, Year II (June 10, 1794), a decree that made almost any criticism of the government an act of treason, punishable by death. Such a loosely written law made the Committee of General Security and many members of the Convention anxious for their safety. Even some of the "Twelve who Ruled" worried Robespierre might turn on them. Robespierre had also alienated many among the sans-culottes when, in late March, he secured the execution of their leaders, the fiery atheist journalist, Jacques Hébert.

Opposition to Robespierre mounted until on the night of 9 *Thermidor*, Year II (July 27, 1794), he and his closest associates were declared outlaws and the next day executed. A number of them committed suicide rather than face the guillotine. Robespierre attempted it, but only managed to blow off part of his jaw. The Reign of Terror was at an end but creating a workable government still remained an obstacle.

THERMIDORIAN REACTION AND DIRECTORY

The Thermidorians, as those who overthrew Robespierre are known, agreed the Terror must end and quickly dismantled its instruments of power. They invited surviving Girondin deputies to return to the Convention. They had to deal with a reaction from the right, young men of the middle class who went around Paris attacking those they suspected of being connected to the Terror. There were also rebels from the left who, on one occasion, invaded the Convention in an attempt to restore the Terror. Clearly, the Thermidorians did not want to return to the Terror or to monarchy, but what exactly they did want was not so clear.

The bourgeois of Paris wanted the economic restrictions of the Terror abolished, and the Thermidorians complied with their wishes, which led to an almost instantaneous inflation. Some food items rose 500 percent and food riots became common. By this point, the value of the assignats was virtually nil. The Thermidorians also made the first step toward restoring religious practices in France. Catholic churches were unbolted and priests, under state supervision, were allowed to resume saying mass.

Even if they had known what they wanted to accomplish, the Thermidorians' task would have been almost impossible. They did create a new government, approved by the Convention in August 1795, the "Constitution of the Year III," the third since the revolution began. It was, of course, the last act of the Convention. It also represented a move away from popular democracy, as property qualifications were reintroduced for voting.

We know it as the *Directory*. Inspired by ancient Greece, it consisted of a two-house legislature, the Council of Five Hundred and the Council of Elders. The former nominated people to be the candidates for the Directory. The latter chose the five who were to serve from those nominated. After that, the Directors pretty much ran things to suit themselves.

The first winter of this new government was especially harsh, not only because of the inflation and food shortages, but also because of especially severe weather. People later remembered this time as the worst since the revolution had begun. The harsh conditions produced more disorders, especially around Paris. A young Corsican artillery commander, Napoleon Bonaparte, serving the new government, dispersed a royalist uprising with what he later termed a "whiff of grapeshot." And an uprising from the left, led by a "socialist," Gracchus Babeuf (1760–1797), was crushed shortly thereafter, bringing to an end the sans-culottes in Paris as an effective revolutionary force.

Happily for the regime, the next year saw a return of good harvests. It also enjoyed an influx of revenues from the conquests of French armies. The assignat, now worthless, was repudiated, along with much of the national debt, and the Directory established a new currency, the *franc*, which would remain the nation's currency until France adopted the euro early in 2014.

The Directory proved to be very unstable. Competition between the Directors and members of the two legislative chambers created a situation in which everyone came to be seen as corrupt, manipulating power for his own gain. Some have suggested that following the austerity of the years of the Republic of Virtue and Terror, some such relaxation of morals and ethics was to be expected.

In 1792, the armies of France had solemnly sworn never to engage in a war of conquest. By 1795, conquest was very much what the Directors were after. It swelled their coffers and some imagined that reaching France's "natural borders" was necessary for the nation to be safe. The military situation was made easy for France because of internal disagreements among her enemies. In particular, between 1793 and 1795, Austria, Prussia, and Russia were busily completing the partitioning of Poland they had begun just before the revolution began. As a result, they feared one another more than they feared France. By 1795, only Austria and Britain remained at war with France. To deal with Austria, the Directory turned to the same young Corsican who had saved them before and directed him to drive the Austrians out of Italy. Little did they dream he would do a great deal more!

NAPOLEON BONAPARTE

Napoleon was born Napoleone Buonaparte on the island of Corsica in 1769, shortly after France had acquired it from Genoa. As a youngster he attended a military school in France. He was said to have spoken French with an accent and that his command of the written language was never especially good. Napoleon first served the revolution as an artillery commander in December 1793, when he recaptured the port of Toulon from the British. This service for the Terror landed him in prison briefly during the Thermidorian Reaction. He was soon released, however, and his service to the Directory in 1795 against the royalist uprising, along with his fortunate marriage to Josephine de Beauharnais, by most accounts a mistress of one of the Directors, caused him to be chosen for the Italian command.

Napoleon made short work of the Austrians in Italy, and by 1797 had forced them to accept the Treaty of Campo Formio, which he negotiated without recourse to the Directory. As a result, Austria lost Belgium, and Napoleon created two puppet states in northern Italy: the Ligurian and Cisalpine Republics.

Britain alone remained at war with France. Napoleon conceived the idea of attacking Britain by invading Egypt. He invited a number of scholars and archeologists to accompany his armies. Their job was to study ancient Egypt. Among the artifacts found was the Rosetta Stone, the key to deciphering hieroglyphics in the nineteenth century.[17]

The campaign did not go as well as he had hoped. His armies defeated the Mamluks, but his navy was destroyed by the British Admiral Horatio Nelson (1758–1805). This meant he was cut off from supplies. Realizing his situation in Egypt was hopeless, Napoleon simply abandoned the campaign, along with his soldiers, and returned to France.

France was ripe for a *coup d'état*. The Directory continued to be challenged from the left, and the right as well. Additionally, a second coalition of Britain, Austria, and Russia had formed against France because the Directory had established four satellite republics in Italy. By Napoleon's return, the French armies had been expelled from all four by the Russian general, Alexander Suvorov (1729–1799).

Despite the outcome in Egypt, Napoleon was given a rousing welcome upon his return to France. The French people only knew of his many victories there. Some of the Directors were now convinced the Directory needed to be replaced and they thought Napoleon could help them accomplish it. The coup was launched November 9 and 10, 1799, and Napoleon and two of the Directors formed the Fourth Revolutionary Government, the Consulate.

Consulate and Empire

The Directors who conspired with Napoleon assumed they would control the new government, and Napoleon as well. At first, the executive was shared by three "Consuls," but in reality, only Napoleon, the "First Consul," enjoyed real authority. By 1802, Napoleon had persuaded the legislators to make him First Consul for Life. In 1804, he transformed the Consulate into the empire, with himself as the emperor. His coronation took place December 2, and was attended by the pope, although Napoleon placed the crown upon his own head. This, of course, was France's fifth revolutionary government.

The government Napoleon created included a four-house legislature whose membership he controlled. Each of the four had only one function. The "Council of State" could propose laws. The "Tribunate" could debate them. The "Legislative Corps" voted on them. Finally, the "Senate" reviewed legislation passed and could veto it. This was a sham legislature, meant to look democratic while leaving all the power in Napoleon's hands. In the end, he could not even tolerate the Tribunate debating his legislation so, in 1807, the Emperor Napoleon simply abolished it.

Whenever Napoleon revised the government, he submitted his actions to a vote of the people, a *plebiscite*, and his wishes were always overwhelmingly approved. This too was a democratic sham as there was no other option as France was in the midst of a war. Yet the evidence seems to suggest Napoleon enjoyed the support of the nation. First, he was prepared to welcome into his service anyone, Jacobins or royalists, who possessed ability and would serve him loyally. Those who did were well paid and given grandiose titles. Napoleon even brought back a semblance of nobility by creating a class he called "the Notables," which included many former aristocrats, but also men of wealth from the *bourgeois*.

---

17   He also carried an Arabic language printing press for propaganda purposes. When he fled Egypt, he left it behind and the Egyptians used it to begin printing *Qur'ans*.

It might be best to liken Napoleon to an enlightened despot. He created a uniform law code for France, "Code Napoleon," that is the basis of law in many nations today, not to mention our state of Louisiana. In some ways, this code preserved the gains of the revolution. All men were to be equal before the law; divorce was legal, as was the exercise of religion. But torture was reintroduced, and the laws that had protected women and children were replaced by laws making the man of the family the supreme authority. Slavery was also reintroduced into French colonies (although not into France itself).

Napoleon could be quite ruthless when he faced internal opposition. A royalist uprising was put down, and the rebels massacred. The Duke d'Enghein, a truly apolitical descendent of the Bourbons, living in Germany, was mistakenly thought to be involved in anti-Napoleonic activities, including assassination attempts. Napoleon had him kidnapped and summarily executed, though he knew he was innocent. It had a salutary effect, as the assassination attempts came to an end.

By the early nineteenth century, the French people were weary of anti-clericalism and anxious for the restoration of the Catholic Church. Napoleon accomplished this with the "Concordat of 1801." While Napoleon gave up some control over religion as a result, the church gave up even more and became, in effect, a ward of the state. Furthermore, Napoleon did not abandon non-Catholics since his law recognized the Catholic Church only as "the church of most Frenchmen." In truth, the pope became a virtual prisoner of the emperor, but most Frenchmen were very glad to have their priests and masses restored to them.

Education had always been in the hands of the church and so it remained at the primary level. But Napoleon was anxious that education at the secondary level be under state control, and created the system of *lycées* that, in modified form, exist in France today.

Napoleon also sought to bring the economy under control. The stability he brought to France improved the economic well-being of most people. Seaport towns suffered as a result of war, but peasants found his rule generally beneficial. The revenues of the state were kept flush by Napoleon's military victories. There can be little doubt that most Frenchmen who voted "yes" in Napoleon's plebiscites were supportive of their ruler and military conqueror. Their economic well-being was much improved under his reign. The same cannot be said for those forced into Napoleon's empire or forced into an alliance with him. Their one ambition was to be rid of the French and their emperor. That meant a steady stream of wars.

Napoleon's Wars

Shortly after Napoleon became First Consul in 1799, the second coalition broke up. The need for peace was recognized by everyone, including his only remaining adversary, England. In 1802, France and England concluded the Peace of Amiens. It was rather one-sided, and Napoleon had no intention of honoring it; consequently, it lasted only a year before war with Britain resumed. Shortly thereafter, the "Third Coalition" of Austria, Prussia, and Russia joined England. In 1803 and 1804, Napoleon dispatched nearly one hundred thousand men to suppress the Haitian uprising led by Toussaint L'Ouverture. The Haitians were far more effective fighters than Napoleon had expected, and yellow fever a more formidable opponent than the Haitians themselves, resulted in severe losses for the French. Beyond that, the new coalition presented a threat to France itself. Napoleon decided to abandon his American project. At the same time, he sold the Louisiana Purchase to the United States for about sixteen million dollars, about one dollar per acre.

The first round in the conflicts with the Third Coalition was a disaster for France. In a decisive sea battle at Cape Trafalgar (October 1805), during which Admiral Nelson lost his life, the English defeated the French navy and gained control of the seas, ending thereby any hope Napoleon might have had of a cross-channel invasion of Britain.

The situation on the continent, however, was just the opposite. Here Napoleon swept all before him. In 1806, after the battle of Austerlitz, the Holy Roman Empire that had existed for eight hundred years came to an end. This once proud ruler now became only the emperor of Austria, as Napoleon was the emperor of France.

By 1807, Napoleon was at the pinnacle of his power. At a meeting with Russian Tsar Alexander I, at Tilsit, the two men drew up a map of Europe, a result of which France was recognized as master of Central and Western Europe, while Russia controlled the East. Austria and Prussia were much reduced in size and made subordinate to France. Only England, Sweden, and Turkey were outside the system.

The grand empire of Napoleon consisted of three types of political units. First, there was France proper, much enlarged as a result of the revolution and of Napoleon's victories. Second, there were areas controlled by relatives of Napoleon: Spain, the Netherlands, the kingdom of Italy, the Swiss Republic, a reconstituted Poland—the Grand Duchy of Warsaw—and parts of Germany–the Confederation of the Rhine. The third

Figure 6.3: 1812 Map of Europe[18]

18   https://commons.wikimedia.org/wiki/File:Europe_1812_map_en.png Fig. 6-3

group consisted of states outside France's direct control: Austria, Prussia, and Russia. All of the states in Europe were diplomatically linked to Napoleon (Figure 6.3).

Napoleon's empire did not last the century he had hoped. Indeed, it fell rather quickly; yet, much he had accomplished remained thereafter. Napoleon and his armies brought the "democratic revolutions" to the rest of Europe. Everywhere, ideas of legal equality and religious toleration were introduced. As in France, careers were made open to talent, and privileges of nobility and clergy were discounted, at least as long as he was there. The geographical area we call Germany today, before conquered by Napoleon, included well over two hundred territorial units; after Napoleon's defeat, the number was reduced to thirty-nine. Napoleon and his armies changed Europe forever.

His obsession with defeating England put strains upon the system, which ultimately led to its demise. In particular, Napoleon conceived of an economic way of defeating the British now that the naval option was no longer available. He called it the "Continental System." Since he controlled almost all of Europe in one way or another, he decided he could starve the "Nation of Shop Keepers," as he called the British, into surrender by depriving them of continental ports. Unfortunately for his plan, Europeans had come to rely upon the British to supply them with much of what they needed. Even Napoleon depended on English merchants to supply him with wool for his soldiers' uniforms. The result was hardship all around, constant evasion, and deception. And growing resentment against Napoleon.

A seemingly minor annoyance also helped undermine Napoleon's position. Spain had been under Bourbon rule since the end of Louis XIV's reign. When the French sought to take over Spain, they encountered a stubborn opposition. No matter how many troops Napoleon sent to Spain, the uprisings could not be subdued. This "Spanish Ulcer," as it was called, could not be salved, and served as an inspiration to the other nations weary of French domination. By the end of the decade, a new sense of nationalism had grown in Austria, Prussia, and Russia out of the opposition to France, which is all the more ironic since nationalism was created by the French revolutionaries themselves.

In 1809, a revived Austrian Empire sought to break out of Napoleon's system, only to be defeated at Wagram. This defeat led to yet another humiliating treaty that led to the marriage of Napoleon (having hastily divorced Josephine) to the Austrian emperor's daughter.

By 1811, Alexander I of Russia, persuaded that Napoleon had to be defeated, withdrew from the Continental System, which was tantamount to a declaration of war. Napoleon began to prepare a massive army of about six hundred thousand men of many nationalities and his invasion of Russia followed in 1812. The Russian approach was to retreat, burning everything as they departed. The French followed after them, but soon found themselves far from any supplies with nothing to requisition locally. One major battle was fought at Borodino, but it was indecisive. When winter came, the French were in serious trouble as they had no winter supplies for the men or their horses. Many froze. Now the Russians counterattacked. Napoleon decided the cause was lost and abandoned his army to return to France.

The campaign's group of six hundred thousand that reached Poland in early 1813 had been reduced to a mere forty thousand men. The revived armies of Europe pursued them and in March 1814, Paris was captured, Napoleon abdicated and was sentenced to exile on the island of Elba, off the coast of Italy. The Bourbons were restored in the person of Louis XVIII, a brother of Louis XVI. The victorious allies, meeting at Vienna, immediately began to quarrel over how the spoils of war were to be distributed.

It looked as though yet another conflict between them would break out. Seizing the opportunity, Napoleon escaped from Elba, returned to France and raised yet another army that was defeated at Waterloo on June 18, 1815. This time Napoleon was exiled to a more distant place, the British island of Saint Helena in the South Atlantic, where he remained until his death in 1821.

Napoleon is buried at *Les Invalides* in Paris. If you visit the site you will find his entombed body suspended in the middle of the room. You may either look up at his sarcophagus in awe, or you may go above it and look down in reverence. You may not look upon it directly. To some, he was the "man on horseback" predicted by Edmund Burke, to others the destroyer of the revolution, but for many Frenchmen he was and remains the greatest hero France has ever produced. No matter how you evaluate Napoleon, it was his reign as emperor of France from 1804 to 1815 that spread the French Revolution throughout Europe.

To finish this chapter, we must now turn to some reforms and revolutions that resulted from both the French and the American revolutions in the period covered by this chapter.

ENGLISH EIGHTEENTH-CENTURY REFORM

During the course of the eighteenth century, the system of government devised in 1688, through which the king and Parliament shared power, remained relatively unchanged. This system guaranteed the landed gentry continued to control the government and governmental policies. They also controlled the local affairs where they resided, as they were judges and sheriffs in their counties.

Yet, Britain itself was changing radically. As we have noted, this was the beginning of industrialization. Its population was growing rapidly, and many people settled in towns often new and totally unrepresented in Parliament. At the same time, many places with once large populations that entitled them to send representatives to the House of Commons were now abandoned, taken over by the seas, or turned into sheep runs. In other words, no one lived there to be represented. These came to be known as "rotten boroughs," or "pocket boroughs," since an aristocrat who owned the no-longer inhabited land was entitled to name his own personal candidate for the seat. Not surprisingly, these changes led to calls for reform in Parliament.

No significant changes will be made in the Britain parliamentary system of government or in the distribution of power there until 1832, but the fact there were men and women agitating for change in the period before and during the American and French revolutions is an important part of the story we are telling in this chapter.

One of the earliest manifestations of a need for reform came from John Wilkes, a Parliament member for Middlesex, in London. Wilkes was a somewhat disreputable gentleman where women, whiskey, and gambling were concerned. He published a newspaper, the *North Briton*, that nettled the privileged and raised questions about the existing social system. In issue No. 45, however, he went too far, at least as far as the government and royal family were concerned. On this occasion, he made the charge that King George III was a liar and that his mother was a minister's mistress. He was arrested on a "General Warrant" (no specific charges were named), his offices were ransacked and his newspaper was closed down. He was put in prison and expelled from Parliament.

Each time Parliament attempted to replace Wilkes in a new election, he ran again and won, even while still in prison. A popular cry of the times in London became "Wilkes and Liberty." When his case came before the courts in 1766, the justices found the use of general warrants to be illegal, which since has been seen to have been a blow for freedom of the press. In the end, Parliament managed to deny Wilkes his seat by arbitrarily placing a losing candidate in it, claiming it was the right of Parliament to determine its own members.

There were others outside London who disliked the arbitrary way government behaved on this occasion. They formed the "Supporters of the Bill of Rights," held mass rallies, raised subscriptions to pay Wilkes's debts, and petitioned Parliament on his behalf.

In the following decades, the desire for reforms grew, as did the organizations attempting to bring them about. In part, the American and French revolutions were responsible because both caused hardships among privileged and poor alike, which promoted an interest in changing the way Parliament worked as a means of solving those ills.

Higher taxes were especially resented, as the war for the colonies was ultimately lost. In one case, the attack on the status quo came from conservative country gentlemen who formed the "Association Movement" of 1779–80. Their most prominent spokesman, Christopher Wyvill, was a clergyman and landowner who argued for the elimination of rotten boroughs, the extension of the franchise, and the introduction of the secret ballot. This movement was at its height in 1789 when it managed to secure sixty thousand signatures on its petitions. But when economic conditions began to improve, it faded away.

Another early voice for reform came from John Cartwright. In 1780, he organized the Society for Constitutional Reform, which lasted until 1794. A retired seaman in the Royal Navy, he refused to serve against the American revolutionaries, ending his naval career. Although he worked with Wyvill on occasions, his ideas were more radical. In particular, he was prepared to work with middle-class carpenters, mechanics, and laborers, along with country gentlemen. In 1776, he published a pamphlet, *Take Your Choice*, in which he championed universal suffrage, equal electoral districts, the secret ballot, and annual parliaments. In later editions, he called for salaries for members of the parliaments and the abolition of property qualifications for voting. These are precisely the ideas that a nineteenth-century group known as the Chartists will strive to obtain.

Sometimes the discontent boiled over into ugly violence, as during the "Gordon Riots" of 1780. To encourage more Catholics in Ireland to enlist in England's armies, Parliament passed a rather mild Catholic Relief Act. The ostensible purpose of the rioters was to secure repeal of this act, but when their petition, submitted to Parliament, was not acted upon promptly, they rioted. For four days, London mobs roamed about in search of Catholics. They attacked chapels attached to private homes and then the homes of wealthy Catholics themselves. They stormed Newgate Prison and set prisoners free. To be sure, behind their anger toward Catholics were economic grievances, the harsh conditions created by the recent American wars. The disorder was genuinely frightening to authorities. Even Wilkes joined the government in opposing them. When order was restored, Gordon spend several months in prison, but twenty-five of the rioters were hanged. More than three hundred Londoners had been killed and thousands injured.

When it began, reformists found the French Revolution to be as inspiring as the American. One such group was the London Corresponding Society, founded by Thomas Hardy. Having many of the same goals as Cartwright, at one time it boasted a following of three thousand dues-paying members who were artisans, tradesmen, and shopkeepers. His organization so frightened Prime Minister Pitt that he had

Cartwright and his chief supporters tried for treason on the trumped-up charge they were planning to kill the king. The jury found them not guilty; however, this did cause many to think twice about continuing in the organization.

Joseph Priestly, a Unitarian minister and chemist, remembered as the discoverer of oxygen, was driven from his home by government-inspired rioters because of his sympathy for the political ideas of the early French revolutionaries. He ultimately fled England and sought refuge with Ben Franklin in America until his death in 1804.

Richard Price, another radical reformer, inspired by "the Declaration of the Rights of Man and the Citizen," supported expanding the franchise and the use of the secret ballot. He further maintained the king was after all no more than the first servant of the public and responsible to it.

Both Priestly and Price were clergymen who saw their ideas for reform as a part of God's caring order of the universe. They were hardly supporters of the Terror or of the violence that resulted from the revolution in France.

One of the most radical among these reformers was Thomas Payne, already known for his defense of the American Revolution in his pamphlet *Common Sense*. In 1791, he published *The Rights of Man* in response to Edmund Burke's scathing attack on the French Revolution, *Reflections on the French Revolution*. Payne, a republican, dismissed the king as a descendent of robber chieftains. He called for the elimination of waste in government and the creation of a welfare society. For this polemical efforts, he had to flee to France to escape prosecution.

Equally important as a manifestation of the new ideas about freedom and liberty that were aborning in England was the work of Mary Wollstonecraft, whose *Vindication of the Rights of Women* was a direct rebuttal to the misogynistic ideas of Rousseau. She later married William Goodwin, an early proponent of anarchism.

William Pitt the Younger, the prime minister who led Britain through the Napoleonic Wars, responded to these ideas during this time of national crisis by crushing those who expressed them. In 1793, he banned all seditious publications and arrested the leaders of the Constitutional and Corresponding societies. He suspended habeas corpus, had Parliament pass laws forbidding the meeting of more than forty people, and made it treason to incite contempt for the constitution or king. In the end, he won. The discontent did not go away, but underground, to resurface in better times.

We should also mention a crusader of a different sort who labored unsuccessfully for reform in this period: William Wilberforce. For more than twenty years he worked tirelessly to end the slave trade in the British Empire. He had to abandon his campaign during the Napoleonic Wars—after all the French Jacobins had freed their slaves. But once the war ended, he returned to the fight and lived to see the practice outlawed in 1833, shortly before he died.

The pressures against reform in England were made even more powerful than they would have been otherwise because of the American and French revolutions. All the same, those revolutions also fed the desire for change, and in the early nineteenth century Britain led the way in introducing democracy to its citizens.

IRELAND

The story of Ireland in the early modern period was one of increasing subjugation to Britain. Three groups made up the inhabitants of this island. The majority were Gaelic Irish, Roman Catholic, and proud descendants of the Celts. They lived mostly in the south. In the north, in addition to the Gaelic Irish, were two groups of Protestants: the "Anglo-Irish," who were English and Catholic and could trace their ancestry to the thirteenth century; and the "Scots-Irish," Presbyterians from Scotland who came during the reign of William and Mary. Also living there, mostly in Dublin, was a small group of career bureaucrats who ran the British imperial administration. Normally, they returned to England once they retired.

Not surprisingly, both the American and French revolutions affected these groups in different ways. Some of the Protestants hoped to be able to advance their economic and religious interests at the expense of the British, as the Americans had done. The Catholic Irish saw their own situation as being rather similar to that of the American colonials. When the Americans not only rebelled but gained their independence, Irish patriots began to think about the possibilities of doing the same themselves.

The British, for their part, realized, in light of the current circumstances, that they would have to make concessions, at least to the Anglo-Irish and the Presbyterians. Some members of Parliament were even supportive of the predicament in which Catholic Irish, mostly poor farmers, found themselves. Prominent Englishmen, such as the novelist and essayist Johnathan Swift, who served as dean of Trinity Cathedral, Dublin, also supported their cause. His satirical pamphlet, *A Modest Proposal* (1729), suggested a solution to Irish poverty. The Irish should sell their excess children to the English for food. It would reduce the population on the island and bring in additional revenue as well.

Parliament passed some legislation that improved the lot of most Irishman. But the Gaelic Irish desires for legislative independence within the British monarchy did not garner much support in England, or with the members of the Irish parliament (mostly Anglo-Irish) in Ireland either.

Following the fall of the Bastille, the Irish reformers, most of whom were Catholics, began to look to France as a possible vehicle for gaining their freedom. Particularly important to this cause was a young Irish Protestant, Wolfe Tone, who hoped to unite Catholic and Protestant Irishmen against a common English enemy. Making his way through America to France, he sought to enlist the aid of French forces in the liberation of Ireland. When, by March 1798, help from France did not arrive, a frustrated group of Catholics, the United Irishmen, rose in rebellion. They were ill prepared and easily defeated by Royal forces. Shortly thereafter, a French contingent set sail with Tone aboard. Unhappily for the Irish and Tone, the ship was picked up at sea by the British. Tone was turned over to the Irish government, tried, and hanged.

Pitt did realize he had a problem on his hands. Finally, the Irish were granted religious freedom in their own country, although they still could not hold elective office. Pitt also engineered the union of Ireland with Britain, forming the United Kingdom in January 1801. The struggle for freedom would continue until the end of World War I before the southern part of the island, at least, finally achieved independence.

HAITI

The last revolutionary experience we look at in this chapter occurred in what is Haiti today. To the French it was Saint-Domingue, which had been added to their Caribbean empire in 1697. They valued it because it produced sugar, coffee, indigo, cacao, and cotton on its plantations, worked by slaves from Africa. The English and Spanish coveted it for the same reasons. It may well have been the wealthiest colony in the world at that time. It is important to our consideration because the story of this small island in the half century this chapter covers brings together, in one small place, all the intellectual, economic, and cultural strains we have been discussing. It also helps us understand the limitations of the "Atlantic Revolutions," so that, in subsequent chapters, you can understand why later revolutionaries will espouse different ideas.

By the late eighteenth century, Saint-Domingue's social class structure consisted of four distinct groups. The wealthiest group were Frenchmen who owned large plantations, the *grands blancs*. Many of them did not spend a lot of time on the island because of yellow fever. When they did, they were mostly concentrated in the north, around what on the map, below, is called Cap-Haitien; it was then Cap-Français. A second group, somewhat larger in number, the *petits blancs*, were white and free, but not wealthy. Many of them had arrived after the Seven Years Wars and taken jobs in what might be called the service sector and the military. A third group, equal in size to the second, was the free people of color (*gens de couleur libres*, or mulattoes). They were partly of white descent and often times competed with the petits blancs for the same jobs. The poor whites saw themselves as superior to the free blacks. The mulattoes, for their part, were frequently educated, some more so that the poor whites whom they resented, and not surprisingly, they, as freed men-of-color, looked down upon the blacks who were slaves.

Roughly nine of ten people on the island were slaves of African descent. Some were born in Saint-Dominque (Creoles) and others were imported, as the work and the disease required the supply of laborers be replenished regularly. These were the plantation workers responsible for the great wealth this French colony produced.

But class and race are not the only complicating factors to consider. When the Democratic Revolutions began, these different groups responded very differently to its message. To the *grand blancs* it was a chance to free themselves from French influence, much as the Americans had done from the British. To the mulattoes it was an opportunity to be treated as equals. They were looking at "Declaration of the Rights of Man and the Citizen." To the slaves, of course, it was a chance to gain freedom.

Finally, the situation was complicated by the ambitions of the powers around Haiti. France vacillated between being true to its revolutionary ideals on the one hand and seeking to maintain slavery on the other. England, involved in war with France, saw real possibilities, both to weaken the enemy and to gain some valuable real estate. Spain, which controlled the other half of the island, wanted to hold on to its possession in a situation that became increasingly complex. Finally, the young United States, with its slave-based economy in the South, looked nervously, not only at the more extreme measures that came out of the French Revolution, but also at the political events occurring in Haiti that might lead to the freeing of slaves and the creation of a black state.

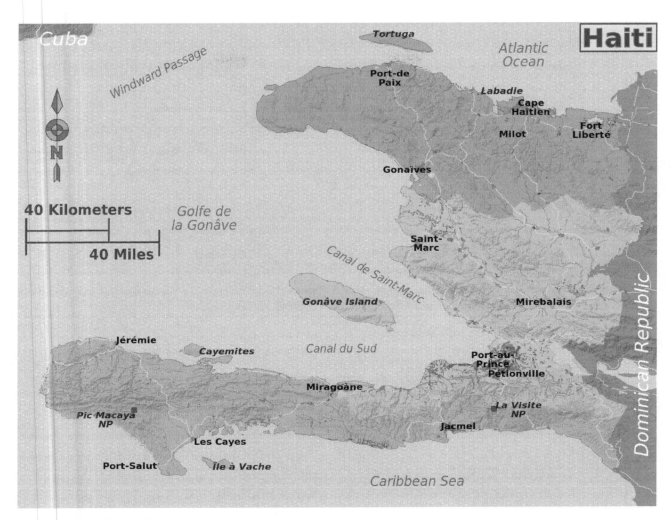

Figure 6.4: Map of Haiti[19]

There is one other factor that should be recognized. In all the slave colonies of the New World, some slaves escaped by running away and forming settlements of their own (Maroons). In Brazil, the space was so vast that many such settlements existed, some for decades, before they were destroyed by the whites. Haiti had such groups as well. At times, they played a role in the course of events.

When the Estates General convened in 1788, Saint-Dominique sent representatives, totally elected by the grands blancs. Freed blacks protested they had not been included and, as the revolution progressed, they began to gain support in Paris.

Back in Haiti and despite the best efforts of the whites to prevent it, news of what was happening in France reached their slaves who, in May 1791, led by a Maroon voodoo priest, rose in rebellion. By 1792, the rebellious slaves controlled two-thirds of the island. Two thousand whites had been killed and one hundred eighty plantations destroyed. Fearing for France's economic interests there, the newly constituted Legislative Assembly passed a law granting full citizenship rights to all free mulattoes.

---

19   https://commons.wikimedia.org/wiki/File:Haiti_regions_map.png

This response was not what the grands blancs expected, and it genuinely shocked the United States. France was now at war with Britain and Spain, so the Haitian whites attempted to transfer their sovereignty to the British. The Spanish invaded from their half of the island, aided by the rebellious slaves.

By this point, France had become a republic under the Convention, and it moved quickly to end slavery in all French colonies and to grant full citizenship to blacks. What Saint-Domingue needed was a national hero, and in the person of Toussaint L'Ouverture, he appeared.

Toussaint had fought with the Spanish until the Convention ended slavery, something the Spanish were unwilling to do. He commanded a large number of slave soldiers and, when he joined forces with the French, they were able to drive the Spanish from their part of the island. He also expelled an English expeditionary force in 1798.

In 1801, Toussaint convened an assembly to prepare a constitution for Saint-Dominique, which he promulgated in July. It was clearly modeled on French constitutional principles. Furthermore, he was governor-for-life, not king or president. His new state would be a "self-ruling" colony under France. Slavery was abolished, commercial freedom protected, and Catholicism was made the religion of the nation, although the pope chose not to recognize what he had done. He was also careful not to threaten the lives and property of French whites.

Recall that things moved fast in France during this period. By 1801, Napoleon was in power. He was unsympathetic to blacks and eventually restored slavery to the colonies. Seeing how powerful Toussaint had become, he decided to bring him down. In July, Napoleon sent an army under his brother-in-law, Charles Leclerc, to restore French control and, secretly, slavery as well.

It was easier for the French than you might suppose, because once Haiti's enemies had been defeated, the confederates who had joined Toussaint to accomplish it resented his assertions of power and fell to fighting him and one another. Naturally, the British and Americans were only too happy to assist them in their quarrels. When Leclerc arrived, he soon managed to divide his opponents, win some over with promises of power, and ultimately isolate Toussaint. In 1802, Toussaint himself was persuaded to surrender and retire to France, where he died in 1803.

When it became apparent to the Haitians that the French planned to restore them to slavery, they rebelled again. As we pointed out earlier, the costs of controlling the island were more than Napoleon could afford. On January 1, 1804, the new leader of the freed blacks, Dessalines, declared the state of Haiti[20] a free republic.

Haiti has the distinction, not only of being the first independent nation to arise in Latin America, but also the first nation in which former slaves fought for and gained their freedom. What followed was a purging of all whites, in particular those who were French. Between February and April 1804, Dessalines traveled about Haiti to see that his orders were carried out. In some cases, he was persuaded to spare the lives of Frenchmen who were said to have treated their former slaves well. Some whites escaped, hidden by Haitians. A Scottish merchant ransomed about twenty-four hundred Frenchmen. The number killed is estimated to have been between three thousand and five thousand.

---

20   "Haiti" is an indigenous Arawak name.

Eleven years later, the French recognized the independence of Haiti in return for an indemnity of one hundred fifty million francs. Thereafter, recognition came from other nations.

Historians have speculated as to whether things might have turned out differently. To be sure, the Haitians were free, but the massacres it took to get them there, and the massacres that Dessalines promulgated, left a mark on the society not soon erased.

In subsequent chapters, the lessons of this half century, its accomplishments and its failings, will be debated and discussed, not only by historians and politicians, but by ordinary citizens as well. The Age of Democratic Revolutions changed Europe and, ultimately, the world forever; yet, as the Haitian story makes clear, there were many reasons why the ideas of this period seemed inadequate and in need of change in the future.

FOR FURTHER READING

Maurice Ashley. *A History of Europe, 1648–1815*. New Jersey: Prentice Hall, 1973.

Jack W. Censer. *The French Revolution and Intellectual History*. Chicago: Dorsey Press, 1989.

Euan Cameron. *Early Modern Europe. An Oxford History*. New York: Oxford University Press, 1999.

William Doyle. *The Old European Order, 1660–1800*. New York: Oxford University Press, 1978.

Lynn Hunt. *Politics, Culture, and Class in the French Revolution*. Berkeley: University of California Press, 1985.

Wim Klooster. *Revolutions in the Atlantic World. A Comparative History*. New York: New York University Press, 2009.

Paul Langford. *Eighteenth-Century Britain. A Very Short Introduction*. New York: Oxford University Press, 2000.

Mona Ozouf. *Festivals and the French Revolution*. Translated by Alan Sheridan. Massachusetts: Harvard University Press, 1988.

William B. Wilcox, and Walter L. Arnstein. *The Age of Aristocracy, 1688–1830*. 4th ed. New York: Houghton-Mifflin, 2001.

Alan Winks, and Thomas E. Kaiser. *Europe from the Old Regime to the Age of Revolution, 1648–1815*. New York: Oxford University Press, 2004.

CHAPTER
SEVEN

The Flowering of Modernity: Political Transformations in the First Half of the 19th Century

INTRODUCTION

The first half of the nineteenth century was a time of much change, a fact attested to by the many revolts and wars of various kinds that were widespread around the globe. There were indeed many social, political, and economic grievances from large segments of the world's people. The world in many ways was divided into two large camps: the privileged and the marginalized. Much of the conflict in the early 1800s, regardless of global region, pitted those who wanted to improve the lives of the marginalized against those who sought to preserve the status quo. No doubt, Napoleon Bonaparte's conquest of Europe in the first decade of the nineteenth century sparked an Enlightenment-era discourse on progress that affected people throughout that continent. At the same time, Napoleon's defeat also produced a reactionary response in Europe over what role a government should play in the lives of citizens. At the time, new ideas also emerged over other sensitive issues, such as slavery. In fact, as the century wore on, the idea of abolishing the slave trade increasingly took root in Europe and the Americas. In addition, the idea of republicanism unleashed a series of wars for liberation against colonial repression that forever changed the political structure of Latin America. Lastly, in the Ottoman-controlled Middle East, and in East Asia, the tendency for governments to want to preserve tradition in the face of modern impulses for change hampered those regions' development.

PEACE AND TENSION IN POST-NAPOLEONIC EUROPE

With his monumental wars of conquest, Napoleon Bonaparte had wreaked enormous havoc on much of Europe in the early nineteenth century. Morale among leaders, citizens, subjects, and soldiers across the continent had indeed become low after more than a decade of fighting. Not surprisingly, as Napoleon's defeat at the Battle of Waterloo (1815) was approaching, European leaders were determined no wars of such magnitude would ever again threaten the glory of the continent. Put simply, most European policymakers insisted any future megalomaniac dictator with expansionist aims like Napoleon had to be stopped, but there needed to be some system put in place to safeguard each kingdom's national security and political stability.

Against this backdrop emerged the Congress of Vienna (1814–1815), a momentous conference that came to shape European diplomacy and politics over time. At Vienna, representatives from most of the major nations on the continent assembled to discuss what a post-Napoleonic Europe would look like. Russia's tsar, Alexander I, was represented by his foreign minister, while Lord Castlereagh, the foreign minister of Britain, served his nation's interests. In addition, the Austrian Empire's foreign minister, Prince Klemens von Metternich, officiated as the host of the conference. At the same time, despite being vanquished, France was represented at the conference by its new foreign minister, Charles Maurice de Talleyrand. Plenipotentiaries from other nations and kingdoms also attended, making the Vienna negotiations one of the largest diplomatic conferences in Europe's history up until that time.

One of the major issues Congress addressed was the reestablishment of postwar national boundaries in the wake of Napoleon's defeat. For the most part, the conference re-established the boundaries of states to match those of the pre-Napoleonic era. Yet a major area of concern still centered around the Holy Roman Empire. A loose confederation of dozens of mostly German-speaking kingdoms, the Holy Roman Empire collapsed in 1806, when Napoleon won the decisive Battle of Austerlitz. The Congress attendees decided not to recreate this empire, which was perceived as too divided to serve the continental goals of peacekeeping. Instead, the Holy Roman Empire was reorganized into the German Confederation, consisting of thirty-nine German states, along with the Netherlands and Denmark. In creating the Confederation, the goal of the conference was to build solidarity among the German states. After all, one of the major problems of the Napoleonic Wars had been the fact some of the German-speaking kingdoms in the Holy Roman Empire had actually allied themselves with Napoleon, while others fought against him. The conference decision to foster unity among the Germans, above all, was aimed at fostering togetherness among these people should the French ever again set out on a path of conquest.

No doubt, one of the hallmarks of the Vienna Conference was also the importance of balance of power considerations in shaping diplomacy. Because one of the goals of the conference was to ensure no single nation became so strong as to exercise a disproportionate amount of power over continental affairs, it was important that nations work together to preserve a general balance of power. Alliances, whether formal or informal, thus had to be established. As a result, one of the main effects of Vienna was the development of the Holy Alliance between Austria, Russia, and Prussia. This informal alliance, which later became formalized in 1822, took its name because of its desire to safeguard an autocratic Christian monarchy against the liberal and nationalist ideas unleashed by the French Revolution. Led by Metternich, the

Holy Alliance became known for its reactionary outlook on European diplomacy (Figure 7.1). In essence, the term *reactionary* came to mean returning Europe to the way it was before the French Revolution and the Napoleonic Wars. Above all, the alliance was aimed at ensuring that revolutionary France did not mount another conquest of Europe.

At the same time, France had much value from the vantage point of Holy Alliance members, a fact that explains the relatively lenient treatment of that nation at the conference. Significantly, when victors in war take balance of power calculations seriously, they may be less inclined to impose a harsh peace on the vanquished because they might need the defeated power as an ally in the future. Napoleonic France was not punished harshly for Napoleon's actions because even the Holy Alliance members had reservations about one another and considered France to have some use in checking other powers. Austria's Metternich and Britain's Castlereagh were concerned about a Russian and, to a lesser

Figure 7.1: Oil Portrait of Klemens von Metternich by artist Thomas Lawrence, 1815.

degree, Prussian power grab, and so they made sure a delighted Talleyrand partook in what was a negotiated settlement. Although Russia, Austria, Britain, and Prussian soldiers occupied France after Napoleon's defeat, this occupation never was meant to be a long-term development. Instead, the goal at Vienna was to restore France to an equal among European powers, provided the nation reverted to its prerevolutionary status quo.

In many ways, France did indeed revert to its prerevolutionary status quo after the Vienna Congress, a development that delighted the reactionary European powers. The Bourbon dynasty was restored to power in France, for example, with Louis XVIII becoming king. In addition, the Catholic Church regained much of the power and privileges it had lost during the revolution, and the wealthy classes received compensation for the losses of their property during the preceding decades of chaos. Just as important, in opposition to the revolutionary ideal of universal manhood suffrage, voting rights were sharply limited to ensure the moneyed classes had a disproportionate influence in France's restoration domestic politics. Approving of the changes taking place in France, the foreign armies that had occupied France after Napoleon's defeat withdrew in 1818. Subsequently, the major European powers treated France as an equal in continental affairs.

What became known as the Concert of Europe, or the concert system, soon emerged as the main institutional framework for European diplomacy. Although Europe had numerous kingdoms and nation-states at the time and representatives from several European states were involved in the concert system, the major decisions were reached by the great powers: Britain, Austria, Russia, Prussia, and later France. Sometimes referred to as the Vienna system because of Metternich's powerful reactionary influence, the concert system sought to stamp out any civil unrest popping up in Europe to ensure the ideas of the French Revolution did not challenge the status quo. Britain, which was much less sympathetic to the autocratic and anti-liberal policies of Metternich, often did not agree with the actions of the other powers. Consequently, the Holy Alliance members and France often took up the task of enforcing concert decisions.

Although the Holy Alliance had hoped to remove from Europe's memory the French Revolution, the liberalism associated with it continued to pop up across the continent beginning in the 1820s. At the time, the term *liberal* had several shades of meaning in Europe, but what they all had in common was the promotion of middle-class power at the expense of the historically privileged noble classes that had dominated the continent's political and economic activities. Liberals included the great masses of people who sought greater political participation—even universal voting rights—and the curtailing of the privileges associated with nobility. In addition, economic-minded liberals promoted *laissez faire* econom-ics, the capitalist notion that the government should take a hands-off approach to market activity in order to maximize individual profit. Some early factory workers, representing the working classes, sought to improve their plight as well, calling for reform in terms of better wages, working conditions, and the right to have a say in the fruits of their labor. All of these liberals mounted a multifaceted critique of the traditional European power structure.

In fact, the 1820s saw several open liberal revolts throughout the continent, most of which the Holy Alliance and France suppressed. Developments in Spain serve as a prime example. After the Bourbon King Ferdinand VII was restored to power in Spain in 1814, he refused to recognize the legitimacy of the Spanish constitution, which had been drawn up while Napoleon's brother Joseph was in power in the kingdom. In fact, Ferdinand openly repudiated the idea of a limited or constitutional monarchy. Not sur-prisingly, an opposition movement to Ferdinand led by liberal merchants and lawyers grew over time and produced a bloody revolt by the early 1820s that temporarily removed the king from power. In response, the Holy Alliance and France decided to intervene. Specifically, the French army invaded and defeated the liberal rebels at the Battle of Trocadero (1823). Ferdinand was restored, while the rebels became victims of reprisals in the aftermath. A similar situation also broke out in the Italian-speaking Kingdom of the Two Sicilies in 1820. There, an anti-monarchist secret society known as the Carbonari led a revolt against Ferdinand I, but the Holy Alliance intervened and crushed it. Nevertheless, influenced by the liberal message of the Carbonari, the neighboring Kingdom of Sardinia established a constitutional monarchy, thus showing the limitations of the Holy Alliance's effectiveness in combating the new challenge of liberal revolts. Switzerland, a small nation organized in autonomous regions known as cantons, also became a major region of liberalism around the same time and later experienced indirect Holy Alliance intervention. Given its geographical proximity to Austria, Metternich was concerned with liberalism taking root in Switzerland and spreading to Austria. Through skillful diplomacy, though, he successfully worked to place limits on freedom of speech and the press in Switzerland.

At the same time, however, cracks emerged in the concert system over Greek nationalism. Long part of the Ottoman Empire, Greek independence fighters began challenging the authority of the Ottomans by the 1820s, seeking the creation of an independent Greece. Given that the Greeks were Christian subjects within a Muslim empire, many peoples throughout Europe supported the independence movement. Russia especially supported such efforts in part because the Greeks belonged to the Orthodox Christian Church, just like the majority of Russians. In addition, the Ottoman Empire had been the long-time enemy of Russia, as evidenced by a series of wars dating back hundreds of years. Large segments of British and French citizens also became champions of an independent Greece, but Austria's government under Metternich opposed Greek independence because he feared nationalist movements within Austria might likewise demand independence. With the greatest amount of ethnic diversity in Europe, Austria indeed was highly sensitive to the fear of nationalism. Metternich thought that Hungarians, Poles, Czechs, Slovaks, Ruthenians, and others would demand autonomy from Austria should Greece obtain it from the Ottomans. Yet, in the end, the other great powers had their way on the Greek question. In 1827, the British, Russians, and French destroyed much of the Ottoman navy, a development that was much to Metternich's chagrin and foreshadowed Greece's independence a few years later.

But despite the cracks in the concert system, the Holy Alliance still remained stalwart defenders of Christian autocratic rule during the mid-nineteenth century. Instead of promoting nationalism, Austria, Russia, and Prussia largely decried the phenomenon and instead promoted the principle of dynastic legitimacy to foster a sense of commonality among the various ethnic groups within their nations. Although the Holy Alliance best exemplified the dynastic legitimacy principle, both France and Britain maintained that legitimacy was grounded in monarchical tradition as well. But the Holy Alliance nations mostly sought the preservation of the *status quo* in domestic political and social relations, and was against liberal reform and nationalism. Their actions, no doubt, were not only influenced by a desire to maintain political power at home but also were influenced by broader European politics, as each controlled a slice of the former Polish-Lithuanian Commonwealth and did not want nationalist and liberal movements to cause rebellion, particularly since Polish nationalists had a history of rebellion and, in fact, revolted again in 1830. The Holy Alliance worked together to put down that movement. Indeed, more than anything else, thwarting the goals of Polish nationalists in the 1830s brought the members of the Holy Alliance together with a renewed vigor. The principle of dynastic legitimacy remained strong until the mid-nineteenth century when liberalism and nationalism eroded it. Even Lord Palmerston, a British Whig, found the principle unappealing for the changing times.

More than anything else, the revolutions that broke out across Europe in 1848 marked the zenith of mid-nineteenth century discontent with the reactionary social order imposed on the continent after Napoleon's defeat. Widespread dissatisfaction among the middle and working classes emerged over a variety of issues. To begin, large segments of Europe's population were increasingly angry over restrictions on speech and the press, and demanded constitutional governments with checks and balances on monarchs. A vocal minority of political activists even demanded universal manhood suffrage to ensure all men had a voice in political affairs, not just the elites and moneyed classes. In addition, workers in city factories demanded better wages, fewer hours, and improved working conditions. Furthermore, the peasants in the countryside, long exploited through an aristocratic landowner system, sought to end all vestiges of feudalism and own the land they worked outright themselves. Crop failures and the emergence of bread riots in kingdoms far and wide only exacerbated the problems for all. Lastly, various nationalist discourses sparked many segments of Europe's people to entertain new visions about how to create a more just political and social order. The result was a new wave of revolutionary furor that was kindled in places as far and wide as France and the Balkans.

Significantly, the revolutions of 1848 in France came to be known as the Second French Revolution, as depicted in Figure 7.2. Disillusioned with reactionary policies and swept by a wave of nostalgia for the earlier French Revolution, the masses forced Louis Philippe of the House of Orleans from office and declared the establishment of the Second French Republic. In an interesting turn of events, free elections resulted in Napoleon's nephew, Louis Napoleon (later known as Napoleon III), becoming the president of France. The 1848 revolution was transformational in French political history. It ushered in universal manhood suffrage, which remained a bedrock of French politics in subsequent eras. In the process, France became one of the first nations in Europe to extend this Enlightenment-era goal to its populace. While the Holy Alliance was no doubt disappointed with such French developments, Austria, Russia, and Prussia were in no position to thwart the apparent triumph of liberalism under Louis Napoleon. After all, these powers also experienced revolutions within their kingdoms in 1848. Consequently, putting out the fires of revolutionary furor domestically became a much more pressing issue than what was going on in France.

In Prussia, which had historically granted few political rights to the vast bulk of citizens, an alienated and increasingly hungry population took to the streets in spring 1848 demanding revolutionary change to the kingdom's system of governance. As mob violence swept the cities, Prussian King Frederick Wilhelm IV used his soldiers to fire on the crowds. In the process, the Prussian king became associated with tyranny and repression, although he was hardly the first Prussian monarch to have that unenviable distinction. To his credit, though, Frederick Wilhelm was forced to deal with the pro-democracy movement sweeping his kingdom, and he broke from the reactionary mind-set of his predecessors. In a compromise, Frederick Wilhelm introduced a bicameral legislature and a three-tier voting system for his citizenry. In reality, however, Frederick Wilhelm's reforms were a far cry from universal manhood suffrage. Like with Britain, the upper house was reserved for the elites, while the masses of middle- and lower-class people could vote for politicians to serve in the lower house. More problematic, the three-tier voting system was based on the amount of taxes that men paid. The relatively small moneyed classes, which paid a higher amount in taxes per annum, thus had a larger voice in all political affairs. In effect, their votes carried a much greater weight than that of poor men.

The situation in the Austrian Empire was even more dire in 1848. Given the great ethnic diversity in the kingdom, it was not surprising much of the mob violence became associated with distinct varieties of ethnic-based nationalism. Magyars (Hungarians), Bohemians (Czechs), Poles, and Italian-speaking Catholics in Austrian-controlled Venetia were all key groups that demanded outright independence from the Crown, headquartered in Vienna. As violence swept the empire—seen in large cities such as Vienna and Budapest, and in the poorer agricultural regions such as Polish Galicia—a disappointed Metternich was forced to resign as chancellor (Figure 7.2). At the same time, Austrian Emperor Ferdinand remained steadfast in his refusal to accede to the demands of those engaged in revolt. In fact, the emperor took their actions as a personal slight against what he believed was his legitimate right to rule. In the end, as the revolutionary violence got out of hand, the king also resigned in favor of his nephew, Franz Joseph. The new emperor was also determined to use the Austrian army to stamp out the revolts, but he had to rely on Russian military support to do so. Violence in Hungary was especially conspicuous, but the Russians aided the Austrians in stopping the revolt there. As a result, the monarchy was saved at last, while no single nationality within the empire achieved its immediate revolutionary goal of total independence.

Figure 7.2: A Painting by Johann Passini detailing the violence of the revolutions of 1848 in the Austrian Empire.

At the same time, the revolutions of 1848 produced some victories against the reactionary political order in other places. Not only did France obtain universal manhood suffrage but similar developments also occurred elsewhere. Denmark, like other kingdoms in Europe, had a long tradition of absolute monarchy. But in 1848, King Christian III faced growing liberal protests from the Danish middle class. Although there was some violence, Christian in large part acceded to the demands and protests of his citizenry and allowed not only the creation of a parliament but also granted every Danish male the right to vote in elections. Similarly, in Switzerland, many cantons extended universal manhood suffrage to their citizens in 1848.

In the final analysis, however, most of the radical goals of the 1848 revolutionaries did not meet with immediate success. Even by the late nineteenth century, universal manhood suffrage did not exist without qualifications in most places. Even Britain, long the strongest voice of liberalism, required its male citizens to pay a fee to vote. This situation was similar in other places. Adding to the problem was the fact that women remained totally disenfranchised. They would have to wait until the twentieth century to see their suffrage aspirations realized. Likewise, the urban factory workers did not reap immediate tangible rewards from their revolutionary activities. As factories popped up all over the continent in the mid-nineteenth century, the owners of the means of production continued to profit heavily and workers were treated as mere cogs in the industrial machine. Complaining about poor working conditions or inadequate wages more often than not resulted in the offending party's termination and replacement than any meaningful improvement in the lives of the masses who toiled in the factories to make ends meet.

One conspicuous effect of the 1848 revolutions, though, was the beginning of the end of the concert system. Within four years of coming to power in France, Louis Napoleon had himself declared emperor of France. It seemed that one of the major goals of Vienna thus came to a failure with that outcome. More important, the forced resignation of Metternich, long the leading voice of the reactionary perspective, meant the old system had lost its strongest voice. Put simply, the revolts of 1848 revealed that the concert system did not effectively anticipate and address the growing clamor for liberalism and nationalism. At the same time, the concert system had worked well in other areas. From 1818 until the early 1850s, the continent largely had been characterized by peaceful relations between nation-states, even if there were periodic outbreaks of domestic strife. For a continent that frequently saw wars between nation-states in the century before, the congress system in a key way had served a valuable purpose in peacekeeping.

Yet after the momentous events of 1848, war between the nation-states of Europe returned, as evidenced by the Crimean War. This war started as a conflict between the Ottomans and Russians over control of the holy sites in Jerusalem. Specifically, Russia's tsar, Nicholas I, wanted to serve as the protector of Eastern Orthodox pilgrims visiting the city's shrines, but the Ottomans preferred having the French serve as the protectors of Christians in the region. With strong personalities, both Nicholas and Napoleon III of France did not compromise on the matter; instead, Nicholas declared war over this unique issue in 1853. But the Crimean War, which lasted three years and resulted in hundreds of thousands of casualties on all sides, saw Russia face off not only against the French and the Ottomans but also the British. In fact, the British feared Russian dominance in the Mediterranean Sea, a development that threatened to cut off Britain's access to the strategically important Suez Canal and the crown jewel of its empire: India. In the process, several major naval battles pitting the Russians against the British occurred in the Black and Baltic seas. Not surprisingly, with the strongest navy in the world, Britain won most naval battles (Figure 7.3). At the same time, many ground-based battles occurred in the Balkans, Crimean Peninsula, Anatolia, and southwestern Russia. Significantly, the British nurse Florence Nightingale rose to prominence amid the battles and popularized the profession of nursing, showing a deep level of care for the wounded. In the end, Russia lost the war, revealing to the world the dominance of British naval power and the effectiveness of European coalitions against any single power.

Figure 7.3: Artist depiction of British bombardment of Russians at Bomarsund in the Baltic Sea (1854).

THE ABOLITION OF THE SLAVE TRADE

As the nineteenth century dawned, Africa had become a continent hampered by the scourge of slavery. For more than two centuries, millions of the continent's men, women, and children had been kidnapped and forced to make the arduous journey across the Atlantic Ocean to become slaves on the various sugarcane, rice, tobacco, and cotton plantations in the Americas. Shackled in chains and forced to lie prostrate in the bottom decks of the slave ships, the conditions for these Africans were horrible. Many suffered from thirst and hunger on the journey, in addition to being exposed to urine and disease-spreading fecal matter. Furthermore, some even went blind from the darkness below the decks. The life of bondage that awaited the captives in the Americas underscored a major crisis of conscience for many who opposed the horrific institution as the nineteenth century dawned.

The growing effort to end the transatlantic slave trade had its roots among Enlightenment thinkers, although there still existed a wide variety of opinion on the matter at the time. Many intellectuals, especially in France, took up the cause of abolitionism as the Enlightenment got under way. The French philosopher Jean Jacques Rousseau, for example, expressly condemned slavery as an inhumane institution in his writings on the social contract theory of government, while his contemporary Baron de Montesquieu likewise became a vocal advocate for the end of all forms of bonded servitude. On the other hand, the

Enlightenment philosophers from the British Isles were more ambivalent on the issue. John Locke, the most vocal proponent of a natural rights theory of ethics, did not extend such rights to non-Europeans and never condemned the transatlantic slave trade. The German philosopher Immanuel Kant also sidestepped the issue. On the one hand, Kant developed a sophisticated system of thought on morality. Yet he also saw Africans as naturally different and inferior to Europeans. Given the range of opinions on the slavery of Africans, new developments in addition to Enlightenment thought had to take root for a successful abolitionist movement to emerge.

Figure 7.4: Eighteenth-century portrait of Olaudah Equiano. Artist unknown.

One such major development was the growing role of former slaves in promoting an abolitionist discourse. By the nineteenth century, the best example included the proliferation of anti-slavery writings by former slave Olaudah Equiano (Figure 7.4). Equiano's autobiography, first published in 1789, detailed the author's horrible experiences as a slave before his later freedom. Kidnapped as a child from his Igbo village by slave traders, Equiano experienced the notorious voyage aboard the slave ships to Barbados, where he entered a life of bondage. He later was sold to a number of masters, living and toiling in such diverse places as Virginia and South Carolina before securing his freedom in 1767 and moving to England and acquiring an education that allowed him to bring attention to the subject. In his writings on slavery, Equiano recounted the brutal floggings that slaves in the Americas were subject to, as well as the humiliating forms of punishment for offenses. Toward the end of his life, Equiano was devoted to ending the slave trade. In fact, Equiano and others like him became regular speakers who were frequently sought out among Britain's emerging abolitionist movement.

As it turned out, the abolitionist movement in Britain at the dawn of the nineteenth century was largely led by individuals of deep religious conviction. Equiano himself had been a strong Christian. Others like him wanted to end slavery, as they viewed it as an institution in opposition to the Gospel's message of loving one's brother as oneself. Founded in 1787, the Society for Effecting the Abolition of the Slave Trade became the main vehicle promoting change. A significant number of popular British ministers, including Anglicans, Methodists, and Quakers, became members over time and increasingly used their power to lobby Parliament to end the slave trade. The Society also engaged in a pamphleteering campaign to spread the message, which in part succeeded thanks to the new religious revivalism sweeping the British Isles at the time. In the United States, a similar Protestant revivalism occurred simultaneously, and a robust abolitionist movement began to emerge there as well.

More than any other British parliamentarian, William Wilberforce (1759–1833) devoted his life to the cause of abolitionism. A strong Christian, he brought up the issue of abolishing the transatlantic slave trade year after year in Parliament, refusing to accept defeat on the matter. The more Wilberforce's colleagues urged him to drop the matter, the more resolve he showed in seeing his aim realized. A man of courage and conviction, Wilberforce privately recruited his fellow parliamentarians to the cause over time. Significantly, Wilberforce's efforts paid off in 1806, when Parliament passed the Slave Trade Act, which ended Britain's involvement in the transatlantic slave trade and charged the Royal Navy with the duty of patrolling the West African coasts to intercept slave ships and arrest slavers.

To be sure, the Slave Trade Act had immense influence on curbing the transatlantic slave trade. Its implementation sharply reduced the number of slave ships acting in the Atlantic and the west coast of Africa by the mid-nineteenth century. Additionally, Britain's decision to end the slave trade led other European nations to follow suit after the Napoleonic Wars. Between 1815 and 1818, France, Spain, and Portugal all ended their participation in the slave trade as well, a fact that proved abolitionism was beginning to take firm root in Europe. By the 1840s, most European nations were actively patrolling the seas to intercept illegal slave ships. The Ottoman Empire also ended its African slave trade as well during this decade. At the same time, however, slavery continued in most of Europe's overseas empires, even though the British were among the first to outlaw slavery outright in their empire, doing so in 1833—the same year Wilberforce died.

Although the transatlantic slave trade was coming to an end by the mid-nineteenth century, it neverthe-less produced long-term scars among the peoples of Africa. Centuries of warfare between the continent's numerous tribes to acquire slaves to sell to Europeans and Arabs produced a certain ethnic factionalism among Africans that was not easily overcome. When Europe was experiencing a wave of nationalism in the mid-1800s, tribalism prevented such a discourse from taking root in Africa. It was not easy for different ethnic groups who had long made war on one another to come together and begin the process of modern state-making. Adding to the problem was that slavery continued to exist inside Africa after the Europeans and Ottomans stopped purchasing slaves there. The factionalism, made much worse by the continuation of slavery, later made it easy for outside nations to conquer large swaths of the continent in the latter part of the nineteenth century.

THE LATIN AMERICAN WARS OF INDEPENDENCE AND EARLY REPUBLICANISM

Napoleon's conquests had unforeseen effects not only in Europe but also in the Americas. In 1803, the United States doubled its size with the Louisiana Purchase. A significant reason for this development had been Napoleon's desire for money to help finance his continental conquests in Europe. As for policy, the United States never became actively involved in the Napoleonic Wars, choosing instead a strict policy of isolationism. As a young nation still plagued with lingering fears the British might try to reassert control of their former colonies, the US policy proved prudent. At the same time, other parts of the Americas came to feel the effects of the European conflict in significant ways. More than any other region, Latin America was forever transformed by the developments thousands of miles away in Europe during the first decades of the nineteenth century.

To elucidate how Napoleon's conquests in Europe affected Latin America, it is important to understand the historical backdrop of the growing grievances within Spanish America. Spain had long administered its colonies in the Americas through its viceroyalty system. Specifically, Spain's territories consisted of most of Central and South America, along with prominent islands in the Caribbean. The lands in Central America and the Caribbean were part of the viceroyalty of New Spain, while Spain's territory in South America had historically been called the viceroyalty of Peru. Each viceroyalty was governed by a viceroy appointed by the Spanish king. For centuries, the Spanish kings from the Habsburg dynasty had allowed *Creoles* (men of Spanish ancestry born in the Americas) to play a vital part in administration. Although not typically viceroys, Creoles served the Spanish Crown as judges, bureaucrats, military leaders, and statesmen. By the eighteenth century, however, the Habsburg dynasty no longer produced kings for Spain. Instead, the house of Bourbon had ascended to the Spanish throne. With this development, a change emerged in the allocation of offices and leadership positions in Spanish America. The Bourbon kings tended to make a sharp distinction between Creoles and *peninsulares* (people living in Latin America who were born in Spain). The Bourbon Spanish leadership believed peninsulares were more loyal to the Crown than Creoles and would serve Spain better in administrative duties such as tax collection. Thus, when doling out bureaucratic offices, the Bourbon leadership preferred granting leadership roles to the peninsulares, much to the chagrin of the Creoles. As a result, by the early nineteenth century, Creoles had become increasingly disenchanted with Spanish rule, as they found themselves increasingly marginalized. This development was significant, as the leaders of South America's independence movement in the early nineteenth century were largely comprised of disaffected Creoles.

Furthermore, the Enlightenment had immense influence on the educated classes within Latin America, fostering a strong proto-independence discourse among them. Such notions as representative government, checks and balances on political leaders, and freedom of speech and the press all became central tenants among those elements demanding change in Spain's administration of Spanish America. In addition, the Enlightenment notion that people should face no punishment for their mere ideas held a special sway for many. Indeed, the ability to protest perceived injustices without fear of repercussions from the Crown was a top priority among the Creole elite. Such fear was quite palpable, as Spain had executed various rebels throughout the empire as the nineteenth century dawned. In fact, the proto-independence movements of the last decades of the eighteenth century had all failed, and the leaders were often drawn-and-quartered to serve as a deterrent to revolt against Spanish authority. Yet if the Crown was not willing to reform, many of the disaffected increasingly believed, it was time to throw off the yoke of Spanish oppression and bring liberty to Latin America.

Significantly, the American Revolution against Britain also served as a prominent source of inspiration for Latinos to take seriously open revolt against Spain. After all, the US colonists had successfully won their freedom, even if war was required to achieve that aim. If the British colonists could overcome, so could others in the Americas. More than anything else, too, the discourse used by the Founding Fathers of the American Revolution had a profound influence on those likewise seeking to establish independent republics in Latin America. Like the American colonial subjects before them, some Latinos now decried monarchy altogether, rightfully pointing out at the time that such a system had a terrible track record of producing tyrant kings. Many elites believed only a democratic system where the people controlled their political affairs would work. The days of absolute monarchy and the invocation of the divine right of kings should be tossed into the dustpan of history. Not only that, but the idea of no taxation without representation, a rallying cry for US independence, won over many Creoles who had long decried arbitrary tax increases imposed by the Crown, despite a decline in silver mining and production in Spanish America.

As it turned out, Napoleon's conquest of Europe during the first decade of the 1800s produced the right conditions for the disaffected to rise up against Spain for independence. In 1808, Napoleon went to war with Spain, invading that nation and driving the frightened Spanish king, Ferdinand VII, into exile. The French forces overwhelmed Spain, and Napoleon soon installed his older brother Joseph as the new king of Spain. This unexpected development produced a political crisis in Latin America. On the one hand, large segments of individuals did not feel obligated to show allegiance to Joseph, as it was clear he was not the legitimate king. On the other hand, the rightful king had abandoned the people in a time of crisis. In the eyes of many, Ferdinand thus was a coward who likewise did not deserve obedience or even respect. If ever the time was right for revolt, it was now.

Against this backdrop, a Venezuelan Creole and military leader named Simon Bolivar led a movement to liberate north-western South America from Spanish rule (Figure 7.5). Bolivar knew Napoleon personally and had spent time with him in Europe. Initially impressed with the French leader, Bolivar soon changed positions, recognizing that Bonaparte was not a force for liberty but tyranny. An ardent admirer of the United States, Bolivar had been deeply impressed with the republican form of government he heard about in the newly independent nation and often cited it as a model for what a successful revolution should produce in his homeland. Over time, Bolivar worked tirelessly for independence and republicanism in his homeland as the first decade of the nineteenth century drew to a close. By 1810, he had a significant following that enabled him to declare the lands around Caracas independent. In the process, Bolivar continued to recruit soldiers to his cause, formulated battlefield strategies, and expounded on his republican vision as an alternative to Spanish rule. Thus, as the second decade of the nineteenth century went on, his movement grew and was able to win decisive battles against Spanish troops.

Figure 7.5: Portrait of Simon Bolivar, the liberator of South America.

In fact, Bolivar proved skillful in persuading many Spanish soldiers to switch allegiances, a strategy that proved fruitful in his development of a formidable army. Slowly, Bolivar's forces conquered larger swaths of land in the northwestern part of the continent, promising to establish a republican nation tentatively called Gran Colombia. By 1813, Bolivar had obtained the nickname El Liberator (the liberator) because of his successes and popular support.

In the southern part of the continent, an Argentine Creole named Jose de San Martin shared Bolivar's fervent desire for liberation. His background, though, had been different from Bolivar's. As a child, San Martin had left Spanish America to study in Spain, where he received a first-rate military education. San Martin then became a general in the Spanish military and had fought around the world for the glory of the Crown. But he became disenchanted with Spain when Joseph was installed as king and traveled back to the Americas to liberate the place of his birth. Upon arrival in 1812, he pledged loyalty to an independence movement in the United Provinces of Rio de la Plata (modern-day Argentina). Thereafter, San Martin organized an army to fight the Spanish, which had a relatively minor presence in the region. Like Bolivar, San Martin proved skillful in persuading regiments of royalists to support the independence movement and switch allegiances. By the middle to late 1810s, San Martin had helped drive the Spanish troops from the area and even won battles in modern-day Chile. In the process, San Martin developed the same reputation as a liberator in the southwestern part of the continent that Bolivar had developed in the north.

As Bolivar achieved victories in the north and San Martin drove out the Spanish in the south, the two military leaders decided to meet to discuss how to drive out the Spanish from the continent once and for all. Both leaders knew that the greatest Spanish military strength was headquartered in Peru, and success of the continent's independence depended on liberation there. At a secret conference at Guayaquil, Ecuador, in 1822, both men discussed integrating their armies to liberate the area. Bolivar and San Martin, however, did not share the same vision of a post-independence government for the continent. Although Bolivar heavily favored a republican form of government similar to that found in the United States, San Martin was a fervent constitutional monarchist. San Martin genuinely believed international recognition from the major European powers was necessary for any independent movement to succeed. Given that the predominate form of government in Europe at the time was monarchy, San Martin believed such a form of government was best to serve the aims of liberation. In fact, San Martin even preferred the new monarchy in independent South America come from the established European royal dynasties. Such a suggestion, though, only rankled a disappointed Bolivar. Given the disagreements at the conference, military integration never took firm root, despite overtures from San Martin. In reality, an embittered San Martin later journeyed back to Europe, where he lived out the rest of his days.

In the end, Bolivar's lieutenant and friend, Antonio Jose de Sucre, took it upon himself to drive the Spanish out of Peru. In 1824, the Battle of Ayacucho occurred, pitting the Spanish Royalist forces of Viceroy Jose de la Serna against Sucre's soldiers. Although the two sides had near parity in terms of strength, Sucre won the day and took a high percentage of Royalists as prisoners of war. This development led to a sharp decline in morale among those who sided with Spain in the wars of liberation. As a result, Ayacucho spelled the effective end of Spain's presence in the Americas. Within two years, the last holdouts of Spain's political authority had vanished. In the process, the long-term dream of independence initiated by the Creoles and others had been realized at last. In fact, in the aftermath of liberation, Bolivar and Sucre became heroes throughout the region. The nation of Bolivia took its name after the liberator, while that nation's capital city, Sucre, would later be named in honor of the hero of Ayacucho.

While the wars of independence were occurring in South America, a similar development was taking root in Mexico and Central America (the heart of the viceroyalty of New Spain). Unlike with South America, though, disaffected Creoles were not the bedrock of the early independence movement in Mexico. Rather, the *mestizo* (mixed race) and Indian population became the strongest segment clamoring for liberation early on, given the exploitative nature of Spanish rule to which they had long been subjected. Large numbers of such people toiled on the *haciendas* (large ranches and farms) just to make ends meet, providing farm labor and tending to cattle and other animals. Sometimes the peasants found themselves in debt to the *hacendado*, or hacienda owner, and were not legally allowed to vacate the hacienda until they paid off their debt. Thus, in some ways the poorest classes of mestizos and Indians were subjects of a debt peonage system. They had little voice in shaping the affairs of their own lives and almost no opportunity for social mobility. Consequently, despite lacking formal education, the poor peasant class increasingly made their grievances known as the nineteenth century dawned.

Disgusted with the social inequality that plagued New Spain, a Catholic priest named Miguel Hidalgo led the rally cry for independence in the viceroyalty (Figure 7.6). As a child, Hidalgo had grown up on a hacienda that his father oversaw. Although Hidalgo had been a privileged Creole, he developed strong affection for the exploited peasants who worked the farmland and tended the livestock on the haciendas, a development that shaped his life's course. In addition, when his family's fortune vanished over a tax dispute with the Crown, Hidalgo increasingly viewed Spanish authority as repressive. As the first decade of the nineteenth century ended, Hidalgo increasingly believed the time was right to foment a rebellion for independence. Against this backdrop, Hidalgo in 1810 issued from the pulpit his famous "Cry from Delores," a battle cry for armed insurrection against Spanish authority in the region. A highly popular and influential priest, Hidalgo attracted the attention of hundreds of supporters among

Figure 7.6: Father Miguel Hidalgo in military uniform.

the peasants who took up arms and joined the cause. Hidalgo was no military leader, however, and his men constituted more of a mob than a disciplined army. Nevertheless, the rebels attacked Spanish forces and spread the message of revolution, popularizing the cause of freedom. But the priest did not live to see his dream realized. Less than a year after the Cry from Delores, the Spanish had captured Hidalgo and executed him for his rebellion. Significantly, unlike in South America, the Creole elites in Mexico were Royalists who continued to support Spanish rule. These same Creoles played an instrumental role in undermining Hidalgo's efforts.

At the same time, Hidalgo's actions influenced a younger generation of Mexican freedom fighters who vowed to carry on insurrection until independence was attained. Fellow popular priest Jose Morales, a mestizo student of Hidalgo's, stepped up to lead the insurgency. He was especially instrumental in promoting the message of independence among the disenchanted poorest classes. But like Hidalgo, Morales also was captured and in 1815 put to death for treason. By the early 1820s, the independence movement had attracted broader segments of the population, especially the Creole elites. The Creoles believed Ferdinand VII of Spain was about to be overthrown in Spain and decided to establish a monarchy in Mexico, rather than a republican form of government. The leader of the Creole rebellion against Spanish rule, Agustin de Iturbide, was decisive in removing Spanish presence from the area. In 1821, he negotiated a treaty with Spain to establish an independent empire in Mexico and Central America. According to terms of the Treaty of Cordoba, the empire would become a monarchy modeled after Spain. Although the Bourbons were supposed to provide a king, Iturbide had himself declared king of the newly established Mexican Empire in 1822.

Yet monarchy did not endure in the new empire of Mexico, which included not only the modern nations of Mexico but most of Central America as well. A group of disaffected generals led by Antonio Lopez de Santa Anna had political ambitions and believed realization of such ambitions could only come about through the establishment of a republican form of government in Mexico. Consequently, the generals overthrew Iturbide, abolished the empire, and established a republican government in 1823. The Central American provinces, however, did not approve of the move, in part because of distrust of the new leaders. Instead, amid the chaos of the coup, they seceded from Mexico, forming the United Provinces of Central America. Although there were high hopes for democracy in the United Provinces, regional warlordism there undermined the central government as well. As a result, within a few years the United Provinces collapsed. In the process, several independent nations emerged, such as Guatemala, Honduras, Costa Rica, and El Salvador. Thus, the historical basis for the independent Central American states had their root amid a time of intense political factionalism, a development that did not vanish as the decades passed.

Meanwhile, the United States took the unprecedented action of shoring up republicanism in the newly independent nations in Latin America. The greatest fear from the US perspective was that Spain would try to reassert control over its former colonies. If Spain succeeded in such an attempt, as many American politicians feared, Britain might also attempt to follow suit in an effort to reclaim its former colonies. Indeed, US tenacity in securing the successful establishment of the South American republics was driven as much by domestic fears as it was about a general desire to see the expansion of republicanism as an alternative to the perceived tyranny associated with monarchy. The Monroe Doctrine, issued in 1824 and named after US President James Monroe, stated that the United States would intervene militarily if European nations attempted to reestablish colonial rule in the independent regions in Latin America. Above all, the overt message from Washington served as a warning to Spain not to engage in any reactionary campaign to undo the results produced by the wars of independence. Put simply, a new day had dawned in the Americas.

Yet the reality of strong republicanism in Latin America proved elusive in the decades after Latin American independence from Spain. In many of the new countries, democracy was little more than a sham, while constitutional rights accounted for mere words on paper. Although Bolivar established his Gran Colombia, factionalism and infighting among various groups for political power led to its disintegration by 1831. The political jockeying for position was so prominent that Bolivar survived some close assassination attempts before resigning in disgust as his envisioned nation collapsed. As it turned out, the southern part of Gran Colombia was always facing raids from the Peruvians over a border dispute, and military men who had idolized Bolivar formulated plots to unseat him themselves. In the end, Gran Colombia did not survive and split into three separate nations: Colombia, Venezuela, and Equator. In the aftermath, a disheartened Bolivar died of tuberculosis, while his lieutenant Sucre fell victim to assassination.

Indeed, such developments reflected a major problem that undermined the early Latin American republics: warlordism. As a general rule, most of the newly independent republics had weak central governments from the outset. Although the presidents of the various nations did indeed wield considerable power, that power was largely confined to the capital cities and the immediate surrounding regions. In general, the farther from the capital one found oneself, the weaker the influence of the central government. This problem enabled military men in the peripheral regions to emerge and morph into regional warlords, sometimes referred to as *caudillos*. These warlords engaged in all sorts of criminality, such as train robberies, banditry, and cattle thievery to raise money to finance their anti-government activities. At the same time, some warlords distributed their loot to obtain followers, thus endearing themselves to the masses in ways the official heads of state could not. The lack of adequate centralization no doubt stymied the effectiveness of the republics and, for many citizens, shattered any confidence that positive change had emerged after independence.

To be sure, republicanism in mid-nineteenth-century Latin America was a far cry from the expectations of the masses who had fought for independence a generation earlier; however, in some ways, Latin America had achieved progress in ways the United States had not. Many Enlightenment thinkers of the previous century had condemned the inhumane institution of slavery, stressing that it violated natural rights and was cruel. Interestingly, anti-slavery rhetoric had been a prominent feature of the liberation campaigns in Spanish America from their inception. Bolivar, in particular, had abhorred the practice and promised to abolish it. Many educated Creoles came to share this view, including Mexico's Iturbide. Not surprisingly then, slavery was abolished much earlier in the newly independent republics that won their independence from Spain than it was in the United States. In 1820, for example, Mexico ended slavery, while Bolivar's Gran Colombia did so the following year. In addition, Chile followed suit two years later and, in 1831, Bolivia ended the practice. Significantly, in none of these republics did war break out to preserve the institution. By contrast, the United States only ended slavery in 1865 after a bloody civil war that resulted in the deaths of hundreds of thousands of people.

At the same time, as the case of Mexico shows, the exploitation of the poor (especially the mestizos and Indians) continued in the new republics, just as it had under Spanish rule. The majority of Mexico's population in the mid-nineteenth century still was employed in agriculture, and the cultivation of maize was common in the northern part of the country, while sugarcane was planted in the south. Essentially, farmhands worked the large haciendas and plantations, toiling to make ends meet. But, as in the past, debt peonage continued. The hacendados sometimes had a general store on their property from which their workers purchased basic necessities such as toiletries, spices, salt, cooking oil, along with tobacco and alcohol. To keep the field hands tied to the hacienda, the prices for such goods were exorbitantly high, ensuring the workers fell into debt to the landlords. In addition, some landlords overcharged for rent, taking advantage of the very people whose labor was needed for them to earn a profit. As a result of such unscrupulous tricks, large numbers of Mexican workers in the mid-1800s found themselves in a constant cycle of debt. The fact that most workers struggled with literacy and lacked a formal education only complicated matters, as they often lacked the requisite skills to argue on their own behalf. Many, placing trust in their bosses, simply signed contracts without knowing the terms and, thus, were taken advantage of. If a worker thought he was cheated and actually escaped the hacienda, the hacienda owner had a legal right to have the police arrest the fugitive worker and return the person to the fields to continue working to pay off the balance of the debt. For countless peasants, this unfortunate scenario had become a reality in the new republic.

Napoleon's conquest of Europe in the first decade of the nineteenth century not only forever changed Spanish America but also brought path-altering developments to Brazil. A Portuguese colony since the 1500s, Brazil had a unique historical trajectory over the centuries. Early on, the large colony was not considered important from Lisbon's point of view. In fact, one of the few valuable products the Portuguese had acquired from the colony was brazilwood, which became widely used in the construction of violins and tables. But over time, the Portuguese discovered gold and learned sugarcane grew well on the coast in the provinces of Bahia and Pernambuco. Consequently, by the 1700s, Brazil was slowly emerging as the brightest jewel in Portugal's colonial crown thanks to its economic contribution. At the same time, by 1800, no Brazilian king had ever traveled to Brazil, and the colony was still largely viewed as an exotic, frightening place in the eyes of the Portuguese elite.

Yet the Napoleonic Wars transformed Brazil's position within Portuguese affairs. As Napoleon's forces defeated the Spanish, Portuguese King Regent Joao VI feared he too would be deposed. After all, the French invaded Portugal in 1807. As a consequence, Joao did something unprecedented: he, along with several thousand government officials, fled that same year to Brazil for safety and decided to govern Portugal in exile from the colony. Remarkably, this development led to the entire dismantling of the old colonial governmental structure of Brazil. Now the king regent himself was present in the colony, and he and his court in Rio de Janeiro went about running Brazil. In the process, Brazil was given the new official status of kingdom and was no longer considered a colony. As time went by, Joao increasingly fell in love with Brazil. He admired the climate, environment, and, most of all, the people. In fact, the more he stayed in Brazil and was away from Portugal, the dearer the Brazilian people became to him. In fact, Joao remained in Brazil well after Napoleon's defeat, a testament to the happiness he felt there. He only returned in 1821, when Portugal was in a constitutional crisis and demanded his presence in Lisbon.

Meanwhile, Joao's son, Pedro, was laying the foundation for Brazil's independence from Portugal. Significantly, Pedro remained in Brazil after his father's return to the mother country and emerged over time as a leading voice for Brazil's independence. Pedro, who like his father before him thought highly of the colony, worked to establish increasing autonomy for Brazil, much to the chagrin of the established Portuguese elites. His tireless efforts paid off in 1822, when he proclaimed Brazil an independent empire and defeated the few battalions of soldiers loyal to Portugal. Pedro subsequently ruled Brazil himself as emperor until 1831, when he abdicated in favor of his son Pedro II. At the same time, the older Pedro introduced a constitutional monarchy for the young nation and was known for his championing of human rights.

Known as the "Magnanimous," Pedro II ruled the empire of Brazil for an astonishing fifty-two years. Although opposed to slavery like his father, Pedro II's early efforts to end the practice met with failure. The Brazilian economy in the mid-nineteenth century depended in large part on agriculture, especially the cultivation of sugarcane and coffee. As it turned out, the Brazilian elite did not permit any changes on the slavery issue. Like in the United States, conflict over the issue risked sinking the young empire into civil war. Had he forced the matter, Pedro II no doubt would have fallen victim to a coup. In the meantime, Pedro II turned his attention to modernizing the nation. In fact, under his leadership, Brazil developed some of the finest universities, hospitals, and railroads in all of Latin America. Toward the end of his life, Pedro II took up traveling, journeying to both Europe and the United States. Significantly, against this backdrop, the nation's slavery issue was settled once and for all. While Pedro II was abroad in 1888, he left his daughter, Isabel, in charge of the empire's internal affairs (Figure 7.7). A staunch abolitionist, Isabella issued a decree

Figure 7.7: Isabella, princess of Argentina, who in 1888 abolished slavery in Brazil.

ending slavery in the nation. Isabel's courage to act while her father was away won her a prized place in Brazil's history, but it also led to the downfall of the empire. In the aftermath, a group of elites, including military officers, overthrow Pedro II and established the United States of Brazil. Thus, Brazil experienced a unique path in charting its course toward republicanism. To its credit, though, the newly formed United States of Brazil did not reintroduce slavery. With Brazil's abolition of the institution, the practice ceased to exist in the Americas.

DEVELOPMENTS IN THE OTTOMAN EMPIRE AND EAST ASIA

Although Europe and Latin America experienced major political turmoil in the early nineteenth century, significant parts of Asia also experienced numerous challenges. This fact was certainly true in the Middle Eastern lands, which the Ottoman Empire had controlled for centuries. In addition, the East Asian powers of China and Japan experienced greater interaction with the world, which in many ways presented new challenges to the traditional political and social structure.

By the start of the nineteenth century, the Ottoman Empire had become the "Sick Man of Europe." Its days of glory and conquest were gone, and merely holding the empire together proved a major challenge for the sultans. As it turned out, the Russians had inflicted a series of defeats on the empire for control of water routes and territory in the late eighteenth century, exposing the military weakness of the Ottomans. In addition, Napoleon's Army of the Orient had wreaked havoc on the Ottoman military during its campaign in Egypt as the century drew to a close. Adding to this situation were the growing internal problems in the peripheral regions. Although the sultans exercised strong power in Anatolia, the empire was so large that effective administration proved challenging. Widespread corruption among the empire's bureaucrats problematized tax collecting. To make matters worse, Ottoman administrators known as mamluks (technically slaves of the sultans) increasingly morphed into warlords in such places as Egypt and Mesopotamia. Against this backdrop, clamors for reform were just as pressing among the Ottomans as they were in other parts of the world by the early 1800s.

In the first decade of the nineteenth century, Sultan Selim III promoted Ottoman modernization, a development that led to his downfall (Figure 7.8). Seeing the need for reform, Selim boldly confiscated the lands of bureaucrats who failed to carry out their duties for the state, such as tax collecting. In addition, Selim established a national education system and reorganized the civil servant system to make it more merit-based. Yet it was Selim's desire to modernize the Ottoman military that proved his undoing. Historically, the Janissaries had formed the elite infantry core of the Ottoman military, but over time had devolved into a hereditary system that was conservative and resistant to modernization. To improve his military's effectiveness, Selim introduced a separate, ultra-elite infantry corps called the *nizam-i-cedid* army. Armed with the best European muskets, the infantry was well trained and played a major role in quelling rebellions in the peripheral regions of the empire. At the same time, the growing importance of the nizam-i-cedid army provoked intense jealousy among the

Figure 7.8: Oil painting, *Sultan Selim III in Audience*, by Konstantin Kapidagli (1803).

Janissaries, who found themselves increasingly marginalized. As a consequence, the Janissaries devised and carried out a rebellion in 1807 that resulted in the assassination of Selim and the disbandment of the parallel army. In the process, the incident revealed that real power in early nineteenth-century Ottoman society was in the hands of the military establishment, not the sultan. In addition, the fate of Selim served as a deterrent to future sultans who likewise might be too reformed-minded.

Nevertheless, the mid-nineteenth century did see reforms introduced within the Ottoman Empire. Significantly, key features of European politics, especially nationalism, served as a major catalyst for change. Inspired by Greek independence in the early 1830s, other non-Muslim subjects within the empire likewise began to demand equal treatment under the law, greater autonomy, and, for some segments, even independence. The growing fires of nationalism forced a series of sultans to introduce reforms to hold the empire together. The reforms, known as the *Tanzimat* (restructuring), began in 1839 and ended the *millet*, which had been the system the Ottomans used to govern non-Muslim religious minorities within the empire. Under the millet, Christians and Jews had been forced to pay a special tax and were treated as second-class citizens. In fact, under the millet system, Christians had a wide range of restrictive laws imposed on them, such as not allowed to build churches taller than the local mosque in a particular locale. By ending the millet, the Ottomans attempted to put out the fires of nationalism among Christian subjects. The newly introduced Rose Garden Edict (1839), which ushered in the Tanzimat, extended equality to all imperial subjects, regardless of religious affiliation.

The Tanzimat reforms, however, had limited effectiveness. Although the reforms calmed nationalist fires within the empire for a while, the same ethno-religious nationalism reemerged in the middle to late nineteenth century. As it turned out, the Ottomans had adopted the same principle of dynastic legitimacy that the European powers under Metternich had fostered to combat nationalism. Metternich's solution did not work to contain nationalism in Europe, and in the end it did not work in the Ottoman Empire either. In the latter's case, the Ottoman sultans' lack of adequate centralization and interaction with their subjects meant that peoples in the periphery of the empire did not identify with the empire or its leadership. With nationalism, they instead increasingly identified with their ethnolinguistic community and sought to advance it at the expense of Ottoman rule.

Perhaps surprisingly, the early nineteenth century was also a major period of turmoil in China. As the eighteenth drew to a close, the Qing dynasty that had ruled the country since 1644 seemed to be at the peak of its rule. The Qianlong emperor had waged several successful frontier wars that dramatically expanded the territory of China. In addition, China had emerged as a major center of culture and learning, in addition to establishing a strong trade influence globally. Yet the domestic situation was not without problems. In some ways, the Qianlong emperor had eschewed the military technology associated with Europe, outlawing the use of guns and promoting swordsmanship as the mainstay of China's military training. Such shortsightedness exposed the Qing leadership to a costly rebellion as the nineteenth century dawned, when a Buddhist millenarian movement known as the White Lotus Society led a tax protest against the dynasty. Although the Qing emperor put down the revolt, the decade-long rebellion showed the weakness of centralized rule in the world's most populous country.

Yet it was the growing presence of Europeans in China in the first half of the century that really contributed to the weakening of China. European merchants, eager to take advantage of the huge market of consumers in the exotic land, established treaties to promote commerce. As time went by, British opium merchants increasingly made their presence known, selling the drug in exchange for money and leading thousands of Chinese people into a cycle of addiction and crime. Chinese men, regardless of social class, also increasingly took up smoking tobacco, mixing it with opium to obtain a "high." Against this backdrop, the Chinese government began to look unfavorably on the presence of European merchants in their land. By the late 1830s, the Daoguang emperor ordered the confiscation of opium from British merchants. This development, however, did not end the growing problem of addiction in the country; rather, it produced war with the British. The Opium War, fought between 1839 and 1842, saw the British navy bombard cities on China's coast and destroy the Asian nation's poorly constructed navy. Just as important, the British victory also resulted in trade concessions on the part of China, thereby paving the way for the opium trade to continue for decades thereafter.

Figure 7.9: Hong Xiuquan, a major figure of the Taiping Rebellion (1851–1864).

To make matters worse, the Taiping Rebellion (1851–1864) in China ripped the country apart, becoming one of the deadliest civil wars in the nation's history. This rebellion's origins were no doubt fanciful and reflected a growing European presence in the nation's internal affairs. Indeed, the growing presence of European missionaries in China led to large numbers of Chinese conversions to Christianity over time. A low-level Chinese bureaucrat, Hong Xiuquan, became attracted to the new faith and became convinced he was Jesus Christ's younger brother (Figure 7.9). Allegedly seeing a heavenly vision, Hong believed it was his mission to establish heaven on earth to usher in Christ's triumphant return. Over time, he attracted a sizable following, which went to work trying to strip China of its Confucian heritage and promote Hong's version of Christianity. Significantly, European and American missionaries in China at the time often smiled favorably on Hong's actions. Acts of violence between Hong's followers and the Qing army, however, began occurring, resulting in a war that over fourteen years claimed millions of lives. In the end, Hong's movement was defeated, but it exposed the weakness of the nation's central government.

In the aftermath of the rebellion, the Qing leadership had become increasingly weak. Problems with tax collecting and bureaucratic corruption plagued the nation. In addition, other European nations besides

Britain increasingly made their presence felt in the nation as well. In fact, by the late 1890s, many of the major European powers had negotiated their own trade concessions and spheres of influence within China. The Qing dynasty's leaders, with an obsolete military that had incurred numerous defeats in the first half of the century, tended to grant European concessions as a means of avoiding conflict that might jeopardize their continued existence.

Japan's experience in the first half of the nineteenth century was likewise full of new challenges. Ruled by the Tokugawa *shogunate* since the 1600s, Japan had an emperor whose power was merely nominal by the dawn of the nineteenth century. Like the Chinese Qing emperors, Japan's military leaders had been highly distrustful of Western ideas and technologies. Firearms, although playing a pivotal role in uniting the islands centuries before, had been long cast aside because they were seen as an affront to the honor of the *samurai* warrior class, who were skilled swordsmen. The feudalistic social structure of the islands also increasingly became a source of internal tension, as there was no possibility for social mobility for peasants in the shogunate. To make matters worse, Westerners began to take interest in the insular islands, best shown by American Admiral Matthew Perry's voyage to the islands in 1853. Aware of the technological superiority of Westerners and fearful the islands might become subject to outside influence, large segments of Japanese society demanded dramatic political and social change.

Amid all this emerged the Meiji Restoration. In effect, an internal revolution in Japan in the 1860s removed the Tokugawa shogunate from power, replacing these military leaders with the traditional emperor. By 1868, the Meiji emperor immediately went to work in building up Japan's military and industrial capabilities. To do nothing, the emperor and many of his advisors believed, would run the risk of subjecting Japan to the same loss of honor that had befallen China, as the Westerners penetrated that land. The modernization of Japan's military was highly successful, as demonstrated by the country's later military victories in the early twentieth century.

CONCLUSION

As this chapter has shown, the early nineteenth century saw the playing out of ideas, not only in the palaces and diplomatic arenas but also on the battlefield. As it turned out, large segments of the world's population, whether in Europe, Africa, the Americas, or Asia, felt in some ways oppressed. Such people believed they were marginalized by political structures that privileged certain classes or groups over them. As a consequence, the first half of the 1800s saw global attempts to redress perceived injustices in order to forge a new order. In the end, progress occurred in some places. For example, the early nineteenth century saw the beginnings of a discourse that ultimately produced the abolition of the slave trade and eventually the institution itself. Not only that, the peoples of Latin America successfully threw off the yoke of colonial oppression, while the Ottoman Empire made strong efforts to correct its mistreatment of historically marginalized religious minorities. At the same time, many of the same problems still plagued the marginalized over time. In post-Napoleonic Europe, voting rights still remained limited, although they did expand. In addition, the growing working classes found themselves still subject to economic exploitation, a major feature of the industrialization examined in the next chapter.

CHAPTER
EIGHT

Negotiating a Changing World: Modernizing Forces of the 19th Century

INTRODUCTION

The nineteenth century saw the flowering of modernity. As the Scientific Revolution and the Enlightenment showed, previous centuries had sown the seeds for the transformation from a premodern to a modern worldview. But during the 1800s, such new developments as industrialization, the rise of capitalism, the advent of mass education, the intensification of nationalism, and the birth of New Imperialism all demonstrated that modernity had come to eclipse the mind-set of the past, especially in Europe and the United States. Indeed, more than any century before, the nineteenth century ushered in an avalanche of change, seen in everything from the transformation in labor, change in cultural values, and priorities in life. Much of the change proved a great benefit to society. The development of technology during the century in many ways made people's lives easier. The rise of science, championed like never before during the century, no doubt facilitated that end. At the same time, the forces of modernity wreaked havoc on the lives of those individuals who preferred the traditional way of life, reducing them to cogs in a machine. Not only that, the new ideas of modernity, coupled with greed and other frailties of the human condition, led to exploitation and cruelties on mass scales. In the end, the world was a much different place at the end of the nineteenth century than it was at the beginning.

INDUSTRIALIZATION

In premodern times, societies used animate sources, whether human, horse, mule, donkey, oxen, etc., to perform the labor associated with farming and construction. With the rise of the modern era, however, there emerged a switch from animate sources of labor to inanimate sources—epitomized by the emergence and widespread use of machines that came to dominate factories. The industrial revolutions of the nineteenth century, which gave rise to factories and mills of various sorts, revolutionized life in Europe and the United States. In fact, industry ushered in the modern world as we know it today, changing the preexisting economic system, politics, leisure, along with social and cultural values. If one thing can be said to have had the most remarkable and far-reaching impact during the nineteenth century, it was no doubt the advent of industry.

Before the rise of industry, the overwhelming majority of people within Europe were farmers. People had to consume food to survive, and much human labor was devoted to the cultivation of grains, root vegetables, and the raising of livestock for the purpose of dietary protein. In 1800, a large segment of Europe's population was the peasantry. These small-scale farmers largely grew enough food to provide for their families and pay their landlords for rent, the use of tools, and other services. To be sure, the peasants were not wealthy. In fact, they really could not be described as commercial farmers, as the bulk of their production was geared toward subsistence, rather than making a profit. Despite their indispensable contribution to Europe's wealth by virtue of their labor, European peasants were of low social status. By and large, they lacked education, were illiterate, and generally were poorly represented in political affairs.

The situation in the United States at the turn of the nineteenth century was somewhat different for farmers. Because of the relatively low population density and seemingly endless supply of land in the United States, even poor farmers often cultivated large tracts of land by the European peasant's standards. As a result, most US farmers were in a position at least to attempt to seek profit from agriculture. Consequently, peasant farming was a much less conspicuous social and economic feature in the United States. But like Europe, farming was vital to the American identity. After all, many of the country's Founding Fathers had been farmers, and agriculture was essential to American President Thomas Jefferson's vision of how the young nation would become a great country. He viewed the United States as an "Agrarian Republic."[1] The future, though, had a different path in store for both Europe and the United States in the nineteenth century: one dominated by industry.

The story of the beginning of the First Industrial Revolution, which was driven by the advent of steam power, is no doubt fascinating. More than anyone else, a little known British preacher named Thomas Newcomen changed the world with his invention of the steam engine. Fascinated with science and mechanical tinkering from an early age, Newcomen in the early eighteenth century attempted to solve a major problem that hindered English tin mining: the accumulation of rainwater in the mines. Manual attempts by workers using buckets to remove the water was a time-consuming process. If Newcomen could devise a machine to do it, the process would go much faster. Newcomen discovered that heating water in a boiler produced steam, which could be harnessed to drive a piston to pump the water vertically from the mines. His invention in 1712, called the Newcomen steam engine, not only solved the mining problem but also served as the prototype for later developments with steam power. The Watt Steam Engine, invented by Englishman James Watt in 1769, eclipsed Newcomen's and became the standard used and produced in factories during the nineteenth century.

---

1   James Gilreath, *Thomas Jefferson and the Education of a Citizen* (Honolulu: University Press of the Pacific, 2002), 302–03.

The rise of textile factories next became a major feature of the First Industrial Revolution. Before the mid-eighteenth century, almost all textiles, whether for clothes, carpets, rugs, etc., were produced domestically, with women providing the labor. At the time, women spun one thread of yarn at a time, which was a time-consuming process. With the invention of the spinning jenny machine in 1760, however, the situation changed. Scores of threads could now be spun at the same time. Businessmen and financiers seized on the opportunity to profit heavily through the mass production of cloth by utilizing the new technology and established factories throughout England that employed the machines. To be sure, the spinning jenny and other later textile machines such as Paul's roller spinner led to the development of a budding textile factory system in England by the turn of the nineteenth century that spread to France and other parts of Europe. Significantly, women and children provided much of the labor in the early English factories, which were exploitative and demanded long hours. The textile industry also became prominent in the northern part of the United States in the first few decades of the 1800s. Lowell, Massachusetts, especially became a hub that employed poor young women who hoped to earn money for marriage.

The steam power associated with the First Industrial Revolution also led to a major revolution in transportation: the creation of the steam locomotive. In 1829, Englishman Robert Stephenson invented the Rocket, the first of such trains. Through tinkering, Stephenson discovered the same steam power that first was used to pump water from mines in a vertical direction could work horizontally by tilting the pistons and attaching wheels and axles to a frame. Stephenson's Rocket, whose speed could nearly reach the unfathomable velocity at the time of thirty miles an hour, produced a frenzied interest among inventors in manufacturing other types of steam locomotives (Figure 8.1). With railroads, as was later discovered, steam locomotives could transport massive amounts of cargo in train cars from one point to another. This realization made transporting goods, whether factory-produced textiles or agricultural products, efficient and exponentially increased the possibilities of economic interaction.

The consequent rise of railroads, beginning in Britain and later extending to the United States and the European continent by the mid-1800s, became a conspicuous development that swept the land. As the birthplace of the First Industrial Revolution and the nation with the strongest economy globally, Britain at first had an advantage in terms of total miles in railroads; however, the United States, France, Germany, and Russia developed impressive rail lines as the nineteenth century drew to a close. Mass-produced steel no doubt helped make the construction of railroads possible. Just as significant, the development of railroads provided literally millions of men with employment, sparking economic and social mobility for many. Men as far off as China and Japan even journeyed to the United States to take up jobs on the railroads along the West Coast.

An indispensable feature of the railroads was the development of steel. Although societies had worked with iron from antiquity, what people today take for granted is that steel did not truly emerge until the mid-1800s with the Bessemer process. Invented in 1856 by Englishman Henry Bessemer, this process involved melting iron at high temperatures and removing all impurities through a complicated process to generate a product that was extraordinarily durable. Pig iron, which was available before the Bessemer process, often suffered from weak spots with impurities that made its use in construction risky. But with the impurities now virtually eliminated, steel became ubiquitous during the latter half of the nineteenth century, seen in everything from bridges, railroads, tools, and buildings. Indeed, the advent of steel led

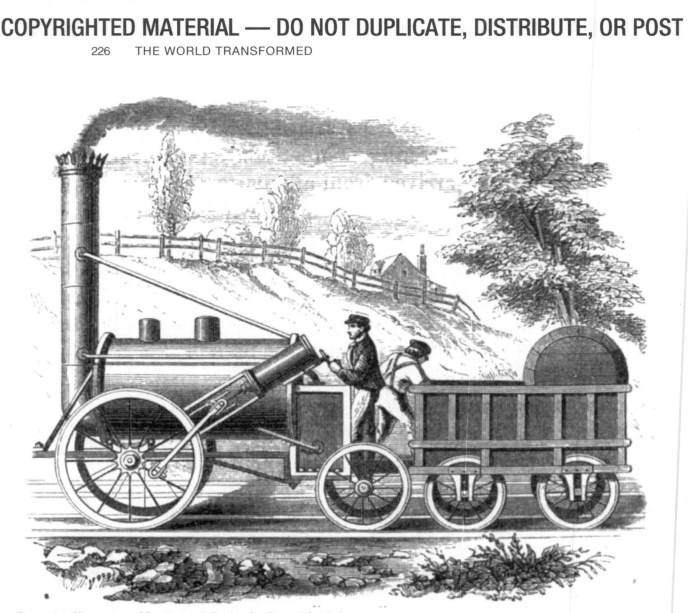

Figure 8.1: Illustration of Stephenson's Rocket (by Samuel Smiles).

to the development of skyscrapers. Now that there was a strong metal for construction, architects could and did design much taller structures for dwellings. As a result, the population capacity of cities rose exponentially, which reinforced urbanization.

Indeed, the industrial revolutions that swept Europe and the United States in the nineteenth century brought dramatic social changes, especially urbanization. No doubt, there was a strong correlation between industrialization and urbanization because of the power brokers of industry. Industrial capitalism depended on a strong working relationship between businessmen, bankers, financiers, politicians, and these individuals for the most part were urbanites. Not surprisingly, most factories and steel mills were situated either in urban centers or near them. Liverpool and Birmingham in England became especially known in this regard, as was Pittsburgh in the United States. As industry thrived, farmers and peasants also left the countryside to take up jobs in the various textile factories and steel mills in urban settings. As a result, the population of cities began to grow rapidly in industrial regions both in Europe and the United States.

At the same time, new social ills ensued. Inadequate sewage disposal systems, along with the pre-modern lack of emphasis on hygiene and sanitation, produced disease and death. Pandemics, especially from cholera, broke out periodically in major cities such as London, Paris, and Berlin in the first half of the nineteenth century. Typhus, which was known in England as the "Irish fever," also infected the poor, who were commonly referred to as the "unwashed" masses. Additionally, urbanization led cities to become hotbeds of vice. With overcrowding, such issues as gambling, drunkenness, prostitution, assault, rape, and murder all became increasingly pronounced. The fear, best represented by the throat-slashing murders by Jack the Ripper in 1880s London, was palpable. Furthermore, the widespread presence of men who had lost their jobs in the factories for whatever reason, whether petty or serious, created a crisis of homeless-ness, vagrancy, and vagabondism in the major industrial towns. All of these developments resulted from the cascade of social change generated by industry.

In addition, one of the most striking changes involved the psychological well-being of the new class of industrial workers, which diminished sharply. The European peasants of the eighteenth century, although poor and of low social status, nevertheless had exercised considerable autonomy over their lives. They had performed field labor often without a supervisor; they worked their own hours, setting their own schedules; and they did not generally need to devote even forty hours a week toward labor and had ample time to engage in leisure, which often included some type of violent activity such as game hunting, cockfighting, bullbaiting, etc. All of these features, however, changed as the peasants began transitioning to factory work. Now they had overbearing supervisors and bosses inside the factories and mills who lorded over them and criticized their work. Now they did not set their own schedule and instead were forced to work in most factories as many as six days a week. And while peasant work did not require many strenuous hours of weekly work, factory work did. It became common for men and women in England, the United States, France, and Germany to work as many as eighty hours a week in textile factories, performing dull, repetitive work. Their time for leisure diminished immensely. Given such dramatic changes, many among the first generation of industrial workers lost self-respect, became depressed, and began abusing alcohol to escape the pain associated with factory life.

Not surprisingly, industrialization also produced some negative changes in family relations. As hus-bands and fathers became depressed and increasingly used alcohol to escape reality, the potential for family violence grew. A direct correlation, after all, existed between alcohol abuse and the propensity for violence. Additionally, wives increasingly saw their husbands using booze, withdrawing from the world, wasting their salary, and neglecting their responsibilities as spouses and fathers. Consequently, many women demanded the outright criminalization of alcohol, and temperance movements dedicated to that goal popped up in Europe and especially in the United States. Prominently supported by preachers during the Great Awakening, most of the major American cities came to have temperance societies by the mid-1800s. Victorian England (1838–1901), known for its prudish moralism, similarly had a strong anti-alcohol movement. More than any single institution at the time, the Church of England espoused the criminalization of alcohol. Although the temperance effort in the United States grew throughout the late 1800s and ultimately produced a brief victory in the era of prohibition in the 1920s, the effort to outlaw alcohol never produced such a dramatic result in Europe. After all, industrialization had introduced all sorts of negative social changes. To make alcohol the scapegoat was a far too simplistic answer.

Another response to the ills of industry was to blame the machines for uprooting the traditional way of life. Given that the industrial revolutions were at their hearts driven by technology, some people naively thought they could destroy technology and go back to the life before. The word "Luddite" refers to someone who is opposed to technology and has its origins with an early nineteenth-century movement in Britain to destroy machines in factories. The Luddites, led by a mysterious figure named Ned Ludd, broke into factories at night and busted up machines and engaged in sabotage and vandalism. This approach, however, was not an effective strategy to combat the perceived social ills of industrialization. In response, the British implemented laws, making such acts illegal.

A stronger response to the new social changes unleashed by industry was Marxism. In 1848, German intellectuals Karl Marx and Friedrich Engels wrote the *Communist Manifesto*, which called for the workers of the world to unite and violently overthrow governments to bring about a classless society in which the means of production (industry) would be owned in common by the working class. While temperance movement advocates had blamed alcohol and the Luddites had faulted the machines for the new societal problems, Marx and his followers were critical of the greedy factory owners and their supporters, which often included wealthy financiers and politicians (Figure 8.2). Industry was not an evil for Marxists. Rather, it was a great good that had the possibility to change the world for the better. The problem was that the factory owners were reaping the economic gains, while the workers were exploited, thus creating a situation of severe economic disparity. For Marx, class hierarchies had been a feature of society throughout history. But industrial capitalism now had produced such economic inequality that the working class, the proletariat, inevitably would take a stand to improve its situation. Influenced by Marx's ideas, many thinkers in the middle to late nineteenth century and thereafter believed a classless society in which industry was owned by workers, not capitalists, would usher in a harmonious world order in the end, even if they deemed violence necessary to establish that world order in the first place. They promoted this idea in various forms relentlessly throughout Europe,

Figure 8.2: Karl Marx in 1875.

especially in the major urban areas. At the same time, no true successful communist revolution occurred in the nineteenth century, although a temporary commune controlled Paris for two months in the spring of 1871.

Despite the changes unleashed by modernity in the nineteenth century, in some key ways life as usual carried on for the vast majority of people. Most Europeans and Americans in the nineteenth century held strong Christian religious convictions. Church attendance remained high, and people turned to their congregations for spiritual and material support in times of personal crises. For many, the new social problems brought new opportunities to demonstrate the depth of their care for the downtrodden, thus reinforcing their faith. In the mid-1800s, Christian socialism emerged in Britain, championed by the ideas of Anglican theologian F. D. Maurice. Under his leadership, these Christians worked tirelessly to ensure the working classes had adequate living conditions and sent their children to school. At the same time, eminent British preacher Charles Spurgeon, among countless other pastors, set up orphanages to care for children lacking families. In France and Belgium, the Catholic Church similarly provided services for the needy. And in the United States, a strong interest in philanthropy developed for the first time among wealthy men and women who were concerned with improving the lives of the unfortunate. Yet few social reformers and philanthropists decried industry. After all, the massive amounts of wealth it generated made philanthropy possible in the first place.

If anything, the latter half of the nineteenth century saw industry increase dramatically. In fact, a Second Industrial Revolution came about as a result of the harnessing of electricity as a power source. While Britain benefited the earliest during the First Industrial Revolution because the steam engine was invented there, Germany benefited immensely as the birthplace of the dynamo. In 1867, German scientist Werner von Siemens developed an effective dynamo, an early electricity generator. His dynamo made possible the use of electricity for factory and home use, eventually replacing the use of steam power in industrial settings. Germany took advantage of this development and rapidly industrialized. Influenced by Siemens, a wide variety of dynamos emerged across Europe and the United States, with the Brush type being common in America. Just as significant, the possibility arose for the first time for mass electrification.

Not surprisingly, electricity introduced all sorts of new possibilities, transforming everything from household appliances to means of communication. In 1881, the American inventor, Thomas Edison, who came to be known as the Wizard of Menlo Park, invented the incandescent light bulb. This development eventually led to the illumination of homes not by the kerosene lamps and candles of the past, but by electrification (Figure 8.3). Additionally, when Scottish American inventor Alexander Graham Bell produced the first telephone in 1874, he called it an electrical speech machine because electricity made this transformative development in communications possible. By the turn of the twentieth century, experiments were

Figure 8.3: The Edison light bulb.

under way that would pave the way for radio communications, a development also made possible by harnessing electrical power. Also, factories throughout Europe and the United States popped up to fill a demand for electrical appliances, including the first types of refrigerators, washing machines, vacuum cleaners, lamps, etc. that everyone today takes for granted. Indeed, thanks to the developments during the industrial revolutions of the nineteenth century, the possibilities seemed endless as the twentieth century dawned.

MASS EDUCATION AND DEVELOPMENTS IN ACADEMIA

One of the major indirect consequences of industrialization and modernism was an unprecedented emphasis on education. Throughout much of history, only a small segment of the populace of kingdoms and states could read and write, knew of history and literature, and studied math and science. The opportunity for education, regardless the region of the world, largely was confined to the privileged elite classes. But with the growth of modernism and industry in nineteenth-century Europe and the United States, there emerged a general shift in opinion: one that championed education for the masses. Science and math played an indispensable role in leading to the inventions that drove industry, so a general optimism led to a widespread belief that more knowledge would produce more technology and a better way of life. For many scientists and consumers, there seemed no limit to the hope for new gadgets and devices. At the same time, businessmen also strongly promoted education. After all, they championed a "scientific" approach to the mass production of goods, focusing on methods to maximize profit, efficiency of resources and time, and marketing strategies. The entrepreneurial focus on education is epitomized in the character of "Mr. Gradgrind" in British novelist Charles Dickens's *Hard Times.* Mr. Gradgrind incessantly praised "facts" and condemned "fancy."[2] Facts represented the industrialists' mind-set that all worthwhile human effort should be toward gaining knowledge, while "fancy" referred to the inefficiency associated with leisure and indulging the imagination. The latter had no place in the modern industrial world.

Throughout Europe and the United States, the mass establishment of schools in the mid-nineteenth century slowly paved the way for compulsory education. In 1846, the British Council of Education established grants for educational facilities to be set up in industry. In addition, as the British economy subsequently thrived thanks to industry, tax dollars were increasingly used to educate the poor. By 1880, compulsory education emerged in England, with all children required to attend school to the age of ten. A year later, France provided a free and secular state education to schoolchildren. In the United States, the individual states decided whether education would be compulsory. Interestingly, in the highly industrialized areas (especially the North), education was indeed compulsory. Yet in the South, which still had an agricultural tradition and was less industrial, education was largely not compulsory. In fact, only a handful of Southern states required compulsory education by the turn of the twentieth century.

While the masses began receiving a formal education, the greatest triumph in the production of knowledge occurred in the universities. Throughout the nineteenth century the number of students receiving a university education grew in proportion to the population of most nations. Although a university degree

---

2   Charles Dickens, *Hard Times* (London: Bradbury & Evans, 1854), 9-11.

remained still a hallmark of the elite classes, the middle classes really for the first time obtained access to this opportunity. The university curriculum of the nineteenth century expanded as well, thanks to major breakthroughs in all the major science fields.

Indeed, in keeping with the spirit of modernism, the major disciplines of academic inquiry at universities throughout the nineteenth century came to revolve around the sciences. Empiricism, the presupposition that one comes to know truth through the senses, had given away centuries before to the scientific method. The scientific method—with its emphasis on observation, the formation of a hypothesis, the testing of the hypothesis with experimentation, and the subsequent development of a conclusion—increasingly became ubiquitous inside universities. Like never before, professors in the nineteenth century championed the method as a tool to both learn the mechanics behind the world and also how to improve the lives of people. As a result, the mass interest in learning led to major developments in the long-established fields of science as well as to new scientific disciplines themselves.

More than any discipline, chemistry thrived, thanks to a revolution in the understanding of the elements. In 1869, Russian scientist Dmitri Mendeleev introduced the periodic table of elements. Having studied chemistry in Germany, the nation that emphasized chemistry in its curriculum the most, Mendeleev arranged the elements by their atomic weights, emphasizing certain groups. He distinguished between the alkali metals, alkaline metals, and halogens, among other groups. Mendeleev's formulation of the periodic table allowed chemists in Europe to begin earnestly studying and cataloging the similarities and differences between the elements, thus contributing immensely to the knowledge of chemistry and helping pave the way for future discoveries. By the 1890s, British chemists, working with nitrogen, had discovered the noble gases. Later, in 1898, French chemists Pierre and Marie Currie discovered the element radium, for which they later won the Nobel Prize. Radium became an early cancer treatment, and Marie Currie devoted much of her later life toward promoting the benefits of the element.

Another scientific discipline that thrived was physics. Often referred to as natural philosophy in the universities, physics before the nineteenth century largely focused on explaining matter and its mechanics. The hallmark of physics in the 1800s, however, was the intense interest in different forms of energy, such as light, heat, and electricity. In 1817, French scientist Augustin-Jean Fresnel proved mathematically that light traveled in waves, overturning previous theories such as Isaac Newton's notion that light moved as particles. In 1822, French mathematician Joseph Fourier elucidated the flow of heat, accurately formulating the laws describing the rate at which objects cooled. By the 1840s, German physicist Julius von Mayer had formulated the law of conservation of energy, according to which energy can neither be created nor destroyed. All of these discoveries helped modernize physics, moving it beyond the past focus on the mechanics of matter. In the process, nineteenth-century physics played an instrumental role in making possible the developments in the discipline in the twentieth century, such as Einstein's theory of relativity and the birth of quantum physics.

The discipline of biology also revolutionized science. The most important development in the nineteenth century involved the cell. In the late 1830s, German botanists developed the cell theory, which maintained that cells were the most fundamental organizing component of living tissues. After publishing their work, other scientists throughout Europe and the United States carried out experiments with microscopes confirming the idea. Cell theory opened an entire new field of discovery. Not long thereafter, scientists had

Figure 8.4: Gregor Mendel, the father of genetics.

identified the major components within the cell's nucleus, including the mitochondria and chromosomes. Other developments in biology included Gregor Mendel's theory of inheritance. Conducting experiments on pea plants in the 1850s, Mendel formalized a theory about dominant and recessive genes that laid the basis for the modern field of genetics (Figure 8.4). Biology also saw the birth of evolution. In his *Origin of Species* (1859), the English naturalist Charles Darwin put forward his theory of evolution by natural selection. Having voyaged to the Galapagos Islands, Darwin cataloged varieties of finches and other animals there. By observing slight differences in species, he speculated they all had a common ancestor. Darwin then extended this idea to suggest all biological life shared common descent. All of these developments attested to the vibrant growth of biology.

Medicine, too, saw many major advances in the nineteenth century. Given the outbreaks of cholera associated with the rapid urbanization of the time, this disease became a major focus among physicians and scientists. By the 1850s, British physicians discovered that the disease spread through contaminated water, thus suggesting a bacterial origin. When English officials began devoting resources to improving sanitation, they found the number and severity of the outbreaks sharply declined. By the 1860s, French scientist Louis Pasteur performed experiments using boric acid to prevent the infectious childbed fever that postpostpartum women often suffered from, demonstrating conclusively that germs produced disease. Consequently, the germ theory of disease emerged, relegating to the dustbin of history traditional notions that sickness stemmed from imbalances of the humors or from bad blood. Additionally, major developments occurred in the areas of surgery and pain relief, with the advent of anesthesia, morphine, and other opiates.

At the same time, nineteenth-century medicine still paled in comparison with the developments of the succeeding century. There were still no effective antibiotics during the 1800s, although scientists did experiment with the elements of the periodic table and often prescribed sulfur and other drugs to combat germ-based disease. Nevertheless, infection control remained a major hurdle to health and life expectancy, and infant mortality rates remained high in Europe. Amputating limbs and arms containing infections and gangrene still was standard care. Also, the medicinal application of certain chemicals and drugs often caused as much harm as good. Morphine was in heavy use in cough syrups. Furthermore, the widespread use of opium and cocaine as pain relievers produced dependency and addiction, which generated an entire new series of challenges. In fact, in late nineteenth-century England, men, women, and children widely used cocaine tooth gels to cure the toothache, and dental health overall actually declined in Europe as sugar became a more prominent feature of the urban diet.

Although chemistry, physics, biology, and medicine (all hard sciences) had a vibrant past as fields of inquiry before the late nineteenth century, new fields emerged as subjects of study for the first time. This fact was especially true of the social sciences (soft sciences) such as psychology, sociology, criminology, and political science. With the hard sciences, observation and experimentation led to results that could be predicted with a great deal of precision. Many thinkers, influenced by the positivist notion of determinism, believed a detailed study of human behavior likewise could produce precise answers in explaining people's actions. For the positivists, with the right knowledge and tools of inquiry, one could predict what a person would do with the same degree of certainty as the law of gravity explained the motion of falling bodies. Influenced by positivism, the late nineteenth century thus saw the birth of many of the social sciences.

Psychology first emerged as a discipline at the time. By the 1880s, philosophers and scientists interested in human behavior had set up labs in many of the major European universities to conduct experiments on human responses to various stimuli. Much theorizing about what drives humans to act, whether reward, punishment, etc., thus ensued. More than anyone else, Sigmund Freud, an Austrian neurologist, came to popularize psychology with his many writings. Significantly, Freud hypothesized that many of the unpleasant features of human behavior had its roots in sexual suppression. Freud, in addition, crafted a wide variety of theories, most of which have few supporters today, and prescribed cocaine as a cure for mental illnesses. Still, Freud's theory of psychoanalysis paved the way for the establishment of psychotherapy as a medical therapeutic tool (Figure 8.5). With strong voices devoted to change, the scientific treatment of mental illness thus came into

Figure 8.5: Sigmund Freud, father of psychoanalysis.

fruition for the first time in history as the nineteenth century came to a close. To be sure, this development marked a dramatic break from the past, which often saw the mentally ill locked away in asylums with little effort made to alleviate their sicknesses.

Sociology and criminology also emerged as disciplines of study. While psychology was concerned with the way individuals acted, sociology sought to discover general behavior patterns of societies at large. Discovering correlations between the economic well-being, education level, and religious attitudes on group dynamics became a major focus of interest among the first sociologists. All of the changes wreaked on society thanks to industrialization, urbanization, and the rise of crime in many areas spurred scientists to inquire about modernity. More than anyone else, French scientist Emile Durkheim breathed life into the nascent field in the 1890s. Considered a father of sociology, his early work addressed the disintegration of traditional social values and explored why the suicide rate was higher among Protestants than Catholics. Such issues of inquiry led others to address crime, paving the way for the scientific study of criminology. Unfortunately, however, much of late nineteenth-century theorizing on crime was tinged with pseudoscientific prejudices, sometimes having a racist or classist bent.

NATIONALISM

During the nineteenth century, another effect of industrialization, urbanization, and education was the intensification of nationalism. To be sure, nationalism existed as early as the first nation-states during the seventeenth century and began to develop strongly in the context of the French Revolution. Yet large segments of Europe's population still did not feel nationalism's effects deeply until the nineteenth century. Indeed, uneducated peasants living in the countryside in many places in Europe often did not consider the nation in which they lived to be a crucial identity-conferring feature in their lives. They often instead had a localized village consciousness because they rarely traveled outside their village, did not read history or newspapers, and did not interact with the upper classes. But as urbanization and education took off, the peasant children of the past became the schoolchildren of the cities. In the classroom, they learned about the glorious histories of their nations and performed national pride-inducing rituals like the Pledge of Allegiance. In the process, the classroom became a key setting for the inculcation of nationalism and patriotism. The ever-present national symbols, such as a nation's flag, heroes, parades, and holidays, fostered that end as well.

A major effect of nationalism was the desire among countless groups of people to establish new nations in Europe in the mid-1800s. In some cases, such as in Greece, Germany, and Italy, these efforts succeeded. In others, like with Ireland and Poland, they failed. Regardless of the results, bonds—everything from a common religion, language, and culture to ethnic identity and shared historical grievances, etc.—united people in a single project of nation-making. Above all, solidarity was the indispensable feature behind the desire to create a new nation.

Among the earliest examples of a new nation taking root—or, more properly, reemerging as a single state—was Greece. Although ancient Greece had been the birthplace of Western civilization, it had not survived as an independent state. In fact, Greece had been occupied by the Ottoman Turks since the fifteenth century. By the early nineteenth century, however, many Greek nationalists had sought liberation and independence of their homeland. This development resulted, in part, from the increasing weakness of the Ottoman Empire, which was called the "Sick Man of Europe." Ottoman society had failed to modernize and lost wars against Russia in the previous century, exposing its weakness and allowing opportunities for Greek resistance.

Just as important were the actions of Greek nationalists in helping secure their independence. In the major Greek urban centers, a generation of young Greek nationalists cited their people's cultural achievements, Orthodox Christian heritage, and common identity to cultivate the concept of an independent Greece, and in the process produced an intense furor for liberation. Thus, in the 1820s, a series of armed Greek revolts broke out, with acts of violence against Ottoman rule. Although the Ottomans put down some revolts, the reaction among Greek nationalists intensified. Foreigners, especially from Russia and England, even traveled to Greece to fight for the independence cause. The British poet, Lord Byron, for example, gave his life for the cause and became a hero among the Greeks. As the revolts intensified, the Ottoman Empire conceded and granted Greece independence, formalized in 1832.

But not all new nations to emerge did so because of a desire for liberation from foreign occupation, as the case of Germany shows. What today is the nation of Germany did not exist before the wave of nineteenth-century nationalism. Historically, the German-speaking lands had constituted the Holy Roman Empire, a loose conglomeration of small kingdoms, principalities, electorates, and duchies. Voltaire had complained there was nothing Roman or holy about the German-dominated empire. After Napoleon defeated the last Holy Roman emperor at the Battle of Austerlitz, the German lands made up the German Confederation. Still, the modern state of Germany did not exist, as the people largely identified with the individual kingdom to which they belonged.

Prussia, which had the strongest economy and military in the Confederation, played a decisive role in uniting the various German-speaking kingdoms, paving the way for German unification. When the revolutions of 1848 broke out in several German states, the Prussians used their power to introduce order, in the process gaining a stronger influence in these states' affairs. In the aftermath, Prussia promoted the creation of a single German state to strengthen order. Not surprisingly, a nationalist discourse emerged that promoted the distinct Germanness of the various states in the Confederation. Prussian Chancellor Otto von Bismarck, who stressed the common blood and soil of the various states, typified this mentality (Figure 8.6). In the mid-1860s, he waged a war to acquire the German-speaking Schleswig-Holstein region from Denmark. After Bismarck's victory, Germany acquired Schleswig, while his ally Austria obtained Holstein. Bismarck's expansionist desire, however, was not quenched. In 1866, he went to war with Austria and obtained Holstein for Germany. Stirring up a militaristic German nationalism, Bismarck next set his sight on the German-speaking region of Alsace, in France. In 1870, he waged war on the French, provoking the bloody Franco-Prussian War. In the end, German military won out, and Germany acquired the territory of Alsace-Lorraine. Having decisively defeated a major power, Germany emerged itself as a major power for the first time in centuries. Bismarck's claim the German-speaking people would be more powerful united, rather than divided, proved true. After all, Germany emerged as the major industrial, military, and scientific center in mainland Europe subsequent to these wars of German unification.

Like Germany, Italy, as it is known today, also did not exist as a single country until the mid-1800s. For centuries, the Italian peninsula had numerous independent small kingdoms, republics, city-states, duchies,

Figure 8.6: Germany's "Iron Chancellor," Otto von Bismarck, 1871.

along with lands controlled by the pope. No single Italianness existed, even though the people of the peninsula overwhelmingly spoke the Italian language and were Roman Catholics. The shared language, religion, and ethnic identity all became features of Italian nationalism during the nineteenth century. A shared history among the peoples, highlighted by the glories of the Roman Empire and the dominance of Christendom, in addition reinforced these push factors toward unity.

As a generation of Italian-speaking schoolchildren in the first half of the nineteenth century learned of their Italian heritage, they began to desire unification, which required throwing off the yoke of foreign control. Austria had controlled areas in northern Italy, such as Lombardy and Venetia, while the Spanish Crown ruled southern Italy's Kingdom of Two Sicilies. In 1832, Mazzini formed a nationalist movement called "Young Italy," which called for a single Italian state for the peninsula. Although this movement, which supported armed resistance, did not achieve immediate victory because Mazzini was sent into exile, it laid the basis for greater Italian nationalism that produced results later. By 1860, the Italian nationalist Garibaldi led an army of Red Shirts that liberated Sicily. He subsequently united his territories under the leadership of King Victor Emmanuel thanks to the skillful diplomacy of nationalist Count Camillo Cavour, who had attracted France's support in expelling Austria from Lombardy. Thus, by 1861, the emergence of a new country that had never existed before came into existence: Italy.

Although Greece, Germany, and Italy all became new nations in the nineteenth century, many nationalist movements did not succeed, as the case of Poland shows. The Polish-Lithuanian Commonwealth had played a strong, powerful role in European history in the sixteenth and seventeenth century. Polish King Jan Sobieski had routed the Ottomans at Vienna in 1688, saving European Christendom from Islamization. The Poles also had been among the first European nations to introduce democratic features in government, having established their parliament, called the Sejm. Nonetheless, by 1795, the Commonwealth had fallen victim of a conspiracy between Russia, Prussia, and Austria. That year the tri-partitioning of Poland occurred, which saw each of those three nations annex a part of Poland. Consequently, Poland did not exist as an independent nation during the entire nineteenth century. Yet the century saw intense Polish nationalism. A shared Polish language and vibrant literature, along with a common Roman Catholic faith, forged bonds of solidarity among ethnic Poles. Dozens of revolts among Poles ensued against the Russians, Prussians, and Austrians in the middle to late 1800s, with the one in 1830 against the Russians being especially deadly. Still, despite widespread Polish nationalism among the peasants, intellectuals, and the working classes, Polish liberation and nationhood remained elusive. The occupying powers worked together to suppress the establishment of an independent Poland.

Like Poland, Ireland also experienced a strong independence movement during the nineteenth century that did not see its immediate hope realized. Long subjugated by the British, the Irish were seen as second-class citizens within their homeland. The overwhelming majority of the Irish were Catholics, and Catholics had few political rights. In addition, the language of the Irish, Gaelic, had been forbidden in the schools, while English became compulsory. Thus, by the mid-1800s, the Irish were losing their language, history, and culture. In response, Irish heritage societies emerged to keep alive the island's heritage. A cultural renaissance later emerged known as the Celtic Revival. Influenced additionally by the waves of nationalism sweeping Europe, many Irishmen such as Daniel O'Connell fought for Catholic emancipation. This goal occurred in 1828, when the British abolished a law that mandated officials take the Anglican Communion to be elected to public office. Emboldened by the victory, the Irish throughout the latter half of the nineteenth century fought for independence but were not victorious. In fact, the Irish faced much persecution, leading many to immigrate to the United States in hopes of a better life.

Yet it was the Habsburg Empire, later known as the Austro-Hungarian Empire, that saw the most intense ethnic-based nationalism in the latter half of the nineteenth century. Of all European nations, the Habsburg Empire had the greatest ethnic, religious, and linguistic diversity. Although the government was in Catholic, German-speaking Austria, the empire included Hungarians, Poles, Serbs, Czechs, and Slovaks, among others. Each of these ethnic groups drew on its people's heritage to promote a discourse championing statehood and independence from the empire. Some minor armed revolts occurred, but the Austrians squelched them. In addition, the idea of Pan-Slavism emerged, which called for creation of a single state for the various Slavic people in the Balkans. Some of the most ardent Pan-Slavists advocated armed violence to achieve this goal. The situation was indeed a powder keg, and the Habsburg Crown largely allowed regional autonomy. At the same time, all of these movements did not succeed in the nineteenth century in realizing their goal of independence.

Another type of nationalism that emerged in the late nineteenth century was Zionism. This movement, which called for the Jews of Europe to unite in hopes of creating a state for themselves in the Middle East, rested in a common faith and ethnic heritage among Jews. During the time of the Roman Empire, waves of persecuted Jews had left their homeland in the Middle East and migrated to Europe, forming large communities in Central and Eastern Europe. For centuries, Jews had become integrated into the European communities in which they lived, despite often facing oppression and mob violence (pogroms). The belief that God had set aside Palestine as a nation for Jews never truly faded from the minds of the most religious believers. Yet Zionism as a well-organized movement did not begin in earnest until Theodor Herzl's publication of *The Jewish State* (1896). In the wake of the book's publication, Herzl and other

Figure 8.7: Father of nineteenth-century Zionism, Theodor Herzl, in 1904.

Zionists attempted to negotiate with the Ottoman Empire for the creation of such a state, but the Ottomans rebuffed such an idea (Figure 8.7). Indeed, Zionism did not take off as most nations deemed the ideas too grandiose and cumbersome. Additionally, a problem stood out: the lands the Zionists desired were not unoccupied but rather the home of hundreds of thousands of Palestinians. Nevertheless, Zionism was a testament to the depth of nationalism as a European cultural phenomenon at the turn of the twentieth century.

NEW IMPERIALISM

The middle to late nineteenth century also saw the rise of New Imperialism; that is, the European establishment of colonies in Asia and Africa between the 1830s and 1914. To be sure, the New Imperialism contrasted sharply with the period of Old Imperialism (1500–1750) in which Europe had conquered the Americas. With Old Imperialism, the Spanish, Portuguese, French, and British had sought gold and glory in the New World and had introduced African slavery to the Americas, while exploiting Amerindian peoples. Yet the Europeans in the middle to late nineteenth century did not journey to Africa or Asia in search of slaves. In fact, by the second decade of the nineteenth century, the Europeans had ended the transatlantic slave trade. The causes and effects of the New Imperialism were multifaceted and the product of modernity.

Without a doubt, industrial capitalism in Europe became a leading force behind the drive for empire. Thanks to the rise of industry, British, French, German, and American factories began to produce a surplus of goods by the mid-nineteenth century, much more than was necessary to provide for domestic consumers. The surplus of goods, especially textiles, led European capitalists to seek overseas markets for profit. Asia, with the largest population in the world, was thus especially attractive. At the time, China by far had the largest population in the world, and India possessed the second largest. Although China did not become a colony of any single European nation during the nineteenth century, Europe acquired concessions from the Qing government to set up spheres of influence in China for markets. In the process, violence and gunboat diplomacy ensued. By the mid-1800s, British merchants had established a major opium market. As a result, many Chinese fell into a cycle of opium addiction, thus moving their leaders in part to want to curtail European influence. Some Chinese began targeting Europeans with acts of aggression. Yet efforts to drive out foreigners were met with British violence, as seen in the Opium Wars. In India, British merchants likewise set up monopolies and even criminalized competition from Indian producers and consumers. It became a crime, for example, for Indians to journey to the sea to obtain salt for food. Rather, they were expected to purchase their salt from British companies. French merchants expected and obtained similar concessions in Indochina, which became the major Asian colony under the control of France.

But the desire for overseas markets was not the only economic motive behind the New Imperialism in Asia. Another motive became the quest for the resources indigenous to that continent. From Burma, the British acquired massive amounts of timber, which helped the construction and furniture industries thrive in England. In addition, the French and British obtained rubber from their respective colonies of Indochina and Malaya. Rubber, it turned out, played a crucial role in driving the electrification process back home in Europe, as rubber was an excellent insulator. In addition, European jewelers profited heavily from the precious stones found on the Indian subcontinent, such as sapphires, garnets, and rubies.

As the New Imperialism in Asia took off, Europe began looking for new places to establish colonies. Setting up colonies again in Latin America was not viable because the United States, with its Monroe Doctrine (1824), had threatened to use military force to prevent Europe's dominance in the Western Hemisphere. Against this backdrop, Africa emerged as the next focus of imperialism. Significantly, despite being the major hub for acquiring slaves during preceding centuries, Africa still had remained a mysterious continent for Europeans by the dawn of the nineteenth century. Malaria, which was rampant in Africa, frightened Europeans and had prevented exploration of the continent's interior. By the mid-1800s, the use of quinine as an anti-malaria drug allowed European penetration of Africa. Yet Britain's famous missionary, David Livingston, who explored much of central and eastern Africa at the time, succumbed to the disease. Still, Africa had become open now for European interaction.

By the 1880s, a scramble for land drove the major European powers to acquire colonies in Africa. At a conference in Berlin in 1884–85, British, French, Belgian, Italian, and German delegates, along with those from other nations, assembled to take action. With little input from Africans, they took out a huge map of Africa and negotiated among themselves the carving up of the continent. The British concentrated their colonies in eastern Africa. One reason for this development was to protect the Suez Canal from Egyptian nationalists and thus safeguard access to India, the crown jewel of the British Empire. Another reason stemmed from the mineral wealth in southeastern Africa. Indeed, influential British entrepreneur Cecil Rhodes, along with other capitalists, sought profit from the rich amounts of copper, tin, and diamonds in the region. Unlike the British, the French came to dominate northwestern Africa. Algeria was especially important to France, as it was becoming a major center of tourism with its Mediterranean climate. From the conference, Germany did not gain dominance in any one region, although it had a presence all over the continent. Tanzania, Namibia, and Cameroon became the Germans' main colonies. Belgium, which had only emerged as a nation in the 1830s, acquired the Congo and Rwanda.

To be sure, altruistic motives on the part of many Europeans reinforced the desire for empire in Africa. Although Europe no longer acquired slaves, the hope of ending the Arab slave trade stirred European sentiment. In addition, many imperialists developed a positive discourse focusing on improving the lives of Africans. With their material wealth, democratic political institutions, and technological and cultural refinement, the British and the French characterized their civilizations as the finest in the world. If given the opportunity to instruct Africans in European ways, many believed, Africans would also acquire a refined culture and become the main beneficiaries of colonial efforts. Thus, British writer and imperialist Rudyard Kipling called on his fellow citizens to take up "the white man's burden."[3] Numerous missionary societies took up the challenge and became champions of empire. Indeed, spreading the Gospel and alleviating the suffering of the unfortunate through charitable acts became a rallying cry for their efforts. And, no doubt, once missionaries journeyed to the "Dark Continent," many set up clinics, dug wells, and established schools for the African masses to benefit from the fruits of Western education.

In creating their empires, however, the European nations were in part responsible for unspeakable atrocities of the indigenous peoples of Africa. In the wars to take the southeastern part of the continent in the 1890s, the British routinely employed Maxim machine guns, mowing down tens of thousands of Matabele people who were defending their land. Although valiant warriors, the Matabele, with their spears and bows, were no match for automated weapons. The British desire for minerals, especially Cecil Rhodes's fixation on the diamonds in the area, overrode any desire for human compassion (Figure 8.8). The British, however, were not alone in the lengths Europeans would go in their thirst for wealth. In establishing the Congo and Rwanda as colonies, the Belgians played enemy tribes off against one another. Murder was prevalent among the Hutus and Tutsis in Rwanda, in part because of the Belgians' pitting them against

Figure 8.8: Cecil Rhodes, founder of Rhodesia, a key British colony in southeastern Africa.

---

3   Rudyard Kipling, *The White Man's Burden* (London: Doubleday and McClure, 1899), 1–8.

each other. But violence became especially rampant and cruel, as the Congo became the personal property of Belgian King Leopold II. By the turn of the twentieth century, the king had benefited handsomely from rubber and ivory, while turning a blind eye as the enemy tribes hacked off the hands of one another, sparing not even children. In fact, the Belgian government censored reports of atrocities, which only became internationally recognized thanks to the work of US missionaries and African activists.

Yet the cruelties did not simply arise out of a desire for European wealth. In German southwest Africa (Namibia), the land was largely barren and partly occupied by the Kalahari Desert. Thus, neither mineral wealth nor markets for consumer goods drove German desire for the land. Nevertheless, when the Germans occupied Namibia, they met fierce resistance from the indigenous Nama and Herrera peoples. What ensued was horrific: the Germans set up concentration camps on Shark Island, a remote island off the coast. Many shackled Nama and Herrera died from execution by hanging, malnutrition, disease, and hypothermia. One historian, Firpo Carr, calls the actions the Germans took against these Namibians "Germany's Black Holocaust."[4] German actions, it turned out, were aimed at the elimination of these races. One might ask, however, "Why?"

The level of violence associated with the New Imperialism no doubt had its roots in social Darwinism. When Darwin published *Origin of Species* in 1859, the book's subtitle was the *Preservation of Favoured Races in the Struggle for Life*.[5] In essence, many took Darwin's idea to suggest some races were superior to others. Before Darwin, British biologist Herbert Spencer had coined the phrase "survival of the fittest." Although Spencer was mainly concerned with economic matters, many took his idea and molded it with Darwin's theory of natural selection and applied it to the races. For these social Darwinists, life was a cold, dog-eat-dog world of competition, with only the most fit races surviving and the less fit dying off.

Social Darwinism, which was antithetical to Christian values of charity and empathy, fueled much destruction. German anthropologists especially took up the idea, even traveling to Namibia to catalog the physiological features of the "inferior" races, like skull size, lip thickness, and hair. The belief among German intellectuals, officials, and soldiers that their race was superior produced a discourse that made the attempt to eliminate the perceived inferior appear more acceptable. It was against nature, social Darwinists suggested, to provide aid and charity to help the unfortunate. Instead, the social Darwinists advocated letting nature do its course. Nature mows down the weak to enable the strong to survive. Such thinking was present in German actions in Namibia.

At the same time, social Darwinism became prominent among many British imperialists as well, as the Great India Famine (1876–78) shows. When bad climactic conditions produced exceptionally poor wheat yields during these years, hundreds of thousands of Indians went hungry. The British governor, Lord Joseph Lytton, rebuffed pleas to stockpile grain to feed the masses, instead sending the food to Europe. To make matters worse, in 1877, the British passed the Anti-Charitable Contributions Act that hampered the distribution of food. British capitalists thought the distribution of food would drive down market prices and thus succeeded in using politics to stop charity. As a consequence, more than a million people in India succumbed.

---

4   See Firpo W. Carr, *Germany's Black Holocaust, 1890–1945* (Kearney NE: Morris, 2003).
5   Charles Darwin, *The Origins of Species by Means of Natural Selection: Or the Preservation of Favoured Races in the Struggle for Life* (London: John Murray, 1859). Note that Darwin meant "races" in the sense of "types." For example, a quote from his book describes "the hereditary varieties or races of our domestic animals and plants."

Significantly, Africans and Asians employed a wide variety of resistance strategies to combat European imperialism. Some of the types of resistance included armed rebellions, the organization of protests, and a wide variety of different acts of private resistance. All of these types of resistance had successes and failures, depending on the local circumstances. To be sure, all forms of resistance sought to provide the colonial subjects with a voice in their political and economic affairs and return to them a greater degree of control over their daily lives. Resistance was about returning Africa to the Africans and Asia to the Asians. To do so, however, required eliminating the European threat.

Although most armed insurrections against the European colonial powers failed because of the supremacy of European weaponry, there were some major successes. The most significant involved Ethiopia's defense of itself against Italian aggression. Ethiopia had long been a major center of political power within Africa. By contrast, Italy had only emerged as a single state in the mid-nineteenth century. Although Italy was no great power, it still sought to acquire colonies in Africa just as all of the other major powers had. Yet the Ethiopians in 1896, under the leadership of King Menelik II, routed the Italian army at the Battle of Adwa. An Orthodox Christian, Menelik courted the Russians, who were also Orthodox, and acquired arms so his nation could defend itself. The Ethiopian defeat of Italy at Adwa showed that Africans could and did indeed protect themselves when they had adequate weaponry.

Given the limitations of armed resistance on the whole, however, Africans engaged in other acts to maintain control over their lives or to affect change. African chieftains often launched formal protests over what they believed were the mistreatment of their peoples. Sometimes, these were successful in bringing change. The British, more than others, were known for such compromise. At the same time, such acts had limited effects. The Germans especially treated their puppet chieftains with contempt, often ignoring complaints and grievances.

As it turned out, the masses of Africans had to improvise to wield control of their everyday affairs. Many engaged in private acts of resistance, called subaltern resistance. Some of these acts were vandalism and petty sabotage against European colonial and administrative offices. These acts also included refusal to cooperate with Europeans by withholding their labor from mines and agriculture, along with refusal to cooperate with European authorities in investigating crimes. By withholding their compliance, these masses of Africans manufactured a discourse that served to delegitimize the presence of the imperialists. Another effective method of such resistance was spreading strategic misinformation or gossip. By exaggerating the negative features of colonial rule, this discourse served to undermine the entire imperial project itself.

At the same time, imperialism remained a feature of life for Europe's colonies in Asia and Africa. By 1900, most nations in Asia had become a colony of some European power. The situation was similar with Africa. In fact, only two nations maintained their independence: Ethiopia and Liberia. Of course, not every industrialized power had a large overseas empire. Significantly, the United States did not acquire a single colony in Africa, even though it obtained the Philippines in Asia after the Spanish-American War (1898). Yet the American failure to become obsessed with empire was an exception to the norm. Indeed, by the dawn of the twentieth century, imperialism seemed to have a vibrant future from the European point of view. To be sure, the colonial project had generated much wealth for the mother countries, and there seemed to be no desire to return to the long-gone days of the past.

CONCLUSION

As this chapter has shown, the nineteenth century saw the flowering of modernity. The revolutionary changes in industry, education, nationalism, and empire all were interconnected. For industry to thrive, the people needed an education emphasizing the sciences. For nationalism to take hold, the masses also required an education stressing the shared experiences of peoples. For imperialism to gain momentum, there needed to be a desire for overseas markets for surplus goods, a development that industrialization gave rise to. Remove one element in the equation and modernity could not have flourished in the way it did.

At the same time, the coalescence of these forces had the potential to unleash considerable hardship and cruelty, as seen in the exploitation of workers in the earliest periods of industry, as well as the often brutal treatment of colonial subjects. By the turn of the twentieth century, the forces of modernity had intensified immensely, leading to fierce competition among the major European nations for wealth, empire, and status in the international arena. As a consequence, the century began with great tension. That tension ultimately produced wars, the likes of which the world had never seen. Not only had society become modern, as the new chapter shows, warfare too became modern.

Making Warfare Modern: The World Wars

INTRODUCTION

From ancient times, conflict has existed and state-organized aggression has reigned supreme. In the process, premodern warfare no doubt resulted in considerable violence. Such warfare, whether fought over land, property, resources, religion, a leadership struggle, or other reasons, produced innumerable atrocities and enduring hardships. At the same time, in the premodern world, individual wars rarely produced casualties in the millions, much less the tens of millions. In addition, premodern wars seldom had far-reaching global effects. After all, most of such wars were confined to a specific region.

With the rise of modern warfare, however, killing on the battlefield became much easier and death tolls reached unprecedented heights, in addition to having larger effects on the international scene. This chapter examines the First World War (1914–18) and the Second World War (1939–45), two of the deadliest wars in human history. These twentieth-century wars were unprecedented in military innovations, strategies and tactics, casualties, and global reach. Above all, World War I and World War II fundamentally changed the nature of warfare and society at large.

THE FIRST WORLD WAR: BEGINNINGS

World War I (1914–18) was a historical event that few individuals living at the turn of the century could have foreseen. Although conflict had been brewing among the major European powers since the 1870s, it would have been difficult for those still in part captivated by the premodern mind-set to comprehend the sheer number of casualties, destruction of infrastructure, and lasting changes associated with the Great War. Yet the war became the first modern war of global proportions. Indeed, it was much different from previous wars, as evidenced by the complicated system of alliances, the depth of nationalistic and imperialistic pride among the belligerents, and the efficiency in killing as a result of military technological advances.

Pact-making was the catalyst that transformed a regional crime confined to the Balkans—the assassination of an archduke in June 1914—into a large-scale European and global war. The Dual Alliance (1879) between Austria and Germany, the Franco-Russian Alliance between France and Russia (1894), the Entente Cordial (1904) between Britain and France, and the Anglo-Russian Entente between Britain and Russia (1907) all prefigured which nations would comprise the two belligerent camps: the Central Powers and the Allied Powers.

In some cases, having been established decades before the war erupted in 1914, these alliances fostered a deep sense of solidarity and mutual responsibility for pact members that grew over time. This fact was especially true in explaining the budding relationship between Germany and Austria. German Chancellor Otto von Bismarck had realized that his nation, whose borders were solidified only after defeating France in the Franco-Prussian War in 1871, needed continental legitimacy, while Austria, which was increasingly bothered by domestic ethnic strife in the Balkans, desired a strong continental ally. Likewise, having suffered a defeat in the Franco-Prussian War, the French needed a nation for support if future conflict with Germany arose. The Russians, who later needed a boost in morale for its military after losing to Japan in the Russo-Japanese War (1904–05), lent their support to France.

In addition to national defense, such pact-making was at the time part of the modern balance of power mind-set in which the major European powers sought to prevent any one nation from ever becoming too powerful—to preclude, in other words, the possibility of another Napoleon ever unleashing havoc in Europe again. With the world's largest economy and navy, the British Empire was the world's superpower at the turn of the twentieth century and thus the target of such balance of power calculations. At the same time, the British believed they did not need formal military alliances and instead established friendship pacts, called ententes, with nations. In 1904, for example, the Entente Cordiale emerged as the triumph of British entente diplomacy, bringing France and Britain together in peace after having almost gone to war over control of the Nile River during the Fashoda Crisis (1898). Additionally, two years after the Entente Cordiale, the British and the Russians established a similar friendship pact, the Anglo-Russian Entente, ending a decades-long conflict over influence in Afghanistan and in Central Asia.

If mutually interlocking alliances and less reciprocal ententes later came to maximize the number of participants associated with the Great War, imperial rivalries and a deep sense of nationalism fostered an antagonistic mind-set among the European powers that produced war in the first place. Despite tension between the French and British for dominance in Africa and Asia, both London and Paris accepted each other's role as a major imperial power. After all, both nations had long histories and storied naval legacies before the time of Napoleon.

Yet Germany's rise as a major imperial power in the 1880s created a new source of conflict that neither France nor Britain accepted. The desire to make Germany the strongest nation in the world, which was widely promoted by the German Naval League beginning in the late 1890s, influenced German Kaiser Wilhelm II's belligerent foreign policy. In 1905, the Kaiser gave a saber-rattling speech aboard a ship in Tangier, Morocco, in support of a local sultan who opposed French rule there. Widely interpreted in Paris and London as a German effort to undermine French power in western Africa, Britain and France united in opposition to such brinkmanship, which became known as the First Moroccan Crisis. Another crisis over Morocco occurred six years later when the kaiser sent his battleship *SMS Panther* to the port of Agadir to challenge French rule. Such provocations again unified the British and French in opposition to what they considered to be an increasingly aggressive German foreign policy under Wilhelm II.

Equally significant, the imperial rivalries reinforced the nationalism that had swept Europe during the late nineteenth century and even sparked new nationalisms, especially the idea of Pan-Slavism. As the twentieth century began, the Austro-Hungarian Empire had been the place in Europe with the most ethnic diversity, containing large numbers of Austrians, Magyars, Slovaks, Czechs, Poles, Serbs, Croats, Romanians, and other groups. In 1882, Serbia had emerged as an independent nation, and many people within Serbia dreamed of a single united country for the Slavs in the Balkans. This vision included liberating the Serbs and other Slavic peoples from the Habsburg Empire and merging them with Serbia to create a single state for the Slavs. Russia, which saw itself as the protector of all things Slavic, promoted this image over time. In the process, the stage was set for conflict between Austria-Hungary and Serbia over the creation of a grand Slavic state in the Balkans.

Against this backdrop, the spark that set off World War I ignited: the June 1914 assassination of Archduke Franz Ferdinand—the heir to the Habsburg throne. Nineteen-year-old Gavrilo Princip, a Bosnian Serb with ties to a Serbian terrorist organization called the "Black Hand," gunned down both the archduke and his wife, Sophie, as their car turned a street corner in Sarajevo (Figure 9.1). Understandably, the assassination of the royal family infuriated the Austrians, who had to figure out the best way to respond. In response, Vienna demanded permission from the Serbian government to invade Serbia to weed out the terrorist organizations. Yet Serbia refused this ultimatum, claiming such a police intervention violated Serbia's national sovereignty. Subsequently faced with the threat of war from Germany and Austria, Serbia sought and won Russian support. Because of the Franco-Russian Alliance, France was drawn in on the side of Russia as well. As a longtime enemy of Russia, the Ottoman Empire sided with Germany and Austria. With their ententes with both France and Russia, the British entered on the side of the Allies. By the summer of 1914, two warmongering camps had thus emerged. On the one side were the Central Powers, consisting of Germany, Austria, and the Ottoman Empire. On the other side stood Serbia, Russia, France, and Britain.

As war became inevitable in the summer of 1914, almost every participating nation believed the war would not last long. According to popular thinking at the time, the technological advances in weaponry that had occurred in the twenty years before, especially the use of automated rifles and machine guns, would make wars much shorter than those of the past. In fact, most soldiers who were mobilizing fully expected to return home by Christmas. And because of the heightened sense of nationalist pride among all of the belligerents, most soldiers felt overwhelmingly confident their nation would be on the victorious side. Yet these expectations would not and could not all be met.

If anything, what became the First World War was just the opposite of expectations. The Germans, situated between Russia and France, had to fight both nations. As for strategy, the Germans intended to make use of the Schlieffen plan: to invade the low country of Belgium and deal decisively with France and then concentrate the bulk of German resources on Russia. Beginning in August 1914, Germany put this

Figure 9.1: Archduke Franz Ferdinand and his wife Sophie, in 1914.

plan into effect. In the first major battle in Belgium, the Germans captured the city of Liege, inflicting nearly twenty thousand casualties on the population of that city. German actions, however, brought a strong outcry internationally. The violation of the longstanding principle of Belgian neutrality, along with the allegations of atrocities perpetrated on the Belgian people, led the British to make war on the Central Powers official. The German soldiers who swept through Belgium, according to British propaganda, were brutes, "Huns," rapists, and child-killers (Figure 9.2). Later, the United States, when it entered the war, employed illustrations of German soldiers kidnapping Belgian children to raise liberty bonds for the war effort. Belgium had become an unwitting victim of a war it played no role in causing. Its misfortune, many lamented, was its geographical proximity to France.

But, for the Germans, defeating France did not turn out as expected. Given Germany's decisive military triumph against France in the Franco-Prussian War, military planners in Berlin expected to defeat France again with ease. The Battle of the Marne (September 1914), however, decisively proved them wrong. Later dubbed the "Miracle of the Marne" by Allied forces, a joint French and British effort repelled German forces in a fierce battle along the Marne River in northern France. Above all, this battle provided the first indication for the Germans of their ill-placed optimism. Nevertheless, the Central Powers did obtain victories elsewhere, including in places where they were the underdog, as evidenced by early Ottoman battles.

Long dubbed the Sick Man of Europe, the Ottoman Empire joined the Central Powers as soon as war broke out because of intense historical antipathy against Russia. An enemy of my enemy is my friend, according to an old adage, and this was true for the Turks, at least during the Great War. For more than two hundred years, the increasingly vulnerable Ottomans had lost multiple wars with Russia, most of which resulted in major concessions in the Balkans. Now that Russia found itself at war with Germany and Austria-Hungary, the Ottomans saw an opportunity to reassert their power in southeastern Europe by saddling up with the foes of Russia.

Although Ottoman military power paled in comparison to that of the great powers, the Ottomans still produced a major victory at the Battle of Gallipoli (April 1915–January 1916). Interestingly, this battle did not see the Ottomans face the Russians but the much stronger British. As the battle began, the British, along with colonial troops from India, Australia, and New Zealand, mounted

Figure 9.2: British anti-German propaganda.

an amphibious assault on Anatolia. But the Ottomans, with minor German assistance, defended their homeland with a feverish zeal, ultimately winning the battle. Many of the British colonial troops protested the campaign, as they found themselves as little more than machine-gun fodder for the Turks. Above all, Gallipoli proved the Ottomans were still a force to take seriously. More important, the battle prompted the Great War to take on a global dimension in the Middle East.

In the Middle East theater, the main Allied strategy became inciting Arab insurgencies against the Ottoman Turks. Faced with a wave of colonial protests after Gallipoli, British war planners decided against calling up more colonial troops to engage the Ottomans. Rather, if the British could stir up Arab resentment of Turkish rule, the Arabs would do the fighting instead. This strategy proved fruitful. The British tapped growing Arab nationalism and presented themselves as a friend who would provide military aid in helping Arabs obtain independence. T. E. Lawrence, known as Lawrence of Arabia, acted as a liaison between the British and the Arabs and played a crucial role in helping foment the Arab Revolt (1916–18) against the Ottomans. A brilliantly calculated diversion strategy by the British, this internal revolt redirected Ottoman attention away from the war effort.

Meanwhile, in Europe, the war increasingly devolved into a stalemate, a fact best demonstrated by the inconclusive Battle of the Somme (July–November 1916; Figure 9.3). As an Allied offensive campaign spearheaded by the British, the British sought to retake lands around the Somme River in France and ultimately to recapture the Belgian coast from the Germans. The British, led by General Douglas Haig, carried out a massive artillery bombardment beginning in July in a bid to break through German lines; however, the Germans, who had a large number of engineers among their soldiers, skillfully dug trenches as a defensive strategy to protect themselves against such bombardments. Although the French were supposed to supply their share of the manpower for the Somme campaign, much of the French military resources instead were devoted to protecting the city of Verdun, the site of a major French-German battle that occurred simultaneously with Somme. Thus, the British did not have adequate manpower to break through German lines. Essentially, both sides got bogged down in trench warfare. British soldiers in one trench faced German soldiers in another. The ground between them was called "no-man's-land." As soldiers tried to cross, the enemy mowed them down with machine-gun fire. More than any other battle, Somme demonstrated conclusively that the war had become a war of attrition, with no end in sight.

Figure 9.3: Trench warfare, Battle of the Somme (1916).

Indeed, the Battle of the Somme epitomized a main feature of many of the Great War's battles: trench warfare. Few military planners had anticipated this feature when making war plans. In fact, trench warfare was an innovation brought on by modern weaponry, especially automatic weapons and heavy artillery. Setting up trenches, essentially for the purpose of cover, was an almost instinctual response to the high risk of fatality associated with entering no-man's-land. As the war went on, more and more trenches were built. They were especially prominent on the western front, but they also were used in the east as well. But the cold, iced-over earth in the east made it more difficult for trenches to be constructed easily and to provide adequate cover to protect against the sub-zero weather.

Although most casualties associated with trench warfare died as a result of direct military engagement, a significant number also fell victim to problems associated with life in the trench. As it turned out, most trenches over time became covered with mud from heavy rains. The soldiers' boots and shoes, which often had holes, let in the moisture, leading many to develop an inflammatory skin and muscle condition known as trench foot. Sometimes, as infection and gangrene set in, soldiers lost a foot and thus became incapacitated from a military point of view. In addition, given the outdoor exposure of the trenches, harsh winters sometimes resulted in such widespread problems as frostbite and even hypothermia. To make matters worse, soldiers were packed into trenches, which often had poor ventilation and inadequate sewage disposal systems. Thus, disease often spread easily. The damp conditions, along with the close proximity of soldiers with one another, meant that a single case of the flu often resulted a unit-wide outbreak. In short, trench warfare explains, in part, why the First World War had a high percentage of disease-related casualties along with the battlefield casualties.

At the same time, the problem of trench combat fundamentally changed warfare. How was it conceivable, military planners on all sides asked themselves, to liquidate enemies in a trench and thus make territorial gains possible again without incurring an unacceptable amount of casualties? Dealing with this problem was a thorn in the side of leaders and military officials. Yet the situation forged new visions about how battles would play out.

Air warfare was one proposed solution. Although European nations, especially France and Germany, had used balloons for reconnaissance well before the First World War, the airplane had not been used as a military weapon. After all, it had only been a decade since the Wright Brothers had invented the airplane, and in that time the airplane was still by and large viewed as an undependable and frightening transportation innovation. At the start of the Great War, several nations used airplanes for reconnaissance purposes. Additionally, the Germans had used zeppelins to drop bombs on Liege as fighting began, a development they employed on numerous other occasions. But trench warfare led to the proposal of using airplanes to strike targets on the ground, initially with machine-gun fire. Yet a problem arose: pilots and gunners could not synchronize their shots with ground targets at altitudes they would need to fly to not risk being shot down.

But by 1915, the nations on the western front had solved the problem of machine-gun synchronization and air combat became feasible. The result was the hasty creation of air forces that played an interesting role in fighting. Rather than attacking ground targets, most of the air battles involved planes shooting one another down. Against this backdrop, the Germans developed a storied reputation with their *Luftstreitkraefte* (Imperial German Air Army Service). Manfred von Richthofen, also known as the Red

Baron, shot down eighty planes in combat and became a national hero among Germans before succumbing in an air battle himself in April 1918. Air combat was used in the Battle of the Somme and the Battle of Verdun, although it played no decisive role in the outcomes of those battles.

Air power played an even less role in the outcome of Germany's battles against the Russians. The Germans had used aircraft for spying purposes as the Russians marched toward Germany in the summer the war began. Thus, the Germans were able to mobilize adequate forces to overwhelm the Russians at the Battle of Tannenberg (August 1914), resulting in massive Russian casualties and the beginnings of Russian despair in fighting the German menace. But because the Russians lacked a large air force, the Central Powers used most of their planes against the Allies on the western front. Just as important, airplanes at the time could not bridge the vast distances from Germany and Austria to reach Russia. Thus, air warfare had a marginal influence in the battles in Eastern Europe between the Central Powers and Russia.

As an effort to break the stalemate of trench warfare, the use of tanks also became a major feature in combat during the war. In 1916, at the Battle of the Somme, the British first employed tanks successfully to take out machine-gunner positions with their Mark I's, an action they would repeat throughout the war with more sophisticated versions of their Mark tanks. The French and Germans soon followed suit with their own armored war machines. Indeed, with their hard exterior, tanks were impervious to machine-gun fire. At the same time, the earliest tanks of the war looked nothing like the typical image of such war machines today. Rather than firing massive shells, most tanks at the time had machine-gun mounts that could take out soldiers but not inflict destructive damage on infrastructure (Figure 9.4). Thus, tanks thus had a limited effect on breaking the stalemate, but they became more prominent from 1917 onward and contributed to several Allied victories late in the war.

Amid the trench-warfare stalemate, poison gas also made its debut as a weapon. Throughout the nineteenth century, chemistry had thrived as a discipline in European universities, especially those in Germany. By 1900, Germany had by a large margin become Europe's leader in chemical research and production. Not surprisingly then, Germany would be the first nation to introduce weaponized gas. Although The Hague Convention (1907) prevented nations from using poison gas in warfare, the German leadership increasingly was convinced its use was needed to obtain advantage amid

Figure 9.4: British tank from the First World War.

the stalemate of the First World War. The major problem, of course, was that little progress could be made as soldiers from all sides became bogged down in the trenches. The German leadership thought the use of chlorine gas would change the situation in its favor. In the spring of 1916, at the Second Battle of Ypres, the Germans first utilized such gas. The strong winds, however, blew back the gas to some extent toward the Germans, who had to employ gas masks to protect themselves from the very same weapon they had intended for their enemies. Nevertheless, the Germans won the battle. Hence, a new feature of the Great War emerged: gas warfare.

As the war wore on, other countries besides Germany employed other types of poison gas. The chlorine gas produced a strong odor and had limited lethality, but other gases were more potent. The French introduced phosgene, which was much more lethal than chlorine gas. In fact, most deaths associated with gas during the war came from it, which smelled like wet grass. The Germans as well quickly adopted this form of gas as their preference, as did the British. But other types of gas were also used. In fact, tear gas, a contemporary choice among riot police to dispel crowds, was first used during the Great War, and it became an effective nonlethal method of gas warfare that had some success in leading soldiers to abandon their positions within the trenches. In addition, the Germans in 1917 introduced mustard gas during the Third Battle of Ypres. Although not especially lethal, it was an exceptionally effective tool of psychological warfare. After all, mustard gas produced massive blistering of the human skin and could even cause blindness.

Despite the technological advances employed during the First World War, these by themselves did not break the stalemate. What did was the entry of the United States into the war in April 1917. When the war broke out three years earlier, US President Woodrow Wilson had pledged his government would be neutral. But the reality was somewhat different. By the time of the war, the US economy depended, in part, on foreign trade, mostly with Europe. Thus, the continuation of commerce was imperative for the United States. When the Germans began employing in earnest unrestricted submarine warfare in the Atlantic Ocean in 1915 to stop British shipments of war material, the situation created tension between the United States and Germany. After the Germans sank the passenger ship *Lusitania* that same year, an international outcry ensued as innocent passengers, including Americans, lost their lives. Soon thereafter, the Wilson administration secured a promise from Germany to stop unrestricted submarine warfare. By all accounts, US neutrality seemed secure.

A couple of major events in early 1917, however, changed the situation. The first reason seemed especially sinister from the US point of view. In January, German Foreign Secretary Arthur Zimmerman sent a telegram to Mexico encouraging that nation to make war on the United States. In exchange, Germany pledged to help Mexico recover lands lost during the Mexican-American War (1846–48), including such states as Texas, New Mexico, and Arizona. Germany had hoped that if the United States was preoccupied with war against Mexico, it would not make the conflict in Europe a priority. The second reason was even more provocative: overconfident but influential German military planners began to think they could win the war, even if the United States entered on behalf of the Allies. It would take a long time, they reasoned, for American soldiers to cross the Atlantic and become integrated into the Allied war effort. By that time, many hoped, the war would be over. Consequently, in February, Germany decided to resume its old policy of unrestricted submarine warfare as a hallmark of the general war effort. The second reason was the official justification the Wilson administration used to justify its entry into war in April 1917.

As US forces mobilized, the Central Powers achieved a pyrrhic victory in Russia's surrender and departure from the war. From a strategic point of view, Russia's Tsar Nicholas II in 1914 had made a mistake in getting involved in the war, as the Russian military lacked much of the modern technology Germany possessed. As a consequence, Russia lost numerous battles against the Germans as time passed, although it won some against the Ottomans. By 1916, public opinion of the war in Russia was at an all-time low, and many Russians blamed the tsar personally for their nation's entry into the war. Russian soldiers, many complained, had been fodder for German machine guns ever since the disastrous Battle of Tannenberg (1914). The public demanded change, and it came. The Russian Revolution of 1917 saw the overthrow of the tsar and the establishment of the Bolshevik regime. Led by the communist Vladimir Lenin, the Bolsheviks had promised to end the war once they solidified power. When they did so in the spring of 1918, the Bolsheviks sent a delegation led by Leon Trotsky to Germany to sue for peace. This surrender, formalized in the Treaty of Brest-Litovsk (March 1918; Figure 9.5), resulted in the Germans acquiring massive tracts of land in Russia, including Ukraine and the Baltic regions. It also resulted in a huge boost to German morale, leading many to think ultimate triumph was in sight.

But fate had something different in store. Although it did indeed take some time for the US military to mobilize, cross the Atlantic Ocean, and set foot in Europe, once it did the outcome of the war became clear: the Allies obtained the upper hand. The American Expeditionary Forces, led by General John J. Pershing, helped turn back Germany's massive Spring Offensive in 1918. Emboldened by Russian surrender on the eastern front, Germany had hoped this offensive would win the war. The Germans, however, did not expect the large number of American soldiers that had arrived in Europe. Berlin had indeed miscalculated. The US presence also was decisive in the Hundred Days Offensive, an allied initiative between August and November. This offensive, which saw allied victories in the Battle of Amiens and the Second Battle of the Somme, pushed back German forces. Thereafter, the Germans were on the defensive militarily. Morale among tired German soldiers for the war effort faded immensely in Germany as a consequence of the failed spring offensive and the Hundred Days Offensive.

Yet it was the sharp decline in morale among the German population that sealed the fate of the Great War. In addition to military defeats, the Germans faced innumerable other problems off the battlefield. One of the most devastating was the Spanish flu pandemic of 1918, which became one of the world's most lethal medical crises in human history. In an age without antibiotics, death rates soared not only in Europe but also globally. To make matters worse, Germans at home lacked adequate nutrition, as civilian rations were cut. The winter of 1916–17 was known as "turnip winter" in Germany, an era of intense civilian hardship in which Germans lived on a dramatic reduction of calories and which the turnip, a staple food for animals, became the principal staple among German civilians because of a shortage of grains. By 1918, Germans often were forced to consume food substitutes called ersatz products. Germans consumed fake bread, dairy products, tea and coffee, and meatless meat. Sawdust, many complained, had become the filler material for German sausages. Essentially, German chemists had developed such food products to feed the population, but they failed to recognize the masses did not embrace these changes.

By autumn 1918, the Central Powers were tired of fighting and sought an armistice, thereby ending the war. The Ottomans stopped fighting in September, followed by Austria-Hungary and Germany in early November. With the greatest military presence, Germany was key in the decision to seek an end to war. Given the decline of both morale among soldiers and civilians for continuing combat, the decision decisively brought fighting to an end. The Great War was over. The Allies had won, and the Central Powers had lost.

Figure 9.5: Lands acquired by Germany from Russia, after the Treaty of Brest-Litovsk (1918).

THE ARMENIAN GENOCIDE

One of the features of modernity in the early twentieth century was the efficiency of killing that made possible episodes of ethnic cleansing and genocide. Racism and enmity between ethnic groups no doubt have existed since the beginning of civilization. But the ability to wipe out a race or come close to doing so was something new. Technological advances in—and the bureaucratization of—warfare rendered killing easy, and the result was often that the number of deaths in such campaigns was exponentially greater than what was possible or even conceivable in premodern times.

A genocide that historians have only recently acknowledged was the Ottoman Turks' slaughter of Armenian Christians during World War I. In the decade before the war, the Ottoman Empire had experienced intense Turkish nationalism, championed by a group of intellectuals and political figures known as the Young Turks. This group had been instrumental in promoting the Turkification of Ottoman society at the expense of such ethnic minorities as Arabs and Kurds, who were Muslims, as well as Armenian Christians. Because of a common Christian identity, Russia had long been the main champion of Armenians who lived within the Ottoman Empire, often demanding concessions and favorable treatment of these Christian subjects. In February 1914, Russia even secured an agreement with the Ottoman Empire to allow Armenians to have greater political control in the two eastern regions of Anatolia where they had a sizable population. For Turkish nationalists, however, such Russian encroachment was unacceptable.

When Russia became official enemies of the Ottoman Empire during the First World War, Armenian Christians became scapegoats and targets for Turkish aggression and racial enmity. This development intensified as the frustrated Ottomans suffered defeats from Russia as the war progressed. In response, the Committee of Union and Progress (CPU), the Turks' body in charge of Armenian affairs, sought to wipe out the Armenian presence from Anatolia. The CPU instituted a forced removal policy according to which no more than five to ten percent of Armenians could comprise the total population of any province. Fearful of Armenian cooperation with Russia, the Young Turks claimed this initiative was necessary to promote Ottoman national security during the war.

By the spring of 1915, the Ottoman military began coercing Armenians in the eastern provinces to evacuate Anatolia by foot for the deserts of Syria. Stripped of their land and property, hundreds of thousands of men, women, children, and the elderly died of hunger, thirst, and exhaustion on the trip to no-man's-land (Figure 9.6). The Armenian populace, which was largely unharmed, could put up little resistance. After all, the CPU had the major Armenian political leaders and intellectuals arrested and put to death. Demoralized, the Armenians who made the journey to the Syrian desert were housed in refugee camps that provided inadequate food and water necessary for survival. Thus, many more perished after completing the arduous trek.

The suffering of Armenian Christians, however, had only begun. As Ottoman frustrations with the war grew in the summer of 1916, the Turks ordered the systematic murder of Armenians in Der Zor, Syria. In fact, the desert camps of Der Zor became the major annihilation center among the nearly two dozen concentration camps holding Armenians in the surrounding region. Tens of thousands died horrifically from mass burning and drowning, while others died from gunshots and the sword. In a bizarre twist made possible by the science associated with modernity, Armenian children were given morphine overdoses and toxic gas. In the end, the total estimated deaths associated with the Armenian Genocide, including the deliberate murders and the loss of lives from the journey to the desert, stood at 1.5 million.

The Turks' treatment of Armenians was more than a campaign of ethnic cleansing. It was also a campaign of *cultural genocide.* In their Turkification campaign of Anatolia, the Young Turks had targeted not only Armenians, but also Arabs and Kurds. But because the Arabs and Kurds were Muslims, they were not sent to the deserts to perish. Rather, they were scattered about and encouraged to assimilate and adopt Turkish culture. Despite a somewhat secular facade, the Young

Figure 9.6: Refugees in Syria, 1915

Turks maintained a common Muslim faith was essential to Turkish identity. Thus, the Arabs and Kurds had hope for integration into broader Turkish society, but not the Armenian Christians. Although the Turks did initially allow Armenians who converted to Islam to avoid forced removal, the CPU abandoned that policy after tens of thousands made pledges to convert. The Young Turks questioned the sincerity of such mass conversions. While the lives of thousands of Armenian children were saved by conversion, these children nonetheless had their heritage wiped away. In fact, many found themselves in the forced-marriage arrangements that were the norm within Turkish society at the time.

Given most of the deaths associated with the Armenian genocide resulted from the forced removal, some might be inclined to view this tragedy not as a modern development but as an unintended consequence of warfare. Such a view, however, not only overlooks the systematic homicidal planning at the top of Ottoman political power but also the vast bureaucracy involved in the forced relocation process. There were numerous Ottoman military resources devoted to the task. In addition, the bureaucracy consisted of thousands of officials who oversaw the numerous deportation control centers, transport stations, and concentration and annihilation centers.

THE CARTHAGINIAN PEACE AND THE INTERWAR PERIOD

After the Central Powers surrendered and brought the Great War to a close, the Allies had different approaches about how to impose a peace. For some Americans, especially President Wilson, the war had been waged to end warfare and to advance democracy. Wilson envisioned a new collective security body, the League of Nations, which would promote diplomacy among the major nations of the world to maintain global peace. Unlike his counterparts, the idealistic American president also sought to forgive Germany and not punish the nation too harshly. For many French, however, revenge was the word of the day. After all, as French President Georges Clemenceau pointed out, the Germans had destroyed much of

Figure 9.7: William Orpen's painting of the signing of the Treaty of Versailles.

France's infrastructure with their invasion, in addition to all of the lives lost. Rebuilding would be costly, and somebody had to pay. The British, who never saw a German invasion during the First World War, were less vindictive, but still wanted to see the Central Powers punished for the war. In the end, the Central Powers paid a heavy price for leading the world to war.

In some ways, the Austro-Hungarian Empire and the Ottoman Empire were the greatest losers of the war. The war's outcome resulted in the total disintegration of these great empires, which had existed for centuries. In the wake, new nations emerged from each. Austria, with its German-speaking population, emerged as a single nation, as did Hungary, with its Magyar population. Out of the Austro-Hungarian Empire too emerged Czechoslovakia, a nation with a Czech majority and a Slovak minority that had never existed in history. In addition, Poland reemerged as an independent nation after having been occupied since 1795. Lastly, a new nation formed in the Balkans, Yugoslavia. As a cruel irony of fate, the creation of Yugoslavia—a Pan-Slavic state—had been what the terrorist who started the war had wanted in the first place. As for the Ottoman Empire, the lands of the Arabian Peninsula and the Middle East became disconnected from Turkey. New states emerged, controlled informally by Britain and France through the League of Nations' mandate system, an imperialist structure. The French exercised political control in Syria and Lebanon, while the British wielded such power in Transjordan, Iraq, and Palestine.

In addition to the destruction of the Austro-Hungarian and Ottoman empires, Germany received a fierce punishment as well. When the leaders of the Allies met at the Paris Peace Conference (1919; Figure 9.7), they forced Germany alone to accept total responsibility for the war: this became the notorious war-guilt clause of the Treaty of Versailles that many Germans detested. In addition, at the behest of the French delegation, Germany was required to pay heavy reparations: one hundred thirty-two billion gold marks. Several key economists of the time, including the internationally respected John Maynard Keynes, criticized the reparations demand, claiming a transfer of such wealth would cripple Germany economically and keep the nation in a perpetual state of destitution. Keynes also maintained the treaty ending the war was a Carthaginian peace, in reference to the overly harsh treaties ancient Carthage imposed on states it conquered.

Meanwhile, Germany, which had a strong authoritarian tradition, became the Weimar Republic. In some ways, the new republic made great innovations with democracy. In 1919, women obtained the right to vote, a year before they did in the United States. There also emerged a number of political parties with various platforms, each appealing to some segment of German society. Despite the hopes for a better life, however, the Weimar Republic faced hardships resulting from the war. By the early 1920s, the reparations burden seemed increasingly onerous. When Germany got behind on payments in 1923, the French and Belgians occupied the Ruhr, the major industrial region of the Weimar Republic. In response, the Germans engaged in an act of passive resistance, printing off money they did not have and devaluing their currency. The result was a massive hyperinflation crisis that beset Germans throughout the year. Money became virtuously worthless, so much that some used large bills for toilet paper.

Amid the hyperinflation crisis, a new figure emerged in Germany who would forever change the world: Adolf Hitler. A corporal during the First World War, Hitler despised Germany's surrender during that conflict. He believed Germany should have fought on but was stabbed in the back by a small clique of various activists who sought capitulation, including the communists, Jews, and others. Seeing his nation facing economic hardship and military occupation, Hitler believed that Weimar Germany was destined to play an insignificant role in world affairs as long as it was a republic. At the time, Hitler became infatuated with the new political philosophy—fascism—that had swept Italy, and whose promoters advocated it as an alternative to both communism and democracy. Hitler studied and fell under the influence of the ideas of Italy's new fascist dictator, Benito Mussolini, who had come to power in 1922. Mussolini, more than anyone else, had faulted democracy as a weak political philosophy that promoted national division, factionalism, and encouraged weakness and mediocrity.

According to fascism, a nation could only thrive with a single charismatic leader who galvanized the nation, emphasizing a common heritage and providing the populace with a grandiose vision for the

Figure 9.8: Italy's fascist dictator Benito Mussolini, in 1937.

future. Mussolini, who had created the Fascist Party, had provided such charisma, attracting thousands of followers who all wore black shirts (Figure 9.8). In 1922, Mussolini and his followers marched on Rome and demanded control of the government. Shockingly, the Italian king, who was tired of the factionalism of Italy's republic, consented, and thus emerged the first fascist state and a powerful example for Hitler to emulate to bring political change.

Following Mussolini, Hitler thought he could galvanize German fascists, who were known as Nazis, to overthrow the Weimar Republic's government amid the hyperinflation crisis. Hitler formed a sizable group of followers, called the Brown Shirts. He also had an important supporter, General Erich Ludendorff, the hero of the Battle of Tannenberg during the First World War. Taking a page out of Mussolini's playbook, in November 1923, Hitler and his followers barged into a beer hall in Munich in which some key government officials had assembled. Hitler fired a shot into the ceiling and told the crowd a new revolution had begun. But rather than overthrowing the government, Hitler and his followers were arrested, put on trial, and sent to prison for brief sentences. Nevertheless, the failed Beer Hall Putsch, as it came to be called, turned Hitler into somewhat of a celebrity among right-wing elements in German society. The media became deeply interested in this bold man and his ideas. For his supporters, the temporarily jailed Hitler had become a martyr for fighting for his homeland, a man who wanted to rectify the perceived injustices associated with the Carthaginian peace.

All the while, most Germans during the mid-1920s viewed Hitler as a maniac and criminal. After all, Germany experienced great prosperity during the roaring twenties, and his radical ideas seemed little more than the deranged ramblings of someone locked in a bygone era. New Weimar Chancellor Gustav Stresemann introduced a new currency that eliminated the hyperinflation crisis. As a result, German industry thrived, especially in steel and chemical production. Even the reparations issue became dramatically less burdensome, as American bankers, through the Dawes Plan, provided necessary loans to allow the German economy to grow as it had never done before. In short, by 1928, the vast majority of Germans were happy with their lot in life. The Nazi Party, which ran in elections, never mounted a major political opposition at the time to the Weimar leadership.

Two events in 1929, however, changed the fortunes for Hitler and the Nazi Party. To begin, highly popular Chancellor Stresemann died unexpectedly at the age of fifty. From the Nazi perspective, this event created an opportunity to fill a political power vacuum. More important, the international stock market crash in October set in motion a European recession that would go down in history as the Great Depression. Unlike with inflation, the primary characteristic of an economic depression is unemployment. Joblessness spread rapidly in the Weimar Republic and in some places reached 50 percent by 1932. In the process, unemployment produced among Germans much hopelessness, despair, intense dissatisfaction with democratic politics, and a tendency to entertain new ideas.

During the early 1930s, the Nazis under the leadership of Hitler exploited the Great Depression to gain widespread support. On one hand, they emphasized the socialist aspect of their platform (the official Nazi name was the National Socialist Party) to present themselves as a party that pledged to provide the unemployed masses with jobs and economic aid. On the other hand, the Nazis stressed the nationalist aspect to attract supporters who identified as ethnic Germans. This strategy enabled the Nazis to define Jews as non-Germans and scapegoat them—many of whom were depicted as bankers—for the Great Depression. In the process, anti-Semitism spread like a wildfire throughout Germany.

The 1932 general elections brought the Nazis to power in Germany, despite a commonly held factual error that Hitler was elected. In fact, Paul von Hindenburg decisively defeated Hitler in the presidential elections that year. Nevertheless, the Nazis became the dominant party in the German Parliament. As a result, they obtained, by law, the right to choose the chancellor, and they selected Hitler (Figure 9.9). Referring to Hitler as a "Bohemian colonel," Hindenburg did not want to appoint Hitler, but the old man's hands were tied. Thus, for the first time in his life, the Nazi leader assumed a prominent leadership role in government.

Over the next couple of years, Hitler morphed into a dictator, in accordance with his fascist ideology. The Reichstag fire of 1933 helped spark this development. After a Dutch communist set ablaze the parliament building that year, Hitler and the Nazis introduced the Enabling Act, which, in the name of national security, gave Hitler almost unlimited powers. Hitler subsequently arrested his most vocal political opponents, especially the communists. When Hindenburg died in the summer of 1934, Hitler abolished the separate political office of president. Instead, he merged the role of president with that of the chancellor, and Hitler subsequently was to the masses simply the "Fuhrer," the German word for leader.

As the years passed, Hitler entranced the German population with his rhetoric, pledging to make Germany the greatest nation in the world. He often spoke about the need for the nation to remilitarize and provided the people with a hope of great things to come. The reality, however, was much different. The Nazis did not effectively deal with the unemployment associated with the Great Depression. Rather, they gave the people a vision to divert their attention away from economic and social problems at home. That vision was an expansionist foreign policy. If Hitler could not provide German men with jobs in factories, he could rebuild their honor by making them soldiers and making war on his neighbors. Given the centrality of military prowess to German notions of manhood dating back to the time of Bismarck and before, many men regained their pride and sense of self-worth.

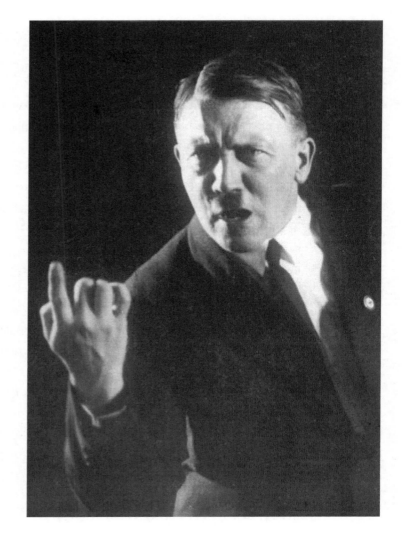

Figure 9.9: Adolf Hitler in 1932.

To be sure, a complex, racialized ideology that was inherently expansionist drove Hitler's foreign policy aims. Hitler viewed the Germans as the strongest, best-fit race whose destiny was to conquer Europe and eventually the world. Thus, the Germans needed *lebensraum,* "living space," for the implementation of the Fuhrer's vision of a Third Reich that would last a thousand years. The lands of Eastern Europe, in Hitler's vision, would provide that space. The Slavic peoples of that region were to perform slave labor because the Nazis deemed them racially inferior. That the masses of Germans fell under the influence of Hitler was, in part, a result of the leader's charisma, as evidenced by his many crowd-enticing speeches and public displays championing the supremacy of German blood and soil.

Yet the racialized thinking was not unique to Hitler. Social Darwinism, with its application of the "survival of the fittest" mentality to different peoples and races, was promoted in the school and university textbooks. When Hitler himself was just a schoolboy, thousands of Germans had already started promoting eugenics, believing that the "weak" elements of society should not be allowed to reproduce. At the same time, many educated Germans later studied the pseudo-scientific discipline of racial hygiene, with some even obtaining doctorate degrees in this field at major German universities. In much of the German scholarly literature in the early twentieth century, too, non-German peoples were portrayed as culturally and intellectually inferior to Germans. Put simply, Hitler did not impose from a top-down position racist thinking on Germans during the Second World War; rather, he tapped into a racism that had been building for more than a generation to provide Germans with a justification for expansion.

That expansion began with a series of events in 1938 that would set off the Second World War a year later. The first step saw Hitler consolidate all German-speaking areas under his control. As an Austrian, the Fuhrer wanted to incorporate his birth country into a greater Germany. At the time, the fascism sweeping Europe had a strong appeal in Austria, so Hitler was able to annex Austria with little effort. At the plebiscite to determine Austria's future, 99.7 percent of Austrians voted to join Germany. This development had a huge influence on Hitler's morale, emboldening him to try to take other parts of Europe with German minorities. The German leader next turned his attention to Czechoslovakia. This nation, with a Czech and Slovak majority, nonetheless had a sizable German-speaking population in the western region known as the Sudetenland. Hitler demanded the right to take the Sudetenland, claiming these German-speaking peoples had a right to self-determination. Yet the Czech government rebuffed such arguments. A conference was held in Munich to resolve the issue. It resulted in British Prime Minister Neville Chamberlain consenting to Hitler's demand to annex the Sudetenland, which occurred later that year. An avid peacemaker and compromiser, Chamberlain maintained he had saved Europe from war.

THE SECOND WORLD WAR BEGINS

Appeasement did not slake Hitler's expansionist ambitions. He next turned his attention to Poland, which many Germans thought did not have a legitimate right to exist as a nation. After all, they argued, no such thing as an independent nation of Poland had existed since 1795, when Prussia, Russia, and Austria carved up the once mighty Polish-Lithuanian Commonwealth among themselves. Poland had only reemerged as a nation after the Central Powers lost the First World War, a loss Hitler and his supporters did not recognize. Sensing the Soviets also did not recognize the legitimacy of an independent Poland, Hitler gambled he could form a pact with the USSR to take back Poland. His gamble payed off. In August 1939, German Foreign Secretary Joachim von Ribbentrop and Soviet Foreign Minister Vyacheslav Molotov signed a secret agreement to invade Poland and split it among themselves; essentially, western Poland would go to Germany, while the Soviets were free to take eastern Poland. This secret deal, known as the Nazi-Soviet Non-Aggression Pact, was the spark that set off the most devastating war in human history.

Indeed, the Second World War began on September 1, 1939, with the Nazi invasion of Poland. London and Paris had warned Hitler that if he invaded Poland, Germany would find itself in a state of war with Britain and France. Yet Hitler, having been appeased earlier by Chamberlain, did not take this warning seriously. But this time the two victorious powers from the First World War followed through with their threat, declaring war on Nazi Germany two days after the invasion of Poland. They did not, however, immediately take military action because there needed to be time devoted to war planning, consultation, and mobilization. Nonetheless, the world stood anxious as it was clear the autumn of 1939 had ushered in another Great War.

In the meantime, the Germans wreaked havoc in Poland (Figure 9.10). Although the Polish military leadership believed their nation could hold out against the Nazis for six months—enough time for the Allies to come to their country's rescue—fate turned out much different. Facing an onslaught from both the Germans from the west and also the Soviets from the east, Poland held out for just a month

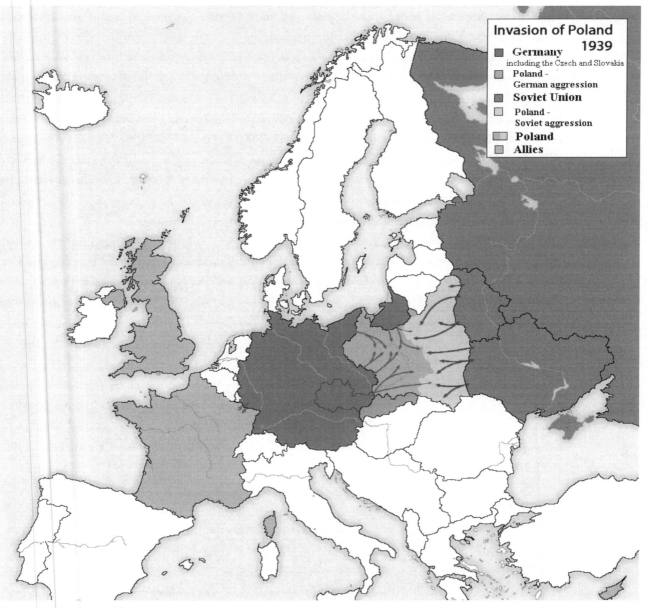

Figure 9.10: Invasion of Poland, 1939.

before surrendering. This development marked the beginning of a brutal occupation that would see millions of Poles experience horrific persecution. The Nazis put Hans Frank, a staunch anti-Semite, in control of their part of the country, and he immediately went to work in expelling ethnic Poles from western and central Poland to make room for Germans, in accordance with Hitler's *lebensraum* aim. Additionally, Jews, who made up a sizable minority in Poland, found themselves in segregated neighborhoods called ghettos. Given inadequate food rations, many starved. This mistreatment foreshadowed what would come later as the war progressed: the Holocaust.

But in the spring of 1940, Nazi Germany, which was allied with Italy and formed the Axis Powers, decided first to deal with the Allied Powers—at this time the French and British. Invading France directly from Germany was difficult because the Ardennes mountains hindered mobilization. Thus, in May 1940, Germany attacked the Netherlands and Belgium, seeking to use the two nations as staging grounds to fight Britain and France. The Dutch and Belgians put up strong resistance, but they both succumbed quickly. Dutch citizens, along with international observers, were especially horrified as the Nazis targeted civilians with the bombing of Rotterdam. From Belgium, in late May, the German military then marched into France. Although the world expected a long fight similar to the trench warfare of the First World War, that did not occur. The French military, which was among the largest in the world, fought the Germans for about a month and then surrendered. Hitler relished the French surrender, using the same train car utilized in the First World War to accept French defeat. The Nazis subsequently occupied Paris and the northern coast of France, while setting up a puppet regime in the southern city of Vichy. The main goal now for the Nazis was taking Britain. Reality, however, was different. The British never faced an invasion from the Nazis, even though the Germans had drawn up plans called Operation Sealion.

Why the French succumbed to the Germans and why the British never did largely have to do with advances in military strategy and technology. World World I had been characterized by trench warfare; however, there was very little trench warfare in World War II. The biggest reason was the advance in military aircraft. There had, of course, been airplanes during the First World War, but the planes of that generation were rudimentary and not designed for heavy combat. Yet, in the interwar period, the major powers all developed air forces, believing rightly the airplane would revolutionize warfare. The Germans, in particular, had in part secretly developed a strong air force called the Luftwaffe. German military strategist Heinz Guderian believed the use of heavily armed divisions (consisting now of infrastructure-crippling tanks, batteries, and other artillery) working in close coordination with fighter and bomber aircraft would promote quick battle victories. This thinking formed the basis of Nazi war strategy, called *blitzkrieg* or lightning war. This warfare strategy overwhelmed the French, precipitating France's surrender in June 1940.

Taking Britain, however, proved an insurmountable task for the Germans for several reasons. To begin, the British Isles, as an island nation, was not subject to blitzkrieg strategy, as the English Channel and the North Sea were effective barriers to a German invasion. Britain, which had the most powerful navy in the world, dominated the marine areas around the Isles, thus preventing the possibility of a Nazi invasion from a tactical point of view. The British also had effective air power with its Royal Air Force, rivaling Germany's Luftwaffe. If anything, the British had an advantage in defensive air combat: radar. In the spring of 1940, the Royal Air Force shot down a high percentage of German aircraft trying to cross the English Channel because the British, unlike the Germans, had integrated this new invention into its defense system. Most important, the strong leadership of new British Prime Minister Winston Churchill helped maintain the morale of the British people. Unlike Chamberlain, whose earlier compromise with Hitler was now met with ridicule, Churchill soothed the British with his firm and confident speeches in times of peril, especially when the Germans dropped bombs on London in 1940. The Nazis never succeeded in conquering Britain, as they had done in France.

Having made little progress against the British, Germany decided to push deeper into Eastern Europe. In June 1941, the German military carried out Operation Barbarossa, its surprise invasion of the Soviet Union. Hitler's military advisers had warned against this move, pointing out the Soviets were no threat to Germany and noting the fact that the USSR had cooperated with Germany on Poland. Yet Hitler ignored this advice. In his autobiography written while in prison, *Mein Kampf*, Hitler had discussed his dreams of conquering the Soviet Union, saying it would be the *lebensraum* for the Third Reich. Russia, in addition, had been Germany's enemy during the First World War, and Hitler despised communism. Marrying communism with his anti-Semitism in a twisted way, Hitler conceived of the Soviet system as a Jewish blight on the world that had to be stamped out. He had built his early Nazi career as an opponent of "Judeo-Bolshevism" and any agreement with the Soviets was never in his mind to be respected.

Operation Barbarossa caught the Soviets off-guard, and millions of Soviet lives, military and civilian, were lost. Although the USSR had industrialized during the interwar period, its military was no match for the Nazis at the time of the surprise attack. The Soviets lacked adequate defense forces, which led the Germans to quickly take huge tracts of Soviet territory in Ukraine, Belarus, and in the Baltic region with blitzkrieg warfare. Mass executions of Soviet citizens occurred everywhere, as the Germans stamped out any resistance and showed no mercy to what they viewed as subhuman Russians. By September, the Germans had laid siege to Leningrad, the Soviet Union's second-largest city and namesake of the USSR's founder, Vladimir Lenin. Conquering the city, the Nazis hoped, would inflict a huge defeat on Soviet morale and precipitate Moscow's surrender. A three-year occupation ensued that saw more than a million casualties, many of them civilians. The Soviet people in Leningrad found themselves without running water, heat, or adequate food. Cannibalism and starvation became major features of life in Nazi-occupied Leningrad. Death, especially among children, the sick, and the elderly, spread everywhere.

Emboldened by the fall of Leningrad in the fall of 1941, the Germans next advanced toward Moscow, hoping to take the Soviet capital. Intense fighting occurred around the city between December 1941 and January 1942. The Soviet leader, Joseph Stalin, had devoted the bulk of the Soviet military resources at that time to defending the capital. Thus, the Germans met an unanticipated amount of resistance. Russian soldiers—many of whom were women—and civilians alike rallied to protect the city in its time of need. Stalin even lifted restrictions on the Russian Orthodox Church to encourage morale in the fight to save the motherland. Blitzkrieg warfare did not work for the Germans, as they lost the Battle of Moscow, the first major German loss during the Second World War in Eastern Europe.

At the same time, however, Hitler amassed two significant allies in Eastern Europe as this fighting occurred: Hungary and Romania. Hungary, which had a strong anti-communist leadership, gave way to fascism under Miklos Horthy. Gaining Hungary as an ally was important for Hitler because that nation had been on Germany's team during the First World War. More important, Romania, now under the military leadership of Ion Antonescu, also became an ally with Hitler. From the Nazi perspective, Romania was significant because of its Ploesti oil fields. Oil, after all, was a resource of which the Germans sometimes had shortages. In a sense, by choosing to ally themselves with Germany, these Eastern European leaders may have saved their nations from the prospect of total subjugation to Hitler's *lebensraum* goal.

THE SECOND WORLD WAR EXPANDS

Unlike Woodrow Wilson during the First World War, the US president during the Second World War, Franklin D. Roosevelt, had pledged not to be neutral. Faced with an American public that nonetheless preferred isolationism, Roosevelt could not declare war early on. But from the start of the war, Roosevelt had favored the Allies because he viewed Nazism as a US national security threat and a scourge that threatened all of humanity. In the mid-1930s, Congress had passed a series of neutrality acts that limited Roosevelt's ability to intervene in foreign wars. Nevertheless, Roosevelt and his secretary of state, Cordell Hull, found ways to circumvent these laws and provide wartime munitions to the Allies. The US Cash-and-Carry policy (introduced in September 1939) allowed warring nations to purchase US arms if they paid for these munitions in cash and came to the United States to retrieve and transport such arms. Because the British dominated the Atlantic, this policy was designed to help London in its fight against Germany. Similarly, the Lend-Lease policy (introduced in March 1941) allowed America to supply Allied nations with munitions and other war materials on a loan and lease basis. Upon implementation, the Soviet Union began to benefit heavily from this policy.

In December 1941, the United States officially entered the Second World War on behalf of the Allied Powers. Japan, which was allied with Nazi Germany, had sought to expand its empire in Asia, just as Germany had done in Europe. In the mid-1930s, Japan had fought the Chinese, taking over a resource-rich region known as Manchuria and perpetrating atrocities on the native inhabitants there and in other parts of China. The United States had been a vocal opponent of Japanese aggression in China, leading Japan to seek an ally in Germany. Yet it was the Japanese attack on the US naval fleet stationed in Pearl Harbor, Hawaii, on December 7 that led the United States into a state of war with Japan. Japanese military planners carried out this attack, which claimed the lives of more than two thousand Americans, to wipe out the US naval presence in the Pacific and thus allow Japan to conquer much of Asia. After the United States declared war on Japan a day after the Pearl Harbor attack, Hitler's Germany declared war on the United States, which, in turn, led the United States to declare war on Germany and the Axis Powers in Europe. The American giant was now at war.

Upon entering the war, the US government had to make a decision on how to fight the war. In essence, the country would be fighting a war in two theaters: in Europe and in the Pacific. There was some debate about which theater the nation should devote most of its attention to first. Most civilians wanted to deal with Japan first. After all, that nation had harmed Americans. There was a fear among Roosevelt's advisers, however, that if the United States did not deal with Germany and let the British Empire fall, the war would possibly be unwinnable. How and whom to fight, therefore, was a conundrum. In the end, Roosevelt decided to fight in both theaters simultaneously. Nevertheless, he adopted the Europe First strategy, not wanting to see Hitler control all of that continent.

At first, in fighting Axis-occupied continental Europe, the United States dramatically increased the war material to the Soviet Union. Roosevelt hoped to get the Soviets to do the bulk of the fighting. In this way, the American president could minimize American casualties. FDR realized the American public might turn against the war effort if he waged combat in a reckless way and the battles against the Axis turned into a war of attrition. With stronger US support, the Soviet Union began setting up factories in eastern Russia specifically for the creation of munitions. This strategy proved fruitful. When the Germans tried to take Stalingrad, they again met an unanticipated amount of resistance from the Soviets.

The Battle of Stalingrad (August 1942–February 1943), a decisive Soviet victory, was also a major turning point in the war in Eastern Europe. Failing to take Moscow, the Nazis turned their attention to a city in southwestern Russia named for the USSR's leader, Stalin. Hitler also hoped to cut off Lend-Lease aid the Soviets received from the Americans through Iran, and acquire access to the oil in the region. At first, the Germans, who dramatically outnumbered Soviet troops around the city, inflicted heavy damage; however, both sides called in reinforcements, so much that each utilized more than a million soldiers. In the end, the Soviets persevered and successfully drove back the Germans. Tactically, the battle had disastrous results for the Germans, as they lost an excessive number of transport aircraft, tanks, and artillery. The Americans indirectly contributed to the battle's outcome through Lend-Lease. One of the most effective pieces of Soviet military hardware, the Katushka rocket, was often hastily thrown together and transported on American Studebaker trucks. They did not look especially menacing, but the Nazis learned that such rockets got the job done. From this point on, the USSR would be on the offense, making gains and taking back lands the Germans had earlier conquered during Operation Barbarossa.

By the autumn of 1942, the United States, which had agreed to integrate its forces with the British, decided to take action in reclaiming Axis-occupied lands. Operation Torch, which saw the Allies retake French North Africa, was the first step. In the process, the Americans and the British established bases in Algeria, Morocco, and Tunisia to dominate the strategically important Mediterranean Sea and launch an invasion of Mussolini's Italy. At the same time, as winter set in, the Allies met fierce Axis resistance in Tunisia. The German *Afrika Korps,* led by Erwin Rommel, fought valiantly to maintain a German presence in the strategic region. But by May 1943, the Allies had won a clear victory largely because of the advantage of sheer manpower, with the Axis accumulating excessive casualties. The stage was set for the conquest of fascist Italy.

Italy, which never truly was a major military power, fell to Allied forces. In the summer of 1943, the Americans, led by General Dwight D. Eisenhower, executed an amphibious assault that took Sicily, despite strong German resistance. By September, the Allies had conquered much of mainland Italy. In response, the German army occupied Italy, but the Italian people rose up against their allies in major cities such as Naples. On the one hand, Italians did not like the prospects of German occupation, as they did not see their nation as Germany's little brother. On the other, they feared the war pandemonium that Mussolini and Hitler had unleashed. Italy turned into a state of chaos, culminating later in Mussolini's flight out of the country. He later was restored as a puppet in Nazi-controlled northern Italy. But for all practical purposes, Allied actions by 1944 had immobilized Italy as a fighting force. At the same time, however, reaching Germany from Italy proved an impractical strategy. For one thing, the Alps mountains hindered

Allied mobilization. More important, Western Europe, including France and the Low Countries, still needed to be liberated from Nazi occupation. Thus, the Allies had another amphibious assault in mind.

The Allied invasion of Normandy, France, on June 6, 1944, also known as D-Day, marked a major turning point of the Second World War in Europe: it allowed the Allies to open up a true second front in the West. The invasion, originally dubbed Operation Overlord, was the brainchild of Eisenhower, the supreme Allied commander after the United States integrated its forces with British and Canadian forces. At D-Day, a combined Allied force invaded five beaches, each with its own code name—Omaha, Juno, Utah, Sword, and Gold—to set foot in France and begin liberating that nation and then others occupied by Germany. The long-term planning for this assault had taken over a year to come to fruition, but it marked the largest number of Allied boots on the western front since the British evacuated more than three hundred thousand troops at Dunkirk after the fall of France.

The amphibious assault on the beaches of Normandy was a huge success for the Allies, but it was costly in terms of human lives. Many World War II films, such as *Saving Private Ryan*, reveal the obstacles that faced Allied troops on the beaches (Figure 9.11). The Germans, for example, used machine guns to mow down thousands of soldiers. In addition, the beaches were strewn with mines and obstacles to hinder tank mobility. In some places, where the Germans expected Allied soldiers to arrive by parachutes and gliders, stood thousands of tall, sharp stakes, called Rommel's Asparagus, to injure or incapacitate soldiers before they touched ground. Despite these obstacles, however, D-Day was a decisive win for the Allies. Having established air supremacy over Germany, thanks to the American contribution, the additional sheer number of Allied ground troops, with a seemingly endless number of reinforcements, overwhelmed Nazi defenses and enabled the Allies to establish a formidable presence on the coast of France within a week.

Figure 9.11: British 2nd Army landing at Juno Beach, D-Day, on June 6, 1944.

In fact, D-Day set the stage for the liberation of Paris and France. As German forces retreated, Allied forces, together with the Free French, took ground. After a week of intense fighting in August, Paris became free, as the Germans abandoned the city. French communists, socialists, and other anti-fascist elements took up arms and helped secure liberation. Meanwhile, the German puppet government in France, stationed in the city of Vichy, fell. Its leaders escaped to Germany, and General Charles De Gaulle, the leader of the Free French, became president of the provisional French Republic. There was much French patriotism at the time, as evidenced by the numerous victory parades that swept the major cities. At the same time, there was an enormous amount of gratitude to the British and especially the Americans for the liberation of France. The summer of 1944 saw French citizens greet American soldiers as heroes, flying the US flag alongside the French flag.

The next major conflict was the Battle of the Bulge, fought between December 1944 and late January 1945. The battle, which began with a top-secret German counteroffensive, sought to retake France and Belgium for the Nazis. Although the Germans initially outnumbered Allied forces and there were tens of thousands of US lives lost, the Allies dug in and brought in large numbers of air and ground reinforcements. In response, under strict orders from Hitler, the Germans sent in large numbers of reinforcements as well. Although the Battle of the Bulge was especially deadly on both sides, it was a huge strategic miscalculation for the Germans. After all, they concentrated so much of their resources to a battle they ultimately lost. As such, they were not prepared to deal with the advancing Soviets from the east.

After winning the Battle of Stalingrad, the Soviets went on the offensive, reclaiming lands from the Germans. Beginning in spring 1944, several successful Soviet campaigns liberated huge swaths of Eastern Europe. In April, the Crimean Offensive was successful and was followed by the Battle of Romania in the summer and the Belgrade offensive in autumn. Emboldened by successes, the Soviets dramatically increased the number of their combat soldiers as they approached Poland. The Vistula-Oder Offensive (January–March 1945) succeeded in liberating Poland, although there were a high number of casualties, civilian and combat alike, on all sides. That success was followed by the first direct Soviet assault on Nazi Germany itself, as the Vienna Offensive (April 1945) saw the fall of Austria to the Red Army.

Spring 1945 saw the Germans retreat toward Berlin in defense of their country. Facing approaching armies from both the Soviets in the east and also the Americans and the British in the west, Germany now was in a fight for its survival as a nation. The dream of a Third Reich that would last for a thousand years no longer dominated the minds of Nazi soldiers; rather, simply living for another day was the hope as the Soviets and Americans competed to reach Berlin first. The Soviet Red Army, it turned out, made it to the German capital by mid-April and destroyed the last vestiges of German resistance at the Battle of Berlin. In the end, Hitler was forced to call up children, the Hitler Youth, in a desperate attempt to protect the city. Yet all efforts failed, and the Nazi leader realized the end had come. In his underground bunker in late April, Hitler married longtime mistress Eva Braun and committed suicide. The Nazis surrendered a week later. The war in Europe, with the tens of millions of deaths it produced, had ended.

THE WAR IN THE PACIFIC

Although the war in Europe officially ended on May 8, 1945, VE Day, the Allies still had to deal with fascist Japan. Allied fighting in the Pacific theater against Japan was just as intense and deadly as in the European theater, but the actors and dynamics were markedly different. Having focused on defeating Nazi Germany, the Soviet Union did not engage in many battles against Japan. In fact, the USSR did not even declare war on Japan until victory in Europe had been secured. As a result, the United States, and to a lesser extent, Britain, shouldered most of the Allied combat burden in Asia between 1942 and 1945 (Figure 9.12). For the Americans, naval battles against Japan characterized the early stage of the war. An intense campaign to liberate Asian nations and islands followed that stage. For the British, with a huge empire in Asia, enlisting imperial subjects to engage in combat became a defining feature of basic military strategy. Occupied with a two-front war in Europe, German soldiers had virtually no presence in the Pacific theater.

Figure 9.12: US recruitment poster after Pearl Harbor attack.

More than any other engagement, the Battle of Midway (June 1942) enabled American forces to establish a presence in Axis-occupied Asia after the Japanese victories at Pearl Harbor and Wake Island. Led by Admiral Chester Nimitz, the United States at Midway sank all four of Japan's carriers and damaged both of that nation's heavy cruisers. In return, Japan sank one of the four US carriers. In the end, the Japanese lost more than three thousand lives, while the Americans lost about three hundred. The battle, however, severely weakened Japan's impressive navy, which had grown dramatically since Japan's victory in the Russo-Japanese War (1904–06). Having thus established naval supremacy after Midway, the main US strategy thereafter involved liberating the various Pacific islands that Japan had occupied.

Between 1942 and 1945, several major battles occurred between American and Japanese forces, including those at Guadalcanal, the Philippine Sea, Guam, Leyte Gulf, Iwo Jima, and Okinawa. Although the United States won most of these battles, there were significant casualties. In fact, Americans casualties in the Pacific theater were almost as high as in the European theater. A major reason for this development was the unique circumstances of Pacific warfare. American military personnel had little understanding of the island topography involved in such fighting. In addition, the Japanese employed guerrilla warfare techniques that bewildered American soldiers, who received training in traditional warfare in the United States.

But, above all, the Japanese prized fearlessness and honor among their soldiers, a fact that spoke much about Japan's persistence in the face of defeats. The kamikaze pilots, who committed suicide by flying into American ships, became heroes among Japanese civilians and were made the stuff of legends. So, too, were the generals who disemboweled themselves after losing battles in order to reclaim loss honor. The Japanese soldiers, and the government in Tokyo, fiercely promoted a no-surrender, fight-to-the-last-man mentality that seemed to render American triumph in the Pacific elusive, despite the numerous battle victories.

Unlike the United States, the British had a huge empire in Asia before the Second World War, but the situation changed as Japan created its own empire during WWII. In February 1942, seeking to eliminate

British military presence, Japan invaded Singapore—the principal British naval base in East Asia—and took a large number of prisoners of war. Just as surprising, the Japanese later invaded and occupied Malaya (modern-day Malaysia), a major colony of the British Empire. Japan held onto Malaya until the end of the war. Occupied with the war in Europe, the British could not and did not devote adequate resources to taking back Malaya.

As it turned out, British fighting in Asia largely was in the China-India-Burma (CIB) theater. Throughout 1942, the Japanese occupied Burma, driving out British, Chinese, and Indian forces in several waves of combat. The occupation of Burma frightened British military planners, who, above all, feared the Japanese would next take India, the crown jewel of their empire. In fact, both sides prepared feverishly in 1943 for battle over India, as engagement seemed inevitable. Unable to send adequate British troops to defend their colony, the British trained and equipped hundreds of thousands of Indians for battle. Some planners viewed this strategy as risky, claiming Indians might use arms to fight for their independence from Britain, rather than against the Japanese. Tactical necessity, however, required the heavy use of Indian troops, and this strategy proved fruitful; however, to emphasize the empire's struggle as a whole, East African soldiers were called up from British colonies to fight alongside their colonial brothers. When the Japanese invaded India in 1944, the Indian soldiers routed them in a series of battles at Imphal and Kohima. The crown jewel was thus safe during the Second World War, but the Japanese did not surrender lands conquered before the India disaster. At the same time, 1944 marked the last Japanese attempt to take unconquered lands, a development that foreshadowed Japan's imminent doom.

After VE Day, the Allies now were in a position to bring their entire military to bear on Japan. American commanders, however, were especially fearful Tokyo would never surrender without a costly, deadly invasion of the Japanese islands. After all, many Japanese units were prepared to fight to the last man. Like Roosevelt before him, new US President Harry S. Truman abhorred the prospect of hundreds of thousands of US soldiers dying in an invasion to produce Tokyo's capitulation. Fortunately, for Truman and the Americans, such an invasion turned out to be unnecessary.

The reason: the United States had developed a new type of weapon, the lethality of which the world had never seen—the atomic bomb. In the early days of the Second World War, physicists had warned Roosevelt that harnessing the power of the atom could magnify the deadly effects of bombs exponentially. In 1938, German scientists had discovered nuclear fission, the ability to split the atom and harness its power. The concerned physicists feared the Nazis, who had many prominent nuclear physicists, including Werner Heisenberg, had a head start in developing such a weapon. As a result, in a joint effort, the Americans and the British recruited many of the world's finest physicists to develop an atomic bomb. The code name for the top-secret research and development of this weapon was the Manhattan Project, which J. Robert Oppenheimer oversaw. Although work began in August 1942, no immediate success in making an atomic bomb occurred. But the enormous amount of experimentation with uranium and plutonium isotopes, calibration, and tinkering in bomb design payed off by the summer of 1945, when Manhattan Project scientists tested the first successful atomic bomb in July: the Trinity explosion. The world was thus ready for atomic warfare, and Japan was the target.

To prevent an American invasion that would have resulted in heavy US casualties, Truman gave the decision in August 1945 to employ the atomic bomb against the Empire of Japan. On August 6,

Figure 9.13: Mushroom cloud from atomic bomb explosion, Nagasaki, Japan, August 9, 1945.

the United States dropped such a bomb from an airplane, the Enola Gay, leveling the city of Hiroshima and claiming more than one hundred thousand lives. Three days later, the United States used another atomic bomb to take out Nagasaki, in the process claiming more than fifty thousand lives (Figure 9.13). The atomic bombings of Hiroshima and Nagasaki created a psychological panic among Japanese people everywhere. Faced with the prospect of more nuclear strikes, Japanese Emperor Hirohito felt compelled to concede defeat and abandon the war. The Japanese public was moved by Hirohito's surrender speech. It had never heard the voice of the emperor, who was viewed as a god in Japan's official Shinto religion. But he assured the public that war could not continue. As a result, the fight-to-the-last-man mentality of the Japanese waned, even though a clique of military officials and civil servants wanted to carry on with war. A week after the attack on Nagasaki, Japan agreed to unconditional surrender, thus ending the Second World War for good. The most devastating war in the history of humankind came to a close.

CIVILIAN DEATHS AND THE HOLOCAUST

A major feature of the Second World War was the civilian death toll, which was much greater than that of the First World War. A main reason for this development owed to the advances in air power. Not only were there thousands of civilian deaths associated with the atomic bombings of Japan, but there also were numerous other bombing campaigns that targeted civilians. The Nazis killed large numbers of civilians with their bombings of such cities as Rotterdam and London. The Allies did likewise with their bombings of such German cities as Berlin, Dresden, and Hamburg. The Americans, who firebombed Tokyo on several occasions during the war, produced more civilian casualties in that city than in either Hiroshima or Nagasaki alone. Targeting civilians with bombing campaigns, while an unpleasant feature of war, was aimed at breaking the national will of a people and producing surrender.

Yet air power alone did not by itself explain the high civilian death toll of the Second World War. Racial enmity was much stronger during the Second World War than in its predecessor, in large part because it was promoted by the new fascism ideology. Fascism, which cultivated a social Darwinist view of racial struggle, produced much of the violence and the atrocities—even against women and children, whom historically have benefited from mercy in times of war. With fascism, there was a belief one's enemies had to be destroyed for national flourishing.

Fascist Japan wreaked, for example, innumerable horrors on the Chinese population during the war. When Japan occupied the city of Nanking, about three hundred thousand citizens of that city lost their lives, according to the Chinese government. In an event known to history as the Rape of Nanking, Japanese soldiers looted, raped, and massacred citizens with no mercy. Japanese soldiers even took photographs of dead babies, who had been bayoneted with rifles. The Japanese, who had long cultivated the idea of their racial superiority and suspicion of foreigners, did not recognize the human dignity of the Chinese people. The horrible treatment of citizens in the Philippines and other Japanese-occupied islands during the war, and the cruelties perpetrated on captured prisoners of war, testified to a Japanese enmity that viewed others as less than human. But it was the Nazis who were the worse in terms of the murder of civilians.

One of the largest contributions to the civilian death toll of the Second World War was the Holocaust—the genocide of Jews perpetrated by Nazi Germany. To be sure, the anti-Semitism of the Nazi regime had been present from its foundations in the early 1930s, resulting in the marginalization of Jews from German society. But the decision to systematically murder a whole race of people during the war reflected the intensity of Nazi racial enmity. There were two stages of the Holocaust: the first, dominated by mobile killing units in the early part of the war; the second, characterized by the extermination camps in the latter. In total, approximately six million Jews, many of whom were women and children, succumbed to a tragedy that revealed the frightening possibilities of modernity.

Viewing Jews as enemies of the Reich, Nazi Germany sought to eliminate this race from the very start of the Second World War. The Germans introduced compulsory ghettoization for Jews, the process of segregating them from other peoples in small neighborhoods. Most of the major cities in Poland had a ghetto, with the ones in Warsaw and Krakow being among the most prominent. Beginning with the Nazi occupation of Poland, Jews who resisted German persecution in the ghettos found themselves arrested and executed. Because of poor rations allocated to Jews in the ghettos, malnutrition and starvation became the main struggles throughout 1940 and 1941. Allowances for children were often not included in family rations, but mothers and fathers shared their own food to help their offspring survive. This suffering, however, only foreshadowed the hardship that came later.

The mass executions of Jews began in earnest after Operation Barbarossa in June 1941. As the Germans conquered Soviet territories in Ukraine, Belarus, and other regions, mobile killing units known as *Einsatzgruppen* rounded up hundreds of thousands of Jews and executed them, often by mass shootings. German soldiers were commanded to spare no person, whether woman, child, or the elderly. At the same time, the Einsatzgruppen also experimented with other means of killing, setting up gas vans to exterminate Jews by carbon monoxide poisoning. The Germans introduced this method of murder to ease the conscious of German soldiers, some of whom had nervous breakdowns when given orders to shoot women and children.

The campaign to exterminate the Jews intensified after the Wannsee Conference in January 1942. This conference, led by Nazi officials Heinrich Himmler and Reinhard Heydrich, established the Final Solution: the policy of rounding up Jews throughout Nazi-occupied Europe and transporting them by train to death camps in German-occupied Poland. The location of Poland for the extermination camps no doubt in part stemmed from a desire to conceal from the German masses the atrocities that would soon occur. Although Germany had numerous labor camps—including such notorious ones as Dachau and Buchenwald—the extermination camps were in Poland.

By spring 1942, the first death camps in Poland became operational. Over the next three years, Auschwitz, Sobibor, Treblinka, Belzac, Chelmno, and Majdanek all became the major extermination camps. When Jews arrived, German camp staff members led them to an underground chamber, telling them they were about to receive a shower. Signs speaking about the benefits of hygiene were in the changing rooms in which people undressed in preparation for a shower after the long train rides. When the Jews entered the chamber, the staff turned off the lights and murdered them with cyanide gas, by dissolving Zyklon-B pellets. This method was how most of the Jews died at the extermination camps, although thousands of others succumbed to starvation, beatings, and disease. In some extermination camps such as Auschwitz, the able-bodied men did not immediately go to the gas chambers; rather, they were sent to a side of the camp reserved for labor. Nevertheless, many of these men fell victims to starvation as they received a food ration consisting of a minuscule amount of bread and vegetable soup.

Jews were not the only victims the Nazis targeted for extermination. The Roma (gypsies), Jehovah's Witnesses, and homosexuals became victims as well, as did individuals who were deemed socially unacceptable, such as alcoholics and the mentally disabled. From the Nazi point of view, such people had no place in Germany. Applying social Darwinism to these groups, the Nazis justified their exterminations on the grounds that such were the weak elements of society, even subhuman, and thus had to be mowed down for the German superrace to thrive. Given the Nazi leadership's view of these targeted groups, they, along with the Jews, experienced unspeakable persecution. Many had barbarous medical experiments performed on them within the death camps and died in terrifying agony.

CONCLUSION

The First World War and the Second World War took the world by surprise. Time and time again, realities did not match expectations in these wars. Rather than soldiers coming home by Christmas, the Great War became a stalemate that produced massive numbers of deaths in the trenches and lasted for years. Rather than establishing enduring empires, the fascist powers that started the Second World War fell in total surrender. Instead of a quick war with minimal casualties, World War I produced about twenty million deaths. Rather than ending merely with the German occupation of Poland and the Japanese occupation of China, World War II became even deadlier, with sixty million deaths, a significant number of whom were unexpectedly civilians.

To be sure, the sheer death tolls of the world wars resulted largely from making warfare modern. The advances in weaponry—everything from automated weapons, airplanes, and poisonous gas to tanks, heavy artillery, Katushka rockets, and the atomic bomb—contributed immensely to the number of casualties. The bureaucratization of warfare, seen in such developments as the complex military planning of generals and the efficiency of mass murder utilized in the Armenian Genocide and the Holocaust, was also a defining feature of making warfare modern.

A scientific world view, a main feature of modernity, shaped the world wars. The advances in weaponry were not battlefield innovations. Rather, they were designed in the work spaces of scientists and engineers. One need look no further than the development of weaponized gas in the First World War and the atomic bomb in the Second World War to understand the ways in which science influenced these wars.

At the same time, though, the world wars presented powerful counterexamples to the modernist claim that a scientific world view promotes progress. These wars proved that devastating possibilities existed, and these wars made those destructive possibilities actual. Rather than promoting progress, the belligerents used science to perpetrate an unprecedented level of destruction on humankind. More than any other events, it was the experience of the world wars that led critics to question the modernist foundations of society, a main theme that the next chapter addresses.

FOR FURTHER READING

Kershaw, Ian. *Hitler, 1889–1936: Hubris*. New York: Norton, 1999.

Murray, Williamson and Allan R. Millett. *A War to be Won: Fighting the Second World War*. Cambridge, MA: Harvard University Press, 2000.

Neiberg, M. S. *Fighting the Great War: A Global History*. Cambridge, MA: Harvard University Press, 2005.

Strachan, Hew. *The First World War*. New York: Penguin Books, 2005.

Weinberg, Gerhard L. *A World at Arms: A Global History of World War II*. Cambridge, 2005.

Challenges to the Dominance of Western Modernity after 1945

INTRODUCTION

Western modernity, as it developed and intensified over the course of the nineteenth and early twentieth centuries, had unleashed many changes over the globe. Liberal democracy, best seen in the political systems of the United States, Britain, and France, seemed to have triumphed after the First World War. Yet the rise of fascism and the Second World War proved not everyone even within Europe desired such a world order. The modern Western nations, having in the process drawn on their science and technology to unleash the bloodiest war in human history, proved the catastrophic potential inherent in the ideas and practices associated with Western modernity. To make matters worse, West European imperialism in Asia and Africa, with all of its flagrant and subtle forms of economic exploitation, showed Western modernity was far from an optimal world order in the minds of many. Not surprisingly then, challenges to Western modernity were bound to happen. Yet the forms these challenges would take were not always clear.

In the aftermath of the Second World War, however, the basic form of such challenges coalesced. The principal challenge to the dominance of the Western way of life came through a struggle known as the Cold War. The Soviet Union, which became a global superpower after the war, sought to spread its Marxist-Leninist ideology as an alternative to the ideas and values of Americans and West Europeans. In the process, the entire globe became an arena for the playing out of a great ideological struggle. Although the Cold War never saw direct military engagement between the United States and the Soviet Union, the conflict generated much bloodshed across the globe.

ORIGINS OF THE COLD WAR

To understand the origins of the Cold War, it is important to go back to the Russian Revolution in 1917. During the First World War, hungry and poor Russians were war-wary after accumulating defeat after defeat in battles against the Germans. By the spring of 1917, these peasants were happy when the tsar stepped down and the provisional government promised to hold elections to determine the political future of the nation. Against this backdrop, a Marxist named Vladimir Lenin, who had been in exile during the war, traveled back to Russia to campaign for a communist movement known as Bolshevism. Calling themselves Bolsheviks, Lenin and his followers promised to get Russia out of the war, and to liquidate the wealthy property-owning classes whose greed Lenin claimed was the source of economic inequality in Russia. Drawing heavily on the ideas of Karl Marx, Lenin promised to bring about a class-less society in which the factory workers and farmers owned the means of production in common. Such a society, Lenin maintained, would produce a happy country, unlike the exploitative capitalist societies found in Western Europe.

Although large segments of Russians fell under the sway of Lenin's movement, no free election to determine the fate of Russia occurred. Instead, the Bolsheviks won over soldiers, police regiments, and armed mobs to its cause, thereby coming to power by force in the autumn of 1917. But not everyone was happy with the Bolsheviks' rise to power, and large segments of Russian society decided to resist. Thus, between 1917 and 1922, a civil war took place in Russia that resulted in the establishment of the world's first communist government. The United States supported the anti-Bolshevik forces during the war, but did not contribute enough troops to defeat Lenin's movement. In 1922, after the Bolsheviks solidified power, Russia became known as the Soviet Union.

The early history of the Soviet Union was filled with much tragedy. Rather than owning factories in common, the Soviet model turned into state-ownership of property. Rather than a classless society that eliminated privilege, communist party members replaced the wealthy classes as the new privileged class. Farmers who refused to turn over their land to the government, known as *kulaks*, were shot or sent to work camps. To make matters worse, Lenin morphed into a dictator, paving the way for future Soviet leaders to follow his model. With Lenin's death in 1924, Joseph Stalin assumed control of the Soviet Union. Known for his ruthlessness and paranoia, Stalin initiated policies that led to the deaths of millions of Soviet citizens. In the early 1930s, for example, he starved millions of Ukrainian peasants, taking their food to feed the industrial workers of Russia. Additionally, Stalin eliminated any perceived threat to his power, whether real or illusory (Figure 10.1). Opponents were accused of various offenses and executed promptly. Such was the Soviet way.

At the same time, the Soviet Union under Stalin succeeded in some key areas. In the 1920s and 1930s, industrialization swept the nation, transforming the country into a modern power. Steel production and mining rose dramatically, and construction projects were ubiquitous across the land. Furthermore, Stalin and the Soviet leadership drilled into the minds of Soviet workers that they were especially important and the bedrock of the Soviet state. Indeed, ordinary workers in the Soviet Union took great pride in their labor and appreciated the recognition they received. Soviet propaganda made them feel they were contributing to the creation of a just project in developing their state. The result, many believed, would offer a great life to future generations. For many Soviet citizens, capitalist nations such as the West European imperial powers and the United States would lose in the end.

Although it may have seemed inevitable for the Cold War to emerge after the Allies defeated the Axis Powers in the Second World War, such an observation was no foregone conclusion. While pro-democratic and capitalistic Americans strongly condemned the authoritarian and communist system of the Soviet Union, strong bonds of solidarity had been forged in the war effort. The American and Soviets had set aside their differences to defeat a mutual threat, with the Americans providing much of the war material and the Soviets doing much of the fighting against the Nazis. Additionally, American President Franklin D. Roosevelt and Soviet dictator Joseph Stalin had developed a strong working relationship with each other. Both remained in constant contact in war planning, in addition to having jovial meetings at the Tehran (November 1943) and Yalta (January–February 1945) conferences. By early spring 1945, as it was clear the war in Europe would soon be over,

Figure 10.1: Portrait of Joseph Stalin, 1937, by Isaak Brodsky.

Stalin and Roosevelt hoped both the Soviet Union and the United States would have a positive working relationship in helping to create a peaceful new world order as soon as the war ended.

Yet fate had a different plan in store. In April 1945, Roosevelt unexpectedly died in Warm Springs, Georgia, and US Vice President Harry S. Truman, a man known for his tough talk and uncompromising behavior, became leader of the strongest nation in the world. This development was the first omen the US–Soviet wartime cordiality might be in jeopardy. After the Second World War ended in Europe, Truman met with Stalin at the Potsdam Conference (July–August 1945) to discuss postwar Europe. And indeed, at Potsdam, much tension existed between the American and Soviet delegations. American policymakers wanted Stalin to allow free elections in the Eastern European nations the Soviets had liberated from Nazi occupation. By contrast, Stalin wanted to maintain firm control over Eastern Europe, claiming his nation needed the region as a buffer zone after facing two German invasions during the world wars. Furthermore, the issue of German reparations provoked strife. Fearing excessive reparations would punish Germans unduly and contribute to future conflict, as the First World War had shown, the United States opposed

Figure 10.2: The Big Three at Potsdam:
British Prime Minister Clement Attlee, US President Harry Truman, and
Soviet Premier Joseph Stalin.

excessive punishment. But the Soviets, having lost twenty million people in addition to the devastating infrastructure damage inflicted by the Nazis, claimed they needed reparations in kind to rebuild their nation.

At Potsdam, the victorious powers in the end agreed to split Germany into four sectors, with the Americans, British, French, and Soviets each administering a zone (Figure 10.2). The reparations issue remained unsolved. But it soon became clear to American observers the Soviets were uprooting German factories in their sector and sending them back to Russia. It also became clear the Soviet soldiers were wreaking all sorts of human-rights violations on the German people in their sector. Widespread rape of German women at the hands of the Red Army revealed the viciousness of the Soviet way of life. It also revealed that having a working relationship with the Soviets was not going to be an easy task.

At the same time, the ideological differences between the American and the Soviet systems produced intense distrust among the leaders for each other. In 1946, US diplomat George Kennan, who had spent much time in the Soviet Union, wrote an article that stressed the impracticality of a working relationship with the Soviets, given their hostile views toward capitalist nations. Certainly, Stalin predicted his nation would inevitably go to war with the United States and the other major capitalist nations. From the Soviet side, capitalist nations were inherently expansive and exploitative. From the American point of view, communism was an ideology that explicitly labeled capitalism an enemy. It was communism, not capitalism, from the American perspective, that was expansionist and a threat. Thus, the ideological divide increasingly seemed unbridgeable. This observation became palpably clear in February 1946 with Winston Churchill's "Iron Curtain" speech before a Missouri college. As Churchill stressed, Europe at the time had become divided into two camps separated by an invisible curtain: Western Europe, which promoted democracy, and communist Eastern Europe, which had experienced coerced Sovietization. Although the Soviets had promised free elections in Eastern Europe earlier, only communist politicians were allowed to run for office in many of these nations under Moscow's direct influence. This fact ensured a huge divide in national character between the two camps.

Not long thereafter, the dispute over Marshall Plan aid also came to strain relations between the pro-democratic nations and the communist ones. Because of the Second World War, Europe was devastated financially. In addition, billions of dollars in infrastructure throughout the continent lay in ruins. Rebuilding thus was on the forefront of everyone's mind, whether civilians or government officials. Against this backdrop, the United States, with the strongest economy in the postwar world, offered to grant generous economic aid and loans to European nations to help them rebuild and recover economically through its Marshall Plan. There were, of course, some strings attached. For example, US businesses demanded and received opportunities to set up shop in Europe and engage in commerce. Yet most Western European countries eagerly accepted the loans, given the dire situation. Although the situation in Eastern Europe was even worse in terms of damage to infrastructure, the Soviet Union did not permit the nations under its control to accept any economic aid from the United States. From the Soviet point of view, such aid was little more than a smokescreen for American imperialism.

To be sure, one of the principal reasons the United States granted Western European nations Marshall Plan aid in the first place was to secure their loyalty to the democratic way of life. Indeed, several of these nations, including France and Italy, had significant numbers of communists among their postwar citizenry. There was indeed a growing fear among American policymakers that the economic turmoil the Second World War had unleashed would produce the right conditions for communism to take root. Homelessness, hunger, and unemployment were all challenges that beset many states. Marshall Plan aid, which totaled more than fifteen billion dollars between 1947 and 1953, was aimed at remedying this situation. It turned out to be an effective strategy. As Western European economies recovered, the communists in those nations found themselves increasingly marginalized.

Yet the use of American economic power in combating the spread of communism was not simply confined to Marshall Plan aid. In March 1947, Truman introduced his policy of containment, which later came to be known as the Truman Doctrine. According to this policy, the United States would provide economic aid to non-communist governments under threat from communist elements within their populations. This doctrine, evoked in the cases of Greece and Turkey that same year, saw the first official US commitment to fighting the Soviet influence in Europe. In response, the Soviets cut off ground-based transportation routes to West Berlin, which the Americans administered but were in the Soviet sector of Germany. This act of provocation, devised by Stalin and known as the Berlin Blockade, sought to test American resolve.

It became a test, however, that the US government passed. If the Americans could not enter West Berlin by road, they could and did provide medical supplies, food, and other necessities to Berliners by airplane. The Berlin airlift campaign of 1948 ended with the Soviet decision to change course, as many East Berliners flocked in mass to the western part of the city in search of the valuable air-dropped cargo. Although West Berlin was reopened to the Americans, doors for US cooperation with the Soviets remained locked, as it became clear a Cold War had emerged.

Nineteen forty-nine turned out to be a decisive year in unleashing the hysteria associated with the Cold War, as the West learned the Soviet Union that year had developed an atomic bomb. Ever since the end of the Second World War, the Americans had exercised a monopoly on this unprecedentedly devastating weapon. Truman had even used the American monopoly as a form of leverage against the Soviets in negotiations. The American president, who sometimes disparaged the intelligence of the Soviets, had believed Moscow would not develop such a weapon for many decades, and the announcement that Stalin had an atomic bomb caught him off-guard. Increasingly, American policymakers feared the Soviets would employ such a weapon against Western Europe in an effort to expand Stalin's sphere of influence and to further the global aims of communist expansionism. As a consequence, to deter such an aggressive act, the formation of the North Atlantic Treaty Organization (NATO) emerged between the United States and its democratic allies in Western Europe in 1949. According to this security pact, if the Soviets attacked any member nation, all would respond militarily. The establishment of NATO helped relieve some of the anxieties associated with the now frightening conflict with Moscow.

But more news soon splattered the newspaper headlines as China fell to communism. Since the 1930s, two factions in China had engaged in a bloody civil war to determine the nation's political future: the nationalists led by Chiang Kai-Shek and the communists under Mao Zedong. Although the civil strife abated during the Japanese occupation of China during the Second World War, the battles between the nationalists and the communists ensued after the war. Because the communists under Mao had fought Japanese occupation more fiercely than the nationalists, the communists had gained a significant numerical advantage over their counterparts over time. By 1949, the nationalists were forced to retreat to the island of Taiwan, leaving the communists in charge of mainland China. Although publicly pledging not to become involved in internal Chinese affairs, Stalin provided Mao with significant wartime munitions to enable the communists to achieve decisive military supremacy in China (Figure 10.3).

As the nation with the largest population in the world, China had immense influence in the international arena; therefore, its fall to communism became a major source of disappointment from the view of NATO. Faced with a nuclear-armed Soviet Union and a communist China, American policymakers in the Truman administration increasingly feared communism would soon sweep the globe, spreading like a plague. Accordingly, they sought to fight such a prospect, whatever the cost. As a result, the United States dramatically increased the amount of tax dollars devoted to defense. Indeed, as the1950s rolled around, a nuclear arms race had also emerged for ever more destructive weapons to serve as a deterrent to war and global catastrophe. A devastating nuclear weapon soon emerged in the nuclear arsenal—the hydrogen or thermonuclear bomb. While a single atomic bomb could liquidate a city, this new weapon could annihilate an entire region. The Soviets also acquired their own version of the hydrogen bomb.

In the meantime, the fear that communism would come to undermine the Western way of life intensified over developments on the Korean peninsula. Seeing communism take hold in China, many segments of the Korean population identified with Mao's form of communism. Unlike traditional

Figure 10.3: Mao Zedong, smiling in Chinese worker's cap.

Marxist-Leninists who stressed the urban working class as the foundation for a workers' revolution, Mao had emphasized the importance of the peasant farmer as an agent for communist change. In Korea, which had a huge peasant population, such ideas took firm root. Consequently, by 1950, a Korean communist movement led by Kim Il-Sung began to court Stalin and Mao for arms to establish a communist regime in Korea. The Chinese, more than the Soviets, were more than willing to aid in fostering Kim's goal. At the same time, large segments of Koreans opposed the threatening specter of communism, thus setting the stage for a civil war over Korea's political future.

In the process, a bloody conflict known as the Korean War emerged. This war, which lasted from 1950 until 1953, came to involve international military intervention. The Chinese supported Kim, whose army made rapid advances in the South and at one point threatened to take over the metropolis of Seoul, Korea's largest city. But not willing to see another nation fall to communism like China, tens of thousands of American soldiers intervened and drove back Kim's forces. Led by General Douglas MacArthur, the American troops launched an amphibious assault at Inchon and pushed the North Koreans back above the 38th parallel. But at this point, the Chinese, who had obtained Stalin's pledge of air power, invaded and promised to bring communism to the peninsula through military action. A deep fear thus emerged among US policymakers that the Korean crisis could involve nuclear weapons. Some American generals, such as Douglas MacArthur, advised Truman to employ such arms to drive the Chinese out of Korea. But Truman refused and fired MacArthur for insubordination. In the end, no victor emerged from the Korean War; the conflict ended in a stalemate. By 1953, a communist North Korea having close ties with China and the Soviet Union emerged, while a democratic South Korea linked to the United States became solidified.

As the Korean War drew to a close, major new developments also occurred that ushered in an especially frightening phase of the Cold War. To begin, new leadership emerged on both sides. Stalin's death in March led to a power struggle within the top brass of the Soviet leadership, which ended with Nikita Khrushchev becoming the USSR's new leader. Unlike Stalin, the unrefined Khrushchev was known as a hothead who lacked self-control (Figure 10.4). Many international observers thus felt the new Soviet leader might intentionally provoke the world into a disastrous game of nuclear brinkmanship. Yet Khrushchev was not the

Figure 10.4: Soviet Premier Nikita Khrushchev with Egypt's President Gamal Nasser, in 1964.

only new leader to emerge on the stage. The Americans also acquired a new president, Dwight Eisenhower. A national hero during the Second World War, Eisenhower provided a tough persona to counter the new Soviet threat.

With tough leaders, the Cold War took on new dimensions. Eisenhower developed a nuclear deterrence strategy known as massive retaliation. According to this policy, if the Soviet Union attacked any NATO member, the United States would unleash its entire nuclear arsenal in response and reduce the Soviet Union to rubble. This strategy was aimed at making sure the Soviets did not even think about employing atomic weapons in warfare. For his part, Khrushchev frequently threatened to wipe the United States off the map. In reality, given the weapons involved, a full-scale nuclear war involving the two superpowers would generate mutually assured destruction. The question that lingered on everyone's minds though concerned whether such a development would take place. In the United States, the fear of a Soviet attack frightened citizens from all segments of society. Schoolchildren were taught to "duck and cover" should they see a flash indicating a nuclear strike was under way. Additionally, Eisenhower ordered the development of the interstate highway system as a means for citizens to escape regions under threat of an attack in a more rapid and orderly fashion. The American president also had the task of reassuring the US people that he would keep them safe. Christian ministers, such as Norman Vincent Peale, encouraged Americans to think positively and not allow Cold War fears to dictate their lives.

Despite the anxieties, the intensification of the arms race and the exploration of new ways to fight a nuclear war ensued. The Soviet Union, which by 1955 had formed an alliance with its satellites in Eastern Europe, known as the Warsaw Pact, took the lead in developing new weapons-delivery technologies. By 1958, the Soviets had developed intercontinental ballistic missiles, thus ushering in a non-aircraft-based means of delivering nuclear weapons. These rocket-propelled missiles put Western Europe in striking range of doom. Understandably, from the American point of view, this development was especially frightening for NATO. To make matters worse, the Soviets also became leaders in the space race. The Soviet Union not only developed the first space satellite, Sputnik, but also saw one of its citizens, Yuri Gagarin, become the first human to venture into outer space. Not to be outdone, the Americans accelerated their nascent space program, promising to be the first nation to put a man on the moon. Despite such lofty aims and realizations, the space race was not simply about obtaining milestones in the history of humankind; rather, the desire to dominate the enemy from outer space emerged as a vital strategy in gaining the upper hand in the Cold War.

At the same time, the NATO countries developed a much stronger relationship with one another than did the Warsaw Pact nations. The bonds of solidarity in Western Europe allowed nations that had been historical enemies, such as France and West Germany, to put aside differences and build solid diplomatic relations. This development helped make possible the beginning of European integration, with establishment of the European Coal and Steel Community in 1958. In this community, member states pooled various resources and traded those resources without burdensome tariffs and fees. The success led to the later development of the Common Market, members of which traded freely with one another. With economic integration emerging by the 1960s, along with a common devotion to democracy and human rights, a single Western European identity emerged. By contrast, the Soviets took a hard-line approach against their allies in Eastern Europe. East German, Hungarian, Polish, Romanian, Czechoslovakian, and Bulgarian leaders always were aware of their subordinate role in their relationship with Moscow. Whenever protests for democracy or human rights popped up in the communist bloc nations, the threat of Soviet military intervention was palpable. To be sure, there was much reason for anxiety, as the Soviets sent their tanks into East Germany (1953), Hungary (1956), and Czechoslovakia (1968) to suppress protests. Rather than building a strong relationship grounded in trust, the Soviets reigned supreme by instilling fear in the leadership of their satellites. For their part, the United States and NATO capitalized on the precarious relationship between the Soviets and their allies through the proliferation of anti-Soviet propaganda. Radio Free Europe, established by the Eisenhower administration, routinely unmasked through the airwaves the authoritarian nature of the communist political system and emphasized the freedom and liberty associated with democratic rule. Such messages no doubt led many in the communist bloc to dream about what life was like in the West.

POST—WORLD WAR II DECOLONIZATION AND THE DEVELOPMENT OF THE COLD WAR IN ASIA, AFRICA, AND LATIN AMERICA

Ever since the nineteenth century, much of Africa and Asia had been administered as colonies of the various West European nations. In Asia, the British controlled India, Burma, and Malaya, while the French controlled Indochina and the Dutch ruled over Indonesia. In Africa, there were various colonial powers involved. The British concentrated their colonial possessions in eastern and southern Africa, while the French exercised dominance in the northern and western parts of the continent. Of course, smaller European nations were involved as well. Belgium had the Congo as its major colony, whereas Portugal controlled Angola and Mozambique. To be sure, imperialism had allowed the nations of Western Europe to profit through the exploitation of its colonies. Those colonies had provided much of the raw materials needed for industrialization, as well as overseas markets for West European consumer goods. In the process, the West European nations had become wealthy, while poverty beset the peoples within their colonies. Not surprisingly, as time passed, peoples within those colonies began to clamor for fair treatment and increasingly sought to drive the Europeans out of Asia and Africa so they could establish their own nation-states.

Before the end of the Second World War, there were several forces championing decolonization that were already under way. Although the West European colonial powers did not desire the end of empire, at least no time soon, they had set up a structure in the League of Nations that helped breed a new sense of "internationalism" into the colonial question. More important, in the early twentieth century the rise of nationalist movements in Asia, the Middle East, and Africa reinforced the desire for liberation among colonial peoples. For Asians, the Russian defeat at the hands of the Japanese showed the white man was not superior. An eighteenth century Egyptian professor, Jamal al-Din al-Afghani, an advocate of a strict interpretation of the Koran, was lionized among Pan-Islamists throughout northern Africa who sought to throw off the yoke of the British colonizers and chart their own course. Significantly, African peoples did not develop on their own a Pan-Africanism because they did not think in those terms. Yet American outsiders, such as W. E. B. DuBois and Marcus Garvey, helped introduce the idea. In India, Mahatma Gandhi became the symbol of anti-imperialism. He advocated nonviolent resistance against the British, urging his people to disobey British laws and even go to jail in the process in order to bring change.

Many colonial subjects, not only in India but as far away as South Africa, took his advice. All of these factors mutually reinforced one another, helping to start a powerful discourse on the end of empire before World War II.

But more than any single event, the Second World War became a powerful indictment of European imperialism. The war was a clear demonstration to colonial subjects that the West did not have a superior way of life. Embroiled in the deadliest war in human history, it now seemed the technological efficiency associated with Western modernity had been harnessed for destructive ends. Not surprisingly, any moral credibility the West was alleged to have came under scrutiny among colonial subjects. Additionally, when Japan occupied parts of Asia that were West European colonies—such as Indonesia, Indochina, and Burma—the Japanese administration promoted the idea they were there to liberate these places from Western control. Although the people subject to Japanese occupation did not want to live under Japanese rule either, they were attracted to Japan's ideas about the impropriety of Asian peoples living under subjugation to West Europeans. Not only that, early Japanese success in conquering large swaths of Asia during the war crushed the notion of West European military invincibility. If the Japanese could win battles against the Europeans, the colonial subjects could do so as well. Of course, in the end, the Japanese saw defeat. Yet the question remained: Would the Asian peoples allow the European colonial powers to return and administer the colonies as they did before the war?

In reality, the answer turned out to be negative. Immediately after the Second World War, the economies of the West European colonial powers had crumbled. Administering overseas empires was a costly endeavor, and these nations did not have the funds to administer colonies in the same way they had before the war. In fact, the bureaucratic presence of these European nations declined, even though such nations worked to reestablish control of their colonies in the immediate postwar period. Furthermore, since many colonial troops served in the war against the Axis Powers, there was an expectation on their part of greater autonomy or even independence after the war. The United States followed through on its commitment in this area, granting full independence in 1946 to its one colony in Asia: the Philippines. Drawing inspiration from US actions, colonial subjects elsewhere looked to the United States to pressure Western Europe to likewise relinquish control. Ho Chi Minh, a Vietnamese nationalist, even wrote to President Truman asking for US support to pressure France to abandon Indochina and allow the creation of an independent Vietnam. Yet Truman never responded to Ho. This rebuff led Ho to court support for legitimacy from the communists, a development that would foreshadow the Vietnam War years later.

At the same time, in India, the independence movement became so strong after the Second World War that the British were forced to relinquish the crown jewel of their empire. On one hand, Great Britain could no longer afford the bureaucracy needed to administer the nation with the second-largest population in the world. On the other, the British, under new Prime Minister Clement Attlee, had vowed to grant independence because of the valiant contribution of Indian and Burmese soldiers during the war. At the same time, not all colonial subjects on the Indian subcontinent were unified in desiring a single independent India. The northern parts of British India had a Muslim majority, which did not identify with the Hindu majority in the core. Inspired by independence advocates such as Gandhi, a sizable movement for the partition of British India gained momentum throughout 1946. In the end, all sides agreed the colony should be partitioned so that new nations could emerge. In 1947, this goal became realized with the establishment of an independent India and Pakistan. Both nations became republics and elected strong leaders. Although a major border dispute between India and Pakistan over the region of Kashmir developed and strained ties between the two newly created neighbors, the anti-colonial sentiment after the granting of independence to India produced great hope for other peoples in their efforts to end empire. The Burmese people, who likewise had fought valiantly for the British against the Japanese during the Second World War, achieved independence the following year.

Indeed, British decolonization in South Asia led other Asian peoples to seek independence, such as the Indonesians. Long a Dutch colony, Indonesia experienced Japanese occupation during the Second World War. Although Indonesian nationalists despised Japanese rule, they did listen to the occupiers' anti-Dutch rhetoric, which emphasized the differences among the Dutch and Indonesian peoples. To be sure, in significant ways, the Dutch and Indonesian people had little in common. While the Dutch were largely Protestant, Indonesia held the largest Muslim population in the world. And whereas the Dutch had a small population, Indonesia had more than one hundred million people and was growing significantly.

Against this backdrop, the Indonesian National Revolution occurred. The revolution, led in part by a charismatic leader named Sukarno, declared Indonesia's independence at the end of the Second World War and vowed not to allow the Dutch to return. From the viewpoint of many Indonesians, the Dutch had no right to return as they had not successfully defended the islands against the Japanese during the war. In addition, the Japanese left huge stockpiles of weapons that the Indonesian nationalists seized. Between 1945 and 1949, the nationalists recruited soldiers tirelessly for the independence movement; the nationalists were determined to fight for their independence, as they realized the Dutch would not hand them their freedom as the British had done with India. Waging guerrilla warfare against the Dutch, the movement won international recognition for the nation's independence in 1949. The Dutch were forced to abandon their longtime colony, and a newly independent nation emerged.

Like the Dutch, the French were hesitant to relinquish their empire in Asia. In fact, the French wanted to administer Indochina as it had done before the Second World War and refused to take the nationalist demands among colonists seriously. Yet the three regions of Indochina—Vietnam, Laos, and Cambodia—each had strong ethnic-based nationalist movements after World War II that pressed the independence question. The Vietnamese nationalists were especially problematic from France's point of view, given leader Ho Chi Minh's increasing Marxist-Leninist rhetoric after the fall of China to communism (Figure 10.5). Although France granted Laos independence in 1949, the French government under Charles de Gaulle was hesitant to do likewise for the Vietnamese, given the prospect of another communist regime rising in Asia. Thus, the French repeatedly used stalling tactics throughout the early 1950s to sidestep the Vietnam question.

Figure 10.5: Vietnamese leader Ho Chi Minh, c. 1946.

The United States also feared a loss of Vietnam to communism would lead all other Asian nations to fall soon as well, just as a stack of dominoes tumble when the first domino falls. Accordingly, the Eisenhower administration supported French opposition to Ho's communist-nationalist independence movement. The US government did not oppose decolonization. Rather, Eisenhower supported Western Europe's withdrawal from Asia, but Cold War considerations ensured NATO would seek the establishment of newly independent nations that were aligned with democracy, not the enemy. Accordingly, as Ho's movement increasingly demanded the use of violence to drive France out of Vietnam, defeating his efforts became a major goal of French and American strategy.

Over time, Ho developed a strong military aimed at establishing a single Vietnamese state. Ho's strongest concentration of support was centered in the North, while pro-democratic resistance to Ho's movement remained solid in the South. The French increasingly saw themselves as the protectors of the movement in the South. As war for the future of Vietnam ensued, the French were driven out of Vietnam after the Battle of Dien Bien Phu (1954). The resultant Geneva Agreement split Vietnam into two states: a communist North Vietnam and a democratic South Vietnam. By the mid-1950s, the situation in Vietnam mirrored that in Korea.

Unlike Korea, however, communist North Vietnam under Ho was determined to unite the country. The Vietnamese people, Ho argued, should not let ideology divide them. Domestically, Ho and his supporters played up Vietnamese nationalism to galvanize people in the South to support him. In the context of the Cold War, however, US policymakers emphasized Ho's communist leanings, not his nationalist message. Although the Eisenhower administration supported the democratic government in the South, Ho, by the late 1950s, was beginning to win the hearts and the minds of the Vietnamese people. In the process, a communist movement, called the Vietcong, within the democratic South emerged, with the Vietcong seeking to unite Vietnam under Ho's rule. As time went by, the nationalist message of the communists increasingly appealed to the poor peasantry in the South. As a result, by 1960, the future of Vietnam had been set: it would be determined by war.

While the Eisenhower administration pledged not to involve the US military in the domestic affairs of Vietnam, his successors, John F. Kennedy and Lyndon B. Johnson, committed US forces to protecting South Vietnam. In fact, by the middle to late 1960s, hundreds of thousands of American troops were inside South Vietnam fighting the Vietcong. The Kennedy administration made a mistake by supporting South Vietnam's hugely unpopular strategic hamlet program, which was aimed at curtailing the ideological message of the North by confining peasants in the South to hamlets and restricting their mobility. Additionally, when Johnson sent huge numbers of US troops to Vietnam in the late 1960s, several blunders undermined American credibility in the eyes of the South Vietnamese. The widespread use of the incendiary agent napalm caused much destruction, and carpet-bombing of targets sometimes resulted in collateral damage. To make matters worse, there was virtually no interaction between American GIs and the South Vietnamese people, thus preventing potential positive bonds of solidarity from forming. A few occasions of gross human-rights violations on the part of US troops, such as the Mai Lai Massacre (1968), further eroded American moral credibility in the war.

For their part, the North Vietnamese proved resilient to American power. Launching the Tet Offensive in 1968, Ho's forces set out to bring together the Vietnamese people (Figure 10.6). Tens of thousands of

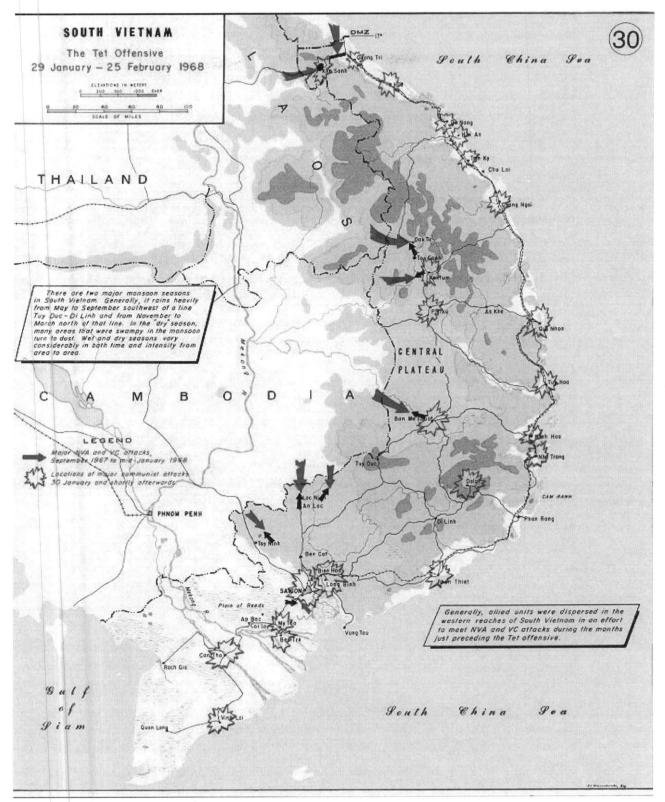

Figure 10.6: Major sites of the Tet Offensive, 1968.

American casualties resulted from a series of North Vietnamese offensives, leading to a sharp decline in morale and support for the war among the American public. Ultimately, the United States abandoned Vietnam in 1973, leaving the South Vietnamese to fight Ho's movement alone. In the end, by 1975, South Vietnam's capital of Saigon fell to the communists and Vietnamese unification occurred. Although incredibly costly in terms of human life, the Vietnam War proved to the world that even superpowers were not invulnerable to the nationalist resolve of a people wanting to chart their own course.

By the 1950s, the West European colonies had for the most part abandoned their empires in Asia, and the newly independent nations faced a decision over whether to take a side in the Cold War. On the one hand, aligning themselves with one of the superpowers had the potential to bring benefits. Siding with the Americans could bring US financial aid, which was vitally needed for the economic development of the newly independent nations. And taking a side in the Cold War could bring protection and military aid from stronger powers, which was especially attractive among many leaders of the vulnerable Asian countries. At the same time, however, forming strong ties with one side in the Cold War could bring hostility from the other side. Thus, foreign policy decision making became a careful calculation that weighed heavily on the minds of Asian leaders.

A wide variety of responses emerged in Asia among the newly independent countries. Some countries, especially those that relied on either overt or covert Soviet support in helping bring about their postwar creation, solidified a strong relationship with the USSR. China, North Korea, and Vietnam (and later Laos and Cambodia) became the major representatives of the Asian communist camp during the Cold War. By contrast, other nations sided with the United States. Notwithstanding Washington's support for South Vietnam, Thailand became American's main ally in Southeast Asia. The Americans needed a strong ally in the region, US policymakers believed, to stop the communist dominoes from falling and reaching the oil-rich Middle East. From the Thai vantage point, US economic aid would enable their nation to modernize, in addition to helping maintain the political status quo. Thus, Thailand received massive economic support and military aid from Washington. Similarly, Pakistan emerged as an early supporter of the United States in South Asia. A strongly Islamic nation, Pakistan was firmly opposed to the secular, atheist agenda associated with the spread of communism. Pakistan also desired US economic and military aid to help modernize and become a significant player in the international arena.

The Middle East, among the most important global regions in the post–WWII world because of its oil, also became a significant arena in the Cold War. Significantly, given the overwhelming Muslim majority of these nations, the United States and NATO had a considerable advantage in reaching such countries. As with Pakistan, most Middle Eastern nations disavowed the Soviet way of life because of its militant anti-theism. Not only that, such West European NATO members as Britain and France had strong ties in the region, having overseen through the League of Nations the development of such new states as Syria, Iraq, Jordan, and Palestine after World War I. In fact, the West European nations were able to obtain a national security arrangement with many Middle Eastern nations, known as the Baghdad Pact. The primary participants included Turkey, Iraq, Iran, and Pakistan, along with the British. Although not a strong alliance like NATO, this pact no doubt solidified Middle Eastern ties with the West in the Cold War.

America's role in the Middle East, however, was somewhat ambiguous. The United States never joined the Baghdad Pact, although it supported its development. The main reason for America's lack of participation in the pact was its fear of alienating Israel, a strong US ally and the only true democracy in the region. Many of the Middle Eastern nations did not accept Israel's right to exist, as the nation had developed only in 1948 as a home for the Jews of Europe who had survived the Holocaust. Most Middle Eastern nations strongly supported the Palestinians, who had to abandon claims to lands they had historically occupied in favor of Jewish settlement. Thus, American pro-Israeli sentiment led US policymakers to weigh decisions carefully.

If anything, American covert power was used to prevent any communist movement from popping up in the region. In the early 1950s, for example, Iran elected a new prime minister, Mohammad Mosaddeq, whose Tudeh Party called for state control of the country's oil industry. In the eyes of US policymakers, nationalizing industries was a smokescreen for pro-communist activity. Although Mosaddeq attracted heavy support from Iran's left-wing faction and communists, he was not an ally of the Soviet Union. Nevertheless, the United States employed the Central Intelligence Agency (CIA) to foment revolt against Mosaddeq, leading to his ouster in a 1953 coup. After the coup, the United States developed a strong relationship with Iran's shah, Mohammad Reza Pahlavi.[1] During the 1960s and 1970s, Iran became one of America's main allies in the region. Although a notorious abuser of human rights, the shah received American economic and military aid by emphasizing his strong anti-communist stance (Figure 10.7). In 1957, the United States formulated an official policy in the region, known as the Eisenhower Doctrine. According to this doctrine, which was an extension of the Truman Doctrine, the United States would intervene militarily to help any nation threatened by international communist influence. In 1958, Eisenhower evoked this doctrine to send US troops to

Figure 10.7: Iran's shah with US President Richard Nixon, in 1969.

---

1   See Stephen Kinzer, *All the Shah's Men: An American Coup and the Roots of Middle East Terror* (Hoboken, NJ: Wiley & Sons, 2003).

Lebanon, when that nation's president requested support in suppressing a communist political movement in the country.

Moreover, with the Suez Crisis of 1956, the Middle East became a major hot spot of the Cold War. Seeing a wave of Egyptian nationalism in the early 1950s, a movement led by Gamal Nasser overthrew Egypt's King Farouk in 1952. A strong Arab nationalist, Nasser sought control over the Suez Canal, arguing it was Egyptian property. Additionally, Nasser had wanted US economic support to build a major dam at Aswan. Although he secured a pledge of funds from the Eisenhower administration, Nasser recognized Mao's government in China and tried to secure economic aid from the Soviet Union at the same time. Such dealings with America's enemies undermined US confidence in Nasser, thus leading American officials to withdraw from its earlier pledge to help construct the Aswan dam. In response, Nasser threatened to take over the Suez Canal, which the British and French jointly operated. In response, British, French, and Israeli troops invaded the area around the canal, thus setting off a crisis many international observers thought would lead to calamity. The Soviet leadership threatened war if the invading nations did not withdraw at once. The American government likewise did not approve of its friends conducting secret military actions without its consent. Thus, both superpowers, in a rare show of solidarity, demanded a resolution to the crisis. In the end, the invading nations backed down and war over a canal was averted. At the same time, the Suez crisis revealed the complex difficulties associated with pact-making that the Cold War had unleashed, especially when economic interests were at stake.

Amid the Cold War, Egypt's Nasser represented in many ways an alternative to taking a side in the global conflict. Although the United States and the Soviet Union courted nations around the world to their side, sometimes a nation refused to be drawn into a conflict not of its making, preferring instead a policy of nonalignment. The origin of the phrase "Third World" originally referred to such nations. Nations of the first world were those aligned with the United States and Western Europe, while countries in the Second World sided with the communist powers such as the Soviet Union and China. But Third World states opted to stay clear of the conflict between the superpowers; they represented a third way or approach of conducting international affairs. By the mid-1950s, the major nonaligned powers included Egypt, India, and Indonesia. Nasser emerged as the leader of the nonaligned movement, and he especially did not want to see Africa drawn into the conflict. Yet the Cold War did come to affect the continent of Africa in significant ways.

Indeed, a major feature of the Cold War in the mid-1950s and early 1960s, especially given the new Soviet leadership under Nikita Khrushchev, was the rhetoric of national liberation in Africa. Publicly, Stalin had emphasized socialism in one country and generally stayed clear of overt statements of support for the establishment of communism in nations around the world. In a way, however, Stalin's approach had been an anomaly. From its inception, Marxist-Leninist thinking had stressed the international focus of its agenda. Lenin had wanted, for example, to extend the Bolshevik Revolution to Germany and Europe and had used his right-hand man Leon Trotsky to try to achieve that goal. If anything, Khrushchev's approach was a return to the early Marxist-Leninist tradition of overt support for the establishment of communist governments worldwide; however, given that Western Europe was in the democratic camp, Khrushchev looked to other parts of the world to promote communism.

Africa, in particular, became the main focus of Soviet efforts to expand ideology and gain global allies amid the Cold War. From the Soviet point of view, the continent seemed especially attractive as a market for Marxist-Leninist ideology for a variety of reasons. To begin, Africa was the poorest continent economically in the world, with most inhabitants living in what would be abject poverty by Western standards. Communism, regardless of its form, sought to unite the poor in opposition to the wealthy. Thus, of all places around the globe, Africa met this particularly important requirement the best. In addition, because the democratic NATO countries were simultaneously the imperial powers that exploited colonies in Africa, the Soviets could easily stir up nationalist and anti-imperialist rhetoric in Africa against West European colonial rule and ensure Africa would not join with the democratic side in the Cold War. Khrushchev, more than anyone else, saw the opportunity to promote communism as a force for the liberation of Africa from imperialist oppression. In doing so, he drew a page from Lenin's playbook. Long before he ushered in the Bolshevik Revolution, Lenin had described imperialism, with all of its exploitation, as the highest stage of capitalism. By contrast, Marxist-Leninism offered Africans an alternative for a better life, one where the means of production would be owned in common and with no privileged class based on wealth.

Not surprisingly, many Africans were attracted to the ideas of Marxism as a means to promote national liberation and decolonization. By the late 1950s, Khrushchev courted political nationalists in such nations as Mali, Guinea, Ghana, and the Congo. Ghana, one of the first nations in sub-Saharan Africa to experience decolonization, became a fully independent nation in 1957. Given Ghanaian leader Kwame Nkrumah's vociferous anti-Western attitude, Khrushchev believed he could steer the new nation into the communist camp amid the Cold War (Figure 10.8). From Ghana, Khrushchev hoped, other nations would embrace communism to liberate themselves and side with the Soviets. The Soviets, however, did not want to appear as if they were imposing their ideology onto Africans. Rather, in official rhetoric, they promoted the notion of Afro-socialism, which was supposed to be a communist system in harmony with Marxist-Leninism but which embraced Africa's indigenous heritage. By 1958, the Soviets had established strong ties with not only Ghana but also Guinea. The latter's leader, Sekou Toure, was especially attracted by Soviet overtures of political, economic, and military aid. As the Soviets made contacts with such leaders of African nations, they offered weapons and munitions. The AK-47 assault rifle, known for its dependability, increasingly found itself in the hands of not only pro-Soviet African governments but also among nationalists in other parts of the continent who had yet to obtain independence. Decolonization, many believed, would only come through armed struggle, just as Marx had argued that only armed revolution would bring about a workers' paradise. Congolese

Figure 10.8: Ghana leader Kwame Nkrumah on a Soviet postage stamp, 1989.

nationalists such as Patrice Lumumba were more than happy to embrace the Soviets as an ally to drive the Belgians out of their homeland.

And yet the Cold War in general and the Suez crisis in particular played one of the most crucial roles in decolonization, insofar as international relations were concerned. In propaganda directed at Africans, the Soviet Union increasingly emphasized Western colonialism and US racism in hopes of discrediting the Western way of life for its own strategic advantage. Many American policymakers believed West European nations had to decolonize or the Soviets would obtain the advantage on the continent. American officials thus often quarreled with their British counterparts after the Second World War, claiming the maintenance of empire only served to foster support for communism across the globe. As Khrushchev increasingly denounced the global oppression associated with Western imperialism, the Suez crisis marked the beginning of the British scramble out of the Middle East and Africa, as the threat of nuclear war over the crisis loomed. Against this backdrop, Washington increasingly applied pressure on the British to take steps toward decolonization. The debate in the United Nations over the Suez crisis, which saw British and French vetoes of various American and Russian resolutions for the withdrawal of Israeli troops, devolved into heated conversations over colonialism.

No time in the past had colonialism been discussed so fiercely. The British, along with the Portuguese, French, and South Africans, became marginalized in the international body for a period after the crisis. At the United Nations, India began to speak out against colonialism, condemning British actions in Egypt while overlooking the Hungarian Revolution (in part because the Soviets had been the strongest advocates of decolonization for some time). Against this backdrop, the United Nations began dealing with the end of empire in a more meaningful way. UN General Assembly Resolution 1514, passed in 1960, called for the immediate liberation of all colonies.

With the international clamor for decolonization, most West European imperialist nations began withdrawing from Africa in 1960. Indeed, that year alone saw seventeen African nations obtain full independence. Within five years after the UN resolution, the vast majority of West European colonies in Africa had now become independent nations. The transitions were not all peaceful, but they did occur. One West European imperial power, fascist Portugal, refused to allow decolonization. Consequently, the Soviets began funneling arms through proxies to support the people in Angola and Mozambique in driving the Portuguese out. In the process, bloody civil conflicts, especially in Angola, emerged.

From the American perspective, the goal was to ensure the newly independent African nations sided with the United States and its allies in the Cold War. For this reason, it became important to win the hearts and minds of Africans to the democratic camp. Accordingly, the Kennedy administration established the Peace Corps to provide humanitarian work such as the establishment of clinics and schools and the construction of wells and sewage disposal systems, etc. Beginning in 1961, thousands of Americans traveled to Ghana and Tanzania, among other places, to prove the West cared about the well-being of African peoples. This initiative, along with massive US economic aid to various nations, played a decisive role in countering the Soviets' influence in Africa.

Indeed, after decolonization, most newly independent African nations chose to have a republican form of democratic government, rather than a communist one. In a way, this was a huge win for the Americans and their allies amid the Cold War. It appeared, after all, that most African states wanted to allow its people to chart their own path of self-determination. At the same time, the Soviets maintained a strong presence on the continent and rarely resisted an opportunity to court new friends and successfully stir up anti-Western sentiment. In fact, at some point or another, Angola, Benin, Congo-Brazzaville, Ethiopia, and Somalia all came to have a Marxist government aligned with Soviet power.

In addition to Africa, Latin America also became a major arena in the Cold War. In fact, the region had several major frightening developments, as the Americans and Soviets sought influence in the region. The widespread poverty that beset Latinos, along with growing anti-US sentiment, meant the Soviets had in some ways an advantage in winning converts to Marxist-Leninism. To understand this development, however, requires knowledge of the deterioration in US-Latin American relations that had taken place over time.

Although the United States itself had not been an imperialist nation in Africa and had a marginal presence in Asia, it nonetheless had shaped Latin American affairs through informal imperialism. Ever since the Spanish abandoned their colonies in South and Central America in the 1820s, the United States had strong ties with its neighbors to the south. Over time, however, US paternalism largely characterized the relationship. Seeing itself as the Latin American countries' big brother, the United States pledged to keep Europeans from conquering the region, as they had done in Asia and Africa.

At the same time, the United States intervened militarily in the region on numerous occasions, especially during the early twentieth century. Given the political instability and large international debts of several Latin American nations, the United States sent its marines to, among other nations, Haiti, the Dominican Republic, and Nicaragua between 1912 and 1917 to restore order. In reality, however, the marine actions turned into long-term occupations. In fact, the United States did not officially end some of the occupations until 1934, when Franklin D. Roosevelt introduced his "Good Neighbor Policy" toward Latin America. In the meantime, a discourse that presented the United States as an imperialist power took root among Latinos. To be clear, the discourse, in some ways, was accurate. American businesses, such as the United Fruit Company, had major economic holdings throughout Central America and the Caribbean. For many people in Latin America, US economic interests, as well as military interventionism in their region, had eroded by the time the Cold War started any sense of trust that had developed in earlier periods.

Fear that Soviet agitation might produce a communist revolution in the Americas first occurred over developments in Guatemala during the early 1950s. After becoming president of Guatemala in 1951, the Revolutionary Action Party's Jacobo Arbenz promoted many leftist, socialist causes. In particular, he was a stalwart champion of land reform and castigated foreign economic penetration into his country. The United Fruit Company, a special target of Arbenz's frustration, owned huge tracts of land across the nation, and Arbenz stirred up peasant sentiment by promoting the idea of redistribution of the company's land. But from Washington's perspective, talk of any land or wealth redistribution was little more than a smokescreen for communist action. Accordingly, the Eisenhower administration labeled Arbenz's government a threat. Thus, in 1954, the CIA sponsored a secret operation known as PBSUCCESS to overthrow Arbenz's government. The coup succeeded, and Arbenz was forced from office.[2] To this day, historians debate whether the United States sponsored the coup primarily out of any legitimate fear of communism

---

2   See Piero Gleijeses, *Shattered Hope: The Guatemalan Revolution and the United States, 1944–54* (Princeton: Princeton University Press, 1991), 244.

Figure 10.9: Marxist revolutionary Che Guevara, in 1959.

or the American government was simply doing the bidding of US corporations, like the United Fruit Company.

Despite Guatemala, the real power keg issue in Latin America was the fall of Cuba to communism in 1959. Ever since the US defeat of Spain in the Spanish-American War (1898), Cuba had been a democracy under the watchful eye of the United States. In the early twentieth century, the United States provided economic aid to Cuban leaders in exchange for US businesses obtaining the right to profit through commerce on the island nation. A prominent Cuban leader during the 1940s, Fulgencio Batista developed a reputation as a corrupt leader who did the bidding of American interests. Not surprisingly then, an opposition movement slowly developed against Batista, and beginning in the 1950s a guerrilla movement led by Fidel Castro and Che Guevara began fighting government forces in the Cuban mountains and elsewhere (Figure 10.9). Shockingly, as Castro's movement grew, he was able to storm Havana in 1959 and drive Batista from power. Calling his coup the Cuban Revolution, Castro hesitated in declaring what type of government he planned to institute in Cuba, but it was obvious he was popular among the poor and appealed to them by promising to expropriate property from the wealthy.

To be sure, the rise to power of Castro caused panic among US policymakers. As it became clearer the new Cuban government was entertaining overtures from the Soviets, the prospect of a communist regime allied with the Soviets ninety miles off the coast of Florida drove American officials into a frenzy. For this reason, the Eisenhower administration sought to use the CIA to overthrow Castro by funneling arms to anti-Castro forces that were planning an invasion in the Bay of Pigs region. Although Eisenhower's successor, John F. Kennedy, carried out the plan in 1961, the result became a monumental failure. To begin, Castro knew in advance about the plan and had prepared accordingly. Besides, the Bay of Pigs was the Cuban leader's favorite fishing spot. Most disappointingly from Washington's perspective, the Bay of Pigs fiasco firmly established Castro as an enemy of the United States. If anything, American covert action drove Cuba into the arms of the Soviets more than any other event.

Against this backdrop, the most intense episode of nuclear brinkmanship during the Cold War emerged: the Cuban Missile Crisis. To protect Cuba from another potential act of American aggression, Castro requested that Khrushchev send Soviet nuclear missiles to the island nation. The Soviets, who also wanted to have the United States remove its Jupiter missiles from Turkey, agreed to the request and secretly transported missiles to Cuba. In the autumn of 1962, US spy planes discovered the weapons, leading the Kennedy administration to panic. Now, the Soviets had nuclear weapons positioned to strike the United States directly. Fortunately, though, Khrushchev and Kennedy resolved the crisis. Through secret negotiations, both leaders agreed to sooth the fears of each other. In exchange for a US withdrawal of its missiles in Turkey, the Soviets withdrew their missiles and the United States pledged not to invade Cuba. In the end, skillful diplomacy averted potential nuclear disaster. At the same time, the Cuban Missile

Crisis solidified Cuba's participation in the Soviet camp and demonstrated a troublesome development for the Americans: a Latin American neighbor, which had a history of strong ties with the United States, had become an enemy.

Yet Cuba would not be the only Latin American nation to embrace the Soviet rhetoric. In the mid-1960s, the Dominican Republic experienced a civil conflict that co-opted the ideological strife inherent in the two main camps of the Cold War. The nation, which had a history of repression under its longtime pro-American dictator Rafael Trujillo, saw the rise of a strong Marxist movement calling itself the Dominican Revolutionary Party. Essentially, this party sought to establish a Cuban-like Marxist regime with ties to the Soviet Union. But not willing to see a second Cuba in the region, the United States, in 1965, sent its military to occupy the nation. In the end, a pro-American government led by Joaquin Balaquer came to power, leading the United States to abandon its occupation after achieving its goal.

The desire not to have a second Cuba also shaped American policymaking a few years later in Chile. When socialist Salvador Allende was elected president, the United States used the CIA to sponsor a coup that overthrew him. Afterward, a brutal military dictator with strong US support named Augusto Pinochet came to power. That the United States would help overthrow a democratically elected Marxist leader but support a pro-American dictator revealed the contradictions associated with Washington's Cold War policy. On the one hand, the United States was the leader of the democratic world and thus supported democracy as an alternative to communism around the globe. On the other hand, if communism came about through democratic means, US policymakers did not accept the results and preferred to support dictators who vowed to support the United States amid the Cold War.

DETENTE, THE REKINDLING OF THE COLD WAR, AND THE COLD WAR'S END

By the late 1960s, the Cold War had generated numerous major conflicts across the globe, even if the superpowers had not directly engaged each other in military combat. At the same time, the military buildup had become a costly endeavor for both the United States and the Soviet Union. Additionally, the proliferation of weapons to parts of the world had produced great amounts of violence, along with political and economic instability in many places. Thus, policymakers in both camps increasingly believed it was time to curtail the arms race and start entertaining the idea of a world characterized by peaceful coexistence.

As such, the 1970s emerged as the decade of detente; that is, the period of the Cold War characterized by a reduction of tensions.[3] A major push factor for detente involved the domestic turmoil inside both the United States and the Soviet Union. In the 1960s, the Vietnam War and the civil rights movement had produced within the United States hundreds of thousands of student protesters who demanded change. The hippy movement, known for its promotion of peace, love, and rock 'n' roll, dramatically countered the violence of the Cold War. At the same time, within the Soviet Union and the communist bloc, there emerged similar protests, best manifested in the Prague Spring's demand for a more humane form of

---

3   For a solid work on détente, see Raymond Garthoff's *Détente and Confrontation* (Washington, DC: Brookings Institute, 1994).

socialism. Stagnating economies further helped produce a reassessment of the arms race. By the 1970s, the economic growth rate of the United States and the Soviet Union had declined, and many worried the extravagant defense budgets had hampered growth and prosperity among the superpowers.

To be sure, the hallmark of detente was a series of bilateral agreements between opposing sides in the Cold War to reduce the arms race. Perhaps the greatest fear among the superpowers was the prospect of nuclear weapons ending up in the hands of irresponsible governments, which in a fit of frustration might unleash doom on humankind. Accordingly, in 1968, the major nuclear powers came together to sign an agreement not to export nuclear weapons to nations. At the same time, the superpowers pressured other nations around the globe to agree to never seek to acquire or manufacture nuclear weapons. Known as the Nuclear Non-Proliferation Treaty, the agreement went into effect in 1970 and came to have nearly two hundred signatories within twenty-five years. Building on the success of this agreement, the Soviet Union and the United States signed two agreements in 1972 to limit their nuclear stockpiles. The Strategic Arms Limitation Talks (SALT), which began in 1969, led both sides to reduce or freeze the number of various classes of intercontinental ballistic missiles. The Anti-Ballistic Missile (ABM) Treaty, which also came out of SALT, limited the number of stations or complexes containing defensive systems that each side could have. Such efforts demonstrated that both sides eagerly sought to put the fear of doom behind them and accept peaceful coexistence.

The 1970s also saw other developments that both strengthened and undermined detente. On the one hand, in 1975, nations both from within the communist bloc and NATO signed the Helsinki agreement, which birthed new concern for human rights into international relations. From the American perspective, obtaining a Soviet pledge to protect human rights marked a dramatic break from the past and was in many ways the high point of detente. But such positive breakthroughs did not continue as the decade drew to a close. The Soviet invasion of Afghanistan in 1979 undid detente and reignited the Cold War. From the American government's perspective, the Soviet actions belied their earlier commitment to human rights.

Thus, as the 1980s rolled around, the stage was set for the rekindling of the Cold War. Ronald Reagan's victory in the US presidential elections that year prefigured a new period of intense conflict between the United States and the Soviet Union. Rather than curtailing military spending as his predecessors had done or accept a world order characterized by peaceful coexistence, Reagan was intent on winning the Cold War. Eschewing the language of detente and calling the Soviet Union the "evil empire," Reagan immediately set to work on strengthening the US military once in power.[4] He even proposed new ideas to maximize American defense capabilities, such as the Strategic Defense Initiative. Dubbed "Star Wars" by critics, the plan sought to establish satellites in outer space that could shoot down incoming Soviet missiles. For Reagan, the plan was designed to cultivate an image of American invincibility (Figure 10.10).

The Soviet Union adopted several strategies, depending on its leadership, in response to Reagan's desire that the Americans win the Cold War. When Soviet leader Leonid Brezhnev died in 1982, two hard-line Bolsheviks came to power. Yuri Andropov, the former head of the KGB, was known for his tough rhetoric and vowed to engage the United States. But Andropov, already an old, sickly man, did not get the opportunity to do so and died in early 1984. Andropov's successor, Konstantin Chernenko, also did not prove

---

4   Andrew E. Busch, *Ronald Reagan and the Politics of Freedom* (Rowman & Littlefield: Lanham, MD, 2001), 197.

a strong leader. In fact, he spent the last few months of his short term as general secretary in a nursing home, before dying in 1985. The quick deaths of the old Bolshevik guard led many Soviet planners to seek fresh, younger leadership that would challenge Reagan.

Mikhail Gorbachev's rise as Soviet leader in 1985, however, did not meet the old Bolsheviks' expectations. In many ways, Gorbachev was his own man and broke from the Soviet ways of governance from the past. Gorbachev realized, for example, that the stagnant Soviet economy was failing and implemented a dramatic restructuring plan known as *perestroika*. In doing so, he had hoped to introduce some nascent market economics into the system, such as greater export diversification, but the economic measures did not remedy the ailing Soviet economy. Gorbachev also challenged the censorship of Soviet history, instituting a policy known as *glasnost* or openness. To be sure, glasnost had far-reaching effects. As Soviet citizens learned about the brutality and gross human-rights violations associated with the early periods of Soviet rule, many became disenchanted with the propaganda

Figure 10.10: US President Ronald Reagan with Soviet Premier Mikhail Gorbachev in Reykjavik, Iceland (1986).

they had been fed. Just as important, Gorbachev denounced his predecessors' hard-line approach toward using force to suppress pro-democratic protests in the communist bloc nations of Eastern Europe.

The latter point, in turned out, became especially important in helping end the Cold War as the 1980s drew to a close. In 1987, Reagan had given a speech in Berlin, Germany, telling Gorbachev to demolish the Berlin Wall. Gorbachev did not do so, but as pro-democratic protests swept Eastern Europe in 1989, the Soviet leader refused to support the crumbling communist regimes in the bloc. Quite remarkably, as pro-democratic and anti-communist movements grew in the bloc, its leaders were forced to allow free elections, a development that paved the way for the end of communism and Soviet domination in Eastern Europe. In November 1989, the Berlin Wall, long the symbol of the divide between the democratic West and the communist East, came tumbling down. With it, the Cold War, in many ways, came to a close. By Christmas of 1991, the Soviet Union had totally disintegrated. The Cold War was over, and the democratic side had proved victorious in the great ideological struggle.

CONCLUSION

As this chapter has shown, Western modernity faced a serious challenge from the Soviet Union and its allies with the development of the Cold War. With its promise of a communist utopia, Soviet ideology shaped not only the way of life of people in Eastern Europe but also had a global influence. The establishment of communist regimes in China, North Korea, Vietnam, and Cuba, etc. all testified to Moscow's worldwide influence. In some ways, the Soviets used longstanding problems generated by Western modernity, such as imperialism and the economic inequality created by capitalism, as rallying cries to promote their communist agenda and gain allies in a frightening global conflict.

Yet in the end the Soviet alternative was a morally bankrupt system in which the realities did not match the propaganda. In no communist state did any kind of utopia arise. Rather, the continual existence of such regimes depended on heavy-handedness, the denial of individual rights and freedoms, and widespread lies that characterized Westerners as the boogeyman. Once the veil was lifted and public criticism of the system was allowed in Eastern Europe, the masses opted for a better life, one not governed by the dictates of Marxist-Leninism.

At the same time, the Cold War had several legacies in the Third World, including the violence associated with the great ideological struggle. Indeed, the militarization, more than anything else, has had long-term negative consequences even to the present. The end of West European imperialism and decolonization also came about as a result of a just critique of Western exploitation and hypocrisy. But those nations that embraced communism did not thrive economically. Indeed, as the next chapter shows, the Third World faced numerous other challenges as well that held back modernization.

The Challenge of Modernization in the Developing World

INTRODUCTION

During the second half of the twentieth century, nations within Asia, the Middle East, Latin America, and Africa experienced tremendous change. As shown in the last chapter, many became involved in the Cold War, while others chose the path of nonalignment. Regardless of their stances in that global conflict, all of these regions faced numerous other challenges to economic development and the promotion of democratic values as the century drew to a close. To be sure, many nations came to prosper economically, such as Japan, South Korea, and some of the oil-rich Middle Eastern nations. Yet the majority of countries in Asia, the Middle East, Latin America, and Africa experienced numerous obstacles that proved difficult to surmount. The hurdles differed dramatically depending on region and the unique historical circumstances of individual countries. At the same time, the proliferation of authoritarian regimes, poor state-introduced economic policies, gross wealth disparity, the problem of drug use and crime, and civil strife all became prominent features associated with parts of the underdeveloped world. In the process, the underdeveloped world became the arena for numerous instances of gross human-rights violations. The failure to resolve such problems in large part explained why the underdeveloped world largely struggled with sustained economic growth, modernization, and conflict resolution as the twenty-first century dawned.

ASIA & THE MIDDLE EAST

As the largest continent, Asia already had a rich diversity of nations with different peoples, traditions, and levels of economic output at the start of the second half of the twentieth century. As a result, making any blanket generalization about Asia's trajectory through the century is bound to be a problematic endeavor. As it turned out, some nations experienced dramatic economic growth and political liberalization from the 1950s onward, while other countries experienced many of the setbacks cited earlier. If there was one common denominator among the Asian nations that failed to thrive, authoritarianism governmental systems, whether communist or military dictatorships, best explained that outcome.

One Asian nation, however, that prospered immensely was Japan, perhaps a somewhat unexpected development given the nation's dramatic loss during the Second World War. Of course, Japan's rise as a major economic power in the second half of the twentieth century drew on developments stemming from earlier eras. For much of its history, Japan had been an insular nation that inherently distrusted foreign ideas and interacted only marginally with other countries in terms of trade and the exchange of culture. In the process, Japan still had a largely feudalistic society by the mid-nineteenth century. This situation changed, however, with the Meiji Restoration era (1868–1912), a period of rapid economic development associated with the reign of the Meiji emperor. The Japanese leadership during this period realized that Europe and the United States were technologically superior states thanks to the industrial revolutions occurring in those places. To modernize and transform Japan from a feudal society into a modern society likewise required industrialization. Just as important, Japanese elites understood the failure to modernize risked putting their nation in jeopardy of European colonization. Consequently, between 1869 and 1912, Japan built railroads across its many islands, set up numerous factories and steel mills, established major universities that promoted science in higher education, and developed a modern military. In fact, the world was shocked at Japan's remarkable victory during the Russo-Japanese War, fought in 1904–05. Japan defeated a major European power, showing the dramatic transformation the island nation experienced in such a small time frame. Japan's military accomplishments during the Second World War only solidified that nation's reputation as a major power.

Yet Japan's eventual defeat in World War II did not impede the nation's economic growth in the second half of the twentieth century. In fact, the Japanese developed strong economic ties with the nations that had defeated them. Doing so, from the Japanese point of view, was aimed at moving forward and putting the past behind. In addition, Japan benefited from a strong export-led economy, while minimizing imports. In fact, by the 1970s, Japan had developed the second-strongest economy in the world thanks to its leadership in automotive engineering and electronics. The Japanese took advantage of the oil crises of that decade to emerge as a global leader in automobile production. With high gasoline prices, consumers around the world demanded automobiles that used less fuel. Consequently, such Japanese carmakers as Toyota, Datsun, Nissan, Mazda, Honda, Mitsubishi, Subaru, and Isuzu all became major manufacturers of fuel-efficient automobiles that obtained stellar reputations for reliability. Additionally, with a society that valued scientific and technological innovation, Japan excelled in producing microelectronics that made possible a bevy of advanced consumer products such as digital cameras, state-of-the-art televisions, and video games. In the process, such Japanese monikers as Fujitsu, Sony, Panasonic, Atari, Nintendo, and Sega all became household names around the globe between the 1970s and the 1990s. Such developments testified to the ingenuity and hard work of the Japanese people.

Japan's neighbor, China, also emerged as a major economic power as the twentieth century drew to a close, but China's much different path after the Second World War presented new challenges for development. After Mao's communist revolution in 1949, China found itself still an agricultural society with only marginal industrialization. Describing himself as a peasant farmer whose greatest support came from the poor farming classes, Mao did not initially seek to change the economic structure of his nation once he came to power. By the mid-1950s, however, China's leadership had realized the nation had to industrialize if it was to become a major player in the international scene. Hence, Mao introduced, in 1958, his Great Leap Forward initiative, which was aimed at modernizing the nation. During the Great Leap Forward, the single most important task was the production of steel, a prerequisite for industry. In fact, peasants were encouraged to construct backyard furnaces to melt down scrap metal for the purposes of industry (Figure 11.1). No doubt, the Great Leap Forward led to a massive output of steel production and a

Figure 11.1: A backyard furnace, 1958—a common feature of Mao's Great Leap Forward initiative in China.

dramatic rise in industrial output throughout China. At the same time, millions of Chinese starved because of poor state-introduced agricultural policies, such as forced collectivization, a fact that undermined Mao's legitimacy in the eyes of many Chinese political elites.

Although China experienced massive industrialization under Mao in the 1950s, the nation still experienced significant hurdles in developing an export-driven economy as Japan had done. Part of the problem stemmed from new tension with the Soviet Union, China's major benefactor. A long supporter of the Soviet Union, Mao split with the Soviets over Khrushchev's rise to power in the USSR. Khrushchev had denounced the brutal policies of Stalin, whom Mao admired. In the process, a debate between the Chinese and the Soviets emerged by the 1960s over the proper course a communist nation should take. In the end, China and the Soviet Union sharply cut ties, an event known as the Sino-Soviet split, which prevented potential markets for Chinese goods. At the same time, the democratic nations of the West did not engage in much trade with China, so strong global exports were out of the question for the most populous nation in the world as the 1960s drew to a close.

But developments, beginning in the 1970s, led China to emerge as a major economic player. In 1972, the United States under President Richard Nixon normalized trade relations with China, opening an enormous American market for Chinese consumer goods. From the US point of view, opening trade with China was aimed at curtailing Soviet power and obtaining cheap products that would benefit American consumers. Also, Mao's replacement as Chinese leader by the late 1970s, Deng Xiaoping, made economic growth the hallmark of his nation's domestic policy. Deng relaxed state control over China's economy, introduced competition among Chinese producers, and courted foreign investment from wealthy democratic nations. In the process, China secured numerous trade deals that allowed the nation to emerge as a major leader in global exports by the end of the 1980s. Subsequent Chinese leaders maintained Deng's economic policies, resulting in continued growth of China's economic influence globally.

At the same time, the products manufactured in China for export differed sharply in quality from Japanese exports. While the Japanese economy depended on the export of highly technical and sophisticated export products, China became known for the mass production of relatively cheap products, such as textiles, batteries, plastics, furniture, electronics equipment, and machine parts. Nevertheless, by the close of the twentieth century, China was beginning to eclipse Japan as the strongest economy in Asia. The sheer population advantage of China over its neighbor in large part explained this development. At the same time, China's per capita income paled in comparison with that of Japan and other democratic Asian nations with strong economies. The history of political repression by the Chinese government, along with the communist system there, continued to be red flags in the eyes of many potential investors in the West who believed free markets and democracy reinforced each other and that authoritarian regimes hindered the success of economic development.

Perhaps better than any example, the sharp contrast between the two Koreas in terms of economic development in the second half of the twentieth century also demonstrated the hardships that beset communist regimes. Given its political outlook, communist North Korea found itself isolated on the world stage, with China being its main trade partner and benefactor. As a result, North Korea did not benefit from broadscale global trade, a fact that contributed to the relative poverty that came to characterize the nation. Intense political repression and gross human-rights violations perpetrated by the North Korean government during the long reigns of the country's founder, Kim Il-Sung (1948–1994), and his son, Kim Jung-Il (1994–2011), further exacerbated the economic potential of the country. Political opponents of the regime, it turned out, often found themselves experiencing torture in the nation's notoriously brutal work camps. Although the father-and-son pair built factories across the nation and developed a menacing military, most North Koreans continued to live in abject poverty. Food shortages, along with rationed electricity and heat, became burdens that plagued their everyday lives (Figure 11.2). This problem became increasingly pronounced after the fall of the Soviet Union, which had engaged in trade with North Korea. Unlike China, North Korea also continued to exercise heavy top-down state control of the economy, so there was little incentive for the populace to innovate and compete to provide consumer choice. In fact, the nation continually struggled with a lack of consumer goods to attract the people's needs and desires.

By contrast, democratic South Korea emerged over time as a major economic power. Developing strong economic ties with the United States and Europe, South Korea experienced massive industrialization in a quick time span. Like Japan, the major centers of higher education in the country privileged a curriculum in scientific and technological learning. The results proved especially successful. By the 1980s, South Korea, which developed one of the most educated populations in the world, became a prominent exporter of automobiles and sophisticated consumer electronics. Hyundai and Kia, two major South Korean automotive firms, became known worldwide for their high-quality cars, while the electronics corporation Samsung later had a global impact as a major manufacturer of mobile phone technology. In the process, South Korea emerged as the leader of the so-called "Four Tiger" nations (along with Taiwan, Hong Kong, and Singapore), a select group of relatively small nations that nevertheless contributed immensely to global commerce. By the 1990s, South Korea also became a world leader in such specialized technologies as robotics and bioengineering. As the twentieth century neared an end, South Korea's fortunes looked increasingly bright.

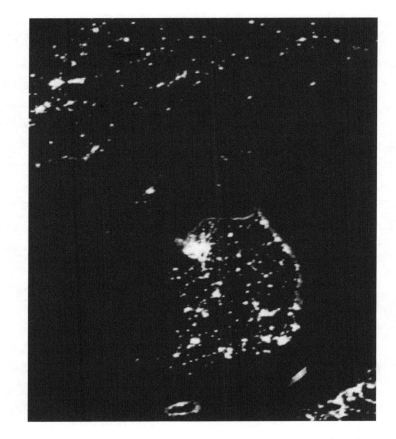

Figure 11.2: Satellite image of the Korean Peninsula at night (2000). Notice the striking contrast between North Korea and South Korea.

Yet other Asian nations faced various challenges that hindered economic development during the second half of the twentieth century. The communist nations of Vietnam, Cambodia, and Laos experienced little positive development in terms of raising the standard of living for their citizenry. Long agricultural societies, such nations did indeed modernize to some extent, at least in the urban areas with prominent textile factories. But while Vietnam and Cambodia became major centers of textile production in the 1980s and increasingly made their presence felt in garment exports, the voiceless workers in the garment factories faced major exploitation. The poor wages, long hours, tedious work, and unsafe working environment that characterized such labor led many outside observers to protest the treatment of workers in "sweatshops." Human-rights activists, especially during the 1990s, initiated a movement to draw attention to the poor conditions that such workers faced, even urging Westerners to boycott products from such countries in hopes of improving the plight of the masses.

Cambodia also experienced a genocide that destroyed much of the potential of the nation. When a communist regime under Pol Pot established control of the nation in the 1970s, masses of struggling peasants hoped for a better life. Yet the communist government, known as the Khmer Rouge, introduced bizarre economic policies. Pot believed communism worked for agricultural societies and that modernization hindered the success of such a system. Consequently, Pot's government forced the masses of Cambodians to relocate to the rural countryside to perform farm work. But the masses did not share the Khmer Rouge's vision of an agrarian utopia for their nation, thus leading to significant resistance. In response, the Khmer Rouge massacred hundreds of thousands of Cambodians in what came to be known as the killing fields. The result became known as the Cambodian genocide, which claimed more than one million lives.[1]

Significantly, Asian nations with histories of military rule proved as authoritarian as the communist regimes, and likewise faced major hurdles in terms of economic growth. Although a republic, Pakistan had a weak democratic tradition from the outset of its independence, in 1947, and subsequently experienced occasional military coups in the latter half of the twentieth century. In 1977, for example, General Muhammad Zia-ul-Haq overthrew the government of Zulfikar Ali Bhutto, claiming Bhutto had rigged elections. Although he promised to hold free elections, Zia stayed in power until his death in 1985. Introducing a rigid authoritarian regime, Zia played to radical Islamist segments of the Pakistani population, many of which denounced the Western way of life. In the process, Pakistan's economic ties with the developed world diminished, while the nation's economy stagnated. Zia's coup and military rule paved the way for later coups and military regimes that hampered political stability in the nation.

Similarly, Myanmar (also known as Burma) experienced military rule from 1962 until 2011, which explains that nation's failure to thrive. The military junta that ruled the nation stamped out all opposition, arresting pro-democracy activists such as Nobel Peace Prize winner Aung San Suu Kyi. The citizens of the nation had few rights and little voice in state affairs. In fact, opponents were often sent to labor camps in the Burmese jungles. The gross human-rights violations resulted in trade sanctions from developed nations that hindered economic growth. As a consequence, Myanmar neither attracted significant foreign investors to help develop the nation's economy nor did it develop a strong export-based economy.

Some Asian countries, such as India, were democratic but nevertheless faced internal issues that plagued economic potential. With the world's second-largest population, India was the largest republic on the planet during the latter half of the twentieth century. At the same time, India remained underdeveloped, in part because of its long subjugation as a colony of Britain. India's neutrality during the Cold War also did not serve the country well economically. By allying with neither side, India limited its potential to attract foreign investment and overseas markets. To complicate matters, India had a rigid caste system, which had been enshrined since ancient times. In essence, the caste system ranked members of Indian society into a social hierarchy and marginalized some peoples, such as the Dalits, known as outcastes or "untouchables" (Figure 11.3). Although the Indian constitution of 1950 officially outlawed discrimination based on the caste system, discrimination continued to exist. The lower castes and outcastes performed menial labor and subsistence farming, while the elite obtained higher education and secured the most lucrative professional

Figure 11.3: A Dalit woman, considered an "untouchable," according to India's historical caste system.

---

1   Ben Kiernan, *Genocide and Resistance in Southeast Asia: Documentation, Denial, and Justice in Cambodia and East Timor* (New Brunswick, NJ: Transaction Publishers, 2009), 271.

jobs. Thus, India became a nation with great economic disparity and a small middle class. The elite were extremely wealthy, while the poor masses struggled just to survive. The sheer economic disparity between the two extremes in India remained unrivaled among Asian nations as the twentieth century was ending.

At the same time, India also emerged as a major Asian center of scientific and technological development, especially involving nuclear energy and computers. In the 1950s and 1960s, Homi Bhabha, a prominent Indian nuclear physicist, promoted nuclear energy as an efficient power source. His devotion to the potential of nuclear power led India to become an Asian leader in nuclear research and development, which later included the acquisition of nuclear weapons. Bhabha also played an instrumental role in India's computer revolution, as he foresaw the potential of the coming digital age long before many of his contemporaries. Bhabha's celebrity status and influence led India to invest heavily in the computer sector during the 1970s onward. Against this backdrop, India emerged as a major hub of computer electronics technology, which, by the 1990s, led the nation to become a global leader in the digital age despite the continuing problem of economic disparity between rich and poor.

After the Second World War, the Middle East emerged as a particularly important region in the global economy because of its vast oil reserves. As people within the developed world increasingly purchased cars for transportation after the war, the demand for crude oil became a pressing issue. Blessed with abundant oil reserves, the Middle East in the 1950s saw numerous Western business interests jockey for contracts to mine and refine its petroleum. In the process, such oil-rich nations as Saudi Arabia, Iraq, Iran, Kuwait, the United Arab Emirates, and Qatar became important players on the world stage. Not surprisingly, these nations realized their growing importance and sought to protect their national interests, and so in the early 1960s formed the Organization of Petroleum Exporting Nations (OPEC), which came to exercise powerful influence in determining the global market price for oil. As a general rule, when OPEC nations exported large volumes of oil, the global price was low. On the other hand, when such countries restrained exports, the market price rose, resulting in greater income in terms of price per barrel.

Among Middle Eastern nations, Saudi Arabia benefited the greatest in the second half of the twentieth century in terms of oil exports. This development owed to the fact that Saudi Arabia overwhelmingly possessed the largest oil reserves in the world and thus wielded the strongest influence among OPEC nations. Beginning in the 1960s, Saudi Arabia used its increasingly strong income from oil exports to modernize. In the process, the nation experienced a rapid transformation from a desert kingdom to a modern nation with state-of-the-art hospitals, universities, and centers of higher education. In some respects, the Saudi government outperformed most Western nations in the provision of social services, as the kingdom became known for providing its citizens with free health care, along with a tuition-free university education. At first, university curriculum tended to emphasize the sciences, especially those associated with geology and resource extraction. The Saudis also developed a reputation over time for their growing cultivation of the humanities and arts.

Despite Saudi Arabia's dramatic economic transformation, however, numerous hurdles also restrained development. Politically, the nation remained an absolute monarchy throughout the twentieth century, ruled by the House of Saud. Ibn Saud, the founder of Saudi Arabia, had ruled the kingdom from 1932 until 1953 and began the nation's path toward modernization. Ibn Saud's sons, including Saud, Faisal, Khalid, and Fahd, were all powerful kings in their own right in the latter half of the twentieth century, but they suppressed pro-democratic reform efforts that threatened their authority. Saudi kings often formed alliances with powerful Muslim clerics to legitimize their power amid clamors for reform. Meanwhile, Saudi royal power grew, with much of the nation's wealth from oil exports concentrated in the hands of the royal family itself. By the 1980s, the enormous number of Saudi princes had developed a reputation for flaunting their extravagant wealth, an embarrassing development that grew over time. In addition, by the 1990s, Saudi society had also developed a negative reputation around the world for its marginalization of women. In accordance with the strict interpretation of Islam that was prominent in the kingdom, women still lacked the right to vote or drive and were expected to have a male escort, usually a family member, while in public. Also, Saudi women were required to cover their faces with the Muslim veil, called a hijab. Although many women obtained a university education, they often found few opportunities for professional employment, though this situation improved as the twentieth century wound down.

An authoritarian governmental system also stymied Iraq's potential to prosper, even as that nation made a name for itself with its strong oil exports after the Second World War. Like its larger neighbor to the south, Iraq had an oppressive history of absolute monarchy in the first half of the twentieth century. Yet monarchy ended in 1958, with the assassination of King Faisal II. Thereafter, a series of strongmen ruled Iraq, the most influential of which was Saddam Hussein. A member of the Bath Party, Hussein came to power in 1979 and morphed into a brutal dictator over time. A Sunni Muslim, Hussein often clashed with clerics representing the nation's Shia Muslim majority. In addition, during the early 1980s, Hussein employed chemical weapons to devastate the dissident Kurdish minority in the north of Iraq. Hussein also waged reckless and costly wars that diminished his nation's economic potential. The Iraq-Iran War, which began in 1980 and lasted almost a decade, saw no clear victor but was costly in terms of wasted resources devoted to fighting, in addition to the loss of lives. Hussein also invaded Kuwait in 1990, accusing the small kingdom of stealing Iraqi oil through slant drilling. Yet an international coalition, led by the United States, drove Hussein's forces out of Kuwait and devastated the Iraqi military. A series of economic sanctions in the aftermath of the event led many Iraqis to struggle with poverty and hunger throughout the 1990s. The United Nations attempted to alleviate the suffering of Iraqis, but drew controversy with its oil-for-food initiative.

Although Iraq was perhaps the best Middle Eastern example of authoritarianism hindering the economic potential of a state, it was by no means the only nation to suffer in this regard. Iran, long ruled by Shah Muhammad Reza Pahlavi, similarly faced obstacles but also had some major successes in the region. A major recipient of US aid during the Cold War in the 1960s and 1970s, the shah modernized the nation's economy. He relied heavily on foreign investment to build railroads and provide the nation with a modern infrastructure, a development owing to the country's rich oil exports. Unlike with Saudi Arabia, women under the shah's reign also experienced a dramatic rise in terms of participation in the labor force, becoming doctors, lawyers, professors, and even entrepreneurs.

Still, Iran's shah ruled his nation with an iron fist. The Iranian government employed a secret police organization, known as SAVAK, which arrested political dissidents, denied them due process under the law, and was known for torture. To complicate matters, Iranians became increasingly anti-American because they thought the United States propped up the shah, especially after America's earlier involvement in removing the democratically elected leader Mohammad Mossadeq in the 1950s. Not surprisingly, by the mid-1970s large segments of Iran's population had become increasingly disenchanted with the shah's rule despite the modernization.

What followed was the Iranian Revolution of 1979, which saw the shah's ouster and the establishment of an authoritarian theocratic government under Ayatollah Ruhollah Khomeini (Figure 11.4). Unlike other forms of authoritarianism, a theocracy is ruled by a religious leader. As an ayatollah, the highest rank for clerics in Shia Islam, Khomeini in the 1980s sharply curtailed the public role of women in the workforce, nationalized many

Figure 11.4: Iran's theocratic leader Ayatollah Khomeini with a child.

of the industries in the country, vociferously promoted anti-Western sentiment, and waged a reckless war against Iraq. The cumulative effect of these policies spelled disaster for Iran's economy. Problems with unemployment became especially burdensome by the 1990s, as an increasingly young Iranian population struggled to find work. To make matters worse, Iran's theocracy became widely known for its brutal suppression of individual freedoms. Public executions by hanging became commonplace, while torture in Iranian jails and prisons elicited an international outcry among human-rights activists. In the process, Iran found itself almost continually the subject of economic sanctions from Western powers, a development that reinforced the economic hardships already unleashed by the initiatives of the theocratic regime.

Yet some of the smaller oil-rich nations, such as Kuwait, Qatar, and the United Arab Emirates, had greater successes in economic development, despite also having somewhat authoritarian governments. Kuwait, which only became an independent nation in 1961, developed one of the highest per capita incomes in the world throughout the 1980s and 1990s thanks to its abundance of oil exports. Remarkably, Kuwait exported enormous amounts of oil, despite being small in size. Because of the nation's great wealth, the Kuwaiti government provided citizens with free health care and other social services. The nation also came to rival major Western nations, constructing major skyscrapers and numerous architectural wonders. By the 1980s, the situation was remarkably similar for Qatar, which became a major hub for the communications industry in the Middle East due to its enormous wealth from liquefied natural gas and petroleum exports. In the mid-1990s, Qatar financed the major media outlet Al-Jazeera, which came to have a global audience. In addition, Qatar, along with the United Arab Emirates, saw a budding tourist industry as the twentieth century neared its end. With relatively liberal laws compared with most other nations in the region, many Westerners flocked to Dubai, the largest city in the United Arab Emirates, to take advantage of a luxury industry that catered to their desires, including shopping, fashion, night clubs, and gourmet restaurants.

Significantly, one Middle Eastern nation came to thrive economically, despite lacking fossils fuels to generate wealth from exports: Israel. As the only nation in the region with a solid democratic foundation, Israel developed a strong trade relationship with the United States and Europe from its inception as a nation in 1948. Over the decades, those trade relations blossomed, and Israel emerged as a major producer and exporter of high-technology products. By the 1990s, Israel had developed the most diversified export economy in the Middle East, profiting heavily from sales in the pharmaceutical and jewelry industries, along with the telecommunications and computer industries. Semiconductors and silicon computer chips especially became a major high-tech export during the decade. Israel also developed a reputation around the globe for its financial and sophisticated banking sectors. Given the wealth generated, Israeli citizens came to have one of the highest standards of living not only in the Middle East but also in the world.

Despite its strong economy, Israel still faced political challenges in the second half of the twentieth century. The main issue stemmed from the Israeli-Palestinian conflict, which dated back to Israel's founding. The land that came to make up the nation of Israel thereafter had earlier been part of British Palestine. After the Holocaust, the British allowed the surviving Jews of Europe to emigrate to a region within Palestine and set up Israel as a state there for the Jewish people. Yet large segments of the Palestinians, both Muslims and Christians alike, did not recognize the legitimacy of Israel's statehood. A series of wars between the Israelis and Palestinians from the 1940s until the 1970s uniformly resulted in Israeli victories and Israel's territorial expansion. In response, the Palestinians increasingly resorted to violence and terrorism to reclaim lands they had lost. By the 1970s, the Palestinian Liberation Organization (PLO), led by Yasser Arafat, had denounced Israel's right to exist and, with some success, sought aid from nations around the world. Most Middle Eastern nations favored the Palestinians and were hostile toward Israel, putting the Jewish state in a precarious relationship with its neighbors (Figure 11.5).

But the United States, with the strongest economy and military in the world, remained strongly devoted to Israel's defense throughout the second half of the twentieth century, even when this position worked against American economic interests. This point became especially clear during the Energy Crisis of 1974. When Egypt and Syria (both stalwart supporters of the Palestinians) went to war with Israel in October 1973, the United States provided Israel with aid and technical support. Although Israel obtained a decisive victory in the war, the OPEC nations overwhelmingly supported Egypt and Syria, and instituted an embargo on oil exports to pro-Israel nations. As a consequence, the price of gas at the pumps in the United States quadrupled, setting off the crisis. The long-term effects of the embargo were felt throughout the 1970s and led to a phenomenon that many classical economists deemed impossible: stagflation. Facing stagflation, the American economy experienced a rise in both unemployment and inflation. Nevertheless, the United States rarely wavered in its resolve to protect Israel. Thus, the American government in the late-1970s worked tirelessly to secure a peace agreement with Israel and Egypt, which resulted in a major diplomatic success with the Camp David Accords (1978). To be sure, American efforts to promote peace reflected, in part, the delicate balancing act that stemmed from the complexities inherent in the Israeli-Palestinian conflict, which remained unresolved and as intense as ever as the twentieth century approached.

LATIN AMERICA

In the second half of the twentieth century, Latin America also faced numerous obstacles that hampered economic development. The reasons, however, were somewhat different from those experienced by Middle Eastern countries. Both regions experienced authoritarianism, but different forms. Rather than have

Figure 11.5: Jerusalem, Israel's capital city. The Blue Mosque in the center is the Dome of the Rock, a sacred site among Muslims.

absolute monarchs or theocrats as several Middle Eastern nations had, many Latin American countries struggled not only under corrupt presidents, but also military and communist dictators. In addition, the problem of drug trafficking and the crimes associated with it in Latin America rose dramatically as the century ended, a development that distinguished the region from other parts of the underdeveloped world.

With rich oil deposits and a diversified economy, Mexico had much potential to become a major economic player in Latin America in the latter half of the twentieth century, but lingering historical problems hampered the nation's progress. To begin, despite being a republic with a strong constitution, democracy never gained the same amount of respect in Mexico as it did in the United States or Canada. In fact, Mexican presidents during the nineteenth century were known for their corruption and often rigged elections, features best represented in Porfirio Diaz's long rule as Mexico's president (1876–1911). Additionally, Mexican presidents often did not wield strong control over the domestic affairs of their country. In reality, by the early twentieth century, the central government's power tended to be concentrated around the capital of Mexico City and the federal district but was weak in the peripheral regions. This weakness made possible the rise of the *caudillos*, regional warlords who wreaked much havoc in the early twentieth century. Prominent caudillos such as Pancho Villa engaged in a wide variety of criminal activities—everything from train and bank robberies to cattle thievery and murder (Figure 11.6). The poor masses sometimes were torn over whom to be loyal to: the central government or the local warlord. After all, caudillos attracted followers and raised armies by distributing loot among citizens in the regions where they wielded influence.

Figure 11.6: Mexican warlord Pancho Villa, a prominent *caudillo* in the early twentieth century.

This quandary had long-term effects into the second half of the twentieth century, as the Mexican government remained weak and the warlords continued to wield influence. The caudillos, however, were no longer mere warlords but had over time morphed into drug lords, as drug cartels by the 1980s had become increasingly common power brokers in Mexican society. Mexico, it turned out, had emerged as a major transport hub of illegal narcotics originating from South America, especially cocaine. The Sinaloa cartel, one of the largest Mexican cartels by the 1990s, expanded its operations over time to include smuggling heroin into the United States and the creation of various money-laundering schemes. By the close of the twentieth century, the number and influence of drug cartels had grown exponentially in Mexico. These illegal organizations, which attracted poor Mexicans with a promise of a better life, often bribed corrupt police and carried out acts of violence against rivals and government informants. Not surprisingly, as the drug problem grew in Mexico, crime and regional instability increased dramatically, factors that discouraged the foreign investment so crucial to economic development.

Amid all this, the problem of wealth disparity emerged as a major issue for Mexico as the twentieth century drew to a close. Because of the ever-present problem of corruption, great amounts of wealth became concentrated in the hands of a small class, while the masses of Mexicans struggled to make ends meet. Monopolies dominated some industries, including telecommunications. Tycoon Carlos Slim, who controlled many of the television and cable stations in the country, became one of the richest people in the world. Yet many Mexicans got by as mere farmhands. They struggled to earn a livable wage and take care of their families. Because of the lack of opportunity for social mobility in Mexico, and the growing problem of crime associated with the drug cartels' rising power, waves of Mexicans emigrated to the United States in search of a better life, a development that became more pronounced over time.

To complicate matters, the North American Free Trade Agreement (NAFTA) produced mixed results for Mexico. This agreement between the United States, Canada, and Mexico, which took effect in 1993, sought to encourage trade among North American nations. No doubt, the agreement led many American corporations such as Ford, General Motors, Whirlpool, Levi Strauss, and Kodak to establish facilities in Mexico, thus creating new employment opportunities for Mexicans. Although factory workers in Mexico developed a higher standard of living than farmhands, the factory workers still faced exploitation. After all, an important reason why US corporations made their presence felt in Mexico was to save dramatically on labor costs. Mexican industrial workers earned far less than their equivalents in the United States, and US corporations took advantage of the agreement to maximize profits. In addition, as American corporations made their presence felt throughout the 1990s, small Mexican businesses struggled, compounding the many economic problems already besetting the nation at the end of the twentieth century.

The Central American nations also experienced major hurdles that hindered development in the second half of the twentieth century. Authoritarianism, political instability, and economic exploitation by foreign nations were challenges experienced in the first half of the century. Such nations as Guatemala, Honduras, and Nicaragua often had military leaders as presidents who were known for rampant corruption and a tendency to want to maintain power for long periods. To complicate matters, such nations faced debt problems and internal chaos that led the United States to become actively involved in the affairs of such nations. A series of US marine occupations of several Central American nations between 1912 and 1934, known as the Banana Wars, resulted in heavy US financial investment in the region. The US-owned United Fruit Company, later known as Chiquita Bananas, purchased huge tracts of land in the various nations. As US economic interests grew in the region, many citizens within the various Central American nations increasingly felt marginalized. By 1950, Central America still remained underdeveloped, and poverty levels, especially among indigenous people, were high. As the decades passed, little progress occurred to change this reality for the region.

In fact, as the twentieth century's end neared, Central America also became a major hub for drug trafficking, a new problem that introduced all sorts of societal ills. In order for illegal narcotics such as cocaine to reach North America from South America, a lucrative business of drug running emerged in Panama, Nicaragua, Honduras, and Guatemala. Faced with few opportunities to provide for their families, by the 1980s many men had begun taking part in illegal drug trafficking to make ends meet. Even Manuel Noriega, the military leader of Panama from 1983 until 1989, became involved in the illegal narcotics trade, a fact that demonstrated the lure of power associated with narco-trafficking. Meanwhile, drug trafficking was devastating the economies of Central America. As gangs and drug cartels popped up, Central America came to have one of the highest crime rates in the world. Homicide and kidnappings became rampant between rival groups, being especially problematic in Honduras by the end of the century. With such crime, Central America faced difficulties attracting foreign investment to spur growth.

Like Central America, the South American nation of Colombia faced some of the most difficult hurdles in Latin America involving political stability and economic development. At the start of the twentieth century, Colombia had emerged as a major global producer of coffee, a product that generated considerable revenue for the nation. Yet the nation inherited long-term historical problems, especially political factionalism that often erupted in violence. In fact, beginning in 1948, Colombia experienced the longest civil war of any nation during the twentieth century. The still ongoing war, known in Colombia for its brutality, saw various guerrilla and paramilitary movements fight the government for control over the nation. By the 1980s, two prominent armed movements, known as FARC and AUC, jockeyed for power, fighting each other and the anti-communist, pro-American government in Bogota. While FARC emerged as a Marxist revolutionary movement that won over many of the poor, the AUC was far less ideological and came to represent the interests of narco-traffickers (Figure 11.7). The violence associated with the armed paramilitary movements produced massive levels of political instability in the country, which prevented sustained economic growth, despite the country having a democratic government.

By the end of the twentieth century, Colombia had become known for its illicit exports of cocaine more than its coffee. The Medellin cartel, headed by notorious drug lord Pablo Escobar, manufactured cocaine derived from Bolivian coca and became the most powerful narcotics producer in the world in the 1980s, supplying a majority of the cocaine that ended up in the United States. In the process, Colombia became a major focus in the war on drugs initiative under US President Ronald Reagan. Narcotics smuggling not

Figure 11.7: FARC insurgents, one of the major paramilitary movements responsible for the civil strife in Colombia.

only produced violent rivalries and a drug-addicted citizenry but also provided the revenue for the Colombian paramilitary groups to fight the government. Realizing the devastating effects of narco-trafficking, the Colombian government in the 1990s arrested Escobar and waged a war against illegal drugs. Nevertheless, problems still remained as the twenty-first century dawned. Narco-trafficking remained a major source of violence, and the paramilitary groups continued their armed struggle against the government and one another.

While Colombia faced the most persistent political turmoil in South America in the latter half of the twentieth century, Argentina also experienced developments that stymied economic potential, a fact that was somewhat surprising given the nation's rich history. At the start of the century, Argentina had one of the strongest economies in South America and was a vibrant republic. The nation had a diversified economy, with strong industrial and agricultural exports, and a prominent tourist sector. The nation had created a well-developed infrastructure with the finest railroads in Latin America. Unlike with other Latin American countries, the democratic process in Argentina had also worked well. The nation was known for its integrity in elections and judicious statesmen, while the problem of corruption that plagued so many other nations in the region was largely absent. The Great Depression, however, set Argentina on a path of hardship. With widespread unemployment beginning in the 1930s and 1940s, Argentina struggled to recover.

Amid this backdrop, a new political phenomenon known as Peronism emerged in Argentina to address the situation. Named after Argentine President Juan Peron (r. 1946–1955, 1973–74), this populist movement opposed both unbridled capitalism and communism and sought to promote Argentina's national interests and improve the status of workers (Figure 11.8). Peronists, who became a dominant political force in the second half of the twentieth century, inherently distrusted foreign influence in the Argentine economy, leading them to institute autarkic economic policies. Specifically, Peron and his followers sought to establish a self-sufficient economy that did not rely on international trade. By producing all goods domestically, Peron's policies were aimed at providing Argentine workers with jobs and combating unemployment. While Peron and his successors effectively addressed the problem of joblessness, the nation's autarkic initiatives led over time to serious inflation problems. Inflation occurs when there is an excess of currency in circulation that drives down the value of that currency. With inflation, which Argentina struggled to combat in the mid-1970s, the wealthy classes became dissatisfied because they had the most to lose when the value of currency bottomed out.

Consequently, Argentine elites formed strong opposition to Peronist policies over the decades, ultimately leading to a military coup in 1976 that removed Juan Peron's second wife, Isabella, from power. A brutal military junta subsequently ruled Argentina until 1983 and waged a reckless war against Britain over control of the Falkland Islands. The military junta failed to correct the economic problems of the nation, which only became worse after Argentina lost the war. Meanwhile, military rule also produced the notorious "Dirty War,"[2] which saw the murder or disappearance of thousands of opponents of the regime, including Peronists. Especially appalling was the military junta's use of death flights to murder opponents. Victims were put on planes and dropped to their deaths from high altitudes into bodies of water from which their corpses were never recovered. Although the military government ended and democracy reemerged in Argentina in the mid-1980s, the nation was no longer the global economic player at the end of the twentieth century that it was at the start. A unique combination of autarky and brutal authoritarianism in the second half of the century had altered the nation's historical path.

Figure 11.8: As Argentina's president, Juan Peron, a popular figure, introduced autarkic policies to address the problems associated with the Great Depression.

Like Argentina, Brazil also faced significant political and socioeconomic changes during the latter part of the twentieth century. A major development centered around the nation's unique experience with military rule. From 1964 until 1985, a military dictatorship ruled the country. But unlike with other military dictatorships, Brazil emerged as an interesting case study of successful economic growth, despite authoritarianism. In fact, between the late 1960s until the early 1980s, Brazil experienced the "Brazilian Miracle," a period of intense economic growth in which the GDP grew at a remarkable rate. The growth stemmed, in large part, from state initiatives to transform the nation into a major industrial power, similar to the initiatives US President Franklin D. Roosevelt carried out in the southern part of the United States amid the Great Depression. Indeed, during the era of military rule, millions of Brazilians obtained work in construction projects, factories, oil refineries, and nuclear power plants. At the time, Brazil even became known for producing automobiles, the first major Latin American nation to become successful in this high-skill industry. But Brazil's notorious human-rights record during the era of military rule spelled disaster for the viability of the system. Large segments of Brazilians desired democracy and repudiated the regime for its use of torture against political dissidents. As a result, the military government transitioned to democracy by the mid-1980s.

---

2   For a good book on the "Dirty War," see Paul H. Lewis, *Guerillas and Generals: The Dirty War in Argentina* (Westport, CT: Praeger, 2002).

Figure 11.9: A Cuban man repairs an old US-manufactured car.

Nevertheless, the problem of wealth disparity remained a challenge for Brazilians as the twenty-first century approached. When Brazil resolved its inflation problem in the early 1990s, the nation attracted a tremendous amount of foreign investment. In the process, such major urban centers as Sao Paulo and Rio de Janeiro came to have financial districts that rivaled those in the large cities in the United States, Europe, and Japan. An elite class of venture capitalists, bankers, and entrepreneurs in Brazil became wealthy as a result. At the same time, the large Brazilian cities also became known for their slums, called *favelas*. Favela dwellers represented the poorest segment of Brazilian society, with favela neighborhoods consisting of poorly constructed dwellings made of scrap metal and wood. Inadequate electricity, running water, and sewage disposal systems within the favelas became major problems, as did the widespread presence of hunger, disease, and crime among inhabitants. Above all, the favelas revealed that Brazilian society at the dawn of the twenty-first century was marked by sharp contrasts. A small elite class at the top thrived, while the poor struggled immensely just to survive.

Not surprisingly, given the poverty associated with Latin American nations in the second half of the twentieth century, many population segments of these countries were drawn to Marxist ideas to address the issues of economic injustice. After all, Marxist ideologues in the region attracted the masses of impoverished people with promises of a fair distribution of wealth. This path, however, did not result in positive developments on the whole. Rather, nations that flirted with Marxism tended to remain among the poorest and most politically unstable of nations in the region, as evidenced by the cases of Cuba, Peru, and Nicaragua.

When Fidel Castro ushered in the Cuban Revolution in 1959, millions of Cubans had high hopes of a prosperous future for their country. Yet the Cold War and the establishment of a communist dictatorship on the island nation shattered the dreams of many. In 1960, in response to the nation becoming communist, the United States imposed a trade embargo on Cuba that came to devastate the Cuban economy over time. Although Cuba exported largely agricultural products such as sugar and tobacco to the Soviet Union and the communist bloc during the Cold War, the amount of income generated did not allow the Cuban people to live a prosperous life. Most Cubans, although receiving free health care and education, lived in substandard housing by American standards. The country relied heavily on Soviet economic aid to survive economically. Those few Cubans fortunate enough to have an automobile obtained older American cars from the 1950s that had come to the island before the embargo (Figure 11.9). To complicate matters, when by 1990 communism had fallen in Europe, a major source of economic aid to Cuba came to a halt. As a result, Cuba experienced a dire economic situation as the twentieth century closed. At the same time, the Cuban people still widely supported Castro and the revolution. In part, this fondness resulted from the indoctrination associated with authoritarian regimes that promoted the cult of personality of the leader and tolerated no opposition. Among Latin American nations, few rivaled Cuba with its people's enthusiasm for Castro as the twenty-first century emerged.

To be sure, Cuba was not the only Latin American state to deal with communism. In the 1980s and 1990s, Peru also became a hotbed of various leftist movements inspired in some way by Marxism, even though the government never became communist. The economic inequality, social marginalization of the poor, government corruption, and perceived inadequacy of democracy led large segments of Peru's population to embrace communist ideas as a way to a better life. In 1980, *Sendero Luminoso* ("Shining Path") emerged as a Maoist movement that garnered massive support from Peruvian peasants who had been historically marginalized and denied opportunities to own land. Led by Abimael Guzman, Sendero Luminoso advocated violent overthrow of Peru's government and was responsible for tens of thousands of murders during the decade. Around the same time, the Tupac Amaru Revolutionary Movement promoted a unique kind of indigenous Marxism that sought to advance Indian rights in the nation through the use of violence. A rival of Sendero Luminoso, Tupac Amaru became known for hostage taking, bombings, bank robberies, and attacks on Westerners. In the 1990s, Peru's government under Alberto Fujimori crushed both movements, but employed illegal death squads to do so. By the close of the century, Peru still struggled with the legacies of the preceding decades' violence, even though the economy improved as the nation become more stable politically. Rather than providing an avenue to prosperity, Peru's flirtation with communist ideas had led to a bloodbath within the nation.

Beginning in the 1970s, Nicaragua also experienced a Marxist movement, but it differed from that later seen in Peru. While communist ideas appealed largely to the indigenous elements of Peru, Nicaragua's population did not include a large Indian segment. Rather, communism appealed to the poor masses of Nicaraguans who wanted to throw off the yoke of the nation's government ruled by the Samoza family since the 1930s. Inspired by the Cuban Revolution, the Marxist-leaning Sandinista National Liberation Front overthrew the government in 1979. Even so, during the 1980s, a bloody civil war emerged, pitting the Sandinistas against a coalition of anti-communist groups known as the Contras. Both sides engaged in gross human-rights violations, including murder, rape, and kidnapping. In the process, the nation was devastated economically, like so many other Latin American nations struggling to forge a unified political identity for their peoples.

Indeed, by the dawn of the twenty-first century, Latin America still struggled with modernization. Argentina, despite overcoming its earlier challenges with inflation, found itself in an economic depression, with massive unemployment. In addition, the slums in the major cities of many of the countries, alongside the state-of-the-art high-rises, still served as visible symbols of the gross wealth disparity that plagued the region. Meanwhile, the continual problem of drug trafficking and crime continued to be major hurdles that drove away foreign investment. At the same time, the region's perseverance in the face of such challenges proved remarkable and testified to a widespread hope among the people for a better future.

AFRICA

Of all regions, Africa experienced some of the most pressing problems that hindered development from the 1960s onward. By the dawn of the twenty-first century, the continent remained the poorest in the world.

To complicate matters, despite having an abundance of natural resources, the continent also remained the least developed according to many indicators. A combination of economic exploitation from foreign nations, the struggle with disease and epidemics, the weak democratic tradition and penchant for authoritarian rule, and ethnic conflicts all presented major challenges to a region many had hoped would have an exceptionally bright future after decolonization. Nevertheless, the possibility for such a future still exists in the present era, if such hurdles can be surmounted.

Even though most African states obtained independence as the old European colonial powers evacuated the continent in the 1960s, the economies of the new African nations largely failed to thrive. Although the continent was rich in copper, gold, petroleum, and precious stones, the mere export of raw materials did not generate adequate income for most citizens to escape poverty. In fact, by the century's end, few nations within Africa exported high-technology products, the manufactured goods associated with wealth generation. Given the failure to establish a sector devoted to high-tech and with their exports focused mainly on raw materials, most African economies were simply not in a position to accumulate the levels of wealth seen in other parts of the world.

In Africa, the problem of disease and health crises also remained a major challenge to development in the second half of the twentieth century. In fact, such diseases as hepatitis B, tuberculosis, cholera, and malaria still wreaked havoc on Africa's population as the century ended. The number of cases of hepatitis B, which is caused by a virus and spread through bodily fluids, declined sharply on a global scale after an effective vaccine emerged in 1982. Unfortunately, the poorest parts of Africa continued to lack access to the vaccine, and Africans with the disease often succumbed to liver failure. In addition, tuberculosis, a bacterial disease that affects the lungs and can be spread through coughing and sneezing, still presented challenges in southern and central Africa as late as the first decade of the twenty-first century. Cholera, a bacterial disease transmitted through the use of unclean water, persisted in parts of the continent as well, especially given the lack of proper sewage disposal systems and access to safe drinking water. Lastly, malaria, a deadly disease spread through mosquito bites, has presented a challenge to Africa throughout history. But with the rise in the use of pesticides during the latter half of the twentieth century, the disease produced fewer casualties; however, central African nations such as Chad and Mali still struggled with the problem.

But the most frightening health-related crises in Africa stemmed from the emergence of such new viruses as Ebola and HIV during the 1970s. The first major Ebola outbreak, which caused its victims to suffer from massive internal bleeding and proved exceedingly deadly, occurred in the Congo in 1976. The virus, experts believed, was spread through the eating of bushmeat, a common source of protein for many Africans. In 1979, Sudan experienced an Ebola epidemic. By the 1990s, Gabon, Cote d'Ivoire, and South Africa also faced outbreaks. But despite its deadliness, Ebola did not become the most devastating virus for Africa. That unenviable distinction instead went to HIV, the virus that causes the immune system-weakening condition known as AIDS. Spread through the exchange of bodily fluids and sexual intercourse, Africa had tens of millions of people infected with the disease at the dawn of the twentieth century. The virus especially wreaked havoc on the populations of southern African nations,[3] such as Zimbabwe, South

---

3   Toyin Falola and Matthew M. Heaton, *HIV/AIDs, Illness, & African Well-being* (Rochester NY: University of Rochester Press, 2007), 353.

Africa, Botswana, Uganda, Angola, and Mozambique, where large numbers were infected and access to antiviral cocktails was limited or too expensive. To complicate matters, some Africans did not trust the use of Western medications that could save their lives, and others denied the existence of the virus. In the process, HIV claimed the lives of millions, while removing from the workforce millions more because of perpetual illness.

The historical problem of racism also continued to be a major issue Africa struggled with in the second half of the twentieth century, long after the end of the transatlantic slave trade and the horrors associated with New Imperialism. Even after the continent experienced widespread European decolonization in the 1960s, a sizable European presence still existed in southern Africa. There was the problem of the continually growing presence of European corporations, which many Africans believed robbed them of the homeland's natural resources. In addition, South Africa and Rhodesia established overt racist governments controlled by the minority white populations of those countries.

Apartheid, the official racial segregation policy of South Africa from 1948 until 1994, reinforced the political power of that nation's white minority. The white government did not recognize black South Africans as citizens or allow them to vote in elections. In addition, the government created controversial reservations known as *bantustans* for the nation's black population to settle. In theory, South Africa's government intended for the bantustans to emerge as independent countries in their own right. Such reservations, however, did not receive international recognition. Instead, by the 1970s, the white-minority government increasingly became the subject of ridicule from the major powers, which decried the institutionalized racism inherent in apartheid. Yet South Africa's government persisted in its hard-line racial policies.

Beginning in the 1960s, the government began forcibly moving blacks to the reservations, an action that resulted in violence. The forced removals of blacks continued into the 1980s, but resistance mounted.

In the process, Nelson Mandela became increasingly revered as the father of South Africa's anti-apartheid movement (Figure 11.10). As a young man, Mandela became associated with the African National Congress, a movement that promoted the advancement of blacks within South African society. While initially drawn to the ideas of nonviolence resistance, Mandela hardened after whites used violence against blacks in the Sharpeville Massacre (1960), which

Figure 11.10: Nelson Mandela meets with US President Bill Clinton, in 1993.

saw sixty-nine anti-apartheid protesters killed. Against this backdrop, the African National Congress changed course and championed an armed struggle against the apartheid government. As a leader of the African National Congress, which became an illegal organization after Sharpeville, Mandela found himself repeatedly arrested for his activism. In 1964, the South African government handed down a life sentence to Mandela, finding him guilty of developing a guerrilla movement that threatened the national security of the country. Imprisoned between 1964 and 1990, Mandela was given offers of early release if he condemned armed insurrection. Yet Mandela refused as long as the government outlawed the African National Congress. Over time, Mandela's self-sacrifice to his cause won over the hearts of millions of South Africans, ultimately resulting in his release, the end of apartheid in 1994, and his becoming the nation's first black president that same year. As the twentieth century drew to a close, Mandela's presidency became known for its policies aimed at promoting racial reconciliation in the country.

The historical trajectory of Rhodesia, later known as Zimbabwe, was much different from South Africa's. In 1965, the British colony's white minority declared itself independent of Britain and rebuffed the decolonization process. The tiny white minority in the nation refused to allow blacks to vote, fearing the black majority would gain control and determine the nation's future. In the process, Rhodesia established one of the most virulently racist governments in the world under President Ian Smith. Its main benefactor was the apartheid regime in South Africa. The Rhodesian Bush War, fought between 1964 and 1979, saw the white minority government face off against a coalition of black-nationalist guerrilla armies led by the Zimbabwe African National Liberation Army's (ZANU) Robert Mugabe. The war ended in a stalemate, but by 1980 the white government had conceded power. With the nation renamed Zimbabwe and the advent of universal suffrage that year, Mugabe became the first black leader of the country (Figure 11.11).

Figure 11.11: Robert Mugabe, president of Zimbabwe since 1980.

Mugabe's rule of Zimbabwe, however, shifted dramatically over time. In the 1980s, Zimbabwe was a budding democracy and had one of the strongest economies in Africa, with a vibrant agricultural and mining sector. In fact, in appreciation of his effective leadership, Mugabe even became the recipient of numerous honorary doctorates awarded from the finest universities around the globe. Even so, Mugabe fell victim to the lure of racial politics over time. White farmers in the country, whose labor produced much of the country's wealth, tended to enjoy a higher standard of living than black Zimbabweans. As a result, Mugabe's ruling ZANU political party by the 1990s increasingly demanded the seizing of white farms and the redistribution of that land to blacks. In the end, Mugabe confiscated the lands of white farmers and reallocated the land to supporters and party members. By the first decade of the twentieth century, the nation had seen its once vibrant economy in ruins, with runaway inflation. In the meantime, much of the country's white population decided to flee the country, concerned about their lack of safety. Once a champion of democracy, Mugabe had over time morphed into a dictator. His leadership became known for the dubious arrest of Mugabe's political opponents and the widespread use of torture against enemies.

Zimbabwe's experience under Mugabe reflected a much broader problem affecting Africa in the last quarter of the twentieth century: the proliferation of authoritarian regimes. Although most nations on the continent became democratic republics after acquiring independence, the continent as a whole did not have a strong democratic tradition. Some Africans were even suspicious of democracy, deeming it a European or Western—but not an authentic African—system of government. Consequently, various forms of authoritarianism, especially Marxist dictatorships and military rule, over time came to saddle the continent with problems that left nasty legacies for people in their wake.

Angola and Ethiopia, for example, were among the most prominent African nations to adopt an overt Marxist government at some point in the twentieth century. Angola had a Marxist regime from 1975 until 1992. The ruling MPLA (Popular Movement for the Liberation of Angola), originally a movement that fought Portuguese rule, imposed a Soviet-style repressive regime. Despite having an abundance of oil, Angola did not thrive economically, as a coalition of pro-democratic elements fought the communist government. A bloody civil war occurred throughout the 1980s, resulting in much tragedy and suffering. When the Soviet Union collapsed, so did the Marxist regime in Angola. In the aftermath, Angola established a fruitful economic relationship with China. Angola traded oil with China, which, in turn, provided the material to help begin modernizing the African nation. The historical trajectory was somewhat similar for Ethiopia. Although the nation had a democratic government during the 1970s, the situation changed the following decade. A massive famine devastated Ethiopia between 1983 and 1985. As people starved, a Marxist government emerged in 1987 promising to alleviate the hunger of the masses. This government attracted Soviet aid, but the Marxist regime also failed once the Soviet Union collapsed and no longer could prop up the state. As these examples show, communism in Africa heavily depended on the success of the Soviet Union. When the USSR's experience resulted in failure, African regimes associated with the Soviets lost legitimacy as well.

Military dictatorships, however, became the most common type of authoritarianism found in Africa during the second half of the twentieth century. Togo, Uganda, Somalia, Gambia, Equatorial Guinea, Senegal, and Nigeria all experienced military rule at some point after decolonization. Although the details differed in specifics depending on the nation, military rule in Africa generally resulted in the violent repression of political opponents and misery for the great bulk of citizens under such leadership. An example was Idi Amin's brutal rule of Uganda between 1971 and 1979. During Amin's years in power, tens of thousands of people became victims of murder, with their bodies sometimes cast into the Nile River to be eaten by crocodiles.[4] Political opponents, including clergymen and the intelligentsia, along with ethnic minorities, found themselves targeted for any perceived opposition to Armin's ironclad rule.

Adding to the problem of authoritarianism was the pervasiveness of civil wars and ethnic strife that affected Africa. Even late into the twentieth century, many African peoples still embraced a tribal identity, privileging it over a national consciousness. In fact, Africa had many major ethnic groups—including the Ibo, Tutsis, Hutu, Nama, Fulani, and Hausa—that often made tribal advancement a central feature in national politics, a development that sometimes produced strife. To complicate matters, European nations, when establishing the boundaries of African states in the era of imperialism, had included tribes that had

---

4   Olusegun Obasanjo and Hans d' Orville, *Challenges of Leadership in African Development* (New York: Taylor & Francis, 1990). 164.

been historical enemies within the same colony. Thus, when these colonies obtained independence and became their own states in the 1960s, lingering tribal rivalries produced tension and violence, harming the prospects of economic development in the new nations. In some cases, as Rwanda showed, genocide even ensued.

Indeed, the Rwandan Genocide (1994) was one of the greatest tragedies of the twentieth century. As for ethnic composition, Rwanda had two dominant groups that were historical rivals: the Hutu and the Tutsis. Although the overwhelming majority of Rwandans were Hutu, the Tutsis had historically held a privileged status in government, dating back to Belgian colonial rule. The Belgians had promoted a discourse according to which Tutsis, being taller, were superior than the Hutus. Many Tutsis internalized this notion of superiority, looking down on Hutus. Thus, tension between the two groups was always present, though in differing degrees at various times. By the 1990s, the two ethnic groups were increasingly at odds, with periodic outbreaks of violence. When Rwanda's president (a Hutu) died in a plane crash in the spring of 1994, the Hutu blamed the Tutsis for shooting down the aircraft. As a result, Hutus went on a rampage between April and June, massacring hundreds of thousands of Tutsis. Spurred on by Hutu politicians and army leaders, organized gangs launched attacks throughout the country, wielding machetes and hacking many innocent civilians to death. No place was safe for Tutsis, not even churches. Men, women, and children all fell victim to the genocidal mind-set that swept the nation.

Although the genocide ended and an era of reconciliation that began in the mid-1990s, justice largely remained elusive for the Tutsi victims. Many of the armed Hutu gangs escaped into the neighboring country of Congo, where they became a source of conflict there.

The brutal civil war in Sierra Leone (1991–2002) likewise emerged as a horrific tragedy as the twentieth century ended. A west African nation known for its rich abundance of diamonds, the nation had great potential to become a major economic player. Yet the country's economy remained poor by the 1990s, with massive unemployment. As such, the Revolutionary United Front (RUF) recruited thousands of young men and even teenagers with a promise of a better life if they joined the movement's armed struggle against the government. As the RUF grew, it became known for inflicting unspeakable brutality against innocent civilians, while drug-addicted teenage recruits increasingly became the agents of terror. Mutilations, such as the chopping off of hands and arms, became signature acts associated with the movement, as did kidnappings, hostage taking, and the rape of women and girls. In addition, the RUF forced civilians to dig for diamonds, the sale of which financed the movement's violent actions. During this time, Sierra Leone's diamonds obtained the name "blood diamonds," given the costs both in human misery and lives associated with the precious stone.[5] Although the civil war ended, the legacies remain today, with the large number of amputees a visible testament to this time of tragedy.

Despite the problems in Africa, the continent's future may well turn out bright indeed. As the twenty-first century dawned, some small countries such as Gabon and Equatorial Guinea began to modernize thanks to their strong oil exports. Also, South Africa became known for its vibrant democracy. One US Supreme Court Justice, Ruth Bader Ginsburg, even praised South Africa for having one of the best constitutions in the world. If the continent can expand its economy to include high-technology exports and

---

5   See Greg Campbell, *Blood Diamonds: Tracing the Deadly Path of the World's Most Precious Stones* (New York: Basic Books, 2004).

rely less on the exports of raw materials to generate income, there is much reason to believe modernization and economic development will occur. In addition, if Africa can overcome its ethnic and civil strife and develop strong democracies that respect individual rights and dignity, the continent's future will no doubt be much better than its experiences with authoritarianism. The good news is that the nations of Africa are young by global standards. Most did not become independent countries until the 1960s. To be sure, it takes time for the blossoming of nations into vibrant democracies with strong economies that make possible a high standard of living for citizens. The twenty-first century may very well see this flowering of Africa, if the many hurdles can be surmounted.

CONCLUSION

As the twenty-first century dawned, Asia, the Middle East, Latin America, and Africa saw a strong impetus to modernize. The West had begun the process earlier, and these regions expected to catch up. Yet the realities in the second half of the twentieth century proved challenging. Forms of political authoritarianism, everything from absolute monarchies in the Middle East to military dictatorships in Africa, Asia, and Latin America, stymied the expansion of individual liberties and economic development. Civil strife, wealth disparity, and crime exacerbated life in such regions. As a consequence, these major global regions largely remained underdeveloped by Western standards by the close of the twentieth century, although there were some exceptions to this rule.

Meanwhile, the underdeveloped regions became a major arena for the playing out of ideas. The propensity of many nations and political movements to embrace or reject Marxism in the second half of the twentieth century certainly bore testament to this fact. In addition, as the next chapter shows, a growing emphasis on both the maintaining of cultural traditions and also the promotion of deeply held religious convictions continued to shape the lives of people in their daily struggles.

CHAPTER
TWELVE

A Return to Traditionalism? New Issues in the Era of Globalization

INTRODUCTION

As the twenty-first century dawned, the world had changed considerably from the past. With the verdict of the Cold War in, many people were optimistic about the global expansion of democracy and free-market economics. In fact, the political scientist Francis Fukuyama optimistically declared the "end of history" in 1993.[1] With the predicted post-Cold War expansion of democracy and free enterprise, the world was expected to experience an unprecedented level of prosperity and peace. Democratic-peace theory, the notion that democratic states do not go to war with one another, was promoted widely in global policy forums as a panacea to cure the world's ills.

Yet unforeseen developments, beginning in the 1990s, cast grave doubts on the optimism of such observers. To begin, large parts of the world proved reluctant to embrace democracy. Authoritarianism carried on as usual in many places. Rather than the expansion of free-market economies, a new phenomenon known as globalization also emerged and unleashed a bevy of unanticipated economic and social problems across the globe. In addition, technological advances such as the Internet led to a new attack on traditional sources of authority and ushered in mass consumption of postmodern ideas. Amid all this, many turned to traditional world views to cope with the new changes sweeping the globe.

---

1   Francis Fukuyama, *The End of History and the Last Man* (London: Penguin, 1993).

TECHNOLOGY, POSTMODERNITY, AND CULTURE: A LATE TWENTIETH-CENTURY RETROSPECTIVE

The birth of the Internet, the hallmark of the digital age, unfolded over several decades. Computer technology had made rapid advances since the 1950s, as vacuum tubes were replaced with complex circuit boards that later included semiconductors (Figure 12.1). In the process, information storage and central processing became exponentially easier, making possible increasing levels of computation. Computer enthusiasts, referred to sometimes pejoratively as geeks or nerds by the 1970s, increasingly developed a reputation for championing the unlimited possibilities of the budding digital age. At the same time, the traditional lives of most global citizens remained much the same throughout the 1970s and 1980s, given that most people did not own personal computers and lacked computer literacy. Although the US military had developed an Internet platform known as ARPANET in the late 1960s, the public lacked access to this revolutionary means of communication and information sharing. Amid the Cold War, many US policymakers had feared the possibility of espionage and other frightening activities should the public make use of the computer-based platform. Although many universities acquired limited access to the Internet by the 1980s, not until the early 1990s did a major push for the public to have such access succeed. With the Cold War over, many of the lingering fears had subsided. Against this backdrop, the High Performance Computing and Communication Act of 1991, introduced by Tennessee Senator Albert Gore Jr., became the single most important piece of legislation responsible for introducing the American public to what soon became known as the World Wide Web. Yet the creation of the Internet was not simply an American phenomenon. Europe, along with the developed parts of Asia, Latin America, and the Middle East, caught the digital fever at the same time and likewise established Internet access on a global scale.

Indeed, by the middle to late 1990s, the Internet had ushered in a new world in which long-distance communication and computing became dramatically less burdensome. E-mail increasingly became common, so much that the traditional practice of writing letters and using the post office, now known as snail mail, seemed a vestige of the past. Simultaneously, computer games began to rival video game consoles as a major diversionary activity that people all over the world played for fun and to relieve stress. More important, millions of websites popped up, promoting businesses, online banking, and new types of social media, in addition to providing unlimited sources of information on virtually all subjects. No longer did schoolchildren have to take out editions of encyclopedias to learn about the major people and events in history. A bountiful supply of information was now accessible with the simple click of a mouse.

At the same time, unprecedented levels of access to information did not always result in predictable developments. In some ways, the oversaturation of information called into question traditional notions of authority. In the new digital age, anyone, regardless of credentials, could design a website purveying ideas on all sorts of topics. Not surprisingly, a virtually unlimited supply of misinformation competed with authoritative sources on such topics as politics, the daily news, history, medicine, economics, and society. In searching the web, a person with a serious medical condition could easily be led astray by information promising the false hope of a quick cure. Likewise, conspiracy theorists saturated the Internet with all sorts of ideas, calling into question the basic events of history and the motives of government leaders. Indeed, Internet conspiracies increasingly centered around such diverse topics as the assassination of John

Figure 12.1: The Electronic Numerical Integrator and Calculator, also known as ENIAC, was among the earliest and most powerful computers in the 1940s. Its calculations helped make possible the hydrogen bomb.

F. Kennedy, the moon landings, the causes of the AIDS and Ebola viruses, and the existence of so-called secret societies alleged to be micromanaging the global economy and world affairs. Before the Internet, people had largely trusted the information they learned from news media and textbooks, but now anyone could claim to be an authoritative source or at least possess some special insight on matters far and wide. Determining which information to place confidence in became a new problem for many Internet readers as the twenty-first century arrived, especially those lacking expertise in the pertinent areas of knowledge under discussion.

In the process, the Internet in some ways reinforced a development known as postmodernism. Emerging in the second half of the twentieth century, postmodernism was the world view according to which there was no single, absolute foundation for truth claims. Significantly, postmodernism differed fundamentally from both traditionalism and modernism on the foundations of truth. While traditionalists had often referenced religious revelation as the fundamental source of truth, the modernists had emphasized sensory experience and science. Yet the postmodernists, unlike both the traditionalists and the modernists, actually denied the existence of any single foundation for absolute truth. To some postmodernists, such as French philosopher Michel Foucault, all foundations of truth contained power structures that privileged certain groups while marginalizing others. Many postmodernists also championed cultural relativism, the idea that each society shapes its own notions of truth and no single standard exists by which to judge the superiority or inferiority of any given society or culture.

The postmodern world view had far-ranging effects on Western society in the late twentieth and early twenty-first centuries. To be sure, cultural relativism influenced the thought of the university-educated masses throughout Europe, the United States, Canada, and Australia. Rather than judge societies according to Western cultural traditions and levels of technological advancement, students were increasingly encouraged to examine societies within their own historical context. Confronting Western biases became an increasingly common feature in the university curriculum, especially given the negative legacies of Western slavery, imperialism, and patriarchy. As a result, a new generation of college students, beginning as early as the 1960s, had begun to view their histories in more critical ways. Such students also increasingly developed a new respect for the cultural achievements of non-Western peoples.

No doubt, with its view of patriarchy as a male power structure, postmodernism partly underpinned the feminist movement that swept the Western world in the second half of the twentieth century. Individuals throughout history had decried male privilege and the marginalization of women. Yet, by the 1960s, the growing notion that political, economic, and social structures in the West had held back the progress of women ushered in a clamor for gender equality. The feminists of this generation drew inspiration from an earlier generation of women who had fought tirelessly to secure the right to vote for the female gender. Women's suffrage, achieved in the United States and in Europe between the 1920s and the 1940s, had allowed women an unprecedented voice in their nation's political affairs.

Significantly, the feminists of the 1960s and 1970s intended to use their new political power to bring about gender equality in the workforce. This new wave of feminism, known as second-wave feminism, had some vocal advocates who labeled men as threats to the flourishing of women. The historical Western ideals of womanhood—that of the mother and housewife—came under attack from the more extreme feminists who argued women had to become man's equal in the workplace to improve the female lot. Others took a more moderate position, arguing women should not abandon their traditional role as mothers but should simultaneously desire professions outside the home to promote women's welfare. Regardless of the language employed, Western society at large increasingly came to believe both women and men deserved an equal opportunity to provide for themselves, and thus equal access to the workplace. Indeed, with a growing discourse on gender equality during the 1970s, women in the West were increasingly expected to obtain a university education and become doctors, lawyers, scientists, engineers, professors, business managers, and entrepreneurs. As it turned out, second-wave feminism proved highly successful in Europe and in the United States in introducing women into the professional classes. By the twenty-first century, more women were obtaining university educations than men were in the United States, and increasingly making their presence felt in the global economy.

A much more controversial feature of second-wave feminism revolved around reproductive issues. In the Catholic nations of Europe, the Roman Catholic Church came under attack from feminists for its restrictions on birth control and abortion. Many women argued that they themselves should have absolute control over their bodies and the state or the church should not have any voice in such matters. This line of argument increasingly took hold in a postmodern environment where the foundations of truth were questioned. In the United States, abortion became legal with the Supreme Court's controversial

Roe v. Wade decision (1973). Some celebrated the development as an advance in women's rights. Others, however, argued the decision legalized the murder of human beings and paved the way for other nations to engage in genocide against the unborn. In many European countries, abortion rights also became legal, despite intense debates on the subject. In the mid-1970s, for example, Austria, France, and Italy legalized the practice, as did the Netherlands in 1980. At the same time, some nations with a strongly Catholic political presence, such as Ireland and Portugal, continued to outlaw abortion throughout the twentieth century, although they also legalized the practice later. As the abortion issue demonstrated, the relativistic thinking promoted by the postmodern world view had led to a renegotiation of social mores. As the twenty-first century began, many people in the United States and Europe were ardent defenders of abortions rights, while large numbers were strongly opposed to what they viewed to be the murder of the innocent. The camps remained as divided as ever.

In addition to second-wave feminism, postmodernism produced the renegotiation of social mores in other areas, such as in art. Traditional styles of artistic expression in the West had adhered to formal rules for centuries. From traditional religious or landscape art to the sophisticated modernist schools of cubism, muralism, romanticism, and surrealism, societies had judged art based on standards, although different kinds depending on time and place. Postmodernism, however, introduced the notion that such rules were mere conventions. What one person viewed as an artistic masterpiece, according to this view, could be seen as something worthy of the trash heap in the eyes of another.

Postmodern art had its roots in the Dadaist movement in Europe in the aftermath of the Great War. The Dadaists, a widely influential group of artists known for their unconventionality, were opposed to the rules and societal features unleashed by modernity. For them, such rules had provoked a war with unprecedented devastation. As such, Dadaists valued art that celebrated anarchy on the canvas and flouted the traditional forms of the craft. Although the Dadaist movement was short-lived, it paved the way for other postmodern artists. For example, one of the early originators of postmodern art during the 1950s was the American painter Jackson Pollock. He created unconventional masterpieces by allowing paint to drip to create random patterns on the canvas; afterward, with his brush, Pollock introduced structure into the sea of randomness.[2] Similarly, Andy Warhol, another American painter who rose to prominence in the 1960s, reflected the postmodern mind-set with his famous painting *Campbell's Soup Cans* (1962). Depicting thirty-two flavors of soup, the painting highlighted the perceived oversaturation in consumer choice that modern society had ushered in. The painting also was captivating in the sense that something so mundane could have artistic value. As the twentieth century wore down, artists increasingly pushed the boundaries of social propriety. For many, art became acclaimed because of its shock value, just as much as the artist's talent.

Postmodern relativism also shaped developments in music, as evidenced by the new genres that developed beginning in the 1960s. Rock 'n' roll music,[3] with its captivating beats and provocative dance styles and lyrics, shocked older generations who commonly decried the music as indecent. Nevertheless, during the 1960s, the pioneering music of such British rock bands as *The Beetles* and *The Rolling Stones* captivated a younger generation much less apt to issue moral judgments (Figure 12.2). The carefree attitude of the

---

2   Robert Brewer, *Postmodernism: What You Should Know and Do About It* (New York: Writer's Showcase, 2002), 48.
3   Stanley J. Grenz, *A Primer on Postmodernism* (Grand Rapids, MI: William B. Eerdmans, 1996), 36.

Figure 12.2: The Beatles, as they arrive in New York City, in 1964.

time, along with the music, produced unpredictable developments as well. Prominent musicians during the 1960s and 1970s became known for their unconventional lifestyles and social criticism. Increasingly, just as in art, music renegotiated the boundaries of social propriety. For many music enthusiasts, the development of psychedelic rock in the 1970s and heavy metal music in the following decade made the early rock music seem quite tame. Although music had dealt with such controversial subjects as crime even during the jazz age, the overt celebration of criminality, drug use, sexual impropriety, and materialism became increasingly common as the century drew to a close, as evidenced by the lyrics often found in rap and hip-hop music beginning in the 1990s. In many ways, with the foundations of truth in question thanks to the growing internalization of the postmodern world view, the celebration of vice became a defining feature in popular music as in other cultural realms.

Indeed, another area in which postmodernism exercised considerable influence was film and television. Although early twentieth-century filmmakers skirted the boundaries of propriety, the mid-century saw the implementation of strict codes of morality in film and television production. This fact was not only true in the United States but also in Europe. The wholesome American sitcoms of the 1950s, such as *Father Knows Best* and *Leave It to Beaver*, provided moral messages to viewers. Significantly, foul language, obscenity, and indecency were largely absent from the airwaves and the theaters of this era. The situation, however, changed over time. By the 1980s and 1990s, television sitcoms and Hollywood films increasingly redefined boundaries of propriety with an ever-growing supply of profanity, obscenity, and violence. Because film producers believed the earlier generation of film and television did not adequately address the shadow side of reality, they peddled various vices on the big screen to attract an audience. At the same time, Americans adhering to traditional moral codes decried the new developments sweeping film and television.

THE WEST IN THE AGE OF GLOBALIZATION

A hallmark of globalization was the increasing economic interconnectedness among nations after the Second World War. Traditionally, nations had implemented measures that hampered foreign trade, such as import fees known as tariffs. Such measures, policymakers believed, eliminated foreign influence in a nation's internal affairs and maximized employment potential for a country's population. For these reasons, tariffs were widely popular among politicians globally during the early twentieth century. Yet, during the Cold War, an influential argument emerged that economic integration without such measures would promote peace among blocs of nations. If nations traded with one another, bonds of solidarity could form, thus promoting the mutual welfare of all. This argument won over many of Europe's leaders. Thus, economic integration occurred among the various democratic and communist blocs, although in stages. For example, Western European nations established the Coal and Steel Community in the late 1950s and later the Common Market, the latter of which abolished tariffs and promoted free trade among member nations. Similarly, the Soviet bloc countries integrated their economies around the same time through the Council for Mutual Economic Assistance (COMECON). When the Cold War ended, new opportunities for broader integration occurred, as policymakers and political leaders increasingly spoke about the possibilities of a new global economy.

Indeed, globalization as a process reached unprecedented levels during the 1990s. With the Cold War over, many triumphalist capitalists in the West proclaimed their economic system had won the great ideological battle and needed to be promoted far and wide on a global scale to enhance the general welfare of the world's citizens. As such, corporations increasingly pushed for new international markets, a development that saw great success with the marginalization of command economies. Indeed, such firms as McDonalds, Coca-Cola, International Business Computers (IBM), and Starbucks all made their presence felt in the major metropolises of East Asia, the Middle East, Latin America, and Eastern Europe during the decade (Figure 12.3). In fact, such corporations became symbols of the new globalization that was taking the world by storm. In the process, major urban areas across the globe increasingly experienced the fruits of Western consumerism, a development that for many almost had an addictive quality about it. In fact, the desire for new technology, gadgets, electronics, fashion, and food seemed almost insatiable.

At the same time, a major element behind the success of the new global economy was a renewed push for free-trade agreements. On the one hand, such agreements made it easier for corporations to set up businesses in foreign lands. After all, the elimination of tariffs and other fees historically associated with international trade provided an enticement for firms to seek markets abroad. On the other hand,

Figure 12.3: The coffee chain, Starbucks, has become a symbol of globalization. This photo is from Seoul, South Korea.

such agreements were believed to benefit consumers in developed countries by allowing access to cheap products made in countries where labor costs were relatively low. The new focus on Western consumerism, epitomized by the inundation of advertisement and marketing during the 1990s, reinforced free-trade advocacy groups that made the case for the internationalization of commerce. As a result, a wide variety of free-trade agreements across the world emerged at the time.

Against this backdrop, the North American Free Trade Agreement (NAFTA) became a prominent development in the new global economy. Enacted in 1993, the agreement created free trade and eliminated tariffs between the three signatory nations: the United States, Canada, and Mexico. Upon implementation, NAFTA generated a fierce debate between supporters and opponents inside the United States. The supporters, including major US corporations, lobbied politicians to support the agreement, claiming American consumers would have access to more goods. Yet opponents, including unions and organized labor, argued the agreement would lead to a massive loss of factory jobs within the United States, as corporations moved their operations to Mexico, where labor costs were significantly lower. In reality, both sides made valid points that turned out to be correct. As the twentieth century came to a close, American consumers did obtain access to more products from Canada and Mexico, and US manufacturing jobs declined as corporations closed factories within the United States and opened new ones in Mexico. By the first decade of the twenty-first century, for example, such major automobile producers as the Ford Motor Company and General Motors had made a strong presence in Mexico, where factory workers earned much less for their labor than their US counterparts.[4]

Indeed, the experience of NAFTA highlighted a new development within the increasingly globalized economy: the decline in the importance of manufacturing among some of the wealthiest nations, such as the United States. During the 1990s, for example, many consumer goods that had been made in the USA were increasingly produced in such nations as China, Japan, Mexico, Indonesia, and Bangladesh. By the twenty-first century, the ubiquitous "Made in China" label found in shops across the land became a symbol of the decline of the United States as a manufacturing power. The symbol also testified to a growing frustrated segment of American blue-collar workers who felt they had been marginalized in the new global economy. After all, many had lost their jobs and faced a cascade of new problems associated with the developments, such as depression, despair, and a loss of self-worth. In response, some workers chose to return to school to obtain a college education in hopes of finding new work that offered better pay. Yet others lost hope in finding work and feared they had been deprived of their ability to support their families. Still, others found new jobs that paid much less than factory work, such as retail and fast-food labor. In the process, for many Americans, globalism developed a negative connotation.

Still, the United States maintained its position as the strongest economy in the world as the twenty-first century dawned. In fact, the service sector of the US economy grew, while manufacturing declined. Thanks to globalization, the emergence of new professions in international banking and financial services stimulated the American economy. Jobs associated with transportation, such as tractor-trailer driving, also remained strong. After all, goods had to be distributed whether they were produced in the United States or abroad. In addition, the aging US population made possible a dramatic expansion of professions in the health-care sector, and the continuing problem with crime enabled new opportunities for service-based

---

4   Bernie Woodall, "Mexico's Auto Production will soon make up more than 25% of the American Market," *Business Insider*, March 25, 2015, available at: http://www.businessinsider.com/r-us-autoworkers-face-threat-as-car-makers-drawn-to-mexico-2015-3.

employment in the criminal justice field. In fact, by the early twenty-first century, the United States had one of the highest incarceration rates among its citizenry among nations globally.

By the 1990s, Europe also experienced dramatic changes in the new global economy, the most significant of which was the formation of the European Union (EU). Building on the growing economic integration among the democratic Western European nations since the 1960s, the establishment of the European Union occurred in 1993 with the Treaty of Maastricht. The six founding members were France, Germany, Italy, the Netherlands, Belgium, and Luxembourg, known as the "Inner Six." During the 1990s, the EU expanded to include all nations in Western Europe with the exception of Switzerland. In some ways, in keeping with the international commercial mind-set of the time, the European Union was aimed at promoting greater degrees of continental trade. To be an EU member, for instance, a country had to agree to conduct free trade with all other members. In addition, by the dawn of the twenty-first century, most EU nations had abolished use of their historical national currencies in favor of a single EU currency known as the euro (Figure 12.4). The euro emerged as a symbol not only of European economic integration but also the union's collective economic prowess, which came to rival the United States in terms of gross domestic product.

In other ways, however, the establishment of the European Union went beyond mere economic integration. Upon its creation, the EU established not only a central bank but also a parliament and a court of justice. In the process, the political institutions in charge of EU governance acquired the authority to implement policies on all member states, such as the abolition of the death penalty. This supranational feature of EU governance became controversial. Indeed, in the twenty-first century, vocal groups of EU opponents decried what they believed to be the erosion of each country's national sovereignty in favor of the EU's supranational government structure. In fact, all European Union-member states had segments within their populations that were critical of their country's participation within the EU. Although there were periodic clamors for secession, no nation since the EU's founding in 1993 elected to part company from the union—until June 2016, when Britain approved a referendum vote to leave the EU. Up to that point, the growing perception among Europeans that they are part of a continental community, rather than simply a nation, produced the renegotiation of individual identity for many. Nationalism, despite its historical appeal, had become much less relevant in the new age of globalism.

Figure 12.4: The euro, which serves as the currency of the European Union (EU), was adopted by most EU members by the early 2000s.

The European Union also faced other challenges. To begin, a flood of Eastern European nations as members in the late 1990s and early 2000s proved a great source of tension. Among others, Poland, Hungary, Romania, and the Czech Republic had experienced more than forty years of communist rule characterized by poor economic performance, an authoritarian system that violated human rights, and rampant corruption. Integrating countries with such histories into the European Union raised questions about EU members' responsibilities for the mutual welfare of one another. In addition, in times of economic turmoil such as the global recession of 2007, the issue was raised again. Some nations such as Greece, Spain, and Ireland experienced severe economic hardships, while countries with stronger economies such as Germany were forced to bail out the weaker nations.

ANTI-GLOBALIZATION

A combination of various factors produced a strong reaction to the cascade of changes affecting the globe at the turn of the twenty-first century. The economic effects of globalization, for example, produced an anti-Western discourse among peoples in the developing world. Also, the cultural relativist outlook associated with postmodernism undermined Western credibility in the minds of many global citizens. As anti-Western sentiment grew around the world during the late 1990s and early 2000s, a variety of responses ensued. Some individuals peacefully protested what they believed to be new problems associated with the developments, such as economic exploitation of poor countries through the financial institutions associated with globalization. Yet others engaged in a violent reaction to the new order in international affairs. Thus, new crises such as the rise of Islamist terrorism arose.

By the turn of the twenty-first century, large segments of people across the globe bemoaned the effects of globalization, claiming the new global economy benefited the rich developed nations and perpetuated the cycle of poverty in the underdeveloped world. The creation of the World Trade Organization (WTO) in 1995 helped produce such discourse. As an international body aimed at the promotion of free trade, the WTO's policies were criticized for increasing global economic disparity between rich and poor nations. The commerce sponsored by the WTO largely consisted in loans and expensive technological products flowing from the wealthy countries to the poorer nations, with the poor nations supplying mainly cheap raw materials, agricultural products, and resources to the wealthier countries. As it turned out, raw materials and agricultural products were of significantly less economic value compared to other classes of exports. Thus, with a few exceptions such as the oil-rich Middle East, most of the exports of raw materials and foodstuffs from Asia, Africa, and Latin America did not enable the economies in those places to thrive. Rather, the real money generators were in the financial service sectors and sophisticated technological exports, domains in which the United States, Europe, and Japan dominated. Indeed, throughout swaths of Latin America, Asia, and Africa, a growing discontent with the global economy developed in the last decade of the twentieth century. The idea that the Western nations, the old imperial powers, were continuing to exploit the underdeveloped world for its raw materials did not die down in the new global economy but rather remained constant.

Additionally, by the 1990s, a small but vocal movement within the West also protested the institutions associated with globalism, such as the World Bank, World Trade Organization, and the International

Monetary Fund. Globally conscious Westerners also increasingly decried the unjust effects of international commerce on the developing world and targeted corporations that had profited heavily while paying their workers a low wage. Throughout Europe, the US corporation McDonalds often felt the brunt of such ire. Joseph Bove, a French farmer, led a protest in 1999 against the restaurant chain when it tried to establish a franchise in a rural town in southern France. His action, along with other protesters, swept France by storm, bringing attention to the harmful effects of multinational corporations on local business communities.

In the eyes of many, another issue was the use of Western military power to undergird the new global economy. This development seemed especially pertinent in the outcome of the Persian Gulf War (1990–1991). In August 1990, the nation of Iraq, led by Saddam Hussein, invaded and annexed the neighboring country of Kuwait, accusing the small oil-rich nation of stealing petroleum from within Iraq's national borders. The Iraqi invasion and annexation of Kuwait resulted in an international crisis, as the world's largest oil exporter, the Saudis, feared Hussein's forces would attack them next. After all, the Kuwaiti royal family had fled to Saudi Arabia, and Iraq launched Scud missile attacks on the kingdom. In response, given the indispensability of oil to the global economy, a coalition of more than thirty nations led by the United States became involved in the conflict. The coalition had some local support from such Middle Eastern nations as Saudi Arabia, Syria, Egypt, and Qatar. In addition, major European powers including the United Kingdom, France, and Italy also joined in. In the end, the United States-led coalition decisively defeated Iraq, liberated Kuwait, and kept oil-rich Saudi Arabia safe from an Iraqi invasion. In the process, the global oil supply remained protected, a feature that prompted many war critics, regardless of the fairness of such criticism, to argue Western intervention was largely aimed at safeguarding the economic power of wealthy states.

Another major globalization issue concerned whether the phenomenon was a force for international peace or conflict. Many observers in the 1990s believed globalization would actually lead to a world with considerably less conflict, violence, and wars. It seemed self-evident to some that, as nations interacted more with one another through economic integration and the exchange of ideas, bonds of solidarity between peoples with different traditions from around the world would emerge. Put another way, by breaking down the divisions between peoples, globalization would serve as a force for unity. Indeed, with growing talk of a global community at the time, increasingly some of the more optimistic individuals even envisioned a world without violence.

Yet not all experts held such a positive outlook. Some observers, such as political scientist Samuel Huntington, argued that globalization would lead to cultural polarization and potentially greater levels of conflict. As global citizens interacted more economically, he argued, cultural differences nevertheless would remain.[5] In fact, Huntington envisioned not a united world but a globe increasingly split into groups he called civilizations, which shared a common religio-cultural identity. Huntington laid out the various civilizations, including Western civilization (consisting of Europe, the United States, Canada, and Australia), the Eastern world (consisting of nation-based civilizations corresponding to such countries as Japan, China, and India), the Muslim world (consisting of the Middle East, Northern Africa, and South

---

5   See Samuel Huntington, The *Clash of Civilizations and the Remaking of World Order* (New York: Simon & Schuster, 1998).

Asia), the sub-Saharan civilization in Africa, a Latin American civilization, and the Orthodox world (made up of Russia and Eastern European nations; Figure 12.5).

Notwithstanding the ultimate verdict of Huntington's thesis, by the twenty-first century, conflict between the various civilizations indeed seemed as intense as ever. In fact, the global hot spots of tension and violence tended to be the regions where civilizations came into contact with one another. A strong example was growing illegal immigration in the United States. The border between the USA and Mexico, an area that in Huntington's typology split Western civilization from the Latin American world, became an intense focal point of conflict. Some American politicians, highlighting the loss of jobs for US workers to such immigrants, argued for the construction of a wall to keep out undocumented laborers from Mexico and Central America, while others argued such labor was needed to stimulate the US economy. Similarly, the border between Pakistan and India, an area that separated Hindu civilization from the Muslim world, was rife with strife as the twenty-first century began, with the two nations engaged in skirmishes over control of the disputed Kashmir region. In addition, a bloody civil war in Sudan, a nation divided between the Muslim world and sub-Saharan camps, highlighted the growing religious tensions enveloping Africa. The civil war in Sudan saw religious-based violence between Muslims and Christians. Lastly, a new conflict between Russia and Western Europe over control of the former Soviet-dominated nations in Eastern Europe emerged, best seen in Russia's conflict with Ukraine over the Crimean Peninsula. In 2014, Russia annexed a part of the Ukraine with a sizable ethnic-Russian population. In response, Western Europe and the United States instituted economic sanctions against Moscow, a development that rekindled the old tensions of the Cold War.

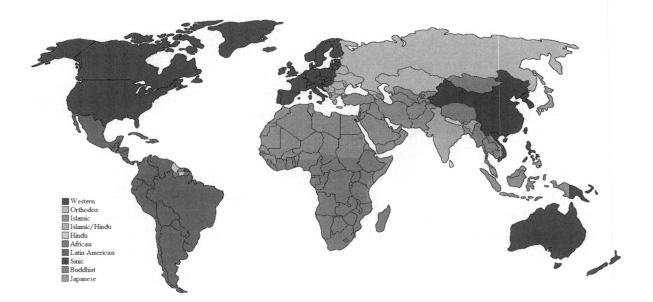

Western
Orthodox
Islamic
Islamic/Hindu
Hindu
African
Latin American
Sinic
Buddhist
Japanese

Figure 12.5: Major world civilizations in Huntington's typology.
Many of the global hot spots since the 1990s have been the areas where the civilizations touch each other.

THE RISE OF ISLAMIST TERRORISM

In the 1990s, the Muslim-dominated parts of the world experienced many internal contradictions and problems that would later pave the way for a major global problem in the twenty-first century: the rise of Islamist terrorism. On the one hand, the Middle East since the 1970s had generated massive amounts of wealth thanks to robust oil exports. At the same time, wealth disparity and unemployment remained a problem in the region, especially among the increasingly young population. To complicate matters, unlike in the democratic West, the strong authoritarian political structure common in Muslim nations stymied the liberalization of individual rights, as shown in the general lack of suffrage, due process, and equality under the law. Many of the Muslim-dominated nations, such as Saudi Arabia and Afghanistan, did not allow religious liberty and expressly outlawed Christian missionary activities. Compared with the West, women in the Middle East and other Muslim-dominated areas also remained politically, socially, and economically marginalized. Thus, in several glaring ways, Western civilization increasingly stood in stark contrast with the Muslim world.

As the twentieth century drew to a close, some segments in Muslim-dominated countries sought reform of their societies along Western lines. For example, a growing number of gender-rights groups in the Middle East sought equal protection under the law for women, greater female participation in profes-sional employment, and the relaxation of restrictions on dress. Likewise, a budding movement backing freedom of speech and the press emerged within such conservative countries as Iran and Saudi Arabia. Some of the more liberal Middle Eastern nation such as Qatar and the United Arab Emirates made huge progress in these areas. Yet clamors for reform fell on deaf ears in many of the conservative states.

In fact, in response to clamors for reform along Western lines, a strong countermovement against reform ensued simultaneously in many places. Conservative Muslim clerics, who tended to wield con-siderable political power, used their voices to champion a traditional Islamic approach to statecraft. In religious schools known as *madrassas*, radical clerics taught schoolchildren in such places as Pakistan and Afghanistan that the problems in their societies resulted not from a failure to adopt Western practices but rather a failure to structure statecraft in accordance with a proper interpretation of Islam. Rather than focusing on the notion of progress—a key development of modern Western civilization since the Enlightenment—radical Muslim clerics looked to the distant past for answers: to the time of Muhammad and the writing of the Koran. In the process, they sought seventh-century solutions to address twentieth-century problems. In Afghanistan during the 1990s, the ultraconservative Taliban regime removed girls from the classroom, outlawed non-Muslim religious expression, and implemented a harsh interpretation of sharia law that saw physical punishment and the death penalty doled out for an increasing number of offenses. This increasing radicalization of Muslims no doubt played an instrumental role in setting the stage for future acts of Islamist terrorism.

As it turned out, the phenomenon of Islamist terrorism took root among extremist Muslims with strong anti-Western sentiment. A variety of perceptions about the West, whether fair or not, contributed to this development. To begin, Western support of Israel drew the ire of large segments of Middle Easterners who believed, regardless of the fairness of such criticism, the Palestinians had been unjustly dispossessed of their homeland. In addition, some Muslims decried what they believed to be postmodern excesses associated with Western culture. As the United States exported its culture abroad—including obscene Hollywood films and music with violent and sexualized lyrics—many fervent Muslims judged Western civilization as increasingly ungodly. In fact, for the more radical Muslims, the United States was more and more labeled the "Great Satan." In their view, Western civilization was not something to be emulated, but rather fought against. The perceived exploitative nature of American and European foreign policy, along with Western military intervention in the Middle East, only intensified such sentiment.

In fact, by the 1990s, some Islamists were vocally calling for jihad, or holy war, against Western civilization. The championing of violence to bring about the expansion of Islamic society emboldened some young Muslim radicals to take violent actions. Significantly, some even believed their death in jihad would not only bring about the expansion of their ideological world view but also lead to rewards in a paradisiacal afterlife. Accordingly, groups of radical Muslims began to engage in violent acts to further their aims. Because civilians were often the targets, the word "terrorism" increasingly became used to describe their actions. Suicide-bombing attacks with improvised explosives, for example, became increasingly common by the mid-1990s, with major urban centers in Israel experiencing several such incidents. Some pro-Palestinian elements even hailed the perpetrators of such acts of murder as martyrs for the cause of Islam, although many moderate Muslims condemned such violence as un-Islamic.

Amid the rising tide of Islamist violence in the 1990s emerged a terrorist organization that would go down in infamy for its targeting of Westerners: al-Qaeda. Known in Arabic as "the base," al-Qaeda was formed and financed by the wealthy Saudi extremist Osama bin Laden. Educated in England, bin Laden became disaffected with Western culture during his years studying abroad. In fact, in the 1980s, he had left the university altogether to fight with the Mujahidin in Afghanistan against the Soviets. At the time, the Mujahidin were engaged in jihad against the Soviet-backed puppet leaders of Afghanistan, who had introduced an increasingly secular culture within the nation. While in Afghanistan, bin Laden formed ties with Islamic militants, who with the covert assistance of the CIA drove the Soviets out of the country by the end of the decade. After the Soviet withdrawal in 1989, bin Laden returned to Saudi Arabia around the time of the Gulf War. Incensed by the presence of American troops in his birth country, bin Laden vowed to attack the United States. Amid this backdrop, he returned to Afghanistan, where he founded al-Qaeda, which he claimed would serve as the base for jihad against the West. In Afghanistan, thanks to his wealth, bin Laden recruited young Islamic militants with little hope of meaningful employment to become fighters for al-Qaeda. The nation's ultraconservative Taliban regime gave tacit approval to bin Laden's actions. Thus, by the mid-1990s, al-Qaeda had evolved into perhaps the world's largest Islamist terrorist organization. Significantly, al-Qaeda fighters first came to prominence in the Yugoslav Wars of the mid-1990s, helping the Muslim Kosovars fight for independence from Albania. Yet al-Qaeda turned its focus on the United States soon thereafter, as evidenced by the 1998 US embassy bombings in Africa.

By 1998, al-Qaeda had established a network within the Muslim-dominated North African country of Sudan. In August of that year, in the first direct assault on US interests, this network carried out truck-bomb attacks on US embassies in Nairobi, Kenya, and Dar es Salaam, Tanzania. In the attacks, more than two hundred people were killed directly, while thousands more were injured. Al-Qaeda justified its attacks by claiming the United States had arrested a group of Islamist fighters in Albania with ties to the terrorist organization. The devastating embassy attacks, which caused a cloud of fear to envelop Africa and

Washington, DC, caught the United States and its leadership off-guard. Once intelligence agencies within the United States determined al-Qaeda had ordered the attacks, Osama bin Laden was for the first time placed on the country's top fugitive list.

In addition, the American president at the time, Bill Clinton, vowed to hunt down bin Laden and destroy the terrorist network around the globe, whether in Afghanistan, the Middle East, or Africa. Accordingly, Clinton ordered a response known as Operation Infinite Reach, which consisted of a series of cruise missile strikes on al-Qaeda's infrastructure within Afghanistan and the Sudan. Although the strikes were partly successful in terms of infrastructural damage to the terror organization, only a handful of terrorists died as a result. In the aftermath, bin Laden and al-Qaeda were able to use the US strikes on Muslim soil as a rallying cry to recruit more terrorists. The American strikes in Sudan, which destroyed a pharmaceutical plant believed to be aiding the terrorist organization, featured prominently in al-Qaeda's propaganda against Washington at the time. Embroiled in an impeachment crisis the next year, Clinton largely ignored or was unaware of the strengthening of al-Qaeda and took no further decisive action to combat the budding terrorist movement.

Unexpectedly, the lack of US resolve to deal decisively with bin Laden and his movement produced new targets and more attacks. In October 2000, for example, al-Qaeda launched an assault on the American naval destroyer the *USS Cole*. While the ship was refueling in the port city of Aden, Yemen, suicide bombers in a small boat pulled up near the destroyer and set off explosives that blew a massive hole in the ship, killing seventeen sailors and injuring nearly forty others. In response, the Clinton administration took no new action against al-Qaeda. The attack, which occurred weeks before the new US presidential election, instead was slated for investigation. In the process, the incoming administration of US President George W. Bush was faced with the task of determining what course of action to pursue.

Emboldened by America's lack of action in response to the *USS Cole* bombing, al-Qaeda soon staged an attack on American soil for the first time: the September 11, 2001, attacks on the World Trade Center buildings, the Pentagon, and other high-profile targets. At Osama bin Laden's urging, nineteen al-Qaeda terrorists from Saudi Arabia boarded four planes on the morning of September 11 at JFK International Airport in New York City. When the planes were in flight, the terrorists took out box cutters and grabbed hostages. Having received flight training in the United States, the terrorists then made their way into each airplane's cockpit and assumed control of each plane. The world was shocked over what occurred next. As it turned out, three of the planes hit their targets, striking both of the World Trade Center's twin towers in New York City and the Pentagon in Washington, DC (Figure 12.6). The news media in the United States covered the events, and Americans across the nation watched in horror as the twin towers collapsed minutes after being struck by the airplanes. A fourth hijacked plane went down in a field in Pennsylvania, when a horde of passengers fought back. Later, observers speculated this plane's target had been the US Capitol or even the White House. In the aftermath of what came to be known as the 9/11 attacks, about three thousand people were dead. The event marked the single highest death toll associated with an act of terrorism in American history.

For many Americans, 9/11 revealed the real danger of Islamist terrorism for the first time. The size of the death toll meant thousands of families were affected directly. Schoolchildren on that day returned home to learn later they had lost a parent, just as husbands and wives learned that they had lost a spouse,

Figure 12.6: The collapse of the north tower, World Trade Center, September 11, 2001.

and parents discovered they had lost sons and daughters. The terrorist events in Africa and the Middle East before had seemed a world away, but the homeland fell victim on that infamous September day. The American pubic rallied around one another in the aftermath. Republicans and Democrats came together in a rare show of solidarity and resolve for justice, in addition to remembering the victims. Church attendance grew, as Americans turned to God for hope and guidance in their time of despair and desperation.

In the aftermath, President Bush vowed for justice, declaring a global war on terror. Within weeks of the attacks, the Bush administration demanded the Taliban government in Afghanistan hand over bin Laden, but the Taliban refused American demands. Consequently, over the next month, the United States formed an international coalition to remove the Taliban from power, root out al-Qaeda's network in Afghanistan, and capture bin Laden. A month after the 9/11 attacks, the Bush administration began overt military actions in the country. The military engagement, known as Operation Enduring Freedom, and which saw robust American air power and ground support in Afghanistan, proved successful. The air campaign took out strategic defenses of the Taliban regime, forcing the government to abandon the capital city of Kabul by November and flee into peripheral areas of the country. In the meantime, the United States aided Afghan anti-Taliban groups such as the Northern Alliance in a concerted effort to find bin Laden and engage al-Qaeda and Taliban forces in armed combat.

Although many Americans in late 2001 were optimistic of bin Laden's imminent capture, such hope proved elusive. Afghanistan's mountainous terrain produced challenges in hunting down the enemy. Many Taliban and al-Qaeda fighters escaped to the caves and hills of the Tora Bora region, which bordered Pakistan. The terrorists knew the terrain well, having used the area to hide during the decade-long war with the Soviets in the 1980s. Although American forces and their allies pursued al-Qaeda, bin Laden escaped Afghanistan, where he hid in a secret compound in Pakistan. Despite some close encounters, it was not until May 2011 that American special forces tracked down bin Laden and killed him. In the decade before his being brought to justice, bin Laden still directed al-Qaeda, popping up periodically in video recordings that urged Muslims to join his cause and make war on the West. Even after bin Laden's death, al-Qaeda and its sympathizers remained a prominent force within Afghanistan and Pakistan. The increasingly radical Islamist segments of the Pakistani population hailed bin Laden as a martyr after his death. Some vendors in the extremist pockets of the nation even sold memorabilia associated with the dead terrorist, such as T-shirts emblazoned with his face and collections of Islamist literature attributed to him. It was therefore increasingly clear the fate of al-Qaeda's founder had not deterred the spread of his violent ideology.

At the same time, the Bush administration in the early years of the war on terror looked at new targets in the global war on terror, including Saddam Hussein's Iraq. A longtime violator of human rights, Hussein had ordered chemical attacks with nerve gas on his country's dissident Kurdish population in the north during the 1980s. After his defeat in the Persian Gulf War in the early 1990s, Hussein had also become a vocal critic of the United States and the West. In addition, the Iraqi dictator frequently threatened to wipe Israel off the map, stirring up anti-Israeli sentiment. Most troublesome, however, was that the Bush administration feared Hussein was not only promoting terrorism but also building weapons of mass destruction (WMDs). By 2003, the fear of Iraq creating nuclear weapons had become a major concern of American policymakers, as reports emerged that Hussein's government was enriching uranium.

Accordingly, the Bush administration sought to eliminate the perceived threat through the controversial use of preemptive action. Essentially, the US government planned to take out Hussein before he was in a position to harm American interests. Although Bush courted nations across the globe to form a coalition to remove Hussein, many nations questioned the wisdom of such a move. Some believed the Bush administration was improperly conflating his nation's hostilities involving Iraq's government with the legitimate global war on terror. Others argued that while Hussein had engaged in gross human-rights violations, he had otherwise kept the nation of Iraq together since the 1970s, in part through his cult of personality. If a strong leader such as Hussein were removed, according to this line of reasoning, the nation could experience unprecedented levels of political instability and civil strife, as the various ethno-religious factions throughout the country jockeyed for power in establishing a post-Hussein government.

Given the trepidation around the world to wage war in Iraq, the Bush administration in March 2003 largely initiated military action with few allies. Although the British, Australians, and Poles became part of what Bush called the "coalition of the willing," the United States bore the brunt of the fighting, which succeeded in toppling Hussein's regime within months. Yet an exit strategy out of Iraq proved elusive, despite the removal from power of the country's longtime dictator. At the same time, American soldiers in Iraq faced pockets of new resistance from a variety of factions. Iran stirred up religious tension in the nation, pitting the country's Shi'ite Muslim majority against the Sunni minority. Additionally, the Kurds in the north fought for self-autonomy. To complicate matters, American forces never found conclusive evidence Hussein was in fact developing weapons of mass destruction, a development that undermined the credibility of the Bush administration in some parts of the developed world and in the Middle East. People increasingly believed the United States had been led into a war under false pretenses. Meanwhile, Iraq became such a hotbed of sectarian conflict that the Bush administration in the mid-2000s requested a surge in terms of soldiers deployed to the nation. This move led to a growing movement of protesters within the United States who sought to end the war immediately, seeing no hope for a peaceful outcome in Iraq (Figure 12.7).

Figure 12.7: Montage of images relating to US military actions in Iraq, mid-2000s.

With all this occurring, a US presidential candidate named Barack Obama, in 2007, won over large segments of Americans who had increasingly become disenchanted with the war. For many Americans, US military actions in Iraq had devolved into a campaign to hold Iraq's weak coalition government in power, despite increasing segments of resistance breaking out throughout that nation. Strongly vowing to bring American soldiers home if elected, Obama swept the nation by storm, becoming the country's first African American president in 2008. Although he initially did not immediately withdraw troops from Iraq out of fears of introducing political instability into the nation, Obama increasingly reduced the presence of American troops in the country. Judging American military action successful in Iraq, Obama declared the American mission in the country complete and withdrew US troops in December 2011.

Yet the American withdrawal produced unanticipated consequences, as the rise of a new terror organization known as ISIS (also known as Islamic State) demonstrated. ISIS emerged as an Islamist movement in eastern Syria amid the civil war that swept that nation in 2013. The Syrian government, led by Bashar al-Assad, was known for its gross human-rights violations, and many Syrians wanted a change in government. Although different factions emerged amid the civil strife, ISIS attracted a large following among disaffected young men who embraced an ultraradical interpretation of Islam. ISIS leaders desired the restoration of an Islamic caliphate, similar to those that existed in the religion's early centuries of expansion. Led by a self-proclaimed caliph named Mohammad al-Baghdadi, ISIS sought to establish a state governed in accordance with sharia law. This vision included the doling out of harsh punishments to individuals who failed to live in strict accordance with the regime's precepts, including the stoning of adulterers, homosexuals, and apostates, and the violent flogging of offenders convicted of numerous offenses such as immodesty. ISIS recruits, who were strongly opposed to all peoples and ideas in opposition to their vision, proclaimed theirs was the purest form of Islam and that all others were heretical. By the spring of 2013, ISIS had established not only a strong presence in Syria but had actually set up a state that included swaths of northern Iraq. The movement largely caught international observers by storm. Against ISIS's growing presence in Iraq, the Obama administration faced new criticism it had abandoned the Middle East to an unconscionable fate. Indeed, when asked about ISIS's growth early on, in 2013, Obama initially dismissed the significance of the movement, labeling it "JV" or a junior varsity-level threat.[6]

By the summer of 2013, however, a change of perception ensued among US leadership regarding the threat potential of ISIS. At the time, ISIS had increasingly conquered swaths of Iraq, including such prominent urban areas as Mosul (Iraq's second-largest city) and Tikrit. The Iraqi army, which had been trained by American forces, showed little resolve in engaging ISIS directly in armed combat, with some soldiers actually switching sides to the terror state instead. Also, ISIS increasingly portrayed itself as a legitimate nation-state, setting up courts, financial centers, and other institutions of government.

To complicate matters, Islamic State increasingly shocked the world with its barbaric propaganda, the likes of which the world had never seen. Indeed, videos of the beheadings of Western hostages in orange jumpsuits began popping up throughout 2014. As time went on, ISIS expanded its depravity with new acts of barbarism. For example, ISIS horrified the world in the fall of 2015 with the burning alive of a captured

---

6   Shreeya Sinha, "Obama's Evolution on ISIS," *New York Times*, July 9, 2015, available at: http://www.nytimes.com/interactive/2015/06/09/world/middleeast/obama-isis-strategy.html?_r=0.

Jordanian pilot. This event was followed by videos of the intentional drowning of captives locked in a cage and submerged in a pool. Significantly, many of the victims were religious minorities, such as Arab Christians and Yazidis. Although depravity had always existed in the history of humankind, rarely had an organized movement openly paraded depravity to the same degree as Islamic State. In fact, even fellow Islamist terror organizations such as al-Qaeda became critical of ISIS, claiming such barbarism would ultimately hurt the Islamist cause. Yet psychological warfare remained a hallmark of ISIS's approach to terrorism.

As ISIS increasingly made its presence felt in Syria and Iraq, the United States and other global powers were forced to take action. Many US critics openly blamed Obama for failing to deal decisively with the movement in its nascent development. Indeed, by 2015, the Obama administration's perceived indecisive-ness still remained a major hurdle of US foreign policy for many critics. Rather than deploy American ground troops to the region, the US response since summer 2013 has largely consisted of air strikes on ISIS infrastructure and military positions. At the same time, the United States has encouraged the world to share the burden in a global fight against Islamic State. The United States provided military support to the Kurdish Peshmerga army, which made some progress against ISIS in the northern parts of Iraq. Russia also began an air campaign against ISIS in the autumn of 2015, targeting the terror state's oil-production facilities. From Moscow's perspective, cutting off ISIS's source of income became an essential pillar in destabilizing the rogue state's power. Nevertheless, by 2016, ISIS still remained in control of large areas in Syria and Iraq, including some major urban areas.

Significantly, ISIS over time expanded its range of operations outside the Middle East. In Libya, a variety of Islamist terrorists even pledged loyalty to Islamic State, vowing to establish a new province. In the process, violence against Egyptian Christian migrants became a major problem in that politically unstable nation. Adding to this issue has been ISIS's success in obtaining radical Islamist recruits from the West. In Europe, where the Muslim population has been increasing since the 1970s, hundreds of second-generation European Muslims who were radicalized have journeyed to Syria and Iraq to fight with ISIS. Islamic State has effectively used social media, including blogs, Twitter, and Facebook pages, etc., to attract recruits. Just as alarming, the growth of ISIS-affiliated terror networks in Europe have become increasingly disconcerting. In 2015, for example, a terror cell led coordinated attacks on citizens in Paris, a development that produced later attacks, such as the airport bombing in Brussels in the spring of 2016. Such attacks resulted in the murder of hundreds of innocent civilians.

At the same time, Islamist terrorism increasingly became a global problem in the twenty-first century, as Africa shows. In Somalia, a terrorist group known as Al-Shabaab wielded considerable power and influence in the impoverished nation. Armed with automatic rifles, Al-Shabaab produced a wave of fear throughout the country, introducing sharia law and perpetrating atrocities on the population. For the crime of stealing, for example, alleged offenders often had their hands cut off. The stonings, whippings, and other violent forms of punishment associated with radical implementation of sharia also became prominent occurrences. Al-Shabaab even recruited second-generation Somalis within the United States to their cause, with several instances of such Somali Americans journeying to the African nation to fight for the terrorists in the mid-2000s. Additionally, Al-Shabaab's rise to prominence led to copycat terrorist organizations, which committed acts of violence in neighboring Ethiopia. As a nation whose population is split roughly equally among Christians and Muslims, Ethiopia faced growing religious tension, with the Islamists perpetrating individual acts of violence in a struggle for the religious future of the country.

Yet the most glaring example of Islamist terrorism in Africa in the twenty-first century was the rise of Boko Haram in Nigeria, another nation with a large Christian and Muslim presence. Boko Haram, which emerged as the deadliest terror organization by 2015, had its origins in 2002, with the spread of the radical ideas of the organization's founder, Muhammed Yusuf. A radical Sunni cleric, Yusuf, in the first decade of the twenty-first century, used his prominent television presence in the nation to demonize the country's Christians, promote jihad against the West, and demand the establishment of sharia law in Nigeria. By 2009, Yusuf had a huge following among radical youth who carried out suicide bombings on high-profile targets. Over time, Boko Haram developed a reputation for its barbaric kidnappings and enslavement of Christian schoolchildren, as well as its murderous attacks on Nigerian Catholics. Large swaths of the country's population had become victims of the terrorist organization by 2015, with many displaced from their homes as sectarian violence swept Nigeria. The growing Boko Haram movement, which pledged allegiance to ISIS in 2015, also developed affiliates in Chad, Cameron, and Niger. In the process, the problem of Islamist terror grew immensely in western Africa, a region with already a long history of violence.

Islamist thought also increasingly affected Asia in the twenty-first century. The Philippines, long a bastion of Catholic Christianity, experienced the rise of the Muslim terrorist organization known as Abu Sayyaf. Like the other Islamist terrorist movements sweeping the world, Abu Sayyaf sought to establish a radical interpretation of Islam in the island country. With its actions largely confined to a few islands among the hundreds that make up the Philippines, Abu Sayyaf nevertheless developed a reputation for kidnapping Westerners, along with suicide bombings and the beheadings of captives. Although initiating military action to reduce Abu Sayyaf's presence, the official government of the Philippines has had limited success. Part of the reason for the lack of decisive action owes to the growth of Islamist ideology in Southeast Asia, especially in such places as Indonesia and Malaysia. With the world's largest Muslim population, Indonesia has felt growing internal pressures to implement sharia law, a development that has taken place in some of the nation's many islands. Like in the Philippines, Western tourists have also been targeted by Muslim extremists in Indonesia, as shown by a series of bombings in Borneo in the first decade of the twenty-first century.

As these examples show, the Muslim world in the twenty-first century has been plagued by the problem of Islamist extremism and terrorism. Of course, in many Islamic parts of the world, large segments of Muslims have embraced a moderate course in the practice of their faith. Such Muslims argue theirs is a peaceful religion and that the extremists do not reflect their personal outlook. Some moderate Muslims have also encouraged interreligious dialogue and openly condemned the extremist acts they say denigrate their religion. In addition, many moderate Muslims quietly abhor the terrorism done in the name of their religion, but fear reprisals if they speak out too strongly and offend religious or political leaders. Thus, many moderates are in a delicate situation, depending on the nation in which they live. To be sure, if Islamist violence continues to grow, it is set to remain a major issue in global affairs as the twenty-first century unfolds.

CHRISTIANITY IN THE LATE TWENTIETH AND EARLY TWENTY-FIRST CENTURIES

In the twenty-first century, religious beliefs have played an instrumental role in galvanizing people to action. Christianity, for two millennia, has been a cornerstone of Western civilization, and it remained the religion with the most adherents worldwide as the new century dawned. Although postmodernism and a variety of other factors contributed to growing secularism in Europe in the twentieth century, in many places throughout the world the religion founded by the followers of Jesus Christ two thousand years ago experienced a renaissance.

A region that has experienced a Christian renaissance, for example, is the former communist bloc of Russia and Eastern Europe. After living through decades of persecution under officially atheist regimes, the region's Christians in the early 1990s obtained the right to freely exercise their religious expression after the fall of communism. Having seen firsthand the moral failures of the authoritarian regimes they had lived under, Eastern Europeans increasingly turned to their Christian religious heritage in hopes of cultivating a brighter future for themselves and their loved ones. In the process, Eastern Orthodoxy and Catholicism grew in terms of power and influence in the region's affairs. In Russia, church attendance increased as the twenty-first century dawned, as did the number of citizens identifying as Christian. The Russian Orthodox Church also rose to a place of national prominence that it lacked during seventy years of communist rule, and new churches popped up throughout Russia (Figure 12.8). Similarly, in Romania, religious fervor swept the nation, so much that it had one of the highest rates of Christian believers in all of Europe. The Romanian Orthodox Church played a crucial role in uniting the country's inhabitants after the fall of communism. In Poland, despite decades of marginalization as well, Catholicism also returned to a new place of prominence in the life of believers, a fact made possible by Pope John Paul II's Polish identity. At the same time, other places such as the Czech Republic largely remained secular, a development that signaled continuity from the Cold War era.

In strongly Catholic Latin America, Christian identity remained strong as well with the advent of the twenty-first century. The preceding century had seen believers in the region experience numerous trials. In Mexico in the 1920s, for example, Catholics faced persecution during the reign of atheist President Plutarco Calles. In fact, tens of thousands of believers lost their lives in a war against Calles's government, known as the Cristero War. Yet later presidents of the nation tended to promote the Catholic Church's interests. Although violent crime became rampant in the region as the century closed due to narco-trafficking, many religious believers increasingly turned to their faith for strength in dealing with life's trials. In the process, the Catholic Church's influence remained strong for those seeking the Christian message of hope.

Nevertheless, new forces did challenge Catholicism's dominance in the region over time. As far back as the 1970s and 1980s, a theological innovation known as liberation theology became prominent in the region. Liberation theologians stressed Christ's solidarity with the poor and the oppressed, and criticized the Catholic Church for not doing enough to alleviate suffering. Yet liberation theology also faced criticism, as some of its most vocal advocates called for the use of violence and force to promote land reform and other issues. Still, liberation theology produced a valuable dialogue in the eyes of many Christians

Figure 12.8: The construction of Orthodox churches such as this one in Moscow, Russia, increased dramatically after the fall of the Soviet Union in 1991.

in the area, with its renewed call for caring for the unfortunate. In response, the Catholic Church in the region increasingly addressed issues of social injustice. More recently, thanks to the actions of Protestant missionaries, non-Catholic forms of Christianity have also been gaining ground in the region. With its charismatic worship style, including speaking in tongues and faith healing, Pentecostalism especially obtained a strong presence as the twenty-first century began. This type of Protestantism has grown among Christians who feel burdened by the rituals of Catholicism and seek what they believe is a truer, Bible-based form of the faith. Pentecostalism has made huge inroads in Brazil, Guatemala, Mexico, and other places. If present trends continue, there could be more Pentecostals in Brazil than Catholics by the close of the century.

Yet the region of the world that saw the greatest rise in Christianity has been sub-Saharan Africa. Although the faith within this area grew in the period of European imperialism in the late nineteenth century, not until decolonization in the 1960s did the number of Christians begin rising dramatically. Indeed, a robust missionary movement in the second half of the twentieth century effectively spread the faith thanks to advances in intercontinental transportation. More than any other development, the advent of commercial airlines allowed waves of American and European Christian missionaries to visit the region by the 1960s. In the process, missionaries forged bonds of solidarity with the peoples they encountered. Missionaries not only spread the Gospel but also engaged in widespread humanitarian work, including the establishment of schools, hospitals, and clinics, and the construction of wells for drinking water and sewage disposal systems to combat disease outbreaks. Such humanitarian work helped reinforce the spread of Christianity, as Africans saw the good deeds of the religion's followers put into practice. As a result, the late twentieth century saw the faith grow rapidly in southern Africa. Indeed, by the early twenty-first century, Zaire, Uganda, Botswana, South Africa, Angola, Kenya, Zambia, and South Africa all had Christian majorities. In fact, the Christian population in such places was higher than in many parts of Western Europe (Figure 12.9).

Still, other regions of the world, especially Asia, saw tremendous challenges in terms of Christian missionary work. Not only did the rise of Islamist terrorism problematize such efforts, but many non-Muslim-dominated nations implemented various anti-Christian initiatives. In communist China, for example, Christians remained a persecuted minority whose public practice of their faith remained curtailed. The exact number of Christians in the world's most populous nation remains unknown. Nevertheless, a robust movement involving house churches gained momentum in the nation by the early twenty-first century. In many ways, these Chinese Christians' courage resembled that of the earliest generations of Christians. After all, the first Christians faced severe persecution within the Roman Empire, but effectively made use of house churches to keep their faith alive. In India, despite having a constitution that allows religious freedom, Hindu nationalism has also made it difficult for Christian missionaries to spread the Gospel. In other places, the situation is much direr. In North Korea, for example, the missionaries who have endeavored to spread Christianity have faced imprisonment, hard labor in work camps, and even execution.

Significantly, Western Europe, long the bastion of European Christendom, saw at the advent of the twenty-first century increasing secularism and a decline in Christian religiosity among its population. One reason for this change was the legacy of left wing, atheistic Marxist thought. Although the Western European nations were never communist, the ideas were widely discussed in the region's major universities. In addition, the postmodern world view, with its attack on the foundations of truth, in part explained this development. Furthermore, with their increasingly busy lives, many Europeans simply turned their attention increasingly to worldly affairs. In the process, the Scandinavian countries of

Figure 12.9: Pentecostal church in Mobassa, Kenya.

Norway, Sweden, and Denmark saw a decline in church attendance, as did others such as France, Germany, and the United Kingdom by the dawn of the twenty-first century.

At the same time, a philosophical critique of postmodern thought has increasingly strengthened Christian apologists in responding to postmodernism. Although postmodernists claim there is no single absolute foundation of truth, they expect others to take their claim as a single absolute truth. Yet if there is no absolute truth, one can counterargue, then postmodernists have no legitimate basis to hold that their statement "there is no single absolute truth" is itself absolutely true. Indeed, for many Christian thinkers, one of the biggest problems with postmodernism is its apparent lack of a solid epistemological foundation. Moreover, in the eyes of many philosophically trained Christians, postmodern relativism produces logical incompatibilities. Christianity affirms, for example, that God became incarnate in the person of Jesus Christ. By contrast, Islam and Judaism deny this assertion. It is not logically possible for both camps to be right. Thus, to assert, as do many European devotees of postmodernism, that truth is relative is to fail to address the incompatibilities inherent in such a world view.

In certain parts of the Western world, especially in the United States, Christian identity has remained stronger. The rise of the evangelical movement, especially since the 1970s, has ensured the faith not only plays a prominent role in the lives of believers but also in national politics. Disappointed with the removal of prayer from public school classrooms and the legalization of abortion, and to growing indecency and obscenity in forms of cultural expression, evangelical Christians increasingly sought political solutions to undo what in their judgment were national moral failures in government. Against this backdrop, the creation of the Moral Majority movement in the 1980s, led by pastor Jerry Falwell and Christian broadcaster Pat Robertson, helped spearhead the restructuring of conservative politics. Such issues as the pro-life position in the abortion debate became increasingly prominent in conservative politics. Indeed, a major constituency of the Republican Party has remained evangelical Christians. In addition, thanks to the Internet, by the 1990s Christians increasingly began sharing their testimonies online and leading others to find faith. Lastly, the growth of Christian apologetics in the twenty-first century in the Anglo-American world has produced the strengthening of faith for many Christians. Apologists defend Christianity's truth claims in the face of secular opposition.

CONCLUSION

Observers hoped the end of the Cold War would usher in an age of global peace and prosperity. The defeat of East European communism by the 1990s became the sign to many people around the glove that democracy and free-market economics produced a more content citizenry than authoritarianism and command economies. Amid all this, democracy and capitalism were promoted like never before. Indeed, as the twentieth century drew to a close, a general optimism about the future swept lands far and wide.

At the same time, the world since the 1990s experienced an unpredictable trajectory. The advent of the Internet took the world by storm, in many ways making the world smaller with instantaneous communications globally. This development reinforced globalization, symbolized by the proliferation of multinational corporations. But rather than promoting global prosperity, new socioeconomic problems arose that led many global citizens to become disenchanted with the new global economy. The rise of the postmodern world view, in part driven by an attack on traditional forms of authority associated with the World Wide Web, also created new tensions to accompany the foundations of truth coming under assault. In the process, in such cultural realms as art, music, and film, the boundaries of social propriety increasingly shifted. In many ways, within their own cultural contexts, people responded with a return to traditional modes of thinking. This neotraditionalism also generated new problems by the start of the twenty-first century, as a growing number of conflicts between various civilizations around the globe demonstrated.

FOR FURTHER READING

Fukuyama, Francis. *The End of History and the Last Man*. London: Penguin, 1993.
Grenz, Stanley J. *A Primer on Postmodernism*. Grand Rapids, MI: William B. Eerdmans, 1996.
Huntington, Samuel. The *Clash of Civilizations and the Remaking of World Order*. New York: Simon & Schuster, 1998.
Stiglitz, Joseph E. *Globalization and Its Discontents*. New York: Norton, 2003.

CONCLUSION

As this textbook has demonstrated, the world changed dramatically between the mid-seventeenth and the twenty-first centuries. Although Asia and the Far East largely wielded dominance in global affairs in the distant past, Europe and the West during these centuries caught up and in significant ways became the regions that introduced many of the new changes, whether positive or negative. In the process, major developments in technology, warfare, politics, society, culture, and economics transformed global affairs with far-reaching effects over time, many of which continue to shape the lives of people around the world today in ways large and small. Indeed, in significant ways, the world increasingly became modern in this transformative period.

Technological advances, seen in everything from the scientific and industrial revolutions in Europe in the early modern era to the global digital age of today, were a hallmark of modernity. With the growing significance of technology, thanks to the cultivation of science, people increasingly looked to make their lives easier over the centuries. The advent of steam power in the eighteenth century revolutionized transportation, as did electricity, mass-produced steel, and breakthroughs in medicine and communications in the nineteenth. Once such developments occurred, they took on a life of their own, producing an unprecedented level of technology in the twentieth century. From the rise of the first mass-produced automobiles, radios, and television sets to the sophisticated spaceships, computers, and smartphones of today, the lives of people throughout the world have increasingly been shaped by technology. At the dawn of the twenty-first century, the possibilities seemed almost limitless.

Accompanying all this, the modernization of warfare increasingly made the world a more frightening place. The widespread embrace of firearms in Europe by the seventeenth century allowed that continent's people to not only transform war-making but also to conquer large swaths of the world, as evidenced by imperialism in the Americas, Asia, and Africa. Furthermore, in a modern world increasingly fraught with competition, the search for ever more destructive means to neutralize enemies on the battlefield and in other places produced new developments over time. Indeed, from the use of weaponized gas and machine guns in the Great War to the advent of devastating air power, Katyushka rockets, and nuclear weapons in the Second World War, the ability to annihilate soldiers and civilians alike became increasingly more efficient throughout the twentieth century. Cold War fears of nuclear fallout and the annihilation of humankind revealed the frightening possibilities of modern warfare, as did the prospect of terrorists obtaining weapons of mass destruction (WMDs) at the start of the twenty-first century.

Economics also changed immensely over the last three and a half centuries. In the seventeenth

351

century, the global economy was largely mercantile. At the time, governments strongly regulated commerce within their nations, and the overall goal of many states was to obtain favorable balances of trade, along with valuable silver and gold bullion. In many ways, the Far East had been the global economic leader in this economic arrangement for centuries. Yet Europe's Enlightenment-era embrace of *laissez-faire* economics, indeed the foundation of modern-day capitalism, breathed new life into the economic might of the West. By the eighteenth century, businessmen in Europe and North America were seeking to maximize profit, a goal governments increasingly championed, realizing that great economic success among citizens also generated larger tax revenues for the state. Of course, the unregulated desire for making money, endemic during the industrial revolutions in Europe, produced grievances. The exploitation of workers, who toiled tirelessly in factories for meager wages and had little voice in political affairs, led to new critiques of the economic changes associated with modernity. One such critique, Marxist-based communism, called for a violent revolution to usher in a classless society where everyone owned the means of production in common. This thinking led to a renegotiation of economic relations in many parts of the world in the twentieth century, as seen in the birth of the Soviet Union and the expansion of communism around the globe. Indeed, more than any other event, the Cold War of the latter half of the twentieth century became the ultimate competition in the playing out of economic systems. As it turned out, far from bringing about a utopia, the communist nations' economies were characterized by poor economic performance, stagnation, the lack of innovation, and rampant corruption. In the end, the centralized economies of the communist countries lost the Cold War. Capitalism had

triumphed. Thereafter, globalization increasingly swept the world, symbolized by the proliferation of multinational corporations.

Although the modern era experienced much change in terms of economic restructuring, many of the old problems from past periods remained. Regardless of the economic system, there have been great levels of wealth disparity throughout the centuries. As shown in everything from the poor peasants in eighteenth-century Europe to the garment workers in Asian and Central American sweatshops today, all economic systems have seen people struggle just to make ends meet. Although capitalism generated great prosperity in the West by the twentieth century, in the less-developed world, the economic system often has evoked negative connotations as the problem of poverty remained. Additionally, the widespread belief, whether fair or not, that the wealthy capitalist nations have cheated the poor countries out of their resources and engaged in unfair trade practices is as rampant in the twenty-first century as it was at the height of imperialism.

In addition to economics, basic features of society across the globe underwent a transformation between the mid-seventeenth and twenty-first centuries. To begin, a greater percentage of the world's population now live in urban areas, a development made possible by many factors, especially industrialization. Also, the old honor-based systems of social hierarchy, common not only in Asia but also the West, gave way to the modern egalitarian social vision. No longer did such titles as duke, marquis, baron, or count carry much significance in European affairs. Just as significant, the world's population today is well-educated by historical standards. Indeed, most of the world's people in the mid-seventeenth century were illiterate and lacked access to primary education, much less the postgraduate opportunities available throughout the world today. Finally, the status of women largely underwent a transformation. In the seventeenth century, women in Europe were largely confined to the domestic sphere, performing such important roles as motherhood, spouse, and the preparer of meals. Their presence in politics and business was largely nonexistent, with the exception of queens. Yet, in the twentieth century, a worldwide critique of patriarchy led to women's enfranchisement and employment alongside men in many professions. Parts of Europe and Latin America also elected women to the office of president. At the same time, women still remain marginalized in many parts of the world, especially in the Middle East, Northern Africa, and South Asia.

Politics also experienced tremendous modernization over the centuries. In some places, such as in Europe and North America, dramatic changes occurred. In the seventeenth and eighteenth centuries, Europe was still a continent of kingdoms ruled largely by absolute monarchs. As it turned out, royal dynasties had justified their absolute rule by evoking the divine right of kings, essentially claiming God had chosen them to lead. Yet the rise of tyranny associated with such a rule produced a response that ushered in modern democracy as we know it today. The triumph of the American Revolution gave rise to an increasingly common form of government in which leaders were not from royal dynasties, but rather those individuals judged most fit for leadership through the electoral process. In the process, the establishment of democratic republics began to sweep Latin America and parts of Europe in the nineteenth century, and other regions in the following century. Even those few nations that retained kings or queens in Europe became constitutional monarchs, if not mere figureheads, with the power lying in the hands of the electorate. Another area of progress was the expansion of voting rights, perhaps the single most important feature of political modernization over time. Nineteenth-century voting restrictions on poor men, as well as virtually all women, gave way in the twentieth century to universal suffrage in large parts of the Americas, Europe, Africa, and Asia as the traditional structures of elitism and patriarchy declined globally.

Meanwhile, the struggle for political modernization did not always meet with success. Even in the early twentieth century, some nations such as China and Japan still had emperors who, like the European kings before them, held absolute power. In fact, by actually claiming to be divine beings themselves, Asian emperors made a much stronger claim than their earlier European counterparts ever did to justify power. By the mid-twentieth century, however, such claims were no longer tenable in the increasingly modern world and gave way to new systems of government, but not always democratic ones. Indeed, a major development was the emergence of new types of authoritarianism in the twentieth century, such as communism, fascism, military dictatorships, and theocracies. The rise of communism in Russia and China had far-reaching effects on not only these nations' populations but also neighboring countries, as did the fascism seen in Nazi Germany and Italy that provoked the world's most devastating war: World War II. Although ostensibly embracing democracy, large swaths of Africa and Latin America experienced military rule as the twentieth century ended, while some nations in the Middle East decried democracy in favor of rule by religious leaders. All of these examples show that parts of the world still struggled with the adoption of democracy.

Numerous factors explain the world's mixed record regarding political modernization. In many places, citizens seek democracy and the expansion of human rights, but the authoritarian governments curtail their expression, thus ensuring the continuation of authoritarianism. Another factor has been cultural differences across regions. Some observers who championed a traditional approach to statecraft decried democracy as a Western phenomenon. The growing material success of the West over the centuries, which in part stemmed from an exploitative relationship with other parts of the world, also undermined everything Western for some traditionalists. Thus, for some, a desire to uphold traditional political structures was deemed a necessity to preserve the cultural identity of peoples throughout parts of the globe.

In fact, of all the major realms of historical exploration, cultural differences have largely remained, despite modernization in other realms. Seen in everything from the types of food people eat, the kinds of music they listen to, and the forms of literature they read, to the religion they practice, and so much more, peoples around the world have consistently viewed the world in which they live and their place in the world through different cultural lenses. Interestingly, since the advent of transcontinental air travel and the Internet in the twentieth century, people have learned more about the cultures of people in lands far away. Some people have embraced the cultural differences, saying cultural diversity enriches human affairs. Yet a growing knowledge of cultural knowledge has led others to view different cultures in a negative light. Indeed, since globalization and the dramatic expansion in global interaction in the late twentieth century, conflicts have remained. And, as it has turned out, cultural differences have played a significant role in the discourses that generated such strife.

What will the future hold as the twenty-first century unfolds? If the experience of history has anything to say, one safe conclusion is that it, in many ways, will be unpredictable. In fact, historians rarely make good prognosticators, as there are too many factors that shape change over time. At the same time, the trajectory of history over the last three hundred years suggests some likely developments. To begin, technology will probably continue to advance as people increasingly attempt to make their lives easier. The possibilities, perhaps fanciful, are worth entertaining. Indeed, civilizations with flying automobiles, the widespread presence of robots, and even space colonization have captured the imagination of many futurists. Whether such developments occur, or even if people desire such things, is uncertain. More likely, advances in medicine and health care could mean people will live longer and more productive lives. Yet what about, one might ask, war and peace? To be sure, history has something to say about that. Despite the well-intentioned efforts of pacifists throughout the ages, conflict has been a feature consistent throughout history, regardless of place and time. In a world with limited resources, human frailties, and competition, the goal of peace seems bound to remain elusive. That does not mean people should not endeavor to promote the general welfare of humankind. In fact, a proper understanding of the past proves an old adage wrong: the claim that history simply repeats itself. Although this claim is partly true, it overlooks the positive changes that have occurred over time. Only three hundred years ago, much of the world was characterized by the presence of gross injustices, as it is today. At that time, the existence of slavery, the abuses associated with patriarchy, and the social marginalization of the poor were widespread. Yet, as people increasingly questioned the moral implications behind such societal features, such injustices increasingly were combated. At the dawn of the twenty-first century, as early evidence suggests, such injustices as gross wealth disparity and the violation of human rights have increasingly become subjects addressed by social critics. As the century unfolds, perhaps global affairs can change for the better. It certainly has that potential, but that goal depends on all people striving to improve the world in which they live.

CREDITS

1. Fig 0-1: Copyright © Morio (CC BY-SA 3.0) at https://commons.wikimedia.org/wiki/File: Skyscrapers_of_Shinjuku_2009_January_(revised).jpg.

2. Fig.1-1: Copyright © Samuli Suomi (CC BY-SA 3.0) at https://commons.wikimedia.org/wiki/File: Versaillespanoraama2.jpg.

3. Fig 1-2: Copyright © Leonardo G (CC BY-SA 3.0) at https://commons.wikimedia.org/wiki/File: Acprussiamap2.gif.

4. Fig 1.3: Copyright © Bizso (GFDL) at https://commons.wikimedia.org/wiki/File:Growth_of_Habsburg_territories.jpg.

5. Fig 1.4: U.S. Central Intelligence Agency, "Map of Russian Empire ," http://www.lib.utexas.edu/maps/cia15/russia_sm_2015.gif. Copyright in the Public Domain.

6. Fig 1.5: Samuel Rawson Gardiner, "Map of Dutch Republic ," http://etc.usf.edu/maps/pages/300/399/399.htm. Copyright in the Public Domain.

7. Fig 1.6: "Map of Poland," ed. Edward Salmon and James Worsfold, https://www.lib.utexas.edu/maps/historical/british_dominions_year-book/pol_claims_map25_1918.jpg. Copyright in the Public Domain.

8. Fig 2.1: http://abyss.uoregon.edu/~js/images/greek_cosmos.jpg. Copyright © 1996.

9. Fig 2.2: https://commons.wikimedia.org/wiki/File:Copernican_heliocentrism_diagram-2.jpg. Copyright in the Public Domain.

10. Fig 2.3: https://commons.wikimedia.org/wiki/File:PSM_V78_D334_Geocentric_system_after_tycho_brahe.png. Copyright in the Public Domain.

11. Fig 3.1: https://commons.wikimedia.org/wiki/File:Africa_Climate_Today.png. Copyright in the Public Domain.

12. Fig 3.2: Copyright © Peter Fitzgerald (CC BY-SA 3.0) at https://commons.wikimedia.org/wiki/File:Saharan_Africa_regions_map.png.

13. Fig 3.3: https://commons.wikimedia.org/wiki/File:Slaveshipposter.jpg. Copyright in the Public Domain.

14. Fig 3.4: Copyright © Moxy (CC BY-SA 3.0) at https://commons.wikimedia.org/wiki/File:America_1000_BCE.png.

15. Fig 3.5: Copyright © Lencer (CC BY-SA 3.0) at https://commons.wikimedia.org/wiki/File:Spain_and_Portugal.png.

16. Fig 3.6: Copyright © Trasamundo (CC BY-SA 3.0) at https://commons.wikimedia.org/wiki/File: Spanish_Empire_Anachronous_en.svg.

17. Fig 3.7: Copyright © OpenStax (CC by 4.0) at http://philschatz.com/us-history-book/contents/m49992.html.

18. Fig 4.1 : Copyright © Michal Klajban (CC BY-SA 3.0) at https://commons.wikimedia.org/wiki/File:Ming_Empire_cca_1580_(en).svg.

19. Fig 4.2: https://commons.wikimedia.org/wiki/File:Chen_Hongshou,_leaf_album_painting.jpg. Copyright in the Public Domain.

20. Fig 4.3: Copyright © Photo by Patche99z (CC by 3.0) at https://commons.wikimedia.org/wiki/File:Room_95-6753.JPG.

21. Fig 4.4: https://commons.wikimedia.org/wiki/File:Eurasian_steppe_belt.jpg. Copyright in the Public Domain.

22. Fig 4.5a: Copyright © Pryaltonian (CC BY-SA 3.0) at https://commons.wikimedia.org/wiki/File:Qing_Dynasty_1820.png.

23. Fig 4.5b: Copyright © Michal Klajban (CC BY-SA 3.0) at https://commons.wikimedia.org/wiki/File:Ming_Empire_cca_1580_(en).svg.

24. Fig 4.6: Copyright © Cacahuate (CC BY-SA 3.0) at https://commons.wikimedia.org/wiki/File:Map_of_East_Asia.png.

25. Fig 4.7: "Climate Map of Japan" Adapted from https://www.japanmeetings.org/why-japan/facts-about-japan.php.

26. Fig 4.8: Copyright © Historiographer (CC BY-SA 3.0) at https://commons.wikimedia.org/wiki/File:History_of_Korea-108_BC.png.

27. Fig 4.9: https://commons.wikimedia.org/wiki/File:Map-of-southeast-asia_1400_CE.png. Copyright in the Public Domain.

28. Fig 4.10: https://commons.wikimedia.org/wiki/File:Indonesia-CIA_WFB_Map.png. Copyright in the Public Domain.

29. Fig 5.1: https://commons.wikimedia.org/wiki/File:Map_of_expansion_of_Caliphate.svg. Copyright in the Public Domain.

30. Fig 5.2: Copyright © André Koehne (CC BY-SA 3.0) at https://commons.wikimedia.org/wiki/File:Ottoman_empire.svg.

31. Fig 5.3: https://commons.wikimedia.org/wiki/File:Gate_of_Felicity_Topkapi_Istanbul_2007_detail_002.jpg. Copyright in the Public Domain.

32. Fig 5.4: https://commons.wikimedia.org/wiki/File:Ottoman_miniature_painters.jpg. Copyright in the Public Domain.

33. Fig 5.5: https://commons.wikimedia.org/wiki/File:Classic_Ottoman_Army_Tents.jpg. Copyright in the Public Domain.

34. Fig 5.6: Copyright © Tangient LLC (CC BY-SA 3.0) at https://ottomans-safavids-mughals.wikispaces.com/.

35. Fig 5.7: Copyright © Fabienkhan (CC BY-SA 2.5) at https://commons.wikimedia.org/wiki/File:Fresque_chehel_sotoun_esfahan.jpg.

36. Fig 5.8: Copyright © Fabienkhan (CC BY-SA 2.5) at https://commons.wikimedia.org/wiki/File: D%C3%A9tail_porte_madreseh-e-chahar_bagh_esfahan.jpg.

37. Fig 5.9: https://commons.wikimedia.org/wiki/File:Plate_pomegranates_Louvre_MAO868.jpg. Copyright in the Public Domain.

38. Fig 5.10: https://commons.wikimedia.org/wiki/File:Mughal_Historical_Map.png. Copyright in the Public Domain.

39. Fig 5.11: Copyright © A.winzer (CC BY-SA 3.0) at https://commons.wikimedia.org/wiki/File:Humayuns_Tomb_Delhi_31-05-2005_pic2.jpg.

40. Fig 5.12: Copyright © Photo by Dhirad (CC BY-SA 3.0) at https://commons.wikimedia.org/wiki/File:Taj_Mahal_in_March_2004.jpg.

41. Fig 5.13: https://commons.wikimedia.org/wiki/File:Princes_of_the_House_of_Timur.jpg. Copyright in the Public Domain.

42. Fig 6.1 : https://commons.wikimedia.org/wiki/File:Troisordres.jpg. Copyright in the Public Domain.

43. Fig 6.2: https://commons.wikimedia.org/wiki/File:Sans-culotte.jpg. Copyright in the Public Domain.

44. Fig 6.3: Copyright © Alexander Altenhof (CC BY-SA 3.0) at https://commons.wikimedia.org/wiki/File:Europe_1812_map_en.png.

45. Fig 6.4 : Copyright © Peter Fitzgerald (CC BY-SA 2.0) at https://commons.wikimedia.org/wiki/File:Haiti_regions_map.png.

46. Fig 7.1: https://commons.wikimedia.org/wiki/File:Prince_Metternich_by_Lawrence.jpeg. Copyright in the Public Domain.

47. Fig 7.2: https://commons.wikimedia.org/wiki/File:HGM_Passini_Angriff_Dragoner.jpg. Copyright in the Public Domain.

48. Fig 7.3: https://commons.wikimedia.org/wiki/File:Bombardment_of_Bomarsund.jp. Copyright in the Public Domain.

49. Fig 7.4: https://commons.wikimedia.org/wiki/File:EquianoExeterpainting.jpg. Copyright in the Public Domain.

50. Fig 7.5: https://commons.wikimedia.org/wiki/File:Simon_Bolivar.jpg. Copyright in the Public Domain.

51. Fig 7.6: https://commons.wikimedia.org/wiki/File:Miguel_Hidalgo_(Vinkhuijzen).jpeg. Copyright in the Public Domain.

52. Fig 7.7: Jhttps://commons.wikimedia.org/wiki/File:Isabel,_Princess_Imperial_of_Brazil.jpg. Copyright in the Public Domain.

53. Fig 7.8: https://commons.wikimedia.org/wiki/File:Konstantin_Kapidagli_002.jpg. Copyright in the Public Domain.

54. Fig 7.9: https://commons.wikimedia.org/wiki/File:Hong_Xiuquan.jpg. Copyright in the Public Domain.

55. Fig 8.1: https://commons.wikimedia.org/wiki/File:Rocket_(Smiles).jpg. Copyright in the Public Domain.

56. Fig 8.2: https://commons.wikimedia.org/wiki/File:Karl_Marx_001.jpg. Copyright in the Public Domain.

57. Fig 8.3: https://commons.wikimedia.org/wiki/File:Edison_light_bulb_with_plate.jpg. Copyright in the Public Domain.

58. Fig 8.4: https://commons.wikimedia.org/wiki/File:Gregor_Mendel_Monk.jpg. Copyright in the Public Domain.

59. Fig 8.5: https://commons.wikimedia.org/wiki/File:Sigmund_Freud_LIFE.jpg. Copyright in the Public Domain.

60. Fig 8.6: https://commons.wikimedia.org/wiki/File:Bundesarchiv_Bild_183-R68588,_Otto_von_Bismarck.jpg. Copyright in the Public Domain.

61. Fig 8.7: https://commons.wikimedia.org/wiki/File:Theodr-Herzl-1904.jpg. Copyright in the Public Domain.

62. Fig 8.8: https://commons.wikimedia.org/wiki/File:Cecil_Rhodes_-_Project_Gutenberg_eText_16600.jpg. Copyright in the Public Domain.

63. Fig 9.1: https://commons.wikimedia.org/wiki/File:Archduke_Franz_with_his_wife.jpg. Copyright in the Public Domain.

64. Fig 9.2: https://commons.wikimedia.org/wiki/File:The_Hun_and_the_Home.jpg. Copyright in the Public Domain.

65. Fig 9.3: https://commons.wikimedia.org/wiki/File:Going_over_the_top_01.jpg. Copyright in the Public Domain.

66. Fig 9.4: https://commons.wikimedia.org/wiki/File:LG_British_tank_WWI_2.jpg. Copyright in the Public Domain.

67. Fig 9.5: https://commons.wikimedia.org/wiki/File:Map_Treaty_of_Brest-Litovsk-en.jpg. Copyright in the Public Domain.

68. Fig 9.6: https://commons.wikimedia.org/wiki/File:Near_East_relief_the_mother_and_children_in_syria.png1. Copyright in the Public Domain.

69. Fig 9.7: https://commons.wikimedia.org/wiki/File:William_Orpen_%E2%80%93_The_Signing_of_Peace_in_the_Hall_of_Mirrors,_Versailles_1919,_Ausschnitt.jpg. Copyright in the Public Domain.

70. Fig 9.8: https://commons.wikimedia.org/wiki/File:Benito_Mussolini_in_1937.jpg. Copyright in the Public Domain.

71. Fig 9.9: Copyright © Heinrich Hoffmann (CC BY-SA 3.0) at https://commons.wikimedia.org/wiki/File:Bundesarchiv_Bild_102-13774,_Adolf_Hitler.jpg.

72. Fig 9.10: Copyright © Listowy (CC BY-SA 3.0) at https://commons.wikimedia.org/wiki/File:Second_World_War_Europe.png.

73. Fig 9.11: https://commons.wikimedia.org/wiki/File:Landings_at_St_Aubin-sur-Mer.jpg. Copyright in the Public Domain.

74. Fig 9.12: https://commons.wikimedia.org/wiki/File:Avenge_Pearl_Harbor-Our_Bullets_Will_Do_It.jpg. Copyright in the Public Domain.

75. Fig 9.13: https://commons.wikimedia.org/wiki/File:Nagasakibomb.jpg. Copyright in the Public Domain.

76. Fig 10.1: https://commons.wikimedia.org/wiki/File:Stalin_portrait_1937.jpg. Copyright in the Public Domain.

77. Fig 10.2: https://commons.wikimedia.org/wiki/File:Potsdam_conference_1945-8.jpg. Copyright in the Public Domain.

78. Fig 10.3: https://commons.wikimedia.org/wiki/File:Mao_Zedong_with_cap.jpg. Copyright in the Public Domain.

79. Fig 10.4: https://commons.wikimedia.org/wiki/File:Nasser_and_Khrushchev,_1964.jpg. Copyright in the Public Domain.

80. Fig 10.5: https://commons.wikimedia.org/wiki/File:Ho_Chi_Minh_1946.jpg. Copyright in the Public Domain.

81. Fig 10.6: https://commons.wikimedia.org/wiki/File:Tet_Offensive_1968.jpg. Copyright in the Public Domain.

82. Fig 10.7: https://commons.wikimedia.org/wiki/File:The_Shah_of_Iran_and_President_Nixon_-_NARA_-_194301.jpg. Copyright in the Public Domain.

83. Fig 10.8: https://commons.wikimedia.org/wiki/File:1989_CPA_6101.jpg. Copyright in the Public Domain.

84. Fig 10.9: https://commons.wikimedia.org/wiki/File:Che_Guevara_June_2,_1959.jpg. Copyright in the Public Domain.

85. Fig 10.10: https://commons.wikimedia.org/wiki/File:Reagan_Gorbachev_Island.jpg. Copyright in the Public Domain.

86. Fig 11.1: https://commons.wikimedia.org/wiki/File:Backyard_furnace4.jpg. Copyright in the Public Domain.

87. Fig 11.2: https://commons.wikimedia.org/wiki/File:Korean_peninsula_at_night.jpg. Copyright in the Public Domain.

88. Fig 11.3: https://commons.wikimedia.org/wiki/File:Dalit_or_Untouchable_Woman_of_Bombay_(Mumbai)_according_to_Indian_Caste_System_-_1942.jpg. Copyright in the Public Domain.

89. Fig 11.4: https://commons.wikimedia.org/wiki/File:%D8%A8%DA%86%D9%87_%D9%88_%D8%AE%D9%85%DB%8C%D9%86%DB%8C.JPG. Copyright in the Public Domain.

90. Fig11.5:https://commons.wikimedia.org/wiki/File:Jerusalem_Dome_of_the_rock_BW_14.JPG. Copyright in the Public Domain.

91. Fig 11.6: https://commons.wikimedia.org/wiki/File:Pancho_Villa_bandolier_crop.jpg. Copyright in the Public Domain.

92. Fig 11.7: https://commons.wikimedia.org/wiki/File:Revolutionary_Armed_Forces_of_Colombia_(FARC)_insurgents.GIF. Copyright in the Public Domain.

93. Fig 11.8: http://commons.wikimedia.org/wiki/File:Juan_Peron_con_banda_de_presidente.jpg. Copyright in the Public Domain.

94. Fig 11.9: https://commons.wikimedia.org/wiki/File:Cuba-old_car.jpg. Copyright in the Public Domain.

95. Fig 11.10: https://commons.wikimedia.org/wiki/File:Bill-Clinton-with-Nelson-Mandela.jpg. Copyright in the Public Domain.

96. Fig 11.11: https://commons.wikimedia.org/wiki/File:Robert_Mugabe_-_2009.jpg. Copyright in the Public Domain.

97. Fig12.1:https://commons.wikimedia.org/wiki/File:World%27s_First_Computer,_the_Electronic_Numerical_Integrator_and_Calculator_(ENIAC).gif. Copyright in the Public Domain.

98. Fig 12.2: https://commons.wikimedia.org/wiki/File:The_Fabs.JPG. Copyright in the Public Domain.

99. Fig 12.3: https://commons.wikimedia.org/wiki/File:Starbucks-seoul.JPG. Copyright in the Public Domain.

100. Fig 12.4: https://commons.wikimedia.org/wiki/File:Euro-Banknoten.jpg. Copyright in the Public Domain.

101. Fig 12.5: https://commons.wikimedia.org/wiki/File:Clash_of_Civilizations_mapn2.png. Copyright in the Public Domain.

102. Fig 12.6: https://commons.wikimedia.org/wiki/File:North_Tower_collapsing.JPG. Copyright in the Public Domain.

103. Fig 12.7: https://commons.wikimedia.org/wiki/File:Iraq_header_1.jpg. Copyright in the Public Domain.

104. Fig 12.8: https://commons.wikimedia.org/wiki/File:Paraskevi_of_Iconium_temple_in_Tugoless.jpg. Copyright in the Public Domain.

105. Fig 12.9: Copyright © Photo by Daryona (CC BY-SA 3.0) at https://commons.wikimedia.org/wiki/File:Pentecostal_church_in_Mombasa.JPG.